CONTENTS

REFERENCE MANUAL

FOR THE OFFICE

8TH EDITION

CLIFFORD R. HOUSE
President Emeritus,
Cincinnati Technical College

KATHIE SIGLER
Dean for Administration and Professor,
Miami-Dade Community College

SOUTH-WESTERN PUBLISHING CO.

Editor-in-Chief:	Robert E. First
Developmental Editor:	Marilyn Hornsby
Coordinating Editor:	Angela C. McDonald
Production Manager:	Deborah M. Luebbe
Production Editor II:	Melanie A. Blair, Thomas N. Lewis
Internal Designer:	Barbara Libby
Cover Design:	Graphica
Photo Editor:	Linda Ellis
Marketing Manager:	Al S. Roane

ISBN: 0-538-61991-0
ISBN: 0-538-61992-9

1 2 3 4 5 6 D 99 98 97 96 95 94

Printed in the United States of America

House, Clifford R.
Reference manual for the office / Clifford R. House, Kathie Sigler, – 8th ed.
p. cm.
Includes bibliographical references and index.
ISBN 0-538-61991-0. – ISBN 0-538-61992-9
1. Commercial correspondence–Handbooks, manuals, etc.
2. Business writing–Handbooks, manuals, etc. 3. English language--Business English–Handbooks, manuals, etc. 4. Office practice--Handbooks, manuals, etc. I. Sigler, Kathie. II. Title.
HF5726.H58 1995
651–dc20 93-45740
CIP

International Thomson Publishing

PREFACE

Every office professional needs to have the latest information and tools to work effectively in today's rapidly changing business environment. The eighth edition of *Reference Manual for the Office* provides you with that extra edge to prepare for the challenges you face on a daily basis. Each page is filled with the latest technology: software, hardware, networks, and telecommunications. The most current of all business practices are presented with numerous examples for each. It is our hope that this *Manual* will launch you into the twenty-first century with an advantage—assistance at your fingertips!

Reference Manual for the Office is a South-Western publication that began in the era of manual typewriters, carbon paper, and mimeograph machines. Over the years, we have responded not only to the technical progress in office work, but to the expanding needs of our users as they entered new areas such as word processing and desktop publishing.

In the seventh edition, we added a substantial section on basic computer concepts. Three trends manifested themselves during the life of that edition. First, the deliberate evolution of *grammar, punctuation,* and *style* continued; they remain as important to office work as ever. Second, the seventh-edition material on *computers* was endorsed by our users, who recommended more of the same. Third, the book continues to be used as a *text,* as well as a reference manual, in growing numbers of business and communication skills classes.

In writing the eighth edition, we discovered the need, not for a change in direction but, for a means of fitting the accomplishments and requirements of a new age—the fallout of the information explosion—into a single, cohesive, affordable volume.

In this edition, we have employed theory only when its applications are useful or helpful in explaining things that are pertinent to today's world. History is recounted only as it pertains to current practical matters. Those things trivial, unnecessarily complicated, or too advanced to be of current practical value are avoided. The emphasis is on utility—on now.

How do theory and history help explain the practical present? There is no better context for the accomplishments of our era than exploration of what life would be without them. For example, without the microchip technology of the late twentieth century, a device emulating the desktop computer would have required floor space equivalent to the area of a football field. Even if such a device could have been constructed, it would have been too slow and cumbersome to have been of practical value; and it would have required an army of operating and service personnel. Its cost would have been truly phenomenal.

The telephone system was revolutionized by microwave transmission, communications satellites, automated switching, fiber optics, and other innovations. There is no better way to illustrate the phenomenal effect of that revolution than to point out that, if the technology of the 1940s were applied today, a telephone system comparable to what we now have would probably require the services of one out of every two high school graduates in the nation.

Understanding the organization of *Reference Manual for the Office* will help you use it effectively. The first three chapters constitute a style manual:

1 Grammar
2 Punctuation
3 Style

Since grammar and punctuation are elements of style, all of this material could have been combined in a single chapter. However, it would have been long and cumbersome. Grammar and punctuation are each significant enough and long enough to merit chapters of their own. Singling out the two most important areas of style for special treatment not only allowed us to give them their due, but made the remainder of the style chapter more manageable.

4 Information Processing
5 Word Processing

Similarly, chapters 4 and 5 could have been combined in a single chapter called Information Processing. It, too, would have been long and cumbersome. Instead, we provide in chapter 4, Information Processing, explanations of the devices, skills, procedures, and the like, that make information processing possible. In chapter 5, we single out the dominant area—word processing (including desktop publishing)—for special treatment.

6 International Business and Travel

Chapter 6 reflects the increased importance of international business in the world economy. International business relationships, travel documents, money, dates, time, and air travel are covered.

7 Getting the Job—Getting Ahead

Those office workers who succeed do so largely because they possess the human relations skills that permit them to get along well with others. Those office workers who fail do so largely because they do not exercise good human relations skills—not because they lack computer skills, clerical skills, and other technical capabilities. Chapter 7 treats the human aspect of information technology: a subject that is as timeless as grammar, punctuation, and style.

8 References

Part of becoming a success is knowing where to go when you need information. No one has all of the facts in her or his head. Chapter 8 provides a listing of source books from almanacs to writing guides, from dictionaries to collections of quotations, from guides on finding a job to guides for personal development, and much more.

We hope you find our efforts to explain these subjects useful and that what you learn from *Reference Manual for the Office* will serve you well as we enter the twenty-first century.

Cliff House
Kathie Sigler

CHAPTER 1

GRAMMAR

NOUNS

1001 **Definition.** A **noun** is a word that names a person, place, thing, or idea. A noun can be used as the subject of a sentence (what the sentence is talking about), or as the object of a sentence (who or what is receiving the action of the sentence).

Persons: Ms. Anabel Farinas, personal trainers, Pat

Places: Detroit, Bayside, classroom

Things: Golden Gate Bridge, manual, mirror

Ideas: ethics, morality, justice

1002 **Nouns tell *who* or *what*.** Since the noun names a person, place, thing, or idea—nouns will always answer the questions *what?* or *who?*

***What* is the best vacation spot?**	***What* are her best qualities?**
Yosemite	honesty
Miami Beach	perseverance
Harbor Point	dependability
Walt Disney World	cheerful attitude

***Who* is leading the group?**
the faculty member
a lifeguard
grandmother
the dance instructor

1003 ***The, a, an:* Signal nouns.** These three words can signal that a noun follows: *the, a, an.*

The woman will take charge.

The mountain is high.

The letter is first class.

The ethics of the group were suspect.

A boy will arrive.

A state will be chosen.

A package was received.

A fear can be real.

An is used as a substitute for *a* before words beginning with a vowel (*a, e, i, o,* short *u*) or beginning with a vowel sound.

An aunt has arrived.

An hour is finished.*
*vowel sound

An envelope is expected.

An expectation is understood.

1004 **Concrete nouns.** A **concrete noun** is a word that refers to something that can be concretely perceived.

The *boat* rides well over the *waves.*

Patrick was riding the *skateboard.*

A *hat* was worn by the first *contestant.*

1005 **Abstract nouns.** An **abstract noun** is a word that refers to an idea or concept: something that can be understood, but not perceived directly.

The victim's mother wanted *justice* in the courtroom.

Freedom is sought by the Cuban rafters.

Above all she valued *friendship.*

1006 **Common nouns.** There are two kinds of nouns: common nouns and proper nouns. A **common noun** names any one of a group or an entire group of persons, places, things, or ideas and is not capitalized.

Common Nouns
teacher
country
company
speech

1007 **Proper nouns.** A **proper noun** names a particular person, place, thing, or idea and is always capitalized.

Proper Nouns

Mr. Sosa, Dr. Charles Klingensmith
United States of America, Zaire
Jeff Brezner Consultants, Inc.
Bermello & Associates

Noun: Function in the sentence

1008 **Subject.** The word or word group about which the sentence is written is the **subject.** A noun, pronoun, or a phrase or clause used as a noun may be the subject of a sentence. Noun subjects may be singular or plural.

A singular subject requires a singular verb.

Singular Subject	Singular Verb	
Jose Mateo	*is*	the best choice for the award.
My *father*	*drives*	carefully since the accident.
The *nurse*	*completed*	the course with honors.

A plural or compound subject requires a plural verb.

Plural/Compound Subjects	Plural Verbs	
Jose Mateo and Sheldon Lurie (two nouns combined)	*are*	the best choices for the awards.
They (plural pronoun)	*drive*	carefully since the accident.
The *nurses* (plural noun)	*completed*	the course with honors.

1009 **Object.** The noun that receives the action of a verb is the **object.**

Subject	Verb	Object
She	threw	the *ball.*
Jerry and Justin	washed	the *car.*

A noun, a pronoun, or a phrase or clause used as a noun may be the object in a sentence.

Subject	Verb	Object
Rebecca	handled	the *computer* well.
Dr. Lopez	examined	*her.*
He	saw	the *running of the bulls* in Spain.

The noun object may be singular or plural without changing the form of the verb providing the action.

Subject	Verb	Object
Rebecca	handled	the *computers* well.
Dr. Lopez	examined	*them.*

1010 **Direct object.** The **direct object** is the noun that answers the question of *who*, or *what* received the action of a transitive verb.

Subject	Transitive Verb	Direct Object
Rick Lambright	passed (what?)	his *CPA examination!*
Sis Smith	called (who?)	*Cristina and Freddy.*

1011 **Indirect object.** The **indirect object** is the noun that receives the action of a transitive verb indirectly. When preceded by a preposition (such as *to, by, at, with*) the indirect object also functions as the **object of a preposition.**

Subject	Verb	Indirect Object
They	sent	the CPA scores to *Rick Lambright.*

(*Rick Lambright* is the object of the preposition *to* and the indirect object of the sentence.)

The school board	presented	the trophies to her winning *team.*

(*Team* is the object of the preposition *to* and the indirect object of the sentence.)

Zoily	gave	*Cary* the new plans.

(*Cary* is the indirect object; *plans* is the direct object.)

1012 **Complement.** The **complement** is the noun that explains, further defines, or completes the description of the noun subject or object.

Subject	Verb	Complement
Rebecca Gomez-Cohen	was named	the new *Dean.*

(*Dean* further describes Rebecca Gomez-Cohen.)

They	found	the play *charming.*

(*Charming* explains how the play was perceived and describes the word *play*.)

1013 **Number: Singular or plural?** Nouns referring to one person, place, thing, or idea are singular; nouns referring to two or more persons, places, things, or ideas are plural.

Singular Nouns	Plural Nouns
book	books
woman	women
operating room	operating rooms
worker	workers
bench	benches
life	lives

The plurals of nouns are usually formed by adding *s* (boys, rooms, workers). However, the plurals of some nouns are formed according to different guidelines (women, benches, lives). Consult your dictionary if you are unsure of the correct plural form of any noun.

1014 **Nouns ending in *s*.** A noun that ends in *s* may be always singular, always plural, or either singular or plural depending upon its use. If you are unsure of the correct usage, consult your dictionary for further information about those nouns that are only singular or only plural.

1015 **Singular noun requires singular verb.**

consensus	process	mumps	dress
summons	distress	mistress	news

Singular noun	Singular verb	
The *summons*	*was delivered*	to Sahir Iman.
"*Mumps*	*is*	a dangerous illness for adults," stressed Dr. Tena Frank.

1016 **Plural noun requires plural verb.**

savings	liabilities	profits	specifics
losings	thanks	credentials	grounds

Plural noun	Plural verb	
Cary Shookoff's *profits*	*were*	unexpectedly high.
The *grounds*	*were landscaped*	by The Good Earth Nursery.

Note: The following words are always plural and require a plural verb, *unless* they are used with "pair of."

Plural Verb Required	Singular Verb Required
shears	pair of shears
slacks	pair of slacks
pliers	pair of pliers
eyeglasses	pair of eyeglasses

The *eyeglasses were* found after the party.

A *pair of eyeglasses was* found after the party.

1017 **Nouns having the same form for singular and plural.** Some nouns have one form that is the same in both singular and plural usage. The correct verb form depends upon the number of the noun—does it represent one or more.

series	species	headquarters	corps
deer	sheep	chassis	moose
gross	means	politics	statistics

The next World *Series is* scheduled to begin here. (one series)

Three opera series are funded this year by the endowment. (three series)

A *moose runs* across the forest. (one moose)

The *moose run* in many directions as the tiger approaches. (two or more moose)

1

1018 **Plurals of foreign nouns.** Foreign words used as nouns are harder to identify as singular or plural because they are not as familiar. Also, there is often more than one way to indicate the plural form. Check your dictionary when you are uncertain.

Singular

The *memorandum* is ready for duplicating.

Plural

The *memorandums* are ready for duplicating.

or

The *memoranda* are ready for duplicating.

1019 **Nouns ending in -*ics*.** Nouns ending in -*ics* are used with either a singular or plural verb, depending upon the meaning of the noun.

civics	statistics	ethics
metaphysics	economics	linguistics
acrobatics	tactics	athletics

When identifying a science, an art, a body of knowledge, or a course of study, such nouns are considered singular and require a singular verb.

Acrobatics is a strenuous class taught by Diane Trapp.

Linguistics is her speciality.

A noun ending in -*ics* is plural if the reference is to individual items, principles, or physical activities.

The *ethics* of their decision *are* questionable. (principles)

New *statistics point* to a poor voter turnout. (individual item)

Calisthenics are good for my mother's sore knee. (physical activity)

His *tactics are* above reproach. (individual item)

Her *gymnastics are* on the programs. (physical activity)

Their *economics are* under discussion. (principles)

1020 **Compound nouns.** A **compound noun** is formed when two or more words are combined and used as a single noun. Compound nouns are written in three different ways. They are

- sometimes hyphenated:

(s)	sister-in-law	middle-of-the-roader	sun-god
(pl)	sisters-in-law	middle-of-the-roaders	sun-gods

- sometimes combined and written as one word:

(s)	pacemaker	downtown	photocopy
(pl)	pacemakers	(singular only)	photocopies

- sometimes written as two or more words:

(s)	delivery room	secretary of state	left guard
(pl)	delivery rooms	secretaries of state	left guards

Since compound nouns are written in three different ways, it is always a good idea to consult a dictionary for the exact spelling if you are not certain of the form. If the compound word is not in the dictionary, it should be written as two separate words. When a compound name is part of a company name, however, always follow the style shown on the company's letterhead. For additional information on compound nouns, see chapter 3, ¶ 3200.

For information on compound nouns containing the word *man* or *men,* see ¶ 1252.

1021 Collective nouns. A **collective noun** is a noun that indicates a group of persons, places, or things. Examples of collective nouns include team, group, department, organization, class, crowd, herd, staff, management, union, public, and majority.

- **Members/Things acting together.**

If the members of the group act together, the collective noun should be used with a singular verb.

The *party wants* to endorse Senator Carrie Meek.

The *majority is* in favor of a change.

Note: *The* precedes *majority* used singularly.

The *herd wanders* toward the watering spot at high noon.

- **Members acting individually or a fraction acting separately from the whole.**

If the members of the group are acting separately, the collective noun should be used with a plural verb.

The *party are* writing letters, driving voters, and speaking on behalf of Senator Meek.

A *majority* of the members *are* coming tonight.

Note: *A* precedes *majority* used as a plural.

The *herd are* lying, walking, eating, and drinking in the pasture.

- **Both collective and individual action.**

Group action and individual action may occur in the same sentence or paragraph. Each pronoun should agree with its antecedent.

Group acting together

The *herd drives* on through the storm until *it* reaches home safely.

The *group chooses its* leader with great care.

MORE

1

Group acting independently

The *herd were* running in different directions from the big cat. *Each feared* for *his* or *her* fawn.

The *department votes* today. *Each* person *wants* the election to be fair.

I hope your *family are* enjoying their separate holidays. *Every one* of them *is* very important to me.

1022 **Geographic locations.** Geographic locations that refer to a single place require singular verbs, even though their form may seem plural.

The *United States of America is* my home.

Massachusetts was the site selected for the national convention.

The *Canary Islands has been* their favorite hideaway.

But: (all of) The Hawaiian Islands have something different to offer. (Reference is now made to the separate islands; thus, a plural form, with a plural verb.)

1023 **Money, quantities, and time.** When reference is made to one sum of *money*, one *quantity*, or one *period of time*, the form is singular (s) and a singular verb is used. When the reference is to more than one amount of money, quantity, or time period, the form is plural (pl) and a plural verb should be used.

(s) Her *$180,000 was* the fourth prize in the sweepstakes.

(s) *Five loaves of nutbread was* her contribution to the dinner.

(pl) *Twelve cars were* unsold at the end of the year.

(s) *Nine months is* a long time to wait for the new baby.

(pl) *Three hours have* passed since you last called.

1024 **Companies and other organizational names.** Write *company* and other *organizational names* as singular with a singular verb. However, when it is important to stress the individuals within the organization, the plural form should be used with the plural verb. Noun, verb, and pronoun must be in agreement.

WordPerfect Corporation is a leader within the computer industry. *It* continues to keep pace with rapid changes in technology. (stressing the entire organization)

Holly McMeekin & Associates have aided greatly in the sale of my property. *They* were always there when I had a question. (stressing individuals within the organization)

1025 **Possessive nouns.** **Possessive nouns** use an apostrophe to indicate ownership. They may be either singular or plural and require corresponding verb forms.

A singular possessive noun requires a singular verb (add *'s* or *'* to noun—see ¶ 3506).

Dr. Suzanne *Richter's* name *was* placed in nomination.

Mary *Calleiro's* flight to New Mexico *was* delayed due to weather.

A plural possessive noun requires a plural verb (add *'* to end of noun).

The *students'* scores on the SAT *are* much improved.

My *employees'* presents *are* to be delivered today.

See ¶ 3500.

1026 **Publications.** Magazine and book titles are considered singular (and require a singular verb), even though they contain plural nouns.

Ladies Home Journal arrives at my Aunt Leota's every month.

Danielle Steel's *Jewels was* on the bestseller list for weeks.

1027 **References to fractional amounts.** When fractional amounts such as

one-fourth one-half one-eighth two-thirds	followed by *of*

or fractional portions such as

may be preceeded by a or *the*	fraction half part percentage piece portion some	followed by *of*

are used, reference is singular, and a singular verb is required *if a singular noun follows or is indicated.*

One-fourth of the *blueprint was* eliminated.

A *percentage* of the *painting is* now complete.

Only a *fraction* of the *work has been* done.

Reference is plural, and a plural verb is required, *if a plural noun follows or is indicated.*

At least *two-thirds* of the doctor's *appointments have been* rescheduled.

Half of the *group have* registered for the examination. (members of the group acting separately)

Some of the *teachers are* in favor of the issue.

1028 **References to *the* number or *a* number.** The expression *the number* is singular and requires a singular verb.

The number of custom homes here *has* increased the value of our home.

However, the expression *a number* is plural and requires a plural verb.

A number of employees *have* used all of their sick leave.

See also chapter 3, ¶ 3300.

1029 **References to *one of.*** The word *one,* followed by an *of* phrase, is singular:

One of them *is* going to win the nomination.

One of the guests *was* the 100th visitor to the park.

One of his papers *has been* accepted for publication.

One of us *is* to be ready for questions.

If a descriptive phrase follows *one of* or *one of the,* you must decide if the phrase modifies just the subject, *one,* or if it modifies the object of the prepositional phrase that follows the *one.*

She has always been *one of those who excel* at everything they do. (*Those* is the subject of *who excel*—because all of those excel, **not** just the one.)

Dr. Geri Ostrow is *the only one* of those graduates *who is* working with multiple personality disorder. (*Who* refers to the *one* person, **not** all of those graduates.)

The *only one of the things* at the garage sale I want *is* the exercycle. (The verb *is* agrees with the *one* thing.)

Note: Both *the* and *only* are required to change the meaning to singular. In the following example without both words, the meaning remains plural and requires the plural verb.

Dr. Geri Ostrow is *only one of those graduates who are* working with multiple personality disorder. (*Who* refers to many graduates.)

PRONOUNS

1051 **Definition.** **Pronouns** are the "shorthand" for writing nouns. When a noun has been previously identified, or is understood, use a pronoun to avoid unnecessary repetition.

The *members* agreed that *they* wanted Sahir Inman as *their* vice president.

Using the pronoun sounds better than repeating the noun.

The *members* agreed that the *members* wanted Sahir Inman as the *members'* vice president.

The pronouns *they* and *their* replace the noun *members*. The noun replaced by a pronoun is called that pronoun's **antecedent** (meaning "coming before"). Pronouns must agree in person, number, and gender with the antecedent they replace. The antecedents are shown all in capital letters in the following examples:

Dr. Kenneth Stringer read the laboratory REPORTS, put *them* in an ENVELOPE, and slid *it* into his briefcase.

The Certified Professional Secretary EXAMINATIONS are given quarterly; *they* last two days; and, *they* are known to be very thorough.

1052 **Personal pronouns.** A **personal pronoun** is a pronoun that changes form to indicate person. You can write or speak from three points of view. In the *first person* you talk about yourself or about a group of which you are a member. In the *second person* you talk about the person(s) to whom you are speaking, and in the *third person* you speak of anyone or anything else.

First Person Singular	**First Person Plural**
I, me, my, mine	we, our, ours

This is *my* new dress.

Our evaluation reveals areas needing improvement.

Second Person Singular	**Second Person Plural**
you, your, yours	you, your, yours

Your check-in at the conference is scheduled for noon.
You all have a chance to aid in the presentation.

Third Person Singular	**Third Person Plural**
he, him, his, she, her hers, it, its	they, them, their, theirs

Her new car is red.
Pass out the tickets to *them,* please.

The pronoun *we* is often used instead of *I* by some who wish to avoid calling attention to themselves. However, *we* should be used only by a representative

MORE

1

speaking on behalf of an organization, a group, another person, and the like; *I* should be used when representing a personal position or opinion.

I feel it is time for us to consider a major reorganization. (a personal opinion)

We shall approve your mortgage application when we have received all of the necessary credit approvals. (speaking on behalf of the mortgage company)

1053 **Indefinite pronouns.** An **indefinite pronoun** is a pronoun that does not refer to a specific person, place, or thing; or, it is one that refers generally to a part or portion of something.

Singular:	another, anybody, anyone, anything, each, either, every, everybody, everyone, everything, much, neither, no one, nobody, nothing, one, someone, somebody, something
Plural:	both, few, many, several, others
Singular and Plural:	all, any, more, most, none, some

Singular indefinite pronouns require singular verbs.

Each of the reports *has its* own summary.
Note: *Each* agrees with *its*—both are singular.

Each has a best way to avoid confrontation.
Note: Avoid the generic usage of the pronouns *his* and *her.*

Avoid: *Each* has *his* own best way to avoid confrontation.

Plural indefinite pronouns require plural verbs.

Both are in charge of the construction crew.

Many nuns *have* completed their doctoral degrees.

Some indefinite pronouns are singular or plural depending upon the noun to which they refer: they are singular when used with a singular noun, plural when used with a plural noun.

Plural: *All* of the *members have* paid their annual dues. (*All* refers to members.)

Singular: *All* of the *term paper is* complete. *It is* due tomorrow. (*All* refers to paper.)

Since indefinite pronouns usually indicate the third person, pronouns referring to such antecedents should also be written in the third person.

Most *parents* want *their* children to be successful.

However, first or second person is used when the group referred to includes a first or second person pronoun.

Most of *us* want *our* children to be successful.

1054 **Compound pronouns.** A **compound pronoun** is created when *-self* (singular) or *-selves* (plural) is added to a pronoun. Use compound pronouns that employ *-self* or *-selves* only in the same sentence as the noun or pronoun they modify.

	Singular	Plural
First Person:	myself	ourselves
Second Person:	yourself	yourselves
Third Person:	himself, herself, itself	themselves

Compound pronouns can further emphasize the noun or pronoun already indicated.

The *students themselves* want to teach the class.

I shall call Dr. McCabe *myself* to discuss this issue.

Reflexive pronouns are those compound pronouns that direct the action of the verb back to the subject.

She has convinced *herself* that she will get the job.

They have satisfied *themselves* that the verdict is just.

The following compound pronouns (which are also indefinite pronouns) are always singular and require a singular verb:

anybody	anyone *or* any one	anything
everybody	everyone *or* every one	everything
nobody	no one	nothing
somebody	someone *or* some one	something

Everybody is required to register in order to vote.

Something strange *was* happening to the phone connection.

Any one, every one, and *some one* are written as two separate words **only** when followed by *of* or when any one of a group or a number of things is implied.

Every one of them was on time.
But: *Everyone* was on time. (*Everybody* was on time.)

Any one of them can win the race.
But: *Anyone* can win the race. (*Anybody* can win the race.)

When two of these compound pronouns are joined (by *and*) as the subject of a sentence, the verb is still singular.

Anybody and everybody is worthy of a second chance.

When *each* or *every* is used **before** two or more subjects joined by *and,* the verb is still singular.

Each customer and employee *was* evacuated when the fire was discovered.

However, when *each* **follows** a plural subject, the verb should be plural.

The managers *each have* high hopes for the sales promotion.

1

1055 **Case of pronouns: Nominative, objective, and possessive.** Not only do pronouns change form to indicate person, they also change form to indicate their function in a sentence. This pronoun function is identified as one of three cases: nominative, objective, or possessive.

The **nominative case** of the pronoun is used when the pronoun is the subject of the sentence (what the sentence is about), or when the pronoun is the complement of the sentence (completing or adding meaning to the verb—such as a predicate nominative [the object of a linking verb—*is, am, was, were, be, been, being, seem, appear, become, thought*]).

Nominative Pronouns: I, we, you, he, she, it, they, who, that, whoever, which, what

As the subject:

She (**not** her) has been elected president of the Michigan Osteopathic Physicians.

They (**not** them) are reviewing the production schedule.

Jose and *she* (**not** her) had a wonderful party last night.

As the complement:

The one with the green striped shirt might be *he* (**not** him).

He was the one *who* (**not** whom) took the personnel reports.

The **objective case** of the pronoun is used when the pronoun is the object (direct or indirect) of a transitive verb (the action of the verb is directed at the pronoun),

or

when the pronoun is the object of a preposition (part of the prepositional phrase),

or

when the pronoun is the subject or object (for exception see ¶ 1057) of an *infinitive* (verb form preceded by *to*).

Objective Pronouns: me, us, you, him, her, it, them, whom, that, whomever, which, what

As the object of the verb:

Eduardo gave Suzanne and *me* (**not** I) help with the billing.

As the object of a preposition:

A complete physical was recommended for *him* (**not** he).

As the subject or object of an infinitive:

The director asked *her* (**not** she) to apply. (*Her* is the subject of *to apply*.)

Did Dr. Richter ask Lila Mae to consult *them* (**not** they)? (*Them* is the object of *to consult*.)

The **possessive case** of the pronoun is used when the pronoun indicates possession. When the **possessive pronoun** preceeds the noun it modifies (or describes), use *my, our, your, his, her, its,* or *their.* When the possessive pronoun is separated from the noun it modifies, use *mine, ours, yours, his, hers, its,* or *theirs.*

My instruments are right here. (preceding noun)

The instruments on the cart are *mine.* (separated from noun)

Use the possessive form of the pronoun immediately before a **gerund** (a verb form ending in *-ing* and functioning as a noun) or before a **participle** (a verb form ending in *-ing* that may show tense or be used as an adjective) functioning as an adjective.

His leaving so soon was quite a surprise. (gerund)
Jan told me of *your winning* bet. (participle)

Sometimes possessive pronouns are confused with similar sounding **contractions** (shortened words in which the apostrophe indicates omitted letters). Avoid this mistake.

Possessive Pronouns	**Contractions**
whose	who's (who is)
your	you're (you are)
its	it's (it is)
their	they're (they are)
theirs	there's (there is)

1056 **Pronoun following *than* or *as*.** When a pronoun is used in a comparison following *than* or *as,* mentally fill in missing words to determine correct case (nominative or objective).

Penny is not paid as much as *she.* (paid as much as she *is paid.*)

The first contestant ran faster than *I.* (than I *ran.*)

Louis rated you higher than *him.* (than *Louis rated him.*)

1057 **Pronouns used with *to be*.** Use the objective form of the pronoun when the pronoun is the subject of, and precedes, the infinitive *to be.*

We need *him* to be here.

Mr. Wilfredo Colon wants *them* to be neat.

Whom do you want to be elected?

Use the objective form of the pronoun when *to be* has a subject (not preceded by a linking verb) and is followed by the pronoun.

Whom do you want to be *me* in the play?

The students mistook the *teacher* to be *me.*

MORE

CONTINUED

Use the nominative form of the pronoun when *to be* has no subject and is followed by the pronoun.

The guilty party was thought to be *I.*

The doctor was thought to be *he.*

Note: While the examples above are grammatically correct, it is clearer to say

They thought *I* was the guilty party.

She thought *he* was the doctor.

1058 **Interrogative and relative pronouns.** **Interrogative pronouns** are used to ask questions. **Relative pronouns** are used to make reference to a noun in the main clause of a sentence. The same pronouns may be used as interrogative or relative pronouns and may be either singular or plural.

- **Interrogative - singular**

Who is coming?

To *whom* is the letter addressed?

- **Interrogative - plural**

Who are coming?

To *whom* are the letters addressed?

- **Relative - singular**

Alex Paradela was the one *who* typed the report. (relative—referring to *one.*)

Kandy Bentley-Baker, *whom* I worked with, is now pregnant.

- **Relative-plural**

Alex Paradela and Gloria Anasagasti were the ones *who* typed the report.

Kandy Bentley-Baker and Richard Janero, *whom* I worked with at North Campus, are now working together.

Note: *Who* and *whoever* are in the nominative case, while *whom* and *whomever* are in the objective case. To avoid confusion, reword the sentence to try *he, she, I, we,* or *they* to test the correct use of *who* or *whoever;* reword to try *him, her, me, us,* or *them* to test the correct use of *whom* or *whomever.*

First, isolate the *who/whom* in its proximate context.

Send the papers to [whoever/whomever] can process the application.

Second, apply the he/him, she/her rule.

She can process; he can process.
Not: *Her* and *him* can process.

Therefore:

`Send the papers to` *`whoever`* `can process the application.`

- **Who/Whoever**

Who is the next President?
(*She* is the next President.)

Carrie is the one *who* we think will do the best job.
(We think *she* [Carrie] will do the best job.)

The applications were sent to *whoever* they thought would be interested in the position.
(They thought *he* or *she* would be interested in the position.)

- **Whom/Whomever**

The Chairperson asked *whomever* to apply for the first chair.
(The Chairperson asked *them* to apply for the first chair.)

To *whom* was the report directed?
(The report was directed to *him*.)

They will welcome *whomever*.
(They will welcome *us*.)

- **Who**

Who refers to an individual person or specific group; use *who* only for references to people.

King Arthur is the one *who* led the Knights of the Round Table.

The knights constituted the group *who* accomplished many feats.

- **That**

That refers to a class, species, or kind of person or group; use *that* for references to things and **types** of people.

That is the type of employee I should like to hire.

or

when referring to places, objects, or animals.

This school is the one *that* I attended as a child.

or

to introduce an essential clause. (See ¶ 2280.)

The purple hat *that* my mother wanted is on sale.

- **Which**

Which refers to places, objects, or animals; use *which* for references only to things.

MORE

Which horse won the first prize?

or

to introduce a nonessential clause. (See ¶ 2279.)

The phone call, *which* I received today, was from my son.

VERBS

1101 **Definition.** The **verb** indicates what the subject does or is, or what is happening to it.

The most common sentence errors occur through the incorrect use of verbs. Therefore, an understanding of the way verbs are used within a sentence can improve your ability to communicate effectively and accurately.

In order for a sentence to be complete, it must contain *both a subject and a verb*. While nouns and pronouns can be the subject of the sentence providing the action (or the object [of the sentence] being acted upon), it is the verb that provides the action.

- **Verbs make statements.**

The building directory *is* now complete.

Dr. Patrick Gettings *will be* our next vice president.

- **Verbs give commands.**

Answer the call, please. (The subject *you* is understood.)

Remain in the office until I return.

- **Verbs ask questions.**

Who *will attend* the secretarial convention?

Is this your briefcase?

1102 **Active voice.** The verb is in the **active voice** if the subject of the sentence is completing the action of the sentence (that is, directing the action toward an object). If the subject acts, the verb is in the active voice.

Subject	**Verb**	
Dr. Coppolechia	*diagnosed*	the illness.

(*Dr. Coppolechia,* the subject of the sentence, is completing the action of the sentence [diagnosing]. Therefore, this verb is in the active voice.)

The insurance agent	*mailed*	the pictures of the accident.

(The insurance agent performed the action indicated by the verb.)

1103 **Passive voice.** The verb is in the **passive voice** if the subject of the sentence is being acted upon.

Subject	**Verb**	
The report	*was delivered*	by courier.

(The *report,* the subject of the sentence, is being acted upon [delivered]. Therefore, this verb is in the passive voice.)

Mario	*was interviewed*	last week.

(The subject, *Mario,* received the action indicated by the verb.)

The passive form of the verb is appropriate when the emphasis of the sentence is on the receiver of the action of the verb or when the person or thing performing the action is not important. In **all** other cases the active voice should be used.

Weak Use of Passive Voice:

It *has been requested* by the manager that a full refund be sent to you immediately.

Stronger Use of Active Voice:

The manager *requested* that a full refund be sent to you immediately.

1104 **Subject/verb agreement.** One of the most common grammatical problems is subject/verb agreement. The subject and verb in the same sentence should agree. A singular subject (one) requires a singular verb. A plural subject (more than one) requires a plural verb.

Singular Subject	**Singular Verb**	
The plan	*is* (**not** are)	almost complete.
He	*is* (**not** are)	the new receptionist.

Plural Subject	**Plural Verb**	
Three women	*were* (**not** was)	in the waiting room.
The technicians	*are* (**not** is) *taking*	golf lessons.

MORE

A compound subject (two subjects used together) requires a plural verb. (For exception, see ¶ 1054.)

Compound Subject	**Plural Verb**	
Bill and Gloria	*have been* (**not** has been)	treated for poison ivy.

When a group that is the subject of a sentence acts collectively with a single purpose, a singular verb is used. See ¶ 1021.

Group Acting Together	**Singular Verb**	
The committee	*recommends* (**not** recommend)	a complete reorganization.

When the members of a group act independently, as many different persons completing the same action, a plural verb is used. See ¶ 1021.

Group Acting Independently	**Plural Verb**	
The staff	*are* (**not** is)	at their desks.

1105 **Helping verbs.** Join **helping verbs** to other verbs to "help" indicate voice (active/passive) or tense (where in time the action takes place—see ¶ 1106). The tense indicated by the helping verb shows whether something *was* happening (past progressive), *had* happened (past perfect), *had been* happening (past perfect progressive), *is* happening (present progressive), *has happened* (present perfect), *has been* happening (present perfect progressive), *will* happen (future), *will be* happening (future progressive), *will have* happened (future perfect), or *will have been* happening (future perfect progressive). Common helping verbs include the following:

are	might	*Might* indicates what was possible
can	might be	
can be	might have	
can have	might have been	
could	must	
could be	must be	
could have	must have	
could have been	must have been	
do (present emphatic tense)	shall	
did (past emphatic tense)	shall be	
had	shall have	
had been	shall have been	
has	should	
has been	should be	
have	should have	
have been	should have been	
is	will	

May indicates action still in question or still possible	may may be may have may have been	will be will have will have been would would be would have would have been

1106 **Verb tense.** Verbs also tell time. The **tense** of the verb indicates the time of the event. Refer to Illustration 1106.1 for assistance with each of the six most common verb tenses: past, past perfect, present, present perfect, future, and future perfect. Depending upon the "time" of what you are writing about, select the appropriate verb tense. Note the use of the helping verbs in all of the "perfect" tenses.

	Time	Form	Examples (Singular)	Examples (Plural)
Past	started and completed in the past	regular verbs* add *d* or *ed* to base form	I ordered you ordered he/she/it ordered	we ordered you ordered they ordered
Past Perfect	started and completed in past before some other past action	*had* + past participle	I had ordered you had ordered he/she/it had ordered	we had ordered you had ordered they had ordered
Present	now	base form (third person singular + *s*)	I order you order he/she/it orders	we order you order they order
Present Perfect	action started in past, continuing in present	*have* or *has* + past participle	I have ordered you have ordered he/she/it has ordered	we have ordered you have ordered they have ordered
Future	will happen in future	*shall* or *will* + base form**	I shall order you will order he/she/it will order	we shall order you will order they will order
Future Perfect	will be completed in future	*shall* or *will* + *have* + past participle	I shall have ordered we will have ordered he/she/it will have ordered	we shall have ordered you will have ordered they will have ordered

Illustration 1106.1 Table of verb tenses

***Note:** For irregular verbs, consult your dictionary for past and past participle verb forms.

****Note:** *Shall* is used with the first person and *will* is used with the second and third persons. However, to express anger or other strong emotion, use *will* with first person and *shall* with second and third.

1

1107 **Regular/irregular verbs.** All **regular verbs** fit the patterns shown in Illustration 1106.1. **Irregular verbs** do not; they vary in form for present, past, future, and past participle verb forms. Always consult your dictionary for assistance, as the principal parts of all irregular verbs are listed. If such parts are not shown, the verb is regular.

Present	Past	Past Participle
am, are, is	was, were	been
become	became	become
begin	began	begun
bring	brought	brought
buy	bought	bought
choose	chose	chosen
come	came	come
do	did	done
drive	drove	driven
fall	fell	fallen
get	got	got
give	gave	given
go	went	gone
grow	grew	grown
know	knew	known
leave	left	left
lay	laid	laid (to place)
lie	lay	lain (to rest)
make	made	made
pay	paid	paid
run	ran	run
see	saw	seen
spring	sprang	sprung
take	took	taken
write	wrote	written

Illustration 1107.1 Common Irregular Verbs

1108 **Verb contraction.** A **verb contraction** is constructed by combining a verb and an adverb, eliminating one or more letters, and replacing the eliminated letter or letters with an apostrophe. See ¶ 2002 and 3533.

Verb	**Adverb**	**Contraction**
would	not	wouldn't
is	not	isn't
could	not	couldn't

Ginny Longmire *couldn't* find our office.

1109 **Verb mood.** The **verb mood** (or mode) indicates the attitude of the speaker in the action of the verb. The action of the verb can be in the indicative, imperative, or subjunctive mood.

1110 **Indicative mood.** The **indicative mood** states a fact or asks a question.

This diamond ring *is* pretty.

Do you *think* this diamond ring is pretty?

1111 **Imperative mood.** The **imperative mood** makes a request or gives a command.

Please *call* me back this afternoon.

Come here immediately!

1112 **Subjunctive mood.** The **subjunctive mood** is used with clauses of

- **Necessity**

It is important that Ray Fernandez *be consulted.*

- **Wishing**

I wish Rebecca Cohen *could preside* at this meeting.

- **Demand**

The marchers demanded their needs *be heard.*

- **Conditions that are improbable, doubtful, or contrary to fact**

If I *were* you (**but** I am not), I *would* apologize.

If you *had* your Masters degree (**but** you do not), you *would get* the promotion.

He acted as if he *were* in charge. (**but** he was not in charge)

She conducted herself as though she *were* already hired. (**but** she was not yet hired)

1113 **Infinitives.** An **infinitive** is formed when the first person singular of a regular verb is preceded by *to*; irregular verbs may form the infinitive differently. The infinitive is used as a noun, adjective, or adverb.

to come   to purchase   to return

When two or more verb infinitives are used together, the preceding *to* may be omitted for the second and subsequent infinitives.

At the closing of our house, we must remember *to read* everything first, *sign* all required papers, *pay* the attorneys involved, and *secure* the buyers' checks.
(*Sign, pay,* and *secure* are infinitives with *to* omitted.)

When the infinitive follows a verb such as feel, hear, help, let, need, and see, the *to* is usually omitted.

Please let me *come* to your Lotus seminar. (**not** to come)

Would you please help Wade Harris *copy* the minutes of the last meeting. (**not** to copy)

Avoid "splitting an infinitive" by inserting an adverb between the *to* and the verb; instead, place the adverb before or after the infinitive for clearer meaning.

My employer wanted me *to proofread* the letter *carefully*.

Not: My employer wanted me *to carefully proofread* the letter.

1

1114 **Gerunds.** A **gerund** is formed when a verb form that ends in *-ing* is used as a noun. Gerunds may be used as subjects or objects.

Studying hard is the only way to get good grades. (subject of the sentence)

He went to the laundry room to do his *washing*. (object of the infinitive *to do*)

ADJECTIVES

1151 **Definition.** **Adjectives** are words used to describe or add additional information about nouns and pronouns. **Descriptive adjectives** add information such as which one, how many, what kind, or what size.

The *little* spot on the patient's X ray was discovered by the *alert* radiologist.

Thirteen students arrived at the *square* building in the middle of the *Calle Ocho* Festival.

1152 **Definite and indefinite adjectives.** A noun preceded by *the* indicates a *specific* person, place, thing, or idea; therefore, *the* is referred to as a **definite adjective** or **definite article.** Use of *a* or *an* indicates *no specific* person, place, thing, or idea; thus, they are referred to as **indefinite adjectives** or **indefinite articles.** Remember to use *an* before all words beginning with a vowel (*a, e, i, o,* and short *u*) and before all words that sound as though they begin with a vowel (such as *hour*). Before all other words, use a.

Definite: *The student* came in for several placement tests.

Indefinite: *An individual* must study hard in order to pass these accounting courses.

A local citizens *group* is supporting a strong police presence in *an area* with *a* high crime *rate*.

1153 **Pronouns as adjectives.** Pronouns may be used as adjectives to modify nouns.

Her score was higher than *his score*.

This research *paper* on computers has many examples of *those errors*.

ADVERBS

1201 **Definition.** Adjectives modify nouns; **adverbs** modify verbs, adjectives, or other adverbs. Adverbs answer the questions when, where, how, or how much. Many adverbs end in *-ly,* making them easy to identify.

When: Susie *now knows* the entire family history.

Ginny's purchase requisition will be *ready soon.*

How: *Lift* the monitor *slowly* onto the desk.

Sidney *carefully prepared* the buffet items.

Where: The essential background work will be *completed there.*

We *found* it *here* in the conference room.

How Much: They *complained vehemently* about the visiting hours.

My report *is mostly* about the latest in technology.

1202 **Comparisons: Using adjectives and adverbs.** Adverbs and adjectives can be used to compare one person or thing with other persons or things. When there is a comparison between two persons or things, the **comparative degree** is used. The **superlative degree** is used when comparisons are made among three or more persons or things. ¶ 1205 provides a quick reference for using adverbs and adjectives in comparisons.

1203 **Comparative Degree—Comparing only two.**

Who is *older,* Naim Nichar or Jose Molina?

This one is *less costly* than the last.

She was *more diligent* in her work than was Patty.

1204 **Superlative Degree—Comparing more than two.**

Who is the *oldest* of the group?

This one is the *least costly* of the lot.

She was the *most diligent* person in the group.

1205 **Comparisons chart: Using adjectives and adverbs.**

	Base Forms	Comparative Degree (comparing two persons or things)	Superlative Degree (comparing three or more persons or things)
One-Syllable Words	**old** **nice**	add *er* to base* **older** **nicer**	add *est* to base* **oldest** **nicest**
Two-Syllable Words	**happy**	add *er* to base* or use *more* or *less* before base form **happier** **more happy** **less happy**	add *est* to base* or use *most* or *least* before base form **happiest** **most happy** **least happy**
Words of More Than Two Syllables	**intelligent**	add *more* or *less* before base **more intelligent** **less intelligent**	add *most* or *least* before base **most intelligent** **least intelligent**

***Note:** There are some minor spelling changes in some words.

***Note:** A few one-syllable words are always written with *more* or *less* before the base form in the comparative degree and *most* or *least* before the base form in the superlative degree.

ELIMINATING BIAS IN WRITING

1251 **Avoid bias—Why?** All individuals are entitled to written materials that present members of both sexes, different ethnic groups, and all races with equal respect, dignity, and balance. To accomplish this, all written material should emphasize the potential of each individual and group. Today's writers are making a real effort to eliminate many of the biases that were common in the past. As you become aware of discriminatory practices in writing, you will find that there are many ways to avoid such bias.

1252 **Sexual identifiers in compound nouns.** Some compound nouns contain the words *man* or *men* and have been used traditionally to refer to men and women alike. Such use is now considered discriminatory when applied to women or to groups of which women are a part. The U.S. Department of Labor helped to lead the way in the use of unbiased language with their 1975 publication, *Job Title Revisions to Eliminate Sex- and Age-Referent Language from the Dictionary of Occupational Titles, 3rd ed.* The latest issue of the *Dictionary of Occupational Titles* (DOT) has been revised to eliminate **all** sexual identifiers.

Some alternative choices for traditionally used compound nouns (and some adjectives and verbs) are listed in the following table. For additional assistance, consult the DOT.

Avoid	Use Instead
man, men, mankind	people, person(s), individual(s), human being(s), human race, humanity, women and men, human(s)
businessman(men)	business executive(s), business person(s), manager(s), merchant(s)
Congressman(men)	Congressional representative(s), member(s) of Congress
chairman(men)	chairperson(s), chair(s), department head(s), moderator(s), group leader(s)
salesman(men)	sales agent(s), salespeople, salesperson(s), sales representative(s), sales force
workman(men)	worker(s)
postman(men), mailman(men)	postal clerk(s), mail carrier(s)
repairman(men)	repairer(s)
foreman(men)	supervisor(s)
spokesman(men)	spokesperson(s)
maid	house worker, housecleaner, housekeeper
manned	staffed
manhandle	maltreat
manhood, manliness	maturity
manly	courageous, honorable
manhole	street utility cover
man of the world	fashionable person, individual of experience

MORE

CONTINUED

In addition, use substitutes for the following words that unnecessarily identify gender:

Avoid	Use Instead
housewife	homemaker
poetess	poet
usherette	usher
co-ed	student
sculptress	sculptor
lady (or female) doctor	doctor
male nurse	nurse

1253 **Sexual identifiers in generic pronouns.** The generic pronouns *he, his,* or *him* have often been used to indicate any member of a group, male or female. This practice is now avoided by many who think that it is unfair to use *he, his,* or *him* when referring to a group that is not all male. Ways to avoid this bias include the following:

Note: When the generic pronouns *they* or *their* are used, the sex of group members is not indicated; therefore such usage is acceptable.

Eliminate the pronoun.

Avoid: Each student is responsible for *his* materials.

Use: Each student is responsible for *personal* materials.

Change from singular to plural.

Use: All students are responsible for *their* own materials.

Use words that do not indicate gender (you, one, person, individual, all).

Avoid: *She* must determine *her* own college major.

Use: Each individual must determine a college major.

Use job titles instead of the pronoun.

Avoid: *She* should be able to transcribe confidential information accurately.

Use: The executive secretary should be able to transcribe confidential information accurately.

Change the pronoun to an article or eliminate the pronoun.

Avoid: The doctor uses *his* patient charts to summarize *his* treatment decisions.

Use: The doctor uses patient charts to summarize the treatment decisions.

Add names to eliminate generic usage.

Avoid: The office manager should determine *his* strengths and weaknesses.

Use: The office manager, Georgianna Stringer, should determine her strengths and weaknesses.

Change from active to passive voice.

Avoid: *He* should inform the supervisor immediately of any emergency.

Use: The supervisor should be informed immediately of any emergency.

(Use this method with caution. See ¶ 1103.)

Repeat the noun instead of using the pronoun.

Avoid: If the visitor has a question concerning the appointment, *she* can check with the receptionist.

Use: If the visitor has a question concerning the appointment, the *visitor* can check with the receptionist.

If the foregoing methods fail, use both pronouns. Do this as a last resort, since including both the male and female pronouns is awkward.

Avoid: A legal secretary's goal is to complete *his* legal secretarial program.

Use: A legal secretary's goal is to complete his or her legal secretarial program.

1254 **Sexual identifiers in bibliographies.** A trend that has gained increasing popularity recently is to eliminate sexual identifiers in published bibliographies by using author initials instead of first names.

House, C. and K. Sigler. *Reference Manual for the Office*. Cincinnati, OH: South-Western Publishing Co., 1995.

1255 **Age identifiers.** Implied age bias in occupational titles should also be avoided.

Avoid	Use Instead
stock boy	stock clerk
busboy	dining room attendant
curb girl	curb attendant

REFERENCE:

U.S. Department of Labor. *Job Title Revisions to Eliminate Sex- and Age-Referent Language from the Dictionary of Occupational Titles,* 3d ed. Washington, D.C.: U.S. Government Printing Office, 1975.

1

COMMONLY MISUSED WORDS

1301 **Confusing Words.** Words that serve both as adverbs and adjectives are often confused. Also, similar-sounding nouns and verbs are often confused with adjectives and adverbs. Use the following guide to avoid misuse of these similar words.

Accede The committee members *will accede* to all of our recommendations. (agree to)

Exceed Remember not to *exceed* the speed limit. (go beyond)

Accept Please *accept* our sincere regrets. (receive, approve—verb)

Except Everyone was present, *except* Armando Ferrer. (with the exclusion of—preposition)

Access Patrick was trying to *access* the data bank. (get into—verb; admission—noun)

Excess The *excess* food was taken to the homeless center. (surplus—adjective; state of surplus—noun)

Adopt Karen and Craig McMeekin will *adopt* a son. (choose—verb)

Adept Roberta and Bill Stokes were both *adept* at learning data processing terminology. (highly skilled—adjective)

Adapt The personnel department will *adapt* this form to fit the purchasing department's new requirements. (adjust—verb)

Adverse Her recommendations caused an unexpected *adverse* result. (contrary)

Averse Dr. Maria Hernandez was *averse* to that kind of action. (disinclined, showing dislike)

Advice Their *advice* was to continue the project. (recommendation—noun)

Advise The school attorney *advised* the board member, Mr. Martin Fine, that there was no conflict of interest. (provide counsel—verb)

Affect	Maureen O'Hara's example began to *affect* Isabel's performance. (to influence, change—verb)
Effect	The *effect* of the test results was a major change in design. (result—noun)
	Rocio Lamadriz wanted to *effect* a rapid change. (bring about—verb)
Aloud	Pam Stringer read the background information *aloud* to her students. (out loud)
Allowed	Children are not *allowed* to enter the Paella cooking area. (permitted)
Almost	We are *almost* ready to begin. (nearly)
All Most	You are *all most* welcome to our home. (each one very welcome)
Already	Have they left the grounds *already?* (before an understood time)
All Ready	Scotty and Holly are *all ready* to go home now. (completely prepared)
Alright	*Alright* is not grammatically acceptable—do not use. (Hint: Just as there is no word *alwrong,* there is no word *alright.*)
All Right	We were relieved to hear that they were *all right.* (satisfactory, certainly)
Alternate	He chose *alternate* treatments of hot packs and cold packs. (first one, then the other in succession)
Alternative	They were left but one *alternative*—to fly home. (one choice that rules out others one might have taken)
Altogether	The results of the survey were *altogether* too good to be true. (entirely)
All Together	The students were *all together* in the auditorium. (all in a group)
Always	Angel Valdes is *always* looking for new parking solutions. (at all times)
All Ways	Geoff has driven *all ways* to his office to determine the shortest route. (every possible choice)

MORE

CONTINUED

Among	They always enjoy being *among* famous politicians. (*Among* is used with three or more persons or things when no close relationship is indicated.)
Between	The choice is *between* Bart and Rebecca for chief of staff. (*Between* is used with two persons or things or with terms such as *treaty, agreement,* or *discussion*.)
Anyone	Has *anyone* seen the budget printout? (anybody)
Any One	*Any one* of these courses will satisfy the requirements. (any particular item or person in a group)
Anytime	Bart Powell was available *anytime* I had a question. (whenever)
Any Time	Did you provide a copy of this report to him at *any time* in the past? (any particular time over a period—always two words as the object of a preposition)
Anyway	*Anyway,* I didn't win the drawing. (in any event)
Any Way	I shall be happy to be of assistance in *any way* I can help. (by any method)
Appraise	Our new house was *appraised* at $250,000. (value)
Apprise	She promised to *apprise* the board of the results. (inform)
Assure	Nora Murrell made it a point to *assure* Linda Pagliaro that all purchasing rules were followed. (declare, reassure, guarantee)
Ensure	To *ensure* prompt arrival, please send the book via overnight delivery. (make certain)
Insure	Nelson wanted to *insure* his new car before driving it off of the lot. (protect against financial loss)
Awhile	Kamala had to wait *awhile* to see him. (one word when used as an adverb)
A While	The patient has been gone for *a while*. (two words when used as a noun)
Badly	This accident victim is *badly* in need of help. (very much—adverb)
Bad	It looks *bad* for our budget reports to be late. (After sensory verbs [look, smell, sound], the adjective *bad* is correct.)
Besides	*Besides* my television, the thieves took the stereo and my new computer. (in addition to)

Beside He sat *beside* me during the concert. (next to)

Between/Among See Among/Between

Both *Both* of the children said, "Mine." (two considered together)

Each *Each* wanted to be first in line. (individuals considered separately)

Bring *Bring* the final totals to me. (to the speaker or the spot where spoken [here])

Take *Take* the final totals to Frank Meistrell. (away from the speaker or the spot where spoken [there])

Can Jose *can* complete his doctorate this year. (ability, power)

May *May* Sally enter the Senate hearings early? (permission, possibility)

Capitol The signing of the new education bill will take place in the *Capitol* at noon. (*Capitol* is used to mean the buildings used by the Congress and by state legislatures.)

Capital The *capital* of Colorado is Denver. (*Capital* is used to mean a seat of government; a term in finance, accounting, and architecture; chief and first-rate; capital letter; and, capital punishment.)

Come Please *come* to my office this afternoon. (to the speaker or the spot where spoken [here])

Go Please *go* to Dr. Brookner's meeting tomorrow. (away from the speaker or the spot where spoken [there])

Command It was a *command* performance. (ordered—adjective; to order—verb)

Commend Sophie Schrager was *commended* on her performance at Columbia University. (praise, recommend—verb)

Comments The speakers *comments* were meaningful to the graduates. (remarks)

Commence The graduation ceremonies will *commence* at 9:00 a.m. (begin)

Comprise The New Music America Festival *comprises* many individual performances. (embraces, consists of)

MORE

Note: *Comprise* and *constitute* are used **obversely.** For example: Many individual performances constitute the New Music America Festival.

Compose	Joseph Celli *composed* the music for the "Escalator" performance. (create music) The mathematics department was *composed* of many creative individuals. (the whole made up of) Esther wanted to *compose* herself before confronting the new problem. (calm)
Contest	The speech *contest* was held in Room 1561. (competition)
Context	The *context* of the sentence will help you determine the meaning of the word. (surrounding or interrelated material or conditions)
Cooperation	The *cooperation* between the two departments was much improved. (common effort)
Corporation	Bernard Fils-Aime signed the papers to formalize the new *corporation*. (an association of persons)
Currently	The temperature is *currently* 75°. (at the present time)
Presently	The class is reading now, but the bell will ring for them to leave *presently*. (in the near future)
Decease	The *deceased* was her neighbor. (dead person, die, cease to exist)
Disease	Her *disease* was diagnosed as a skin infection. (illness)
Deference	In *deference* to your opinion, I shall reconsider. (yielding, respect)
Difference	The *difference* between the two texts was significant. (state of being unlike)
Each/Both	See Both/Each
Effect/Affect	See Affect/Effect
Eminent	She was an *eminent* member of the community. (prominent)
Imminent	The arrival of the hurricane to the seaside community was *imminent*. (about to occur)

Ensure/Insure/Assure See Assure/Ensure/Insure

Everyday This is becoming an *everyday* problem with him. (routine, daily)

Every Day *Every day* we can delay will make our position stronger. (each day)

Everyone Will *everyone* be coming to the meeting? (everybody)

Every One *Every one* of them had a full physical. (each one)

Ex- *Ex*- used to mean former is not standard or formal usage.

Former Charles Rogers is a *former* president of the Wolfson Campus Faculty Senate. (any officer before the current one)

Exceed/Accede See Accede/Exceed

Except/Accept See Accept/Except

Excess/Access See Access/Excess

Farther/Further See Further/Farther

Fewer/Less See Less/Fewer

Formerly She was *formerly* the telecommunications consultant. (previously, before)

Formally Dr. Mathilde Krim was *formally* accepted as a member of the American Foundation for AIDS Research Board. (in a formal manner)

Forward Come *forward* a little into the light so that I can see your new uniform. (toward the front, progressive)

Foreword In the *foreword* of the book, an authority mentions the author's years of careful research. (prefatory comments most often by someone other than the author)

Fortunate We are *fortunate* to have known Ric. (lucky)

Fortuitous Of the 100,000 people, it was *fortuitous* that we saw Larry and Jim in the crowd. (strictly by chance)

MORE

1

Fourth	It was the *fourth* time I tried to call the accounting department. (after third)
Forth	From that day *forth,* she was never the same. (forward, onward in time)
Further	His statement could not be *further* from the truth. (additional; greater distance in time or quantity)
Farther	Your therapist's office is *farther* than I thought. (actual distance)
Go/Come	See Come/Go
Good/Well	See Well/Good
Imminent/Eminent	See Eminent/Imminent
Imply	Sally Buxton *implied* that she did not want to leave the campus. (suggest)
Infer	I *infer* from your comments that we shall not be going to Argentina. (conclude)
Incite	The demonstrators were trying to *incite* the crowd to action. (arouse, provoke)
Insight	Arnold Fleisch demonstrated excellent *insight* into the problems experienced in the science lab. (understanding)
Indifferent	Jay Freeman was not *indifferent* to the concerns of the classified staff personnel. (uncaring)
In Different	We each came to the same conclusion *in different* ways. (separate, other)
Insure/Ensure/Assure	See Assure/Ensure/Insure
Irregardless	Do **not** use—double negative; use *regardless*.
Regardless	The telephones will be installed today, *regardless* of the electrical storm. (without taking into account, in spite of)
Its	Even though the manuscript is finished, we are well aware of *its* keyboarding errors. (belonging to it)
It's	*It's* a big challenge for Reina Welch. (contraction of *it is*)

Latest This is the *latest* announcement about the conference. (most recent)

Last Carmen McCrink was the *last* one to arrive for the Arts Council meeting. (final)

Latter Dr. Karen Paiva and Dr. J. Terrence Kelly were the two contestants; the *latter* was the winner. (second of two)

Later Enjoy yourself; it's *later* than you think. (after another point in time)

Learn I want to *learn* to use the computer. (acquire knowledge)

Teach She loved to *teach* Lotus 1-2-3. (impart knowledge to others)

Leave *Leave* the keys on my desk. (depart, abandon, move away)

Let *Let* Security open the doors to the auditorium. (permit)

Leased Al Schlazer *leased* a condominium near the Omni Shopping Mall. (rented)

Least Arriving on time was the *least* of our worries today. (smallest)

Less Our debt was *less* in those days. (We owed $2,100 then; we owe $4,800 now. [refers to quantity/amount])

Fewer Our debts were *fewer* in those days. (We had 10 debts then; we have 18 now. [refers to number or that which can be counted])

Libel The author was sued for *libel* after the book was published. (injury through written or printed statements)

Liable The hospital is *liable* for the patient's care. (responsible)

Lose The development team did not want to *lose* a minute during the delicate negotiations. (suffer a loss)

Loose The connection was *loose*, and the video reception was affected. (not secure)

May/Can See Can/May

MORE

1

Maybe	*Maybe,* we should call if the equipment doesn't arrive soon. (possibly—adverb)
May Be	Your concerns *may be* different tomorrow. (might—verb)
New	We filled our wing of the research center with *new* furniture. (fresh, unused)
Knew	She *knew* Dr. Joan Schaeffer before taking the professor's class. (acquainted with)
Past	In *past* negotiations, the union responded more quickly. (previous time—adjective, noun, adverb, or preposition)
Passed	To my surprise, I *passed* the legal terminology test. (proceeded beyond—verb)
Percent	Over 50 *percent* of our students are Hispanic. (use when accompanied by a number)
Percentage	A small *percentage* of our personnel still need to complete their withholding forms. (use when not directly accompanied by a number)
Persecute	Teenagers often feel their parents are trying to *persecute* them. (annoy, harass)
Prosecute	Victoria Sigler was selected to *prosecute* the hate-crimes suspect. (to legally take to trial, to pursue until finished)
Personnel	The *personnel* in your department seem very enthusiastic. (employees)
Personal	My decision to leave my position was a very *personal* one. (private)
Precede	Your announcements will *precede* the arrival of the speaker. (come before)
Proceed	Please *proceed* with the meeting. (advance; carry forward)
Presently/Currently	See Currently/Presently
Principle	It wasn't the decision that was made; rather, it was the *principle* of the matter that was important to Dr. Ileana Gonzalez. (basic truth)
Principal	Ms. Mandy Offerle was the very popular *principal* of the school. (chief official, capital sum of money)

Quiet It was a *quiet* day at the office. (still, hushed)

Quite This is not *quite* what I was looking for. (completely, exactly)

Raise Would you please *raise* that corner of the table? (cause to lift up)

Rise The sun will *rise* tomorrow at 6:25 a.m. (ascend, move upward by itself)

Really Are you *really* going to support Social Security reform? (actually, truly—adverb)

Real Dr. Sarah Turbett was a *real* friend. (true, actual—adjective)

Regardless/Irregardless See Irregardless/Regardless

Respectfully The entire situation was handled *respectfully*. (with regard for, in deference to)

Respectively The first, second, and third prizes will go to Mercedes Sandoval, Shirley Gribble, and Glenn Thompson, *respectively*. (in the order given)

Sometimes *Sometimes,* it is hard to understand insurance reports. (now and then)

Sometime *Sometime* later this week, we shall schedule an important staff meeting. (at an unspecified time)

Some Time It was *some time* before the director returned from the presentation. (a period of time)

Sum What is the *sum* of all your travel expenses? (total)

Some *Some* of the audience began to leave the fringe benefits briefing. (part, a portion of)

Surely *Surely* you don't want to quit now? (certainly, confidently—adverb)

Sure I am *sure* you can learn these data processing abbreviations. (certain—adjective)

Take/Bring See Bring/Take

MORE

CONTINUED

Teach/Learn	See Learn/Teach
Then	Wait until the vehicle stops; *then,* you can get out safely. (at that time—adverb)
Than	My performance rating is higher now *than* it was when I first began working here. (as compared to—conjunction)
There	Write it *there* on the check requisition. (in that place)
Their	*Their* interest was in their friend's mental health. (possessive pronoun)
To	Come *to* the cafeteria with me. (preposition)
Too	Ricky wants to come, *too*. (also)
Two	*Two* lab managers were assigned to the same unit. (number following *one*)
Week	This *week* we have a vacation from school to celebrate the Fourth of July. (seven successive days—noun)
Weak	He was too *weak* to climb any farther. (not strong—adjective)
Well	Ann is *well* enough to join Karen at the game. (fortunate, healthy—adjective; or rightly—adverb)
Good	The chili smells *good*. (attractive, bountiful, wholesome—adjective)
Whether	*Whether* or not we vote, our issue still cannot win. (function word indicating alternatives)
Weather	The *weather* remained sunny during our entire conference. (state of the atmosphere)

PREPOSITIONS

1351 **Prepositions as connectors.** **Prepositions** connect or show the relationship of a noun or pronoun to another word in a sentence in what is referred to as a **prepositional phrase**.

The technician moved carefully *between* the two hospital beds.

In this example, the preposition *between* shows the relationship between *technician* (the subject) and *beds,* the object of the preposition.

When pronouns are used as the object of a preposition, they must be in the objective case. (See ¶ 1055.)

Yolanda placed a call *to* her.

Greg searched high and low *for* them.

Please write the telephone number *for* me.

1352 **Frequently used prepositions.** The following listing includes many of the most frequently used prepositions.

about	below	into	to
above	beside	like	under
across	between	of	until
after	by	off	up
against	down	on	upon
among	during	over	with
around	except	past	within
at	for	round	without
before	from	since	
behind	in	through	

CONJUNCTIONS

1401 **Conjunctions as connectors.** **Conjunctions** are words used to connect two words, phrases, or clauses. **Coordinating conjunctions** connect words, phrases, or clauses that are equal in rank or stature. Common forms are *and, but, for, or, nor,* and *yet.*

Dr. Eduardo J. Padron *and* Dr. Roberto Hernandez were honored at the banquet.

The managers like their jobs, *but* they want to continue taking additional classes.

1402 **Correlative conjunctions.** **Correlative conjunctions** are pairs of words that connect two like words, phrases, or clauses. Common forms are *either/or, neither/nor, both/and, not/but, whether/or (not),* and *not only/but (also).*

Either Dr. Vicente *or* his assistant will perform the routine review in the morning.

Neither Lourdes *nor* I remembered the appointment yesterday.

CHAPTER 2

PUNCTUATION

APOSTROPHE

2001 **Uses of the apostrophe.** Apostrophes are used primarily to create possessive forms of certain nouns and indefinite pronouns. Those possessives are discussed in chapter 3, ¶ 3009 and 3501-33.

Apostrophes are also used in contractions, as single quotation marks, as symbols in technical writing, and in creating the plural forms of letters, numbers, and other symbols. These uses are discussed in ¶ 2002-10.

2002 **Apostrophe in contractions.** When an apostrophe is used to replace a character or characters omitted in a contraction, it is placed at the exact point of omission. No letters or other characters are added.

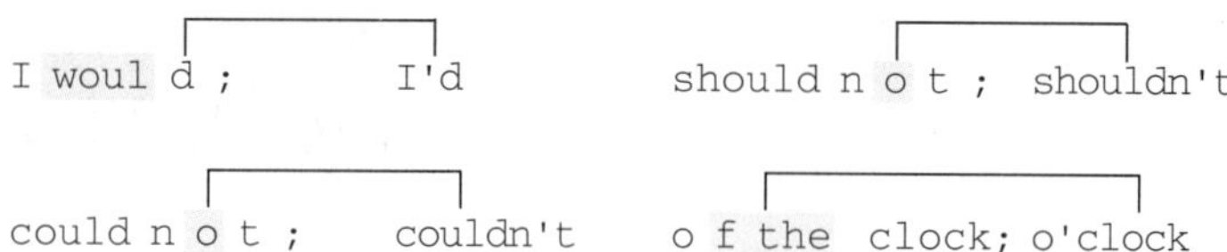

2

An apostrophe may be written in place of the first two digits of a year when using a contraction is appropriate. See ¶ 3304.

`The class of '85 will have a reunion next year.`

2003 **Apostrophes as single quotation marks.** In some cases type fonts, keyboards, and computer printers use a single character for the apostrophe and for left and right single quotation marks. In that case, the character is straight and vertical ' .

In other cases the font, keyboard, or printer employs left and right single quotation marks ‘ ’ . The same character that is used for the right single quotation mark is used for the apostrophe ’ .

See ¶ 2781 for a discussion of single quotation marks.

2004 **Apostrophes as symbols (in technical writing).** Technical (specialized) writing employs symbols, abbreviations, and graphics that may seem out of place in formal writing or ordinary text. Even the most formal documents, however, may have technical *sections* that contain tables, charts, diagrams, specifications, illustrations, and the like. A well-constructed document may contain both very formal and very technical material as long as the appropriate context is clearly established for each section of the document.

Many questions of usage and style simply do not arise if the writer is careful to avoid the haphazard mixing of formal text, ordinary text, and technical material.

In a technical context, an apostrophe may be used to represent *feet* or *minutes*. (A quotation mark is used to represent inches or seconds.)

`29 feet 4 inches: 29' 4"     9 minutes 27 seconds: 9' 27"`

2005 **Plural forms of capital letters.** Addition of a lowercase *s* is the preferred pluralization of capital letters. Use the older form (employing an apostrophe) for letters A, I, and U in order to avoid ambiguity. If the *apostrophe s* form is used to pluralize any capital letter in a context, use the same *apostrophe s* form to pluralize *all* capital letters in that context.

With apostrophe:	A’s	B’s	C’s	D’s
Preferred:	Es	Fs	Gs	Hs
But:	A’s	I’s	U’s	
Not:	As	Is	Us	
Do not mix:	I’s	Js	Ks	Ls
But use:	I’s	J’s	K’s	L’s

2006 **Plural forms of lowercase letters.** Apostrophes are used to form plurals of lowercase letters.

With apostrophe:	a's	b's	c's	d's
***Not* acceptable:**	as	bs	cs	ds

See ¶ 3009 for pluralization of abbreviations written in lowercase letters.

2007 **Plural forms of numbers.** Although *'s* may be added to numbers to pluralize them, the addition of the letter *s* alone is preferred.

Preferred:	9s	12s	100s	1000s
Acceptable:	9's	12's	100's	1000's

2

2008 **Plural forms of symbols.** Apostrophes may be used to create plural forms of symbols.

With apostrophe:	*'s	&'s	#'s	@'s	?'s
Also acceptable:	*s	&s	#s	@s	?s

2009 **Graphic representation of words.** A word used as a word rather than for its meaning may be enclosed in single quotation marks (within a quoted sentence) or quotation marks if the spoken language is implied. However, italics (or underscore) are used in all other cases.

Reference to written word:	Paint the *and* a little higher on the sign.
Reference to spoken word:	Shakespeare uses *"thou"* for *"you"* in dialogue.
Spoken word within quote:	He said, "Shakespeare uses *'thou'* for *'you'* in dialogue."

2010 **Spacing with an apostrophe.** The following examples illustrate spacing with apostrophes. [▮ = space]

That is the Spinozas'.▮▮The Dixons'▮is the last house on the street.

The class of▮'84 will be honored at the reunion.

It's O'Hara who shouted,▮"He said,▮'stop.'"▮▮'Tis time to remember that.

2

2051 **Asterisks identifying footnotes.** Asterisks may be used to refer the reader to footnotes at the bottom of the page. [▮ = space]

Asterisks may refer readers to footnotes located lower on the page.▮▮An asterisk is inserted immediately after the sentence, clause, phrase, word, etc. to which a footnote*▮pertains.▮▮A pair of asterisks, written with no space between them, identifies the second footnote on the page.**▮▮Three asterisks, written with no space between them,***▮identify the third footnote on the page.

---

*In text, an asterisk follows another punctuation mark without intervening space.▮▮At the bottom of a page, asterisks precede the footnotes they identify without intervening space.

**Insertion of an asterisk does not alter conventions for spacing:

a. Leave two spaces after the end of a sentence.*▮▮If the sentence ends with a question mark or exclamation mark, spacing is the same—two spaces following the asterisk.
b. Leave▮one▮space▮between▮words.▮▮Count the asterisk as part of the word it follows.
c. Following a comma,*▮leave one space after the asterisk.

***If more than three footnotes appear on a page, most writers use other symbols in addition to asterisks or use numbered footnotes instead of asterisks. See ¶ 5529 for numbered footnotes.

2052 **Footnotes following tables and other illustrations.** A table, diagram, chart, graph, or the like, may require a footnote to identify its source, or footnotes as comments on its various parts, or both.

Asterisks may be used to footnote such an illustration if it requires no more than three footnotes. The system described in the preceding model is used, except that footnote references appear in the illustration and the footnotes themselves appear immediately below the illustration rather than at the bottom of the page. The following table illustrates footnoting with asterisks; numbered footnotes are discussed in ¶ 5529-36.

2

PRINCIPAL U.S. PORTS
Ranked by Foreign Tonnage

New Orleans, LA**	Long Beach, CA***
Houston, TX**	Philadelphia, PA*
New York, NY*	Texas City, TX**
Norfolk Harbor, VA*	Tampa Harbor, FL**
Corpus Christi, TX**	Port Arthur, TX**
Baton Rouge, LA**	Newport News, VA*
Baltimore Harbor, MD*	Pascagoula, MS**
Los Angeles, CA***	Mobile, AL**
Lake Charles, LA**	Tacoma Harbor, WA***

*Atlantic Ocean
**Gulf of Mexico
***Pacific Ocean

2053 **Asterisks representing unprintable words.** Asterisks may be used to indicate omission of unprintable words. A group of three asterisks without intervening spaces may be substituted for each word, or each omitted letter may be represented by an asterisk.

He was called a *** and a ***.
She said, "******** and ****."

2054 **Spacing with an asterisk.** See ¶ 2051, 2053.

BRACES

2101 **Reproducing braces.** Typewriters can reproduce braces by "stacking" parentheses or brackets. Some word processors and computers use their graphics capabilities to produce a more finished version of braces. Printing processes produce all of these—plus the still-more-finished versions designed by typographers and artists.

MORE

CONTINUED

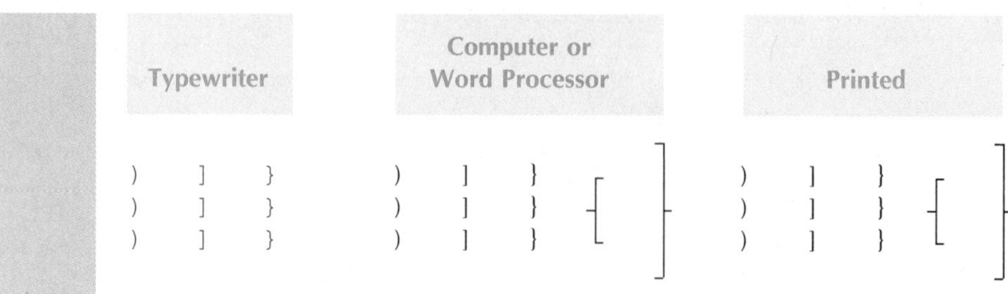

Both braces and brackets can be drawn with plastic templates.

2102 **Braces in illustrations.** A brace may be used to organize data: to illustrate graphically the relationships among the items joined by the brace.

```
                     ┌ Su   74                       ┌ 30 ┐
                     │ M    76                       │ 32 │
                     │ Tu   79                       │ 34 │
Mean Temperatures ───┤ W    75               Sizes ──┤ 36 ├── $32.75 Each
                     │ Th   73                       │ 38 │
                     │ F    72                       │ 40 │
                     └ Sa   73                       └ 42 ┘
```

2103 **Braces in law documents.** Braces are used frequently in the opening sections of law documents to illustrate graphically the nature of the document or the nature of the action the document represents.

```
Earl Flores                      )
               Plaintiff         )

               vs.               )

Ford Green                       )
               Defendant         )
```

2104 **Braces in mathematics and logic.** In mathematics and logic, braces are used to indicate the highest degree of aggregation, enclosing brackets, which enclose angle brackets outside parentheses. The usual order is as follows:

```
{[<(   )>]}
```

```
2{3[4<5(7-2)>-97]-1}=  ► 2{3[4<25>-97]-1}=  ► 2{3[3]-1}=  ► 2(8)=
 2{3[4<5(5)>-97]-1}=      2{3[100-97]-1}=      2{9-1}=       16

 2{3[4<5(5)>-97]-1}=      2{3[100-97]-1}=      2{9-1}=
  2{3[4<25>-97]-1}=          2{3[3]-1}=          2{8}=
```

BRACKETS

2151 **Brackets enclosing parenthetical expressions.** Parentheses are used in ordinary text to set off parenthetical expressions.

`Jessica (the tallest girl in the group) was first in line.`

Square brackets are used to enclose a parenthetical expression within a parenthetical expression.

`Jessica (the tallest girl [but not the tallest student] in the group) was first in line.`

Angle brackets are used (especially in technical writing) to indicate a third level ([< >]) parenthetical expression or to enclose specialized information. In some dictionaries, examples are enclosed in angle brackets; the *swung* dash is used to indicate the word being defined. An example of one use of the word *wash* might be

`<~ ed their hands>`

Angle brackets are also used to identify keys on a keyboard.

`Strike <Shift> + <A> to enter a capital A.`

2152 **Brackets enclosing writer's comments.** Square brackets are used to identify comments or observations inserted in quoted material by the writer. They are particularly useful for the insertion of stage directions into scripts, as in the first example that follows.

"This is my answer: [moving to the right] No! No! No!"

The mechanic said, "It [the engine] will not start."

"My bass [*sic*] is in charge of the entire department."

The word *sic* means "thus" or "so." It tells the reader that, even though there is something unusual—possibly incorrect—about the preceding part of the quotation, it is reproduced exactly (thus or so) as it appeared in the original. The word *sic* is italicized in printed material.

2153 **Brackets enclosing notes on pronunciation.** Square brackets may be used to insert notes on pronunciation.

```
cart ['kärt]                    establish [is - 'tab - lish]
```

2154 **Printing and drawing brackets.** Most typewriters, word processors, and computers reproduce square brackets [ ] and angle brackets < >. Plastic templates for drawing them are available in office supply stores.

Both square brackets and angle brackets can be drawn with a ruler. A fair representation of square brackets can be made on most typewriters using diagonal and underscore keys: /̄ _/.

2155 **Spacing with brackets.** These examples illustrate proper spacing with brackets. [▮=space]

```
My answer, as you know,▮[moving closer]▮is yes.
That was it▮[the book].▮▮She left the room.
Where shall I put it▮[the box]?
Where shall I put the box?▮▮[moving toward exit]▮▮Here?
Please put it▮[the box]▮on the table.
```

See ¶ 2104 for using brackets with braces in mathematics and logic.

2200 COLON

2202 2201 **Colon separates introduction : explanation.** A colon identifies a relationship in which an *introductory expression* (preceding the colon) introduces an *explanatory* or *illustrative* expression (following the colon). See ¶ 2202.

2202 **Introduction precedes colon.** An introductory expression preceding a colon should conform to these conventions:

- The introductory expression should have a subject and predicate.

[Subject and Predicate]	[:]	[Explanation or Illustration]
These *stops are* on the list	:	New York, Chicago, and Seattle.

- The introductory expression should cause the reader to anticipate an explanation or illustration that will follow the colon.

[Anticipatory Expression]	[:]	[Explanation or Illustration]
There are four dry ingredients	:	flour, sugar, yeast, and salt.

- The introductory expression should be near the colon. Intervening words should not distract the reader from the relationship identified by the colon.

Not: *The following paint is needed* because the customers have changed their minds about the colors to be used in the living room and kitchen: 3 gallons 4903 (Arctic White), 5 quarts 1121 (Glengrove Green), and 2 gallons 2112 (Eggshell White).

But: The customers have changed their minds about the colors to be used in the living room and kitchen. Consequently, *the following paint is needed:* 3 gallons 4903 (Arctic White), 5 quarts 1121 (Glengrove Green), and 2 gallons 2112 (Eggshell White).

Note: In specifications such as these and in other technical material all numbers are written in figures. (See ¶ 3302-03.)

- The introductory expression should not end with a verb or preposition unless it is followed by items *listed* on separate lines.

	[Introductory Expression]	[Verb or Preposition]	[:]	[With Verb or Preposition]
Not:	The price	includes	:	delivery, padding and installation, and a one-year guarantee on all materials and labor.
Not:	The unit consists	of	:	the three-piece living room suite, the seven-piece dining room suite, and the five-piece bedroom suite.

MORE

CONTINUED

But:	The price	includes	:	Delivery Padding Installation One-year guarantee
Or:	The unit consists	of	:	Three-piece living room suite Seven-piece dining room suite Five-piece bedroom suite

- The introductory expression may imply—rather than state—that something will follow.

[Implied Introduction]	**[:]**	**[Explanation or Illustration]**
The cause was obvious	:	it had rained two inches in an hour.

2203 **Explanation or illustration follows colon.** An explanatory or illustrative expression follows a colon.

- The expression following a colon may consist of one or more sentences.

[Introduction]	**[:]**	**[Explanatory Sentence(s)]**
The detective recited the facts	:	The jewels belonged to Marcella. She lent them to Gabrielle. The jewels were stolen from Gabrielle.

- The expression following a colon may consist of one or more clauses.

[Introduction]	**[:]**	**[Explanatory Clause(s)]**
He talked of only one thing	:	what the jewels were worth.

- The expression following a colon may consist of one or more words.

[Introduction]	**[:]**	**[Explanatory Word(s)]**
There is one key word	:	stolen.

- The expression following a colon may consist of items on a list.

[Introduction]	**[:]**	**[Explanatory List]**
The elected officers are as follows	:	President Vice President Secretary-Treasurer

- The expression following a colon may consist of a quotation.

[Introduction]	**[:]**	**[Quotation]**
Samuel Goldwyn said:	:	"If you can't give me your word of honor, will you give me your promise?"

2204 **Equal independent clauses require semicolon.** Use a semicolon to separate equally important independent clauses when the second such clause does not explain or illustrate the first.

[Independent Clause]	**[;]**	**[Independent Clause]**
She traveled by plane	;	he traveled by car.

2205 **Semicolon with transitional expression.** Use a semicolon to separate independent clauses linked by a transitional expression. Some examples follow. See ¶ 2803 for others.

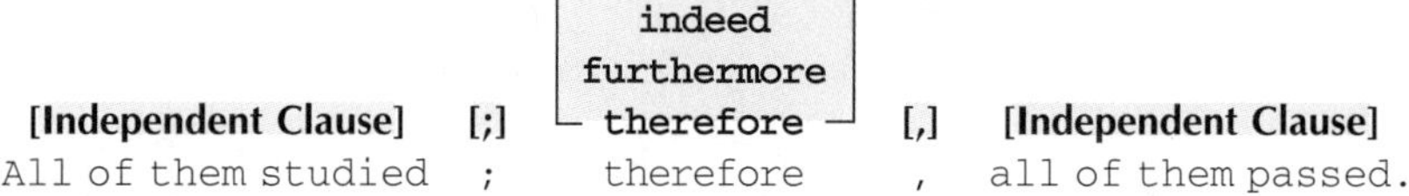

A comma is required after most transitional expressions. A few transitional expressions (thus, so that, yet, hence, and then) require no hesitation in thought or speech and, therefore, require no comma.

[Independent Clause]	[;]	[Transitional Expression]	[Independent Clause]
They were prepared	;	so	they did well.

2206 **Capitalization of the first word after a colon.** The first word after a colon is capitalized only if the conventions for capitalization apply to it. See ¶ 3100-52 on capitalization.

This is the reason:	They were later than you thought.
These are the winners:	U.K., U.S.A., and France.
She is featured in a new mystery:	*Death Takes Liberty.*

2207 **Capitalize a proper noun or proper adjective after a colon.** After a colon, capitalize each proper noun and each proper adjective (adjective made from a proper noun). See ¶ 3101-52.

These names are on the list:	Alfredo, Celeste, and Nanette.
One philosophy held her attention:	Aristotelian.

2208 **Capitalization in a quoted sentence following a colon.** After a colon, capitalize the first word in a quoted sentence.

The guard repeated the warning: "Travel at your own risk."

2209 **Capitalize the first word of dominant clause following a colon.** If the sentence element after a colon is an independent clause that is the *dominant or more general element of the sentence,* capitalize its first word.

- Dominant independent clause follows a colon.

The reason is this: *Southbound traffic is heavy.*

- Independent clause following a colon is not dominant.

Southbound traffic is heavy: *that is the reason.*

- The dominant element following a colon is not an independent clause.

The reason is this: *southbound traffic.*

2210 **Capitalization in two or more sentences following a colon.** If two or more sentences follow a colon, they are punctuated normally.

Acceptable:	The tree should stay:	It will grow fast. We need the shade.
But:	The tree should stay:	It will grow fast; we need the shade.
Or:	The tree should stay:	It will grow fast and we need the shade.

2

2211 **Capitalization in a list following a colon.** After a colon, capitalize the first word on each line of a line-by-line list.

```
The following items were displayed:
       Digital watches
       Analog clocks
       Table lamps
       Radios
```

This convention is not altered by addition of item numbers, quantities, stock numbers, prices, or the like.

```
The following items were displayed:
1. Digital watches       8 Digital watches       1. 8 Digital watches
2. Analog clocks    or   9 Analog clocks    or   2. 9 Analog clocks
3. Table lamps           7 Table lamps           3. 7 Table lamps
4. Radios                6 Radios                4. 6 Radios
```

2212 **Colons in literary references.** A colon may be used in a literary reference:

- To separate title and subtitle. The subtitle must be a secondary title capable of standing alone.

Acceptable: *Bloodbath: Gore in the Afternoon*

Not: *Bloodbath: In the Afternoon*

- To separate volume number and page number in footnotes and bibliographies.

Volume 7, pages 109 through 119 7:109-119

- To separate city of publication and name of publisher in footnotes and bibliographies.

Cincinnati: South-Western Publishing Co.

See ¶ 5514, 5529-35 for bibliography and footnote styles.

2213 **Colons in biblical references.** A biblical reference may be written with a colon separating chapter and verse.

Proverbs 14:13 refers to Chapter 14, verse 13 of the Book of Proverbs.

2214 **Colons expressing ratios and proportions.** A colon may be used to express a ratio or proportion.

The differential has a ratio of 1.7:1. *Or* 1.7 to 1. *Or* 1.7-to-1.

2215 **Spacing with a colon.** Do not space before a colon. Space twice after a colon in normal use. Do not space before or after a colon when it is used in expressing the time of day, in a literary reference, or in expressing a ratio.

COMMA

Comma Separating Main Clauses

2251 **Comma with a coordinating conjunction.** In a compound sentence, a comma is used to separate independent clauses linked by a coordinating conjunction.

[Independent Clause]	**[,]**	**and / but / or / for / nor / yet**	**[Independent Clause]**
They tried diligently	,	and	they were successful.
The model was professional	,	but	the picture was amateurish.

Do not use a comma to separate a coordinating conjunction from the clause it precedes. The only exception to this rule is when the conjunction is preceded by a semicolon or begins an entirely new sentence. (See the example in ¶ 2354.)

Not: You can lead a horse to water, but, you cannot make it drink.

But: You can lead a horse to water, but you cannot make it drink.

2252 **No comma in some short compound sentences.** If both independent clauses in a compound sentence are short and the clauses are closely related, the comma may be omitted.

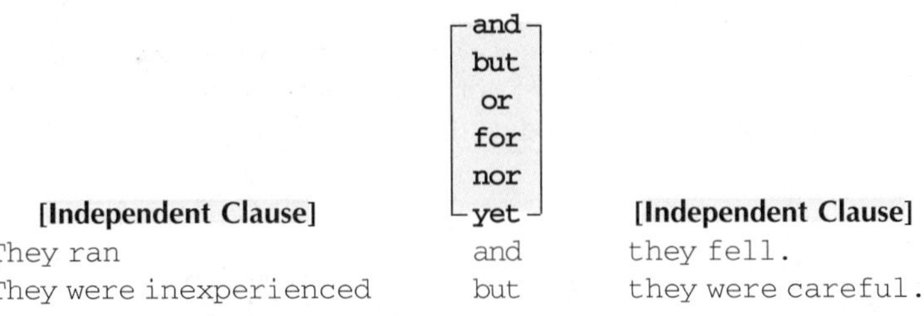

They ran and they fell.
They were inexperienced but they were careful.

2253 **Compound sentence with three or more independent clauses.** If a compound sentence consists of three or more independent clauses, punctuate as you would any series.

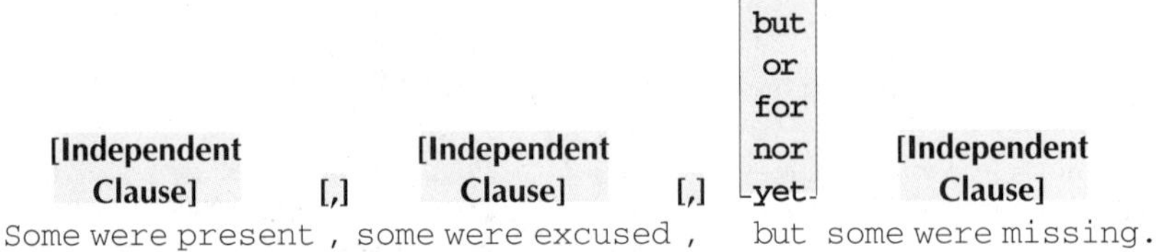

Some were present , some were excused , but some were missing.

2254 **Simple sentence with compound predicate.** A simple sentence with a compound predicate should **not** have a comma between the two predicates. Do not confuse this form with that of a compound sentence. See ¶ 2251-52 for examples of compound sentences.

Barry ran and jumped.

Not: Barry ran, and jumped.

Note: No matter how long the two predicates, a comma is **not** used to separate them.

Barry ran hurriedly across the wet street and jumped clumsily into the backseat of the moving car.

2255 **Simple sentence with compound subject.** A simple sentence with a compound subject should **not** have a comma between the two subjects.

[Subject]	[and]	[Subject]	[Predicate]
Rain	and	snow	make driving dangerous.

Not: Rain, and snow make driving dangerous.

2256 **Comma splice.** If the independent clauses of a compound sentence are not joined by a coordinating conjunction (and, but, or, for, nor, yet) a comma should **not** be used to separate the independent clauses.

Not: The sailboats were tightly bunched, there were no stragglers.

But: The sailboats were tightly bunched, and there were no stragglers.

Or: The sailboats were tightly bunched; there were no stragglers.

Note: The error in the first example is called a **comma splice** or **comma fault.**

Commas Setting Off Nonessential Sentence Elements

2257 ***Nonessential* sentence elements are set off by commas.** A **nonessential element** is an explanatory word, phrase, or clause that is part of the sentence but is independent of the basic structure and meaning of the sentence. It may *contribute* to the meaning of the sentence, but its contribution is *not essential.*

- Nonessential elements are parenthetical. If parentheses are placed around a nonessential element, the sentence retains its meaning—and is still properly constructed.
- If a nonessential element is deleted, the remainder of the sentence stands alone as a properly constructed sentence and retains its meaning.
- A nonessential element interrupts the flow of thought expressed by the sentence.
- A nonessential element is sometimes called a **nonrestrictive element** or a **parenthetical expression.**

[Subject]	[,]	[Nonessential Word]	[,]	[Rest of Sentence]
Words	,	however	,	did not resolve the matter.

[Subject]	[,]	[Nonessential Phrase]	[,]	[Rest of Sentence]
The boat	,	now abandoned	,	sank slowly to the bottom.

[Subject]	[,]	[Nonessential Clause]	[,]	[Rest of Sentence]
Bertha	,	who is a veteran sailor	,	was at the wheel.

Contrast these *nonessential elements* with the *essential elements* in ¶ 2258.

2258 ***Essential* sentence elements are *not* set off by commas.** An **essential element** is a word, phrase, or clause that follows the element it modifies and restricts or limits it. Essential elements are sometimes called **restrictive elements** because they restrict or limit the sentence elements they modify.

[Subject]	[Essential Word]	[Rest of Sentence].
A penny	saved	is a penny earned.

MORE

CONTINUED

[Subject]	**[Essential Phrase]**	**[Rest of Sentence].**
A child	with a temper	is a child who needs help.

[Subject]	**[Essential Clause]**	**[Rest of Sentence].**
Students	who follow the outline	are likely to do well.

An essential element frequently identifies one member of a group:

The car *with the flat tire* is in the shop.

The girl *who has a red nose* sat in the front seat.

Contrast these *essential elements* with *nonessential elements* in ¶ 2257.

2259 **Clause that can be essential or nonessential.** Some sentence elements can be essential or nonessential: writers indicate their intent by using or omitting commas and by using certain key words.

- **Nonessential:** The boat, which was full of water, sank quickly.

(Set off by commas, the clause is *nonessential*. Only one boat is under discussion.)

- **Essential:** The boat *that* was full of water sank quickly.

(Without commas, the clause is *essential;* it identifies the boat.)

Note: *Which* must be changed to *that* in order to make the clause essential since all clauses introduced by *which* are nonessential.

A phrase or clause introduced by *that* must be essential, as illustrated below.

Correct: The boat *that was full of water* sank quickly.

Incorrect: The boat, that was full of water, sank quickly.

2260 **A *hearing test* for nonessential elements.** Punctuation allows a *writer* to guide the *reader* just as dramatic emphasis allows a *speaker* to guide the *listener*. Increasing or decreasing the rate of speech, pausing ever so briefly, pausing profoundly for effect, using gestures and facial expression, employing body language—all help the *listener* interpret what is being *said*. Commas, semicolons, dashes—all similarly help the *reader* follow what is *written*.

Distinguishing between essential and nonessential sentence elements is perhaps the one area in which our ear for the language is nearly as reliable as our ability to interpret the rules. When in doubt about whether or not to set off part of a sentence with commas, read the sentence aloud or to yourself:

- If your voice falls when you read the sentence element in question, the element is probably nonessential and should be set off with commas.

- If your voice rises or remains steady as you read the sentence element in question, the element is probably essential and should not be set off with commas.

Try the accuracy of your ear on the examples in ¶ 2257-59. Notice how difficult it is to pause for incorrect commas or to lower your voice when reading an essential element such as a phrase or clause introduced by *that*.

Comma Setting Off Introductory Nonessential Sentence Element

2261 **General rule for introductory nonessential elements.** Set off an introductory nonessential element by using a comma after it.

[Introductory Nonessential Element]	[,]	[Independent Clause]
Without a doubt	,	that was the best game of the year.

2262 **Comma after introductory element.** Commas are used after these introductory elements:

¶ 2263	Participial or infinitive phrase		
¶ 2264	Dependent clause		
¶ 2265	Prepositional phrase		
¶ 2266	Independent comment		
¶ 2267	Mild interjection		
¶ 2268	Words in direct address	[,]	[Independent Clause]

2263 **Introductory participial or infinitive phrase.** Use a comma after an introductory participial or infinitive phrase. A participle is a verb (other than the principal verb of a sentence or clause) that functions as an adjective.

[Participial Phrase]	[,]	[Independent Clause]
Landing on my feet	,	I continued to run.

An **infinitive** is a verb (other than the principal verb of the sentence or clause) used as a noun, adjective, or adverb. An infinitive usually consists of the word *to* followed by the present form of a verb: *to see, to run, to eat, to read.* A few infinitives do not include the word *to*, but they are not used in introductory phrases. See ¶ 1113.

[Infinitive Phrase]	[,]	[Independent Clause]
To see a panoramic view of the town	,	I climbed the hill.

2264 **Introductory dependent clause.** Use a comma after an introductory dependent clause.

[Dependent Clause]	[,]	[Independent Clause]
When the rain stops	,	we can leave.

Every clause has a subject and predicate. However, an independent clause can stand alone as a simple sentence; a dependent clause cannot.

2265 **Introductory prepositional phrase.** Use a comma after a long introductory prepositional phrase.

[Long Prepositional Phrase]	[,]	[Independent Clause]
Far from the never-to-be-forgotten scene	,	I took stock.

- If the prepositional phrase is short and there is no break in thought or speech, the comma may be omitted.

[Short Prepositional Phrase]	[Independent Clause]
In town	the storm damage was far more apparent.

- A prepositional phrase consists of the preposition, its object, and the words in between.

aboard the ship	beneath the seat	over the river
around the world	from the east	through the woods
because of the wind	inside the shelter	under the bed
behind the barn	instead of the cash	without a reason

- A phrase does not have a subject and a predicate; it functions as a single part of speech. A prepositional phrase can function as an adjective or as an adverb.

2266 **Introductory independent comment.** Use a comma after an introductory independent comment.

[Independent Comment]	[,]	[Independent Clause]
In my opinion	,	the forecast is completely without merit.
Fortunately	,	there is no support for her position.

2267 **Introductory mild interjection.** Use a comma after an introductory mild interjection.

[Mild Interjection]	[,]	[Independent Clause]
Oh	,	to go back to the days of my youth.
Well	,	water is essential to life on the farm.

The comma in the second example additionally prevents misreading the word *well* as an adjective modifying the noun *water*. Compare the example to the same sentence without a comma.

Well water is essential to life on the farm.

Appropriate inflection and the pause indicated by the comma can make the same distinction when the sentence is spoken.

2268 **Introductory words in direct address.** Use a comma after an introductory word or words in direct address.

[Direct Address]	[,]	[Independent Clause]
Tiffany	,	you come here right now.
My friends	,	the time has come for me to speak.

2269 **Comma after introductory word or comment in a second clause.** A transitional expression or independent comment may introduce the second clause of a compound sentence.

[Independent Clause]	[;]	[Transitional Expression or Independent Comment]	[,]	[Independent Clause]
She did her duty	;	however	,	the others did not.
It is a dead issue	;	in my opinion	,	you can forget it.

Commas Setting Off Interrupting Nonessential Sentence Element

2270 **Setting off interrupting (nonessential) sentence elements with commas.** Set off a nonessential sentence element that interrupts the flow of the sentence by using a comma before and after the interrupting element.

[Rest of Sentence]	[,]	[Interrupting (Nonessential) Element]	[,]	[Rest of Sentence]
That was	,	without a doubt	,	the best game of the season.

2271 **Independent comment that interrupts the sentence.** Independent comment, set off by commas, can interrupt the sentence at any logical point.

That, *in my opinion,* was the best game of the year.

2272 **Transitional expressions that interrupt the sentence.** A transitional expression that interrupts the flow of the sentence should be set off by commas.

The debt burden, *however,* is a matter of grave concern.

2273 **Direct address that interrupts the sentence.** An expression of direct address that interrupts the sentence is set off by commas.

Run the tests, *Mildred,* before you reach any conclusions.

2274 **Nonessential and essential appositives.** An **appositive** is a noun or noun equivalent that identifies or explains the immediately preceding noun or noun equivalent.

- Nonessential appositives are set off with commas.

John Wayne, *the actor*, played in many Westerns.

- Essential appositives are not set off with commas.

John Wayne *the actor* was a tall man; John Wayne *the baker* is not.

2275 **Contrasting expressions.** Nonessential expressions inserted for contrast are set off with commas.

The door, *not the window*, was open to the wind and rain.

2276 **Individual word set off for emphasis.** An individual word may be set off with commas to give the word additional emphasis.

He smiled, *mischievously*, and slowly tore the note into pieces.

2

2277 **Interrupting phrases.** Phrases that interrupt the flow of the sentence (nonessential phrases) are set off with commas.

The reason, *a severe drought*, soon became apparent.

Her goal in life, *to become a physician*, will soon be realized.

2278 **Phrases that do not interrupt.** Phrases that do not interrupt the flow of the sentence (essential phrases) are **not** set off with commas.

A special class *on advanced Boolean algebra* has been scheduled.

The horse *with the odd gait* was waiting near the barn.

2279 **Interrupting clauses.** Clauses that interrupt the flow of the sentence (nonessential clauses) are set off with commas.

The boy, *since he now smelled of fish*, went home.

I saw the car, *which was skidding wildly,* crash into the tree.

2280 **Clauses that do not interrupt.** Clauses that do not interrupt the flow of the sentence (essential clauses) are **not** set off with commas.

The plane *that had just landed* taxied to the gate.

The man *who had been reading the newspaper* threw it down and left abruptly.

2281 **Setting off a nonessential final sentence element.** Set off a nonessential element that ends a sentence by using a comma before the nonessential final element.

[Rest of Sentence]	[,]	[Nonessential Final Element]
That was the best game of the year	,	without a doubt.

2282 **Independent comment.** An independent comment appearing at the end of a sentence is preceded by a comma.

[Rest of Sentence]	[,]	[Independent Comment]
Our last performance was our best	,	in my opinion.

2283 **Transitional expression.** A transitional expression appearing at the end of a sentence is preceded by a comma.

[Rest of Sentence]	[,]	[Transitional Expression]
The rain has not hurt the rhubarb	,	however.

2284 **Direct address.** An expression of direct address appearing at the end of a sentence is preceded by a comma.

[Rest of Sentence]	[,]	[Direct Address]
Please see that the door is locked	,	Susan.

2285 **Expressions used for contrast.** A parenthetical expression used for contrast at the end of a sentence is preceded by a comma.

[Rest of Sentence]	[,]	[Contrasting Expression]
We are doing this for fun	,	not for profit.

2286 **Emphasizing an individual word.** An individual word may be set off with a comma at the end of a sentence to give that word additional emphasis.

[Rest of Sentence]	[,]	[Word Emphasized]
The passage came to an end	,	ponderously.
His saccharine smile became a sneer	,	slowly.

2287 **Nonessential phrases.** A nonessential phrase at the end of a sentence is set off by a comma.

[Rest of Sentence]	[,]	[Nonessential Phrase]
They left at last	,	never to return.
We put it back where we found it	,	under the bridge.

2288 **Essential phrases.** An essential phrase at the end of a sentence is **not** set off by a comma.

[Rest of Sentence]	[Essential Phrase]
They were seated	in the rear compartment.
We will try to have the stage ready	for the last act.

2289 **Nonessential clauses.** A nonessential clause at the end of a sentence is set off by a comma.

[Rest of Sentence]	[,]	[Nonessential Clause]
Her thesis interested Goodmont	,	who is an expert in the field.
She returned to the car	,	which was parked under a tree.

2290 **Essential clauses.** An essential clause at the end of a sentence is **not** set off by a comma.

[Rest of Sentence]	[Essential Clause]
They were seated in the rear cabin	because they requested those seats.
We will try to have the stage ready	when the actors return.

Commas Separating Items in a Series

2291 **Basic pattern for series.** In a sentence that includes items in a series, use a comma after each of the items except the last.

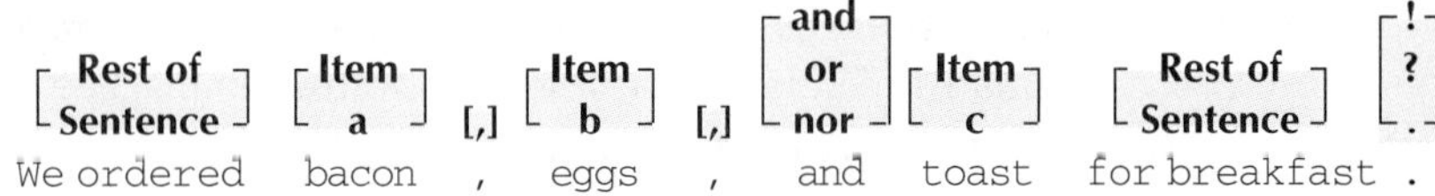

We ordered bacon , eggs , and toast for breakfast .

2292 **Comma after the last item in series.** Use a comma after the last item in a series (item c) only if there is a specific reason for doing so.

Alice, Bette, and Chad, *running for the plane*, failed to see the ticket agent.

[Nonessential phrase]

But: Alice, Bette, and Chad ran for the plane and failed to see the ticket agent.

2293 **Comma after the next-to-last item in a series.** Use a comma after the next-to-last item in a series (item b) to avoid confusion.

Not: These are the choices: blue, blue and gold, red, green, brown and tan. [Five choices, or six?]

But: These are the choices: blue, blue and gold, red, green, brown, and tan. [Six choices.]

Or: These are the choices: blue, blue and gold, brown and tan, red, and green. [Five choices.]

2

2294 **Series of two items.** Do not use a comma between two items that constitute a series.

The plate was full of candy and nuts.

2295 **Items connected by *and, or, nor, but* in a series.** Do not use commas to separate items in a series when those items are connected by *and, or, nor,* or *but.*

The plate was full of candy *and* nuts *and* dried fruit.

2296 **Series ending with *and so forth, and so on, and the like, etc.*** When a series ends with an expression such as *and so forth, and so on, and the like, etc.*, the ending expression is preceded by a comma. The ending expression is also followed by a comma—unless it falls at the end of the sentence.

The plate of candy, nuts, dried fruit, and so forth, was on the table.

The plate on the table contained candy, nuts, dried fruit, etc.

Note: Use *etc.* only at the end of the sentence—except in technical material.

2297 **Preference in organizational names.** Regardless of the conventions that may seem to apply, write the name of an organization as the name is written by those who represent the organization.

Alday, Elizondo, and Fritzner and Co.

Casares and Defloe and Erskine

Gulf + Western Industries, Inc.

Narmalake & Webster Ilkas, Ltd.

2298 **Two adjectives preceding a noun.** When two consecutive adjectives precede a noun, separate the two adjectives with a comma. See also ¶ 2300.

They saw a vast, quiet world that seemed at peace with itself.

But: They saw a vast *and* quiet world that seemed at peace with itself.

2299 **More than two adjectives preceding a noun.** When more than two adjectives precede a noun, use a comma after each adjective that could correctly be followed by the word *and.* See also ¶ 2298 and ¶ 2300.

They anticipated a long [and] hot [and] tiring journey home.

They anticipated a long, hot, tiring journey home.

2300 **Modification patterns.** When two or more adjectives precede a noun, any one of several modification patterns may exist.

- The preceding adjectives may each modify the noun. In this case use a comma after each adjective except the last. The word *and* can be substituted for each of the commas, and the adjectives *happy, carefree,* and *joyous* can be written in any order. See ¶ 2299.

[Rest of Sentence]	[Adjective]	[,]	[Adjective]	[,]	[Adjective]	[Noun]
It was a	happy	,	carefree	,	joyous	era.

- The noun and the word immediately preceding it may be so closely related that they express a single idea. In that case, the other adjectives in the series may modify that single idea.

[Rest of Sentence]	[Adjective]	[,]	[Adjective]	[Adjective Plus Noun]
It was a	long	,	hot	summer day.
There is the	dreary	,	old	county jail.

Notice that the word *and* can be substituted for the commas in each case—but cannot be inserted in the adjective-plus-noun combination (summer day) or between it and the preceding adjective (hot). One would say "It was a long *and* hot summer day." One would **not** say "It was a long *and* hot *and* summer day."

In this pattern, the adjective-plus-noun combination must remain intact: *summer* cannot be interchanged with *hot* or *long*.

Commas with Repeated or Omitted Words

2301 **Words repeated for emphasis.** Words repeated for emphasis are separated by commas.

```
No, no, no, a thousand times no!
That painting is very, very valuable.
```

2302 **Repeated verbs.** Use a comma to separate identical verbs that are next to each other.

```
When you work, work hard; when you play, play hard.
```

2303 **Repetitious words—elliptical sentences.** A comma may be used to replace repetitious words that are easily perceived. A sentence thus shortened is called an **elliptical** sentence.

```
The good oranges are on top; the bad, on the bottom.
```
[The words *oranges are* are omitted.]

2

2304 **Omission of *that*.** Omission of the conjunction *that* can create a definite pause in the sentence. A comma should be inserted **only** if such a pause exists.

Pause: The problem is, no one in the class comes on time.

No Pause: They thought the professor would wait for them.

Note: It is not considered best usage to omit *that* in formal writing.

2

Commas in Personal Names

2305 **Abbreviations and numbers following personal names.** A comma should be used to set off an abbreviation, but not a number, after a personal name.

Seymour Sanford, Jr.
Victoria D. Marabilla, MBA
Dario J. Pennell III
Arthur T. Plummer, Sr.

However, each person should be addressed as that person prefers, whether or not that preference conforms to convention.

Preferences: Purvis Perrotti, III, Esq.
Phillippe S. Reveronne Jr.

2306 **Personal names in sentences.** An abbreviation following a personal name in a sentence is set off with commas.

The program indicates that Earl Sopwith, CPA, is the chairperson.

If the name is normally written without a comma, no comma is used before or after the abbreviation or number—unless the sentence structure otherwise calls for a comma.

Preston Goodnight III is the next person on the program.

In the case of Preston Goodnight III, we can make an exception.

2307 **Transposed names.** When a name is written last-name-first, the transposed portion is set off with commas.

Garcia, Robert E., Jr.
Flondero, Rosa D.
Saltulin, Bartelle R., III
Hawkins, Neville J., Esq.

Commas with Other Punctuation; Spacing

2308 **Comma with other punctuation.**

Dash, ¶ 2361, 2364-67

Parentheses, ¶ 2608-12

Quotation marks, ¶ 2766, 2771-73, 2777, 2789

2309 **Spacing with a comma.** The following sentences illustrate proper spacing with the comma. [▮=space]

Note: These sentences are models used only to illustrate spacing; they would **not** actually be punctuated as shown.

```
Within a sentence,▮one blank space usually follows a comma.
"Quotation marks,"▮she said,▮"sometimes conflict with commas."
The rules for▮"quotation marks,"▮(parentheses),▮and [brackets]
are similar but not identical.▮▮Do not space before or after a
comma in a number:▮▮1,405,247,093.
```

2

DASH

Dash Indicating an Abrupt Break

2351 **Dash indicating an abrupt break in thought.** A dash is used to indicate an abrupt break in thought— and to place emphasis on the expression following that break.

Expressions set off with parentheses "speak" in a lowered voice or a whisper. Those set off with commas "speak" in a normal voice. Those set off with dashes "speak" in a loud voice— or "shout"!

A single dash may be used to set off the latter part of the sentence—or a pair of dashes may be used to set off a sudden break in thought within a sentence.

```
You may eventually learn to do it—but only if you pay
attention.
Keep your eye on the target—the little red circle—all the
time.
```

2352 **Dash indicating that a sentence is broken off.** A dash may be used to indicate that a sentence is broken off before it is completed.

```
Take the morning shuttle to Chicago, then—  No, there is a
better way.
```

If the broken-off sentence is a statement **and** the element that follows is a complete sentence, use two spaces after the dash.

2

2353 **Dash indicating that a question is broken off.** A dash may be used to indicate that a question is broken off. The dash is followed by a question mark; the question mark is followed by two spaces.

Where did I put my—? Oh, there it is.

2354 **Dash indicating an exclamation broken off.** A dash may be used to indicate that an exclamation is broken off. The dash is followed by an exclamation mark; the exclamation mark is followed by two spaces.

I think I have told you—! But, I can see that you are not interested.

2355 **Dash emphasizing a single word.** The dash may be used to emphasize a single word at the beginning of a sentence, within a sentence, or at the end of a sentence.

Power—that is the goal of all his schemes.

Her ultimate goal—power—is increasingly apparent.

There is one thing that never fails to arouse their interest—power.

2356 **Dash indicating restatement for emphasis.** A repeated thought may be emphasized by setting it off with a dash or dashes.

That was a great performance—a truly great performance.

There was an eel—yes, an eel—slithering across the kitchen floor.

2357 **Dash indicating stammering or hesitation.** A dash or dashes may be used to indicate stammering or hesitation in speech.

I'll have number—let me see—number three— No, I'll have number four.

2358 **Dash indicating a summary.** A dash may be used to emphasize a summary of the ideas expressed earlier in the sentence.

Poverty, hunger, suffering, greed, corruption—all were apparent.

But: Poverty, hunger, suffering, greed, and corruption were apparent.

A dash should **not** be used unless the summarizing word (*all,* in this case) is the subject of the sentence.

2359 **Dash with an appositive.** A dash may be used to set off an appositive when an emphatic break is desired.

Clevis Gilmore—the forensic specialist—was on the job.

That is Clevis Gilmore—the forensic specialist.

See ¶ 2274 on nonessential and essential appositives.

2360 **Dash indicating the source of a quotation.** A dash may be used before the source of a quotation.

```
Trickery and treachery are the practices of fools that have not
wits enough to be honest.
                                  —Benjamin Franklin
```

Dash Supplementing or Replacing Other Punctuation

2361 **The dash with other punctuation.** Use the dash alone—not with another punctuation mark—unless it indicates a break so abrupt that the sentence is broken off. See ¶ 2353-54.

Not: The car was moving slowly,—but erratically.

Not: The car moved slowly—but erratically,—down the road.

But: The car was moving slowly—but erratically.

Or: The car was moving slowly—but erratically—down the road.

2

2362 **Dash instead of a colon.** When an emphatic but informal break is desired, use a dash instead of a colon to introduce an explanatory expression.

She guessed the number of beans in the jar and won the prize—a jar of beans.

2363 **Colon instead of a dash.** A colon may be used instead of a closing dash if the colon is followed by an explanatory expression that otherwise merits the use of a colon. Do not use the colon and the dash next to one another.

Dumet understands the problem—one of several he has created: too much overtime and not enough production.

2364 **Dash replacing a comma to emphasize the second independent clause in a compound sentence.** A dash may be used instead of a comma before a coordinating conjunction in a compound sentence; this form provides a stronger break and greater emphasis on the second independent clause.

The reduction is temporary—for the price will be increased Thursday.

2365 **Dashes setting off a nonessential element for emphasis.** A nonessential element that requires special emphasis may be set off with dashes instead of commas.

Only one person—in my opinion—can be held responsible.

2366 **Dashes setting off a nonessential element containing commas.** A nonessential element set off by dashes may contain commas.

Several items—speed, angle of descent, and wind resistance—should be checked.

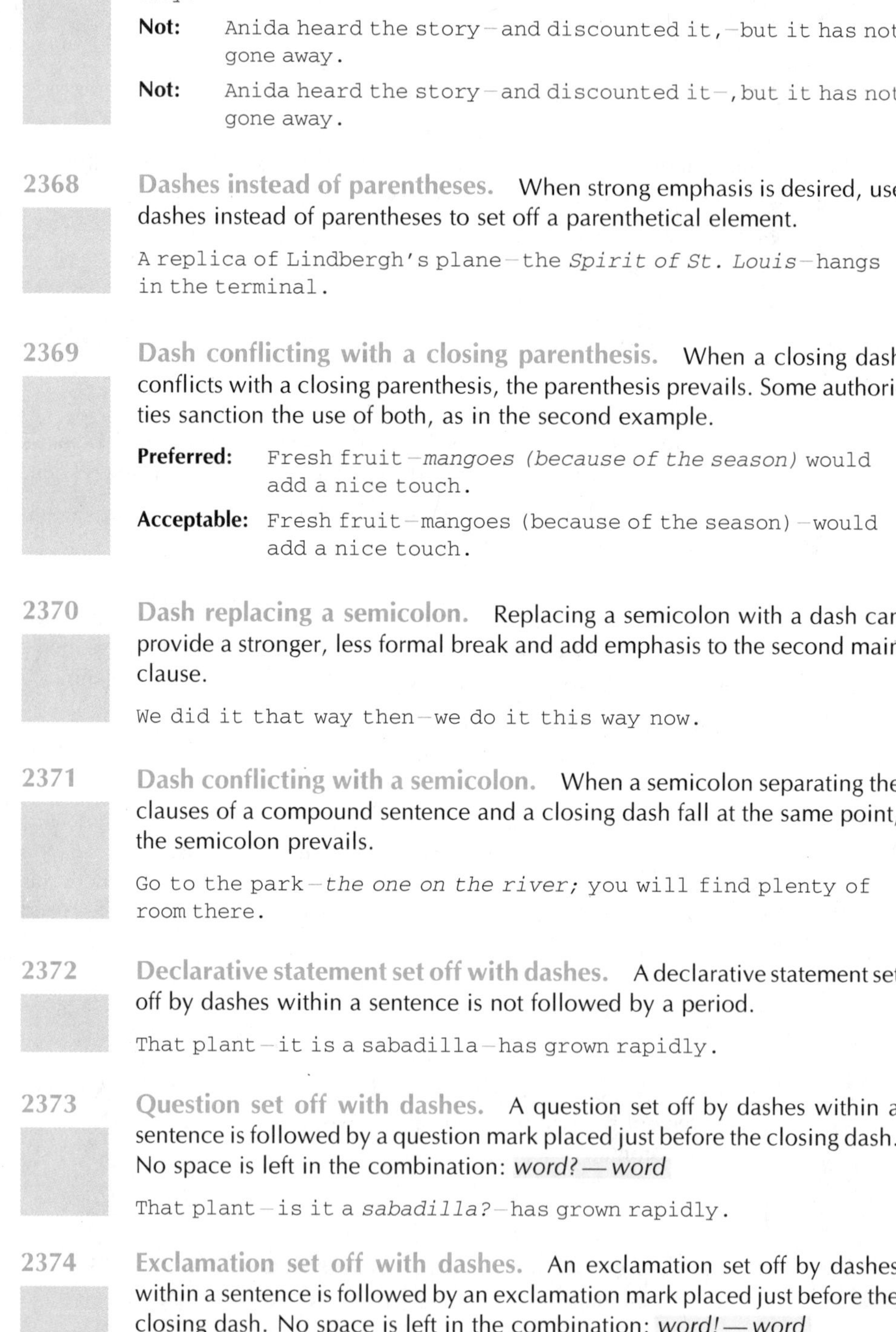

2367 **Dash conflicting with a comma.** When a closing dash conflicts with a comma, retain the dash and eliminate the comma.

`Anida heard the story—and discounted it—but it has not gone away.`

Not: `Anida heard the story—and discounted it,—but it has not gone away.`

Not: `Anida heard the story—and discounted it—,but it has not gone away.`

2368 **Dashes instead of parentheses.** When strong emphasis is desired, use dashes instead of parentheses to set off a parenthetical element.

A replica of Lindbergh's plane—the *Spirit of St. Louis*—hangs in the terminal.

2369 **Dash conflicting with a closing parenthesis.** When a closing dash conflicts with a closing parenthesis, the parenthesis prevails. Some authorities sanction the use of both, as in the second example.

Preferred: Fresh fruit—*mangoes (because of the season)* would add a nice touch.

Acceptable: Fresh fruit—mangoes (because of the season)—would add a nice touch.

2370 **Dash replacing a semicolon.** Replacing a semicolon with a dash can provide a stronger, less formal break and add emphasis to the second main clause.

We did it that way then—we do it this way now.

2371 **Dash conflicting with a semicolon.** When a semicolon separating the clauses of a compound sentence and a closing dash fall at the same point, the semicolon prevails.

Go to the park—*the one on the river;* you will find plenty of room there.

2372 **Declarative statement set off with dashes.** A declarative statement set off by dashes within a sentence is not followed by a period.

That plant—it is a sabadilla—has grown rapidly.

2373 **Question set off with dashes.** A question set off by dashes within a sentence is followed by a question mark placed just before the closing dash. No space is left in the combination: *word?—word*

That plant—is it a *sabadilla?*—has grown rapidly.

2374 **Exclamation set off with dashes.** An exclamation set off by dashes within a sentence is followed by an exclamation mark placed just before the closing dash. No space is left in the combination: *word!—word*

That plant—it *is* a *sabadilla!*—has grown rapidly.

2375 **Dash conflicting with end-of-sentence punctuation.** When a closing dash falls at the end of a sentence, the regular end-of-sentence punctuation prevails.

There it is—our newest model!

Not: There it is—our newest model—!

2376 **Spacing with a dash.** [▌=space]

Note: These sentences are models used only to illustrate spacing; they would **not** actually be punctuated as shown.

Normally, do not space before a dash—or after it.

After a broken off sentence, however—▌▌Space twice after the dash.

After a broken off question?▌▌—Retain the question mark.

After a broken off exclamation!—▌▌Retain the exclamation mark.

After a broken off element *within* a sentence—resume the sentence with no space before or after the dash.

DIAGONAL (Slant, Slash, Solidus, Stroke, Virgule)

2401 **Diagonal indicating choices (and/or).** The diagonal, also known as a slant, slash, solidus, stroke, or virgule, is used primarily to indicate choices.

This boat can be ordered with trim tabs and/or a boarding platform.

This *and/or* expression is suitable **only** for technical writing—and for technical illustrations and technical passages that occur in ordinary text. In ordinary and formal text use the following form.

This model can be ordered with trim tabs or a boarding platform or both.

2402 **Diagonal in abbreviations.** The diagonal appears in several abbreviations used **only** in technical writing—and in technical passages that may occur in ordinary text.

```
w/buttons: with buttons        w/o buttons: without buttons
c/o: in care of                B/L: bill of lading
```

2403 **Diagonal expressing dates and seasons.** The diagonal may be used instead of a hyphen between years to indicate that the years are successive—or, in the same manner, to indicate a single season spanning two calendar years. This form is acceptable **only** in technical writing, but not acceptable in ordinary text or in formal writing. The hyphen is preferred.

Acceptable:	1775/77	377/375 B.C.	the 1985/86 season
Preferred:	1775-77	377-375 B.C.	the 1985-86 season

2404 **Diagonal in quoted poetry.** Lines of poetry quoted within a sentence may be separated from one another by diagonals. Space before and after the diagonal. If more than two lines of poetry are quoted, space the lines as they are in the original poem—or single space and start all lines of the poem five spaces to the right of the left margin.

```
The exact lines were, "Will paint with red the highest rim of
peaks / and write again: Another day must die."
```

2405 **Spacing with a diagonal.** Space once before and once after a diagonal when it is used to separate two lines of quoted poetry within a sentence (¶ 2404). Do not space before or after a diagonal used in any other way.

2450 ELLIPSIS

ELLIPSIS

2451 **Ellipsis within a sentence.** Within a quoted sentence, an ellipsis indicates the omission of a word or words. It is formed using three periods, each preceded and followed by a single space.

The captain, a thirty-year veteran *with a perfect record,* was at the controls.

The captain, a thirty-year veteran . . . , was at the controls.

The phrase *with a perfect record* is omitted in the foregoing elliptical (condensed) example; the ellipsis represents the words omitted. Commas are used in the elliptical version both because their use retains the sense of the original sentence and because they are needed to set off the nonessential phrase *a thirty-year veteran* in the elliptical sentence.

The captain, *a thirty-year veteran* with a perfect record, was at the controls.

The captain, . . . with a perfect record, was at the controls.

The phrase *a thirty-year veteran* is omitted in this condensed version. Normally, the phrase *with a perfect record* could be written as essential (without commas). In this case, however, it should be written as above (nonessential: with commas) in order to retain the sense of the original sentence.

The captain, *a thirty-year veteran with a perfect record,* was at the controls.

The captain . . . was at the controls.

The commas in the original sentence set off *a thirty-year veteran with a perfect record,* a nonessential (nonrestrictive, parenthetical) phrase. With the entire phrase omitted, the commas are not needed in the elliptical sentence.

2452 **Ellipsis beginning a quoted sentence.** The ellipsis may be used to indicate an omission at the beginning of a quoted sentence.

If I take the assignment, I shall need more room to work.

He said that he " . . . shall need more room to work."

2453 **Ellipsis between sentences.** If an omission in quoted matter occurs between sentences, retain the original end-of-sentence punctuation and add the ellipsis.

"Spring training has begun in earnest. Aching muscles are being stretched and conditioned for the demands of the regular season. Although the World Series is a thousand games away, individual performance is already being evaluated."

MORE

2

CONTINUED

"Spring training has begun in earnest. . . . Although the World Series is a thousand games away, individual performance is already being evaluated."

The spaces before and after each of the three periods in an ellipsis are considered part of the ellipsis itself. In this case, the last space in the ellipsis also serves as one of the two spaces required between sentences; another space is added to complete the required two-space interval. [▮=space]

Spring training has begun in earnest.▮.▮.▮.▮▮Although the World Series

Original end-of-sentence punctuation
Ellipsis
Two-space interval between sentences

2454 **Ellipsis following a question.** If an ellipsis follows a question, the question mark is retained: [▮=space]

"Has spring training begun in earnest?▮.▮.▮.▮▮Although the World Series is a thousand games away, individual performance is already being evaluated."

2455 **Ellipsis following an exclamation.** If an ellipsis follows an exclamation, the exclamation mark is retained. [▮=space]

"Spring training has begun in earnest!▮.▮.▮.▮▮Although the World Series is a thousand games away, individual performance is already being evaluated."

2456 **Ellipsis at the end of a sentence.** If a word or words are omitted from the end of a quoted sentence, replace the omitted words with an ellipsis, retaining the end-of-sentence punctuation after the ellipsis. [▮=space]

Spring training has begun▮.▮.▮.▮.▮▮Aching muscles are being stretched and

Has spring training begun▮.▮.▮.▮?▮▮Aching muscles are being stretched and

Spring training has begun▮.▮.▮.▮!▮▮Aching muscles are being stretched and

Ellipsis
Original end-of-sentence punctuation
Two-space interval between sentences

2457 **Ellipsis following a paragraph.** If an omission follows a paragraph that is not broken off, the ellipsis is inserted **after** the closing punctuation of that paragraph. [▮=space]

The last sentence in the paragraph is written—including the end-of-paragraph punctuation—then the ellipsis is added!▮.▮.▮.▮

Original end-of-sentence punctuation
Ellipsis

The *next quoted paragraph* following the omission begins in the normal position.

2458 **Sentence fragment ending a paragraph.** If the last part of the last sentence in a paragraph is omitted, the ellipsis **precedes** the end-of-paragraph punctuation. [▮=space]

```
If the last part of the last sentence in a paragraph is omit-
ted, the ellipsis precedes the end-of-paragraph▮.▮.▮.▮!
```

Ellipsis ——— (points to ▮.▮.▮.)
Original end-of-paragraph punctuation ——— (points to !)

The *next quoted paragraph* following the omission begins in the normal position.

2459 **Nonstandard form of the ellipsis.** A few writers use elongated dashes for ellipses.

```
It was omitted . . . in the abridged text.
It was omitted——in the abridged text.
```

Ellipses formed with asterisks rather than periods are used between paragraphs to indicate the passage of time. The same form is used in quoted material to indicate the omission of a paragraph or paragraphs.

The paragraph *before the omission or passage of time* ends here.

* * *

The new paragraph *following the omission or passage of time* begins here.

Some commentators frown upon the usage described in this paragraph. The asterisk-ellipsis is, however, rather widely used; *Merriam Webster* sanctions the use of both forms: ________ and * * * .

2460 **Short quotation; no ellipsis.** A short quotation that is obviously a sentence fragment does not require an ellipsis.

```
The entire matter was attributed to "poor accounting
procedures."
```

2461 **Ellipsis in displayed quotations.** An ellipsis is not required before or after a displayed quotation that is set in from the left margin—or set in from both margins. Quoted material displayed in this manner is sometimes called an **extract.**

Quoted material may be set in five spaces from the left margin and single spaced, or set in five spaces from the left and right margins and single spaced. Ellipses are used to indicate omissions within and between quoted (inset) paragraphs.

```
     . . . set in five spaces from the left margin and
     single spaced, or set in five spaces from the left
     and right margins and single spaced.  Ellipses are used
     to indicate omissions . . . .
```

If a quotation begins or ends in mid-sentence, it should begin or end with an ellipsis. With this exception, neither quotation marks nor ellipses are used to begin or end the quoted (inset) paragraphs.

2462 **Ellipsis connecting loosely related ideas.** In informal text, ellipses are sometimes used to connect loosely related ideas or to indicate a pause . . . particularly in advertising copy.

```
Look your best . . . for less . . . in the latest fashions.
```

2463 **Ellipsis introducing a list of display lines.** An ellipsis may be used to introduce a list of display lines, or an ellipsis may be used to introduce each line on such a list. The items must be listed on separate lines; they may be capitalized.

Preferred

```
Buy a Cosmic Computer and get
get. . .
     high quality
     low price
     top performance
     professional assistance
     factory service
```

Acceptable

```
Buy a Cosmic Computer and get
      . . . high quality
      . . . low price
      . . . top performance
      . . . professional
            assistance
      . . . factory service
```

2464 **Spacing with an ellipsis.** The ellipsis includes a space before the first period and a space after the last period:

[▮=space]	¶	[▮.▮.▮.▮=Ellipsis]
Between words in a sentence:	2451	word▮.▮.▮.▮word
Between sentences:	2453	sentence.▮.▮.▮.▮New sentence
Following comma, semicolon, dash:	2451	—▮.▮.▮.▮word
Following a colon:		:▮▮.▮.▮.▮word
Following an opening quotation mark:		"▮.▮.▮.▮word
Preceding a closing quotation mark:		word▮.▮.▮.▮"
Following end-of-sentence punctuation:	2453-55	?▮.▮.▮.▮▮New sentence
Preceding end-of-sentence punctuation:	2456	▮.▮.▮.▮!▮▮New sentence

2500 EXCLAMATION MARK

2501 **Exclamation mark expressing strong feeling.** The exclamation mark expresses strong feeling: amusement, disbelief, dissent, enthusiasm, surprise, urgency, or other strong feeling.

Amusement: Look at the nose on that clown!

Disbelief: I can't believe that a bean stalk could grow so high!

Dissent: I object!

Enthusiasm: That was the best vacation ever!

Surprise: Oh! I didn't see you standing there.

Urgency: I must talk to the boss immediately!

Writers who use the exclamation mark sparingly increase its effectiveness, while those who use it at every opportunity weaken its impact. The story of the boy who cried "Wolf!" provides a suitable parallel.

2502 **Exclamation mark following a single word.** A single word before a sentence may be followed by an exclamation mark. The exclamation mark may be used at the end of an exclamatory sentence, as it is in most of the preceding examples. Or it may be placed immediately after the sentence element to which it applies: a word, phrase, or clause.

Bravo! That was a splendid performance.

Congratulations! You deserve the prize.

2503 **Placing the exclamation mark in parentheses.** For precise emphasis, some writers insert the exclamation mark immediately after the sentence element to which it applies. The exclamation mark is enclosed in parentheses.

That was an ingenious(!) solution to a perplexing problem.

Some authorities frown upon this form, recommending that the exclamation mark be placed at the end of the sentence.

That was an ingenious solution to a perplexing problem!

In the latter case, italics, underlining, or boldface type can provide any emphasis that is required.

That was an ingenious solution to a perplexing problem!

That was an *ingenious solution* to a perplexing problem!

Inserting an exclamation mark enclosed in parentheses into a sentence to indicate irony or sarcasm is not a generally accepted practice.

Not: She described it as an intelligent (!) response to the question.

2504 **Exclamation mark following *Oh*.** *Oh* may be used as either a strong or a mild exclamation. As a strong exclamation, it is followed by an exclamation mark. As a mild exclamation, it is followed by a comma. In either case, it is capitalized only when it stands alone or when it begins a sentence.

Oh! What a surprise.

Oh, I think the show is about to begin.

I thought I saw him here, but—*oh,* there he is.

2505 **Exclamation mark following *O*.** *O* indicates direct address. It says, "I am directing this to you." *O* is not followed by any punctuation unless punctuation is called for by the structure of the sentence. *O* is capitalized regardless of its position in the sentence.

O Death, where is thy sting? O Grave, where is thy victory?
—Corinthians 15:55

O Lord, why me? Why me, *O* Lord?

2506 **Exclamation mark following elliptical sentence.** An elliptical sentence is one that has been shortened: a sentence fragment that stands alone as a complete thought because the remainder of the sentence is understood. The elliptical sentence is inherently terse and is, therefore, frequently used for exclamatory statements.

	Where are you?
(I am)	**Here!**
	Where? (are you)
(I am)	**In the cave!**

Elliptical:	*Hurry! Hurry! Hurry!* The show is about to begin.
Full Sentence:	You hurry! You hurry! You hurry! The show is about to begin.

2507 **Exclamation mark with other punctuation.**

Dash, ¶ 2354, 2374

Parentheses, ¶ 2611, 2614, 2617

Quotation marks, ¶ 2770, 2794

2508 **Spacing with an exclamation mark.** [▮=space]

This is an exclamation mark at the end of the sentence!▮▮A new sentence . . .
Exclamation!▮▮A new sentence is shown here.
This is an exclamation mark▮(!)▮enclosed in parentheses.
This is an "exclamation mark followed by another punctuation mark!"▮▮A new . . .

HYPHEN

2551 **Uses of the hyphen.** The primary use of the hyphen is in creating compound forms. Compounds are discussed in chapter 3, ¶ 3200-41.

Hyphens are also used to divide words at the ends of written or printed lines. Word division is discussed in chapter 3, ¶ 3700-28.

Finally, hyphens are used with *numbers,* which are discussed in chapter 3, ¶ 3307.

2552 **Spacing with the hyphen.** [▌=space]

Do not space before or after a hyphen in a compound word such as inter-American.

Do not space before or after hyphens used in a series with commas: short-, medium-, and long-range plans.

Numeric ranges are written with no space before or after the hyphen: 1-10. Alphabetic ranges may be written with no space before or after the hyphen, or with one space before and after each hyphen: A-M or A - M.

Parentheses Enclosing a Parenthetical Sentence Element

2601 **Punctuating parenthetical elements.** Parentheses, commas, and dashes are all used to set off parenthetical expressions:

- **Parentheses** indicate lowering the voice to a whisper, making it seem to apologize for intruding with information so nonessential.

The golden rule (Matthew 7:12) is a civilized principle.

- **Commas** lower the reading voice moderately, indicating that the sentence element they enclose is nonessential.

The golden rule, Matthew 7:12, is a civilized principle.

- **Dashes** raise the reading voice to a shout, emphasizing the sentence element they set off. Dashes may set off essential or nonessential elements or replace other punctuation marks when special emphasis is required.

The ring—a diamond set in platinum—was displayed prominently.

2602 **Parenthetical elements illustrated.** A parenthetical element may be a word, phrase, clause, or sentence. Symbols used generally (£) or those used in special fields such as mathematics (π) or music (#) may also be treated as parenthetical elements.

Word: The report was printed in 12-pitch (elite) type.

Phrase: Elite type (twelve characters per inch) is smaller than pica type.

Clause: Pica type (it is larger than elite type) is easier to read.

Sentence: (Computer printers make many type fonts available.)

2603 **Testing parenthetical constructions.** If you believe an expression to be parenthetical, first enclose it in parentheses. Then read the sentence *without the enclosed expression*. If the sentence is still *correct,* the parentheses have probably been used correctly.

Incorrect: The last plane (was a purple Concorde) to be loaded.

Correct: The last plane (a purple Concorde) was loaded.

The sentence must be *correct* (grammatically complete) without the parenthetical expression. That does not mean that parenthetical expressions are necessarily unimportant. It does mean that they play a subordinate role grammatically regardless of their real importance.

We have expressed our esteem for your work with a small ($5 million) check.

2604 **Parentheses enclosing references.** Parentheses may be used to enclose references to other pages or sections of the same document or references to other documents.

The results are not uniform. (See Henderson, page 17.) Another instance (see page 47) was uncovered in our own investigation.

Parentheses Organizing Information

2605 **Outlines.** Parentheses may be used to enclose numbers and letters in an outline, giving the outline format additional levels of organization.

```
I. First level: roman numeral
   A. Second level: capital letter
      1. Third level: arabic numeral
         a. Fourth level: lowercase letter
            (1) Fifth level: arabic numeral, parentheses
               (a) Sixth level: lowercase letter,
                   parentheses
                   1) Seventh level: arabic numeral, right
                      parenthesis
```

2606 **Enumerations.** Numbers or letters organizing an enumeration may be enclosed in parentheses.

Follow this sequence: *(1)* Insert Tab A into Slot B. *(2)* Insert screw as shown. *(3)* Tighten the screw.

2607 **Numeric information.** Detailed, nonessential numeric information is frequently enclosed in parentheses—particularly confirming (restated) information in law documents.

Date: The tenant was evicted the same year (1993).

Time: The term of the note will be thirty-one (31) days.

Amount: Pay the amount of $37.50 (thirty-seven and 50/100 dollars).

References: The rule is stated in the bylaws (Section 8, Paragraph 2).

Parentheses With Other Punctuation; Spacing

2608 **Punctuation before an opening parenthesis.** Normally, a comma, semicolon, colon, or dash is not used before an opening parenthesis. See ¶ 2606 for an exception.

Not: The same three numbers were under consideration: (1, 3, and 5).
The same three numbers were under consideration—(1, 3, and 5).
The same three numbers were under consideration; (1, 3, and 5).
The same three numbers were under consideration, (1, 3, and 5).

But: The same three numbers were under consideration (1, 3, and 5).

MORE

Or: The same three numbers were under consideration: 1, 3, and 5.
The same three numbers were under consideration—1, 3, and 5.
The same three numbers were under consideration; they are 1, 3, and 5.
The same three numbers were under consideration, 1, 3, and 5.

The preceding *Or* category examples are listed in order of preference.

2609 **No punctuation after an opening parenthesis.** After an opening parenthesis:

- Do not use a punctuation mark unless it is part of the first word in parentheses.

('Twas the night before Christmas . . .)

- Do not capitalize the first word in parentheses unless it begins a complete parenthetical sentence or otherwise requires capitalization.

That chest (it is Chippendale) is a bargain.

That chest is a bargain. (It is Chippendale.)

- Do not capitalize the first letter following the opening parenthesis unless it would be capitalized elsewhere in the sentence: a proper noun, a proper adjective, or the pronoun *I*.

That chest (I believe it is Chippendale) is a bargain.

2610 **Period before a closing parenthesis.** Do not use a period before a closing parenthesis unless

- The parenthetical expression ends with an abbreviation.

The new building will be located on the main street (Fifth Ave.).

- The parenthetical expression ends with or consists of a complete sentence.

The new building will be located on the main street. (That is Fifth Avenue.)

2611 **Question mark or exclamation mark before a closing parenthesis.** Do not use a question mark or exclamation mark before a closing parenthesis unless the mark applies only to the parenthetical element *and* differs from the punctuation mark at the end of the sentence.

Not: Will the game (is it tomorrow?) be televised?

But: Will the game (is it tomorrow) be televised?

And: Will the game (it is tomorrow!) be televised?

Not: The game (it is tomorrow!) will be televised!

But: The game (it is tomorrow) will be televised!

Exception: Punctuate normally a parenthetical expression that stands alone. See ¶ 2615.

(What a great day we have had!)

2612 **No comma, semicolon, colon, or dash before a closing parenthesis.** Do not use a comma, semicolon, colon, or dash *before* a closing parenthesis.

Her article *(Computer Utilities for the 486-SX)*, despite its narrow focus, is very useful.

Run the test again (vibration and torsion); the initial results were inconclusive.

The test was inconclusive (the temperature was not controlled): We must have accurate results.

The field in question (computer technology)—more than any other—continues to develop rapidly.

2613 **Punctuation after a closing parenthesis.** When an element enclosed in parentheses ends the sentence, place the end-of-sentence punctuation after the closing parenthesis.

We shall begin the series tomorrow (Thursday).

Will the series begin tomorrow (Thursday)?

The series must begin tomorrow (Thursday)!

2614 **Punctuation preceding a parenthetical sentence.** If an entire sentence is enclosed in parentheses, the previous sentence is punctuated normally: there may be a period, question mark, or exclamation mark (followed by two spaces) before the opening parenthesis.

This price will not apply after today! (The new model will be available then.)

2615 **Punctuation following a sentence enclosed in parentheses.** When the entire sentence is parenthetical, use no punctuation after the closing parenthesis: place the end-of-sentence punctuation before the closing parenthesis.

(This is a parenthetical sentence.) (Is this a parenthetical question?)

2616 **Question mark enclosed by parentheses.** A question mark—used to express doubt—within a sentence is enclosed in parentheses.

The advertisement promises a lifetime(?) guarantee.

2617 **Exclamation mark enclosed by parentheses.** An exclamation mark—used to emphasize a word or other sentence element—is enclosed in parentheses. This use of the exclamation mark is **not** universally accepted.

The advertisement promises a lifetime(!) guarantee.

2618 **Spacing with parentheses.** [▌=space]

```
Treat opening parentheses▌(and brackets)▌as part of the word
they precede.
```

```
Treat closing parentheses▌(and brackets)▌as part of the word
they follow.
```

```
(An entire parenthetical sentence, including closing punctua-
tion, is enclosed within parentheses.)
```

```
A question mark(?)▌or exclamation mark(!)▌within the sentence is
enclosed in parentheses to indicate doubt(?),▌uncer-
tainty(?),▌astonishment(!)▌or the like.
```


PERIOD

2651 **Period at the end of a sentence.** Use a period following a statement that is a sentence. The sentence may be a simple statement of fact, or it may affirm, assert, avow, or state an opinion.

```
There are three eggs in the basket.
```

```
The seascape is the best painting in the exhibit.
```

2652 **Period following a request phrased as a question.** A period is used to punctuate a request phrased as a question.

```
Will you lay the book on the table.
```

```
Will you lay the book on the table?
```

Both sentences are punctuated correctly. The first is a polite request only *phrased* as a question. The person to whom it is addressed is expected to respond by complying with the request. The second is a question; the person to whom it is addressed is expected to reply—probably with a yes-or-no answer.

2653 **Period following a command.** A mildly stated command, in which the writer does not wish to display a sense of pressure or urgency, may be punctuated with a period.

```
Put the book back on the table when you have finished.
Do not walk the dog through the neighbors' yards.
```

Forceful commands, particularly those meant to convey a sense of pressure or urgency, are punctuated with an exclamation mark.

```
Stop where you are!
Come out of there with your hands up!
```

2654 **Period following an indirect question.** Use a period to mark the end of an indirect question.

```
He asked why runways 9 and 27 are never used at the same time.
The most important question is what will happen tomorrow.
```

2655 **Period following an elliptical sentence.** An elliptical sentence is one in which a word or words are omitted, but understood.

```
(You) Stop that. (My answer is) No. (The time is) Now.
Without a doubt (what you say is true).
```

2656 **Periods in outlines.** Use a period after each number or letter that identifies a division or subdivision in an outline (except where a parenthesis or parentheses are used). Do not use a period at the end of a line in an outline unless the end of a sentence falls at that point. See ¶ 2605 for a more detailed model outline.

```
I.  Paleolithic artifacts
    A.  Stone instruments
        1.  Ax heads
```

2657 **Period after a run-in heading.** A period or other appropriate end-of-sentence punctuation is used after a run-in heading. A run-in heading usually starts at the left margin, but may be indented. It or its paragraph number is the left-most item on the line of text. Although it begins a paragraph, it may be a sentence fragment rather than a complete sentence.

This is a run-in heading. A run-in heading is followed (on the same line) by the text of the paragraph. The text does not rely on the heading for any of the meaning of the paragraph. Therefore, the first sentence of the paragraph usually repeats the thought (but not the exact words) of the heading.

2658 **Periods in enumerations.** Listed items may be identified by letters or numbers followed by periods.

```
1. Disks                 A. Disks
2. Printer ribbons       B. Printer ribbons
3. Paper                 C. Paper
```

MORE

Some of the common conventions for writing enumerations are

1. Leave two spaces after the period following the identifying number before each item. The identifying number may be placed at the left margin, or indented. In this model enumeration, item 1 is indented; item 2 is written flush with the left margin; item 3 is indented (including all lines in the item); in item 4, the item number is written flush with the left margin and the other lines in the item are written flush with the first word in the first line.

Note: In practice, the styles are not mixed: All items in the same enumeration are written in the same style.

2. This is an example of an enumerated item written flush with the left margin.

3. The entire enumeration may be set in from the left margin. In this case, the lines after the first line are written flush with the item number.

4. The text, starting with the second line, may be written flush with the first word of the first line.

Be consistent in the use of periods at the ends of items.

2659 Other uses of the period.

Decimals, ¶ 3324-29

Abbreviations, ¶ 3008

Acronyms, ¶ 3012

Contractions, ¶ 3017

2660 The period with other punctuation.

Dash, ¶ 2375

Parentheses, ¶ 2609, 2610, 2613, 2615

Quotation Marks, ¶ 2794

To form an ellipsis, ¶ 2451-64

2661 Spacing with a period. [▮=space]

Space twice after a period at the end of a sentence.▮▮An abbreviation within a sentence is treated as a full word:▮▮i.e.,▮et.▮seq.,▮FDIC,▮ISBN,▮etc.▮▮

For more on periods in abbreviations, see ¶ 3008.

For information on a period after a letter or number in an enumeration, see ¶ 2658.

For information on a period as a decimal, see ¶ 3324-29.

2

QUESTION MARK

2701 **Question mark ending a full sentence.** Use a question mark to indicate a direct question.

```
Does the bus stop here?
Is there a restaurant near the park?
```

2702 **Question mark ending an elliptical sentence.** Treat an elliptical sentence as though it were a full sentence. An elliptical sentence is one in which one or more understood words have been omitted.

```
"I opened the package that was addressed to you."
"Why?"
(The complete sentence is, "Why did you open the package
addressed to me?")
```

2703 **Question in the form of a statement.** A sentence that is phrased as a statement may be identified as a question by its context or by the fact that it is spoken with rising inflection. Such a sentence is punctuated with a question mark.

```
You were satisfied with the service you received?
This flight will arrive on time?
```

2704 **Indirect question (no question mark).** Do not use a question mark following a sentence that describes a question but is, itself, a declarative sentence.

```
She asked if the quiz is scheduled for Thursday.
```

2705 **Direct question within a declarative sentence.** Use a question mark immediately following a direct question within a declarative sentence.

Will there be a surprise quiz Thursday? is the question.

When you have thought it over, ask yourself Why did I act so foolishly?

Note: In the second example, the question mark serves as end-of-sentence punctuation even though the sentence is declarative. Capitalization of the first word of the question is optional.

2

2706 **Converting a declarative sentence to a question.** A short question within a longer declarative sentence may convert the longer sentence to a question. The longer sentence, having become a question, is followed by a question mark.

The sentence: It is true that the inspector has been here.

The question: It is true, *is it not*, that the inspector has been here?

or

It is true that the inspector has been here, is it not?

2707 **Sentence element introducing a question.** A question within a sentence may be introduced with a comma or a colon. The colon is preferred if the introductory element is long or formal.

The question is, What happened to the surplus we thought we had?

This is the question that must be answered: What happened to the surplus we thought we had?

2708 **Questions in a series as a single sentence.** A series of brief questions with a common subject and predicate may be treated as a single sentence, using question marks or commas.

Are we scheduled for golf? tennis? swimming?

Are we scheduled for golf, tennis, swimming?

2709 **Questions in a series as separate sentences.** A series of brief questions may be treated as elliptical sentences.

Are we scheduled for golf? If so, where? When?

2710 **Series of independent questions.** A series of brief questions not sharing the same subject and predicate must be treated as independent questions.

Is the game over? Did we win? What was the score?

2711 **Expressing uncertainty or doubt.** A question mark enclosed in parentheses may be used at any appropriate point in a sentence to express the uncertainty or doubt of the writer.

They were said to have become engaged(?) in 1989.
[Expresses doubt that they were or are engaged.]

They were said to have become engaged in 1989(?).
[Expresses uncertainty about the date of the engagement.]

2712 **Question mark with other punctuation.**

Asterisk, ¶ 2051

Dash, ¶ 2353, 2373, 2376

Ellipsis, ¶ 2454

Parentheses, ¶ 2611, 2614, 2618

Quotation Marks, ¶ 2767, 2794

2713 **Spacing with a question mark.** [▮=space]

This represents an interrogative sentence ending with a question mark?▮▮This represents a new sentence immediately following that interrogative sentence.▮▮A question mark may follow a question?▮within a sentence. Doubt (?)▮may be indicated by enclosing a question mark in parentheses.

QUOTATION MARKS

Direct and Indirect Quotations

2751 **Enclosing a direct quotation.** Quotation marks are used to enclose the exact words spoken or written.

"Where did you put my tools?" asked the plumber.

"I can fix your nose," the doctor said at last.

2752 **Indirect quotation.** An indirect quotation conveys what the quoted person said, but not the exact words of the quotation. Indirect quotations frequently begin with *if, that, whether,* or *why*. Indirect quotations are **not** enclosed by quotation marks.

Margarita asked *if* the tour bus will be here by eleven.

She asked *whether* or not lunch will be served.

He wants to know *why* there are so many questions.

2753 **Direct questions and direct quotations.** A direct quotation may be an indirect question.

She said, "I would like to know what time the bus stops here." [direct quotation; indirect question]

She said that she would like to know what time the bus stops here. [indirect quotation; indirect question]

She asked, "What time does the bus stop here?" [direct quotation; direct question]

2754 **Selective quotation.** A selective quotation contains the *exact* words of the speaker or writer, but **not** *all* of the words spoken or written.

The other golfer shouted "over the hill."
[The other golfer actually shouted, "Your ball went over the hill."]

See ¶ 2451-58 and ¶ 2460-61 for use of ellipses in quotations.

2755 **Quoting *yes* and *no*.** Do **not** use quotation marks around the words *yes* and *no* unless there is a need to emphasize the fact that they are the exact words of the speaker or writer.

If the guide says *yes,* we should take the longer route.

It is apparent that the director enjoys saying *"no."*

2756 **Well-known sayings.** Do not use quotation marks around well-known sayings, mottos, proverbs, and the like.

It demonstrates *that a bird in the hand is worth two in the bush.*

Quotation Marks for Emphasis

2757 **Quotation marks identifying humor.** A play on words may be enclosed in quotation marks. Any other form of humor is usually not treated in this manner unless it is (or contains) a direct quotation.

She looked at the jumble of tools and asked him to put his "playthings" away.

2758 **Slang and other nonstandard expressions.** A nonstandard expression used by a writer for special effect may be enclosed in quotation marks if it is the writer's intent to call attention to the expression itself or to the fact that the expression does not represent the writer's normal style. Such usage is often pretentious, since there is normally no need to apologize for or call attention to the apt use of a nonstandard expression. Also, this usage is soon dated, since—in time—the best slang becomes standard, the worst is forgotten, and the remainder becomes unfashionable.

Once you see his "rancid" personality in action, you know that he has an "attitude."

Overworked adjectives regularly pass into and out of fashion. *Rancid* has been applied to anything undesirable; *radical,* to anything out of the ordinary. Having an *attitude* is shorthand for having a *bad attitude*.

In the foregoing example, it might be better to use (without quotation marks) a more precise adjective instead of *rancid*—perhaps spiteful, repellent, or the like—depending upon the writer's precise intent. The quotation marks enclosing *attitude* are probably superfluous since this usage has passed into the common lexicon.

2759 **Coined words.** Words that are coined by a writer for special effect usually should be placed in quotation marks.

One look at the workshop tells you that she is doing better at the "takeaparts" than she is at the "puttogethers."

2760 **Colloquialisms.** A colloquialism is an expression that is suitable for informal, familiar speech rather than for writing. A colloquialism may be placed in quotation marks. This form is particularly appropriate if the writer believes the colloquialism may not be familiar to readers.

This kind of stove is known as a "woodburner."

An older aircraft that has landing wheels slightly forward and a single wheel or skid aft is known as a "tail-dragger."

2761 **Definitions.** A word defined is italicized or underscored, and its definition may be enclosed in quotation marks if the definition is a formal one.

To *schmooze* is "to converse informally."

If many definitions appear in the same material, it may be desirable to emphasize only the words that are defined and print the definitions themselves in ordinary body type.

To <u>schmooze</u> is to converse informally.

Or

To *schmooze* is to converse informally.

See also, ¶ 2854.

2762 **Technical terms.** In normal text, technical terms that may be unfamiliar to the reader should be introduced with definitions, using one of the styles illustrated in ¶ 2761.

Every microcomputer is built around a *microprocessor*, "a computer processor on a single semiconductor chip."

2763 **Translations.** When a definition follows foreign words, the definition is enclosed in quotation marks or parentheses. The foreign words being defined are italicized.

He claimed that it was a *lapsus linguae*, "a slip of the tongue."

See ¶ 2761 for other forms.

2764 **Following *marked, labeled, signed, headed,* etc.** Expressions following introductory words such as *marked, labeled, signed, headed,* and the like, are enclosed in quotation marks.

The memorandum was marked "Urgent."

The bottom package is labeled "Fragile."

The love letter was signed "Your Secret Admirer."

The last column was headed "Net Loss."

2765 **Graphic representation of words.** Underscore or use italics to represent a word used as a word rather than for its meaning. Enclosure in single quotation marks is acceptable when the spoken language is implied.

Reference to written word: Paint the *and* a little higher on the sign.

Reference to spoken word: Shakespeare uses "thou" for "you" in dialogue.

See ¶ 2009 and ¶ 2858.

Punctuating Sentences Containing Quotations

2766 **Quoted statement at the beginning of a sentence.** When a declarative sentence is quoted at the beginning of a longer sentence, replace the period that follows the quoted declarative sentence with a comma.

"Do not expect that kind of service again," she said.

"I can be ready in half an hour," said the chef.

2767 **Quoted question at the beginning of a sentence.** When a quoted question begins a sentence, retain the question mark. A comma is **not** added; the question mark is written before the closing quotation mark.

"Will refreshments be served at the reception?" he asked.

"Can we meet the deadline?" the pressperson asked.

2768 **Quoted exclamation at the beginning of a sentence.** When a quoted exclamation begins a sentence, retain the exclamation mark. A comma is **not** added; the exclamation mark is written before the closing quotation mark.

"That's enough for today!" said the road worker as she laid down her shovel.

"Don't ever try that again!" said Carter.

Formatting and Punctuating Quoted Material

2769 **Quoted word or phrase beginning a sentence.** When a quoted word or phrase begins a sentence, it is followed directly by the closing quotation mark—unless the structure of the sentence requires additional punctuation before the closing quotation mark.

"Time for Arrest" was the title of the detective's speech.

"Time for Arrest," the title of the speech, was appropriate.

2770 **Quotation that does not interrupt the host sentence.** The period at the end of a single quoted sentence may be dropped to keep the quotation from interrupting the flow of the host sentence.

I do not think that "I will if I can" is an appropriate answer.

An exclamation mark or question mark at the end of such a quotation is retained.

I do not think that "I absolutely refuse!" is an appropriate answer.

I do not think that "What if I refuse?" is an appropriate answer.

2771 **Quotation that is an essential element in the host sentence.** Do not set off with commas a quotation that is an essential element of the host sentence.

You may not say "It is easier said than done" after you have tried to pronounce it.

2772 **Quotation that is a nonessential element in the host sentence.** A quotation that is a nonessential element in the host sentence is set off by commas.

The words for which Garbo is remembered, "I want to be alone," were spoken then.

2773 **Introductory elements such as *she said* and *he said*.** When an introductory expression such as *she said* or *he said* occurs before a quotation, the introductory element is usually followed by a comma.

She said, "Put the books away before you start the game."

He said, "Where did you put the eggs?"

2774 **Colon after a long or formal introductory element.** An introductory element that is long or formal may be followed by a colon.

Cecilia summarized her statement in this manner: "He is guilty."

2775 **Longer quotations.** Quotations of more than one sentence are introduced with a colon.

The dean then said: "Some made the dean's list this term.

Others, struggling to keep afloat in a sea of Fs, are in danger of capsizing—academically."

2776 **Displayed quotations.** An extract, displayed in a panel (set in from the left margin or from both margins) is introduced with a colon and not enclosed by quotation marks. See ¶ 2461.

Regarding education, Benjamin Franklin said:

> As to their studies, it would be well if they could be taught everything that is useful and everything that is ornamental. But art is long and their time is short. It is therefore proposed that they learn those things that are likely to be most useful and most ornamental, regard being had for the several professions for which they are intended.

2777 **Quotations interrupted by *he said, Matilda said,* etc.** When a quoted sentence is interrupted by an expression identifying the speaker, follow this pattern:

"This is the third time," said Steven, "that you have been told."

Do not capitalize the first word of the resumed quotation unless it is capitalized in the original sentence being quoted.

2

2778 **Quotations spanning sentences.** When a quotation with an interrupting expression spans two sentences, each sentence is punctuated separately.

"This is the third time I have told you," said Steven. "Please see that it does not happen again."

2779 **Quotations spanning paragraphs.** When a quotation consists of two or more paragraphs, open each paragraph with a quotation mark. Use a closing quotation mark after the last paragraph **only.**

"First paragraph.

"Second paragraph.

"Last paragraph."

2780 **Quoting dialogue.** Dialogue is writing in which two or more people are represented as conversing. Quote the expressions attributed to each participant in turn. Start a paragraph for each new expression, but double space only before and after paragraphs of two or more lines. Quotation marks are used in ordinary dialogue. In plays, scripts, and legal transcripts, the name of each speaker (usually in italics or all in capital letters) appears before each expression and quotation marks are not used.

Ordinary Dialogue	Plays, Scripts, and Legal Transcripts
"How can you do this to me, Alice?	*Herb:* How can you do this to me, Alice?
"It is the least I can do, Herb.	*Alice:* It is the least I can do, Herb.
"The least you . . . ."	*Herb:* The least you . . . .
"Yes, I wish I could do more."	*Alice:* Yes, I wish I could do more.

2781 **Single quotation marks.** Single quotation marks are used to punctuate a quotation within a quotation.

Sheila said, "The story 'Miss Wimple's Garden' is one of my favorites."

If another level is needed, use double quotation marks again.

Edward reported, "Sheila said, 'The story "Miss Wimple's Garden" is one of my favorites.'"

2782 **Poetry and quotation marks.** Poetry may be quoted by reproducing the entire poem or part of the poem and crediting the author before or after the quotation itself. Permission should be obtained to reproduce more than one line of a poem protected by copyright. The poem should be reproduced line for line and centered on the page.

```
There was an Old Man with a beard,
Who said: "It is just as I feared!
Two owls and a hen,
Four larks and a wren
Have all built their nests in my beard."
```

—Edward Lear

2783 **Minor titles enclosed in quotation marks.** Minor titles are enclosed in quotation marks when they appear in text. Major titles are italicized in printed text, underscored in typewritten text.

The title of the article is "A Way With A Will."
Find the answer in *Reference Manual for the Office.*

See ¶ 2852

2784 **Omissions in quoted material.** See ¶ 2451-58 and ¶ 2461 for the use of ellipses to indicate omissions.

2785 **Quotation within a quotation.** See ¶ 2781 for punctuating a quotation within a quotation.

2786 **Insertions in quoted material.** See ¶ 2152 on the use of brackets to insert explanations into quoted material.

2787 **Capitalization in quoted material.** See ¶ 3103 and ¶ 3141-42 on capitalization in quoted material.

Quotation Marks with Other Punctuation

2788 **Quotation mark with a colon.** A colon is placed **outside** (after) a closing quotation mark.

She said, "You have no taste": her definition of the word reflects her own prejudices.

2789 **Quotation mark with a comma.** A comma *preceding* a quoted element is placed before the opening quotation mark. A comma *following* a quoted element is placed before (inside) the closing quotation mark.

His new article, "Touching Bases," deals with the subject thoroughly.

In the British system, a comma is placed *after (outside)* the closing quotation mark unless it is part of the quoted sentence.

2

2790 Quotation mark with a dash. The position of a dash relative to quotation marks depends on how the dash is used.

- When a quotation is part of a nonessential element set off with dashes, and the closing dash and closing quotation mark occur at the same point, the dash is placed **outside** (following) the closing quotation mark.

`See if you can find Mattie's manuscript—the one entitled "Seeing the Town"—in that stack on the table.`

- If the sentence breaks off immediately after the quotation, place the dash **outside** (following) the closing quotation mark.

`I am not positive, but I think the title is "The Grass Grows Greener"—`

- If the sentence within the quotation breaks off, place the dash **inside** (before) the closing quotation mark.

`I heard her say, "I simply cannot remember—" But that is another story.`

2791 Quotation mark with parenthesis. A closing parenthesis may belong inside (preceding) or outside (following) the closing quotation mark.

- When the quotation is part of the parenthetical element, place the closing parenthesis **outside** (after) the closing quotation mark.

`He has given that speech (called "Trying Times for Trying People") more times than I can remember.`

- When the parenthetical element is part of the quotation, place the closing parenthesis **inside** (before) the closing quotation mark.

`She agreed to the wording "Paid (By Check)" until the contract is signed.`

2792 Quotation mark with a period. A period is placed **inside** (before) a closing quotation mark.

`After a long pause, she answered, "Ready."`

In the British system, a period (full stop) is usually placed **inside** (before) a closing quotation mark if it is the ending punctuation of the quoted matter. The period is placed **outside** (after) a closing quotation mark if the quotation is a short statement and the host sentence has greater weight.

British usage: `Often, have people quoted Garbo's famous words, "I want to be alone".`

2793 Quotation mark with a semicolon. Place a semicolon **outside** (after) the closing quotation mark.

`She said, "I do not like the way you behaved"; however, she looked as though she could have said more.`

2794 **Quotation mark with end-of-sentence punctuation.** Use the following patterns to resolve conflicts between the end-of-sentence punctuation of quoted material and that of the entire sentence in which the quoted material appears.

- **Quotations other than titles:** When a conflict between punctuation marks arises, the stronger mark prevails.

Duplicate punctuation marks are not used (!"! ?"? or .".").

Pattern	Example	Excluded By Rule
statement "statement."	He said, "Move along."	."."
statement "question?"	She asked, "What time is it?"	?".
statement "exclamation!"	The driver shouted, "Move over!"	!".
question "statement"?	Did she say, "I was"?	."?
question "question?"	Did he ask, "What time is it?"	?"?
question "exclamation!"	Did the driver shout, "Move over!"	!"?
exclamation "statement"!	He shouted, "Almost"!	."!
exclamation "question"!	She demanded, "Can you fly it"!	?"!
exclamation "exclamation!"	You must not shout, "Wolf!"	!"!

- **Quoted titles:** Titles are quoted exactly, including punctuation marks. A period is dropped in favor of an exclamation mark or question mark. The exclamation mark and question mark do not replace one another.

Duplicate punctuation marks are not used (!"! ?"? or .".").

Pattern	Example	Excluded By Rule
statement "title/statement."	We saw "This Old House."	."."
statement "title/question?"	She read the poem "Is Heaven Next?"	?".
statement "title/exclamation!"	I read a review of "Hit the Deck!"	!".
question "title/statement"?	Did you see "This Old House"?	."?
question "title/question?"	Would she like the poem "Is Heaven Next?"	?"?
question "title/exclamation!"	Did he see "Hit the Deck!"?	?"?
exclamation "title/statement"!	He must see "This Old House"!	.!.
exclamation "title/question"!	I really enjoyed the poem "Is Heaven Next?"!	
exclamation "title/exclamation!"	They will like "Hit the Deck!"	!"!

See ¶ 2862-63 on underscoring and italicizing punctuation marks.

2795 **Spacing with quotation marks.** [▌=space]

```
This is the previous sentence.▌▌"This is the quoted sentence."
A quotation may follow a colon:▌▌"This is a quoted sentence."
A quotation may follow a dash—"This is a quoted sentence."
("A quoted sentence may be parenthetical.")
"A quoted sentence may precede one that is not quoted."▌▌This
is the subsequent sentence.
```


2800 **SEMICOLON**

SEMICOLON

2801 **Semicolon replacing a coordinating conjunction between closely related clauses.** A semicolon may replace a coordinating conjunction between closely related independent clauses.

Coordinating conjunctions are and, but, or, nor, yet, *and* for. *An* independent clause *has a subject and a verb and can stand alone as a sentence.*

```
The wind is blowing and the water is rising.
The wind is blowing; the water is rising.
```

Do not replace a coordinating conjunction with a comma. This error is called a *comma splice* or a *comma fault*.

Not: `The wind is blowing, the water is rising.`

2802 **Independent clauses *not* closely related.** If the independent clauses of a compound sentence are not closely related, the elements should be reformed as separate sentences in order to provide a stronger break between the clauses.

`Time seemed to stand still. Neither wanted to be the first to speak.`

2803 **Semicolon with transitional expression.** When independent clauses are linked by a transitional expression, use a semicolon before the transitional expression and a comma after it.

`Time moved in slow motion; indeed, the second hand seemed to lurch forward by the minute.`

Partial list of transitional expressions:

accordingly	first	however	second	third
besides	furthermore	indeed	then	thus
finally	hence	meanwhile	therefore	yet

See ¶ 2804.

2804 **Which transitional expression between independent clauses?** Using appropriate transitional expressions and punctuation marks between independent clauses is a key to writing effective compound sentences. For example:

- *Indeed* expresses certainty and frequently foreshadows additional comment on the subject.

`The water is cool; indeed, it is downright cold.`

- *Therefore* cites the foregoing statement as a basis for the statement about to follow. *Hence* and *thus* are used similarly.

`The water is cool; therefore, the sand feels warm.`

`The water is cool; thus, the sand feels warm.`

- *However* suggests contrast.

`The water is cool; however, the sand is quite warm.`

- *Furthermore* advises the reader that an additional point is about to be made regarding the foregoing statement.

`The water is cool; furthermore, it is expected to remain cool.`

See ¶ 2803.

2805 **Conjunction, comma, semicolon, period, colon, or dash?** Each punctuation mark creates a break or pause of different duration and intensity.

- A conjunction between short, closely related independent clauses can cause the sentence to flow smoothly—without a pause.

`The water is cool and the sand is warm.`

MORE

- A comma lengthens the pause.

The water is cool, and the sand is warm.

- A semicolon lengthens the pause and may create contrast.

The water is cool; the sand is warm.

- Creating separate sentences further lengthens the pause and may intensify contrast.

The water is cool. The sand is warm.

- Use a colon when the expression beginning the sentence introduces and is explained or amplified by the following expression.

Several consecutive cold days have brought winter conditions to the beach: the water is quite cold and there is no warmth to the sand.

- The dash indicates a sharp break in thought.

We went to the beach hoping to bask and splash—but the frigid water and chilling wind soon dashed those hopes.

2806 **Semicolon between independent clauses containing commas.** A semicolon should be used between independent clauses if the commas separating items in series would otherwise make the sentence unclear or difficult to read.

Unclear: I ordered lettuce, tomato, and mayonnaise, and parsley, tartar sauce, and pickles were put on my sandwich.

Better: I ordered lettuce, tomato, and mayonnaise; parsley, tartar sauce, and pickles were put on my sandwich.

Or: I ordered lettuce, tomato, and mayonnaise, but parsley, tartar sauce, and pickles were put on my sandwich.

2807 **Semicolon used to separate series.** For clarity, two (or more) series—which contain commas—in the same sentence are separated by a semicolon.

The cook promised to remove the parsley, tartar sauce, and pickle; toast, scrape, and butter the bread; and add lettuce, tomato, and mayonnaise.

2808 **Semicolon with other punctuation.**

Dash, ¶ 2370-71

Parentheses, ¶ 2608, 2612

Quotation marks, ¶ 2793

2809 **Spacing with a semicolon.** Do not space before a semicolon. Use one space after the semicolon in all applications.

2

UNDERSCORE AND ITALICS

2851 **Underscore or italics?** Some computers and word processors print italics. Characters entered and printed in italics may appear as italics on the screen, or they may just be highlighted in a distinctive color. Italics and normal (upright) fonts can be mixed. Virtually all typesetting processes can produce italics.

Since most typewriters and some computer printers cannot print italics, underscoring is frequently substituted for italics. When a typewritten manuscript is published, underscoring is automatically converted to italics unless manuscript notations to the contrary are made.

2852 **Major titles underscored or italicized.** In running text, major titles (books, periodicals, long poems, plays, operas and long musical compositions, paintings, drawings, statues and other works of art, movies, and musicals) are italicized when italics are available, underscored when italics are not available. Minor titles (articles, speeches, short stories, manuscripts, essays, dissertations, theses, lectures, television and radio programs, and songs) are enclosed in quotation marks when they appear in running text.

See ¶ 2853, 2783.

2853 **Word endings added to titles.** Do not underscore or italicize word endings added to the titles of books or other publications.

<u>Gone With The Wind</u>'s sales	the May and June <u>TV Guide</u>s
Gone With The Wind's sales	the May and June *TV Guide*s

See ¶ 2852.

2854 **Definitions.** The correct form for definitions is italics (or underscore) for the word defined and quotation marks for the definition.

The noun land means "the solid part of the earth's surface."

The noun *land* means "the solid part of the earth's surface."

A **semiformal definition** may be written:

Land is the solid part of the earth's surface.

An **informal definition** may be written:

Land is the solid part of the earth's surface.

See also, ¶ 2761.

2855 **Technical terms.** Technical terms that may be unfamiliar to the reader should be introduced with definitions, using one of the styles illustrated in ¶ 2854 and 2761.

Every microcomputer is built around a *microprocessor:* "a computer processor on a single semiconductor chip."

2856 **Foreign expressions.** Foreign expressions that have **not** become part of the English language are underscored (or printed in italics). Those that have been accepted as part of the English language are written normally.

She spoke *ex-animo,* "from the heart."

But: The inequities were resolved on a quid pro quo basis.

2857 **Names of individual ships, aircraft, and spacecraft.** The names of individual vehicles are underscored or written in italics.

The Constitution and the Independence are the only remaining U.S. passenger ships.

The boat was named *Rosinante,* after Don Quixote's horse.

2858 **Graphic representation of words.** In order to express certain thoughts, it is necessary to distinguish between a *word* and *what the word stands for*. The sign painter who says "Move the *cow* to the top of the sign" probably means the word *cow* or a picture of a cow, not Bossie herself.

Move the *cow* to the top of the sign.

2859 **Underscoring or italics for emphasis.** *Italics,* when available, may be used to call attention to an expression that deserves emphasis; underscoring is used similarly when italics are not available. Both should be used **sparingly** to conserve their impact.

2860 **Underscoring a complete sentence.** If a complete sentence is to be emphasized, underscore the entire sentence, including the end-of-sentence punctuation.

He turned, looked at the stranger, and saw—himself!

Note: Entire sentences are rarely underscored.

2861 **Underscoring selected sentence elements.** Underscoring usually emphasizes part of a sentence, not the entire sentence.

He turned, looked at the stranger, and saw—himself!

2862 **Underscoring punctuation marks.** When underscoring part of a sentence, underscore only the punctuation that is part of the underscored sentence element.

The book is called What's in it for Me? (? punctuates the title)

Is the book called That's it for Me? (? punctuates the sentence)

I am reading That's it for Me! (! punctuates the title)

I really enjoyed Good Grooming! (! punctuates the sentence)

Did you read What's in it for Me? (? punctuates title and sentence)

Contrast this with ¶ 2863; see also, ¶ 2794.

2863 ***Italicizing* punctuation marks.** Generally, printers set each punctuation mark in the style of the word it follows. Therefore, if the last word of the sentence is italicized, the end-of-sentence punctuation is italicized as well. (This does not apply to parentheses, brackets, and braces.)

The book is called *What's in it for Me?* (? punctuates the title)

Is the book called *That's it for Me?* (? punctuates the sentence)

I am reading *That's it for Me!* (! punctuates the title)

I really enjoyed *Good Grooming*! (! punctuates the sentence)

Did you read *What's in it for Me?* (? punctuates title and sentence)

Contrast this with ¶ 2862; see also, ¶ 2794.

CHAPTER 3

STYLE

ABBREVIATIONS

3001 **Definition of abbreviations.** **Abbreviations** are shortened forms of words or phrases. They are used to save space and time. While a few abbreviations are permitted in general business writing (*Dr., p.m.,* and the like), most are confined to illustrations within documents, such as tables and graphs, or to items internal to an organization—such as computer reports, personal notes, and informal memos.

3002 **Basic uses.** Use the following basic guidelines for abbreviations.

- **Easily recognized abbreviations.** Use easily recognized abbreviations instead of writing out an entire word.

Dr. Patrick Gettings **instead of** *Doctor* Patrick Gettings

- **Symbols in tables and graphs.** In technical tables and graphs, use abbreviations instead of writing out an entire word.

Stock #	**Weight**		**Stock *Number***	***Weight***
78992	750 *lbs*	**instead of**	78992	750 *pounds*
4267	97 *lbs*		4267	97 *pounds*

- **Note taking.** When taking notes, abbreviate words by eliminating all nonessential letters, taking care to leave enough of the word to be recognized later.

Remem: Pls get brfcse frm hm tonit.

3

3003 **When to use abbreviations.** Avoid excessive use of abbreviations. Use only those abbreviations that readers will recognize. Do not sacrifice the clarity and meaning of your writing by forcing a reader to pause to try to determine the meaning of an abbreviation.

Some abbreviations are used so consistently that they are preferable to the full word or words, in all but the most formal writing.

- **Titles and degrees before/after names.** Abbreviate titles before names and degrees after names.

Dr. Liz Samuels
Oscar de Zayas, M.B.A.
Mrs. Ida Gropper

Armando Corominas, Ph.D.
Ms. Jill Mangold
Craig McMeekin, Ed.D.

Note: The kind of titles illustrated in these columns are not for formal writing, such as engraved invitations.

- **Official part of a company name.** Abbreviate parts of a company name such as Incorporated, Corporation, Company. However, you should always follow the preference of the company as indicated on their letterhead.

ZCM Productions, Inc.
Hi-Lu Corp.
Jaffer Sprinkler Co.

- **Time.** Abbreviate designations used with time in ordinary text. (See ¶ 3376 for exception.)

5:00 a.m.

1220 B.C.

10:00 p.m., PST
(See ¶ 3007 Exceptions)

Note: These expressions are not for formal writing, such as engraved invitations. See ¶ 3030.

3004 **Consistency.** Be consistent! Use the same form of each abbreviation throughout the same document.

The Center for Business and Industry (*CBI*) was recognized for its work with business executives in Miami. Together with the Miami Trade Center, *CBI* sponsored popular speakers such as John Nesbitt and Tom Peters. In a survey done by *The Miami Herald*, *CBI* was rated "very helpful" by 90 percent of those responding.

Exception: When using an abbreviation for the **first time** in a document, you may wish to use the complete form followed by the abbreviation in parentheses for clarity. Throughout the remainder of the document, however, only the abbreviated form will be used.

The *Miami Bookfair International (MBFI)* was held for the sixth consecutive year in 1991. *MBFI* had a total attendance of 600,000 people, including 150,000 children.

3005 **References.** Check a dictionary or other reference for acceptable forms of abbreviations not listed in this unit. Many references have a section on abbreviations; some of them include alphabetic lists. One caution—the correct punctuation and capitalization may not be indicated in the dictionary listing of the abbreviation. In such cases, follow the rules provided in this unit.

3006 **Preferred over contractions.** Like abbreviations, contractions are shortened forms of words or phrases. Unlike abbreviations, however, contractions use an apostrophe to indicate where letters have been omitted. Since abbreviations are often easier to read and understand, the use of abbreviations is generally preferable to the use of contractions.

Note: In formal writing the contraction o'clock is used with the word *morning, noon, afternoon, evening, night,* or *midnight* rather than *a.m.* or *p.m.*

Word	Abbreviation	Contraction
national	natl.	nat'l
association	assoc.	ass'n

Exception: Some verb and date forms have no easy abbreviation. In such cases, use the contraction.

wouldn't can't didn't '85 (for 1985)

3007 **Capitalization of abbreviations.** The capitalization of abbreviations generally follows the capitalization of the words being abbreviated.

Mothers Against Drunk Driving	MADD
New York Stock Exchange	NYSE
revised	rev.

Abbreviations of proper nouns are generally capitalized, following the rules used for capitalization of unabbreviated proper nouns.

Beginner's All-purpose Symbolic Instruction Code BASIC

MORE

CONTINUED

Abbreviations of common nouns are not capitalized.

minute min.

amount amt.

Exceptions: These abbreviations are written in all caps:

eastern standard time	EST
anno Domini	A.D.
collect on delivery	COD

3008 **Punctuation and spacing in abbreviations.** The modern trend is toward the elimination of periods in abbreviations. Some of these abbreviations without periods have passed into common usage; others have not.

3

- **Use periods at the end of single words.**

Dr. Ms. Chas.

- **Shortened words (not really abbreviations) are not followed by periods.**

memo	photo	math
3d	steno	auto

- **Use no periods and no spaces with abbreviations that are written in all capital letters.**

IRA NAACP CBS

Exceptions:

See ¶ 3010 for	Academic Degrees	B.A., B.S., M.A.
See ¶ 3020 for	Geographic	U.S.A. (*or* USA)
See ¶ 3030 for	Time	B.C., A.D.

- **Use periods and no spaces with abbreviations that are written in all lowercase letters.**

p.m q.v. o.m.

Exceptions:

See ¶ 3023 for	Measurements	mm, mph (*or* m.p.h.), psi, wpm

- **Use periods and spaces for abbreviations written with two words.**

op. cit. gr. wt. *loc. cit.*

Exceptions:

See ¶ 3010 for	Academic Degrees	Ed.D., Ph.D.
See ¶ 3019 for	Foreign Expressions	ad hoc, *et al.*

Within a sentence, an abbreviation is followed by one space.

Please place the *AIB* code immediately after the banking course description.

The *NAACP* provided an excellent speaker for the Martin Luther King luncheon.

A mark of punctuation following an abbreviation within a sentence is placed **immediately** after the abbreviation, with no space between the abbreviation and the punctuation mark.

`I was concerned; it was 3:05` *a.m.*`, and he had still not come home.`

If the abbreviation ends the sentence, two spaces follow the end-of-sentence punctuation.

`The new dean was introduced as Cristina Mateo,` *Ph.D.* `A meeting was discussed . . .`

Note: If the abbreviation ends with a period, that period also serves as the end-of-sentence punctuation.

`My new car averaged 25 m.p.g.  The design . . .`

Note: If the sentence does **not** end with a period, insert end-of-sentence punctuation following the abbreviation. A question mark or exclamation mark following an abbreviation at the end of the sentence is placed immediately following the abbreviation, with no spaces between the abbreviation and the punctuation mark.

`The president emphasized that the meeting would begin at exactly 2:00` *p.m.!*

`The contestant who won typed 125` *wpm!*

`Will the next international congress be held in the` *U.S.A.?*

3009 **Plurals and Possessives.** The plurals of most abbreviations are formed by adding *s*.

mgr. → mgrs.	Dr. → Drs.	ave. → aves.
*MD → MDs	*DO → DOs	CPA → CPAs

*See ¶ 3011.

Some abbreviations, particularly those of weights and measurements, have the same form in the singular and plural.

ft	in	m	qt

Plurals of some single-letter abbreviations are formed by doubling the letter.

p. 105 →	pp. 105-107	(referring to pages)
l. 8 →	ll. 8-10	(referring to lines)

The plurals of some abbreviations are formed irregularly.

Mr. → Messrs.

Note: This plural abbreviation is most properly used **only** in addressing unmarried brothers, business partners, or members of a firm. However, some people use it for any pair or group to whom *Mr.* would apply individually.

MORE

```
Messrs. Smith and Jones
Messrs. Adams and Berger
Mrs. → Mmes.
```

Note: The use of this plural abbreviation (Mmes.) is **not** considered good form.

```
Ms. → Mses. or Mss.
```

Note: This plural (Mses. or Mss.) is **not** standard. Since *Ms.* is not truly an abbreviation for a longer word, a plural is illogical.

However, the following is acceptable:

```
the Misses Smith and Jones
No. → Nos.
```

3

For clarity, add *'s* to form plurals of lowercase letters and lowercase abbreviations with punctuation.

```
changing the c's to e's
c.o.d.'s
```

Possession in abbreviations is indicated by adding *'s* when the abbreviation is singular, *'* when the abbreviation is plural and ends in *s*.

Singular	Plural
CORE's convention	CPAs' annual training
U.S.A.'s treaty	D.O.s' residency program
R.N.'s resume	M.D.s' graduation

3010 **Academic Degrees.** Academic degrees are written with periods following the abbreviation for each word and no spaces. A list of common abbreviations for academic degrees follows.

A.A.	Associate of Arts
A.S.	Associate of Science
B.A. (*or* **A.B.**)	Bachelor of Arts
B.B.A.	Bachelor of Business Administration
B.C.E.	Bachelor of Civil Engineering
B.D.	Bachelor of Divinity
B.Ed.	Bachelor of Education
B.L.S.	Bachelor of Library Science
B.S.	Bachelor of Science
D.B.A.	Doctor of Business Administration
D.D.	Doctor of Divinity
D.D.S.	Doctor of Dental Surgery
D.O.	Doctor of Osteopathy Medicine *or* Doctor of Optometry
Ed.D.	Doctor of Education
J.D.	Doctor of Jurisprudence (*Juris Doctor*)
L.H.D.	Doctor of Humanities
Litt.D.	Doctor of Letters *or* Doctor of Literature
LL.B.	Bachelor of Laws
LL.D.	Doctor of Laws
LL.M.	Master of Laws

M.A.	Master of Arts
M.B.A.	Master of Business Administration
M.D.	Doctor of Medicine
M.E. *or* **M.Ed.**	Master of Education
M.S.	Master of Science
Ph.D.	Doctor of Philosophy
Th.D.	Doctor of Theology

When the Masters of Business Administration is referred to as a type of training program, it is sometimes written without periods.

The *MBA* training program is the kind of preparation our junior executives should have.

The Certified Professional Secretary (*CPS*), Certified Public Accountant (*CPA*), Certified Financial Planner (*CFP*), and Chartered Life Underwriter (*CLU*) designations are generally written in capitals and without periods.

The *CPS* examination is administered once a year there.

We administer the *CPA* exam in our computerized testing area.

However, when combined with other academic degrees, add periods for consistency.

Bonnie Anderson, Ph.D., C.P.A.

When academic titles follow an individual's name, do not use titles such as *Dr., Mr., Ms., Mrs.* or *Miss* before the name.

Sis Smith, M.D. *or* Dr. Sis Smith
(**Not:** Dr. Sis Smith, M.D.)

Other titles that do not duplicate a degree following the name may be used in front of the same name.

Dr. Irene Lipoff, Professor of Social Science
or
Professor Irene Lipoff, Ph.D.

the Reverend Ned Glenn, D.D.
or
the Reverend Dr. Ned Glenn

Vice President Bill Stokes, CPA

3011 **Medical Degrees.** The American Medical Association and the American Osteopathic Association prefer that no periods be used in medical abbreviations. Within the medical profession, titles such as MD, DO, RN, and FACS (Fellow of American College of Surgeons) are often written without periods.

Marcia Beth Stringer, RN James McCormick, DO

3012 **Acronyms.** A shortened, pronounceable word created (usually) by using the first letter of each word in a longer title is called an **acronym.** Acronyms save time and space in writing and time in speaking, especially when a title is particularly long. Most acronyms are written with capital letters; some common acronyms are written in lowercase letters. Spaces and punctuation marks are eliminated.

National Organization for Women	NOW
College Level Examination Program	CLEP
World Health Organization	WHO
Students Against Drunk Driving	SADD
Environmental Prototype Community of Tomorrow	EPCOT
light amplification by stimulated emission of radiation	laser
zone improvement plan	ZIP or zip

Commonly used acronyms are included in ¶ 3031. They are followed by the designation *ac*.

Note: *Acronyms* are different from ordinary abbreviations, as they are pronounced as one word. The following *abbreviations,* however, are pronounced letter by letter.

ATT	YMCA	YWHA
TVA	SAT	MDT

3013 **Addresses.** In the inside address of business letters, or in an envelope address, the following terms are commonly abbreviated to balance address lines. (See also, ¶ 3316-19.)

Avenue	Ave.	Boulevard	Blvd.
Building	Bldg.	Court	Ct.
Drive	Dr.	Highway	Hwy.
Lane	La. *or* Ln.	Parkway	Pkwy.
Place	Pl.	Road	Rd.
Square	Sq.	Street	St.
Terrace	Terr.	Turnpike	Tpk.

Within the context of a letter or report, however, such terms are written in full. For geographic abbreviations, see ¶ 3020.

3014 **Broadcasting stations and systems.** Radio and television broadcasting stations and broadcasting networks and systems are abbreviated in capital letters with no periods or spaces.

Detroit—WXYZ-AM
↑ ↑
station system

Miami—WLYF-FM
MGM Studios
NBC
CBS
UPI News Service

ABC News was the first to declare the winner last night.

3015 **Chemical and mathematical abbreviations.** Do **not** use periods with symbols representing chemical elements and formulas.

```
Au = Gold                    Ni = Nickel
Cu = Copper                  Zn = Zinc
```

Do **not** use periods with symbols representing mathematical abbreviations.

```
sin = sine                cos = cosine
log = logarithm           pi  = the value given to the
                                nonending, nonrepeating decimal
```

3016 **Compass directions as nouns and adjectives.** When a compass direction is used as a noun, write it in full and begin with a capital; do not abbreviate.

You could tell by her accent she is from the *South.*

When a compass direction is used as an adjective, write it out; do not abbreviate and do not capitalize.

We put up the sails and headed our boat, Bandolera, to the *south* bay toward Elliot Key.

Note: Different uses require different capitalization. For additional information, please refer to ¶ 3120.

- **Compass directions in addresses.** When a compass direction *precedes a street name,* it is generally written out. (See also, ¶ 3316-23.)

Dr. Kenneth Stringer
114 *East* Michigan Boulevard
East Lansing, MI 48864

However, when doing so would cause the inside address to be out of balance (or in tables where space is limited), it is also permissible to abbreviate a compass direction before a street name.

Ms. Bonnie McCabe 11621 *S.W.* 112 Street Miami, FL 33176	*or*	Ms. Bonnie McCabe 11621 *SW* 112 Street Miami, FL 33176

Note: For special U.S. Postal Service rules for addressing envelopes, please refer to ¶ 3316-23.

When a compass direction *follows a street name,* insert a comma to separate the street name from the abbreviation and then abbreviate in capital letters. Follow local practice in determining the spacing or use of periods. In the absence of a local preference, eliminate periods and spaces.

Mrs. Castell Bryant
6919 Liberty Street, *NE*
Philadelphia, PA 19126

MORE

- **Compass directions in technical material.** When a compass direction is included in technical material, use all capital letters and omit all punctuation and spacing.

SSW	NE	W
(south-southwest)	(northeast)	(west)

3017 **Contractions.** Abbreviations and contractions are both shortened forms of words and phrases; do **not** confuse them. When writing contractions, an apostrophe is inserted at the point where any letter or number is eliminated. See ¶ 2002 for more information on contractions.

shouldn't	we'll
gov't	'92

3018 **Dates.** Days of the week and months of the year should be written in full. In technical matter where space is limited (as in charts, tables, and the like), however, the following uses are permissible:

Jan.	Feb.	Mar.	Apr.	May	June	
July	Aug.	Sept.	Oct.	Nov.	Dec.	
Sun.	Mon.	Tues.	Wed.	Thurs.	Fri.	Sat.

On forms or in computerized reports, it may be desirable to abbreviate days and months even further. In such cases use the following:

Ja	F	Mr	Ap	My	Jn	
Jl	Au	S	O	N	D	
Su	M	Tu	W	Th	F	Sa

3019 **Foreign expressions.** Foreign expressions are followed by an *f* in the section on business abbreviations commonly used. (See ¶ 3031.)

3020 **Geographic abbreviations.** Try to avoid geographic abbreviations—except in forms, tables, computerized reports, or in other technical material where space is extremely limited. Exceptions to this rule are extremely long names such as U.A.R. (United Arab Republic) and U.S.A. (United States of America).

When geographic names are abbreviated in capital letters, periods (but no spaces) follow each letter.

Philippine Islands	P.I.
United Kingdom	U.K.
New York City	N.Y.C.
British West Indies	B.W.I.

- **State and Province Abbreviations, U.S.A.** The following table shows the names of the states, districts, and territories of the United States; the standard abbreviations of the names; the two-letter abbreviations that are used with zip codes; and the capital cities.

Name	Standard Abbreviation	Two-Letter Abbreviation	Capital
Alabama	Ala.	AL	Montgomery
Alaska	Alaska	AK	Juneau
Arizona	Ariz.	AZ	Phoenix
Arkansas	Ark.	AR	Little Rock
California	Calif.	CA	Sacramento
Colorado	Colo.	CO	Denver
Connecticut	Conn.	CT	Hartford
Delaware	Del.	DE	Dover
District of Columbia	D.C.	DC	Washington (National Capital)
Florida	Fla.	FL	Tallahassee
Georgia	Ga.	GA	Atlanta
Guam	Guam	GU	Agana
Hawaii	Hawaii	HI	Honolulu
Idaho	Idaho	ID	Boise
Illinois	Ill.	IL	Springfield
Indiana	Ind.	IN	Indianapolis
Iowa	Iowa	IA	Des Moines
Kansas	Kans.	KS	Topeka
Kentucky	Ky.	KY	Frankfort
Louisiana	La.	LA	Baton Rouge
Maine	Maine	ME	Augusta
Maryland	Md.	MD	Annapolis
Massachusetts	Mass.	MA	Boston
Michigan	Mich.	MI	Lansing
Minnesota	Minn.	MN	St. Paul
Mississippi	Miss.	MS	Jackson
Missouri	Mo.	MO	Jefferson City
Montana	Mont.	MT	Helena
Nebraska	Nebr.	NE	Lincoln
Nevada	Nev.	NV	Carson City
New Hampshire	N.H.	NH	Concord
New Jersey	N.J.	NJ	Trenton
New Mexico	N.Mex.	NM	Santa Fe
New York	N.Y.	NY	Albany
North Carolina	N.C.	NC	Raleigh
North Dakota	N.Dak.	ND	Bismarck
Ohio	Ohio	OH	Columbus
Oklahoma	Okla.	OK	Oklahoma City
Oregon	Oreg.	OR	Salem
Pennsylvania	Pa.	PA	Harrisburg
Puerto Rico	P.R.	PR	San Juan

MORE

CONTINUED

Rhode Island	R.I.	RI	Providence
South Carolina	S.C.	SC	Columbia
South Dakota	S.Dak.	SD	Pierre
Tennessee	Tenn.	TN	Nashville
Texas	Tex.	TX	Austin
Utah	Utah	UT	Salt Lake City
Vermont	Vt.	VT	Montpelier
Virgin Islands	V.I.	VI	Charlotte Amalie, St. Thomas
Virginia	Va.	VA	Richmond
Washington	Wash.	WA	Olympia
West Virginia	W.Va.	WV	Charleston
Wisconsin	Wis.	WI	Madison
Wyoming	Wyo.	WY	Cheyenne

3

- **U.S. Place Names.** *Saint* is generally abbreviated within the United States by using *St.*

St. Paul St. Louis St. Thomas

Port, Point, Mount, Heights, and *Fort* are **not** generally abbreviated within the United States unless space is limited.

Fort Meyers Shaker Heights
East Point Mount Vernon

Outside of the United States, however, follow local customs and preferences regarding the use of such abbreviations.

- **Canadian Provinces.** The following table shows the names of the Canadian provinces, the standard abbreviations of the names, the two-letter abbreviations of the names, and the capitals of the provinces.

Name	Standard Abbreviation	Two-Letter Abbreviation	Capital
Alberta	Alta.	AB	Edmonton
British Columbia	B.C.	BC	Victoria
Manitoba	Man.	MB	Winnipeg
New Brunswick	N.B.	NB	Fredericton
Newfoundland	Newf./Nfld.	NF	St. John's
Northwest Territories	N.W. Ter.	NT	Yellowknife
Nova Scotia	N.S.	NS	Halifax
Ontario	Ont.	ON	Toronto
Prince Edward Island	P.E.I.	PE	Charlottetown
Quebec	Que.	PQ	Quebec
Saskatchewan	Sask.	SK	Regina
Yukon Territory	—	YT	Whitehorse

3021 **Government and international agencies.** Abbreviations for government and international agencies are generally written in all capital letters with no periods and no spaces. (See also, ¶ 3031.)

SSA	FHA	UNICEF
OPEC	NASA	GSA

3022 **Information processing.** Information processing expressions are followed by an IP in the section on business abbreviations commonly used. (See ¶ 3031.)

3023 **Measurements.** Units of measure are abbreviated when they occur frequently in documents.

- **Standard form**. Abbreviate standard units of measurement in lowercase letters. Periods are not usually employed.

in	inch(es)*	ft	foot/feet
sq in	square inch	mph	miles per hour
wpm	words per minute	yd	yard(s)

*When using this abbreviation for *inch* within a sentence, make certain it cannot be confused with the preposition *in*. In such cases either add a period (*in.*) or spell out *inch*.

In measurements including abbreviations and numbers, a space is included between the number and abbreviation. In simple measurements, the abbreviation may be inserted at the end of a series of numbers.

34 sq ft		80 x 92 in
17 ft 3 in	*or*	17' 3" (See ¶ 2004.)

In measurements including symbols, however, there are no spaces between number and symbol, or symbol and letter abbreviation.

78°F	62°C

- **Metric.** Abbreviate metric units with lowercase letters and no periods. (See also, ¶ 3352-56.)

meter	m	gram	g
liter*	L		
square**	sq	cubic**	c

*Liter uses a capital *L*, to avoid confusion with the number *1*.

**These forms are used in combination with base units in English measurements; however, in metric measurements they are represented as powers:

One cubic centimeter = 1 cm^3

MORE

- **Metric prefixes.** Add the prefix to the basic metric units provided above. (See also, ¶ 3354.)

deka	da	(x10)	hecto	h	(x100)
kilo	k	(x1000)	deci	d	(1/10)
centi	c	(1/100)	milli	m	(1/1000)

She wanted to figure out her weight in *kilograms;* she weighed 57 *kilograms.*

The ball measured about 15 *centimeters* around.

Note: Metric abbreviations represent both singular and plural forms.

In expressing per hour measurements with metric abbreviations, use the / to represent *per*.

60 km/h = sixty kilometers per hour

3024 **Medical abbreviations.** Commonly used medical abbreviations are included in ¶ 3031. Each one is followed by the designation *m*. See ¶ 3011 for the preferences of medical associations.

3025 **Numbers.** (See ¶ 3300.)

3026 **Organizations and groups.** Many organizations and groups are best known by their abbreviated names.

WDW	AFL-CIO	VISTA
NOW	UPI	MADD

The foregoing abbreviations may be used except in formal writing. In addition, many parts of organization or group names may be abbreviated.

Co.	Company	Inc.	Incorporated	Ltd.	Limited
Corp.	Corporation	Mfg.	Manufacturing	Bros.	Brothers

Always write the name of an organization or group as its members prefer. The letterhead and other printed material of the organization provide a good example.

3027 **Personal names and initials.** Abbreviated forms of given names are often used in writing lists of names and in other places where space is limited; they are usually not pronounced. Nicknames are shortened forms of names that may be spoken or written (but not in formal communication).

	Abbreviated Form	Nickname
Richard	Rich. *or*	Dick *or* Rick
Thomas	Thos. *or*	Tom
Elizabeth	Eliz. *or*	Liz
Suzanne	Suz. *or*	Sue

Note: Periods are included with abbreviations, but not following nicknames. Whenever possible, follow an individual's personal preferences in using both abbreviations and nicknames.

Initials within a name should be capitalized. Each initial is followed by a period and one space.

Alyce P. Neji	J. M. Molina
M. Duane Hansen	Robert A. R. Blood

When using initials only, use all capital letters with no periods and no spaces.

	KSS	PWG
	STM	for Sylvia T. McCarty
But:	ZEZ	for Zoila E. de Zayas

3028 **Titles.** Some title abbreviations are always acceptable, even in formal correspondence.

- **Personal**. Abbreviate the following titles when they are used with personal names.

Singular	**Plural**	
Mr.	Messrs.	(See ¶ 3009.)
Mrs.	—	(See ¶ 3009.)
Ms.	—	(See ¶ 3009.)
Dr.	Drs.	

Note: Since *Miss* (singular) and *Misses* (plural) are not abbreviations, no period is used after these titles. *Ms.* is a title commonly used in business writing wherein identification of a woman's marital status serves no purpose.

When *Saint* is part of a name, follow individual preference for writing out or abbreviating.

Professor Delphine St. Thomas
Anabel San Lorenza

Note: In Hispanic names *San* may represent *Saint*.

Always abbreviate *Jr.* and *Sr.* following personal names (except on formal invitations and the like). *Esquire* may be spelled out or abbreviated (Esq.)—except in formal use. These abbreviations should be used with full names. A personal title may also be used **before** the full name with *Jr.* and *Sr.*, but never with *Esq.*

Lourdes Hidalgo-Gato, Esq.* Dr. Dale Romanik, Jr.

*Esq. is used by lawyers within the U.S.A. It is most correctly applied to males; however, some females now use it.

Designations such as *II, III, 2d,* or *3d* follow full names. No periods or commas are used; however, if an individual wishes to use a comma, follow that preference.

Preferred:	Nickson Benedico III
Acceptable:	Nickson Benedico, III

MORE

CONTINUED

- **Professional.** Professional titles should be written in full whenever possible.

Vice President Arcie Ewell	Professor Joyce Crawford
the Reverend Kenneth Long	Vice Mayor Dewey Knight

When titles are long, or when space is limited, professional titles may be abbreviated if the full name or last name and initials are used.

First Lieutenant Lynn Forrester	1st Lt. Lynn Forrester
Father Leonard Bryant	Fr. Leonard Bryant

Note: When titles begin with *the,* do **not** abbreviate.

The Honorable Dewey Knight	The Reverend Harriet Spivak

3

3029 **Business symbols.** (See ¶ 3304.)

3030 **Time and time zones.** Use the abbreviations *a.m.* and *p.m.* with numerals in expressions of exact time in ordinary text.

4:01 p.m.	3:35 a.m.	8:32 p.m., EST *or* 8:32 p.m. (EST)

Use *o'clock* with spelled-out numbers for the hour, the quarter-hour, and the half-hour in ordinary text. Use *o'clock* with spelled-out numbers in all formal writing. When *o'clock is used,* eliminate *a.m.* and *p.m.* (See ¶ 3375-79.)

six o'clock in the evening
Not: 6 p.m. o'clock

Time zones are abbreviated in all caps without punctuation.

Standard Time		**Daylight Savings Time (DST)**
Eastern	EST	EDT
(eastern standard time)		(eastern daylight time)
Central	CST	CDT
Mountain	MST	MDT
Pacific	PST	PDT

Note: In the travel industry (especially on airline tickets), the following abbreviations are commonly used:

a.m.	=	a	p.m.	=	p

See chapter 6 for additional information.

3031 **Business abbreviations commonly used.** The following list contains abbreviations for common medical terms (m), governmental agencies, common academic degrees, information processing terms (IP), common English phrases, common foreign phrases (f), acronyms (ac), and time zones.

A.A.	Associate of Arts
AAA	American Automobile Association
AAMA	American Association of Medical Assistants
A.A.S.	Associate of Applied Science
ABA	American Bankers Association
	American Bar Association
abbr.	abbreviation
ABC	American Broadcasting Company
abr.	abridged
acct.	account
ACLU	American Civil Liberties Union
A.D.	*anno Domini* (in the year of the Lord) (f)
ADC	Aid to Dependent Children
	analog to digital converter (IP)
add.	additional
ad hoc	for a particular purpose, (f) Latin meaning "for this" —**not** an abbreviation, no periods.
ad lib.	as desired; at pleasure—(f) for the Latin *ad libitum* meaning "at one's pleasure"
admin.	administration
ADP	automatic data processing (IP)
ad. val. *or* **A/V**	*ad valorem,* (f), Latin, meaning "according to worth"
ad *or* **advt.**	advertisement
AEC	Atomic Energy Commission
AFA	Advertising Federation of America
AFB	Aid For the Blind
	air force base
AFD	Aid For the Disabled
	Association of Food Distributors
afft.	affidavit
AFL-CIO	American Federation of Labor - Congress of Industrial Organizations
agt.	agent
AIB	American Institute of Banking
AICPA	American Institute of Certified Public Accountants
AIDS	Acquired Immune Deficiency Syndrome (ac)(m)
aka	also known as
ALGOL	algorithmic-oriented language (IP)
ALU	arithmetic and logic unit (IP)
a.m.	*ante meridiem* (before noon)
AMA	American Medical Association
Amer.	America, American
AMEX	American Stock Exchange (ac)
amt.	amount
anon.	anonymous
ans.	answer
ANSI	American National Standards Institute
AP *or* **a/p**	accounts payable
AP	Associated Press
API	American Petroleum Institute
APL	a programming language (IP)
approx.	approximately

MORE

CONTINUED

appt.	appoint, appointment
APR	annual percentage rate
apt.	apartment
aq	aqueous (water) (m)
AR *or* **a/r**	accounts receivable
ar.	arrive, arrival
ARC	American Red Cross
ARM	Adjustable Rate Mortgage
ARMA	Association of Records Managers and Administrators (ac)
ASA	American Standards Association American Statistical Association
ASAP *or* **asap**	as soon as possible
ASCAP	American Society of Composers, Authors, and Publishers (ac)
ASCE	American Society of Civil Engineers
ASCII	American Standard Code for Information Interchange (ac) (IP)
asgmt.	assignment
ASME	American Society of Mechanical Engineers
assn.	association
assoc.	associate
asst.	assistant
ASTA	American Society of Travel Agents, Inc. (ac)
ASTD	American Society of Training Directors
astd.	assorted
ATM	automatic teller machine
att.	attached, attachment
AT&T	American Telephone & Telegraph
attn.	attention
atty.	attorney
A.V. *or* **AV**	audiovisual
ave.	avenue
avg. *or* **av.**	average
B.A. *or* **A.B.**	Bachelor of Arts
bal.	balance
BASIC	Beginner's All-purpose Symbolic Instruction Code (ac) (IP)
B.B.A.	Bachelor of Business Administration
BBB	Better Business Bureau
BBC	British Broadcasting Corporation
bbl	barrel(s)
B.C.	before Christ
BCD	binary-coded decimal (IP)
B.Ed.	Bachelor of Education
B/F	brought forward
BIA	Bureau of Indian Affairs
bid	twice a day (m) [Latin *bis in die*]
B.I.D.	Bachelor of Industrial Design
BIOS	basic input/output system (IP)
bit	binary digit (IP)
bl	bale
B/L *or* **BL**	bill of lading

bldg.	building
blvd.	boulevard
BP	blood pressure (m)
bps	bits per second (IP)
bro(s).	brother(s)
B.S.	Bachelor of Science
B/S *or* **BS**	bill of sale
Btu	British thermal unit
bu	bushel(s)
bus.	business
c	centi, as prefix 1/100
	copy
c. *or* **ca.**	circa, approximately (f)
C	100 or Celsius
Ca	Calcium (m)
CA	Cancer (m)
CAB	Civil Aeronautics Board
CAD	computer-aided design (ac) (IP)
CAI	computer-assisted instruction (IP)
CAM	computer-aided manufacturing (ac) (IP)
cap. *or* **Cap**	capital, capitalize
CARE	Cooperative for American Relief to Everywhere (ac)
cat.	catalog
CAT	computerized axial tomography (ac) (m)
	Computer Aided Translation (ac) (IP)
CB	Citizens Band
CBC	complete blood count (m)
CBS	Columbia Broadcasting System
cc	cubic centimeter (m)—cm^3 is preferred in nonmedical copy unless referring to automobile cylinder capacity
	carbon copy
CCP	console command processor (IP)
CCU	coronary care unit (m)
CD	certificate of deposit
CDT	central daylight time
CEO	chief executive officer
cf.	confer, compare (f)
CFO	chief financial officer
cg	centigram(s)
ch.	chapter
chg.	charge
CIA	Central Intelligence Agency
CIC	Consumer Information Center
c.i.f. *or* **CIF**	cost, insurance, and freight
CIM	computer input microfilm (IP)
CLEP	College Level Examination Program (ac)
CLU	Civil Liberties Union
	chartered life underwriter
cm	centimeter(s)
CMOS	complementary metal-oxide semiconductor (IP)
CNS	central nervous system (m)
co.	company

MORE

CONTINUED

c/o	care of
COBOL	common business oriented language (ac) (IP)
COD *or* **c.o.d.**	collect on delivery
COM	computer output microfilm (IP)
comm.	commission
cont.	continued
COO	Chief Operating Officer
CORE	Congress of Racial Equality (ac)
corp.	corporation
CPA	certified public accountant
cpi	characters per inch (IP)
CP/M	Control Program for Microprocessors (IP)
cps	characters per second (IP)
CPS	certified professional secretary
CPSC	Consumer Product Safety Commission
CPU	central processing unit (IP)
cr.	credit
CRT	cathode-ray tube (IP)
CSC	Civil Service Commission
CST	central standard time
ctn.	carton
cu	cubic
cu cm	cubic centimeter—cm^3 is preferred
cu. in. *or* **cu in**	cubic inch
cust.	customer
cwt.	hundredweight
d	deci, as prefix l/10
da	deka, as prefix x 10
D.A.	Doctor of Arts
DA	District Attorney
DASD	direct access storage device (IP)
d.b.a. *or* **DBA**	doing business as
D.B.A.	Doctor of Business Administration
D.D.	Doctor of Divinity
D.D.S.	Doctor of Dental Surgery (m)
dept.	department
dis. *or* **disc.**	discount
dist.	district
distr.	distributor
div.	division
DNA	does not apply or does not answer
	deoxyribonucleic acid (m)
D.O. *or* **DO**	Doctor of Osteopathy (m)
DOS	disk operating system (ac) (IP)
doz. *or* **dz.**	dozen
DP	data processing (IP)
dr.	dram, debit
Dr.	doctor
DSCB	data set control block (IP)
DSL	data set label (IP)
dstn.	destination
dtd.	dated
DX	diagnosis (m)

3

ea *or* **ea.**	each
EBCDIC	Extended Binary Coded Decimal Interchange Code (IP)
ECB	event control block (IP)
ECOM	electronic computer-originated mail (ac) (IP)
ed.	edition, editor
Ed.D.	Doctor of Education
EDP	electronic data processing (IP)
Ed.M.	Master of Education
Ed.S.	Specialist in Education
EDT	eastern daylight time
EEC	European Economic Community
EEG	electroencephalogram (m)
EEOC	Equal Employment Opportunity Commission
EENT	eye, ear, nose, and throat (m)
EFT	electronic funds transfer
e.g.	*exempli gratia* (for example) (f)
EKG	electrocardiogram (m)
Enc.	enclosure
ENT	ear, nose, and throat (m)
EOF	end of file (IP)
EOM *or* **e.o.m.**	end of month
EPA	Environmental Protection Agency
EPCOT	Environmental Prototype Community of Tomorrow (ac)
EPROM	erasable programmable read-only memory (IP)
ER	emergency room (m)
ERIC	Educational Resources Information Center (ac)
ESD	external symbol dictionary (IP)
ESOP	Employee Stock Ownership Plan
ESP	extrasensory perception
Esq.	Esquire
ESS	electronic switching system (IP)
est.	estimated
EST	eastern standard time
et	and (f)
ETA	estimated time of arrival
et al.	*et alii* (and others) (f)
etc.	*et cetera* (and so forth) (f)—Avoid the use of *etc.* in running text
et seq.	*et sequens* (and the following) (f) *et sequentes* (those that follow) (f)
ex.	example
exec.	executive, executor
exp.	expense
ext.	extension
F	Fahrenheit
FAA	Federal Aviation Agency
FAO	Food and Agriculture Organization of the United Nations
FAS *or* **f.a.s.**	free alongside ship
FAX	facsimile transmission (ac) (IP)
FBI	Federal Bureau of Investigation
FBLA	Future Business Leaders of America

MORE

CONTINUED

FCC	Federal Communications Commission
FDA	Food and Drug Administration
FDIC	Federal Deposit Insurance Corporation
fed.	federal
ff.	and the following pages
FHA	Federal Housing Administration
FIFO	first in, first out (ac) (IP)
fig.	figure
fl. oz.	fluid ounce
FNMA	Federal National Mortgage Association (also commonly known as "Fannie Mae")
f.o.b. *or* **FOB**	free on board
FONZ	Friends of the National Zoo (ac)
FORTRAN	formula translation (ac) (IP)
FPC	Federal Power Commission
FRB	Federal Reserve Bank Federal Reserve Board
FRS	Federal Reserve System
frt.	freight
FSLIC	Federal Savings and Loan Insurance Corporation
ft	foot, feet
ft-tn	foot-ton
FTC	Federal Trade Commission
fwd.	forward
FY	fiscal year
FYI	for your information
g	gram(s)
gal	gallon(s)
GAO	General Accounting Office
GI	gastrointestinal (m)
GM	general manager
GNP	gross national product
govt.	government
GPO	Government Printing Office
gr.	grain, gross
gr. wt.	gross weight
GSA	General Services Administration
GTT	Glucose Tolerance Test (m)
GU	genitourinary (m)
gyn	gynecology (m)
h	hecto, as prefix x 100
HBO	Home Box Office
HBP	high blood pressure (m)
hdlg.	handling
hdqrs. *or* **HQ**	headquarters
HGB *or* **hb**	hemoglobin (m)
HHS	Department of Health and Human Services
HMO	health maintenance organization
HOPE	Help Obese People Everywhere (ac)
HP *or* **hp**	horsepower
hr	hour(s)
HUD	Department of Housing and Urban Development (ac)

IABC	International Association of Business Communicators
ibid.	*ibidem* (in the same place) (f)
IBM	International Business Machines
IC	integrated circuit (IP)
ICC	Interstate Commerce Commission
	Indian Claims Commission
ICU	intensive care unit (m)
ID	identification
idem	the same (f)—**not** an abbreviation
IDP	integrated data processing (IP)
i.e.	*id est* (that is) (f)
ILGWU	International Ladies' Garment Workers' Union
IMF	International Monetary Fund
in. *or* **in**	inch(es)
inc.	incorporated
incl.	including, inclusive
INS	Immigration and Naturalization Service
ins.	insurance
inst.	institute, instant
int.	interest
intl.	international
inv.	invoice
invt.	inventory
I/O	Input/Output (IP)
IOC	International Olympic Committee
IOOF	Independent Order of Odd Fellows
IOU	I owe you
IPL	initial program loading (IP)
ips	inches per second
IQ	intelligence quotient
IRA	individual retirement account (ac)
IRS	Internal Revenue Service
ital.	italic
IV	intravenous (m)
J.D.	Doctor of Jurisprudence (*Juris Doctor*)
Jr.	junior
jour.	journal
JP	justice of the peace
JTPA	Job Training Partnership Act
k	kilo, as prefix x 1000
	karat
K	kilobyte (IP)
kg	kilogram(s)
km	kilometer(s)
km/h	kilometers per hour
L	liter(s)
l. *or* **ll.**	line(s)
LAN	local area network (ac) (IP)
laser	light amplification by stimulated emission of radiation (ac)
lat.	latitude
lb(s)	pound(s)

MORE

CONTINUED

lc	lowercase
L/C	letter of credit
LCD	liquid crystal display (IP)
LIFO	last in, first out (ac) (IP)
LL.B.	Bachelor of Laws
loc. cit.	*loco citato* (in the place cited) (f)
long.	longitude
LPN	licensed practical nurse (m)
LQP	letter-quality printer
LS	*locus sigilli* (in place of the seal) (f)
LSI	large-scale integration (IP)
ltd.	limited
m	meter(s)
	milli, as prefix 1/1000
M	1,000 (symbol)
M.A.	Master of Arts
MADD	Mothers Against Drunk Driving (ac)
max.	maximum
M.B.A. *or* **MBA**	Master of Business Administration
MBDA	Minority Business Development Agency
MC	master/mistress of ceremonies
M.D. *or* **MD**	Doctor of Medicine
M.Div.	Master of Divinity
mdse.	merchandise
MDT	mountain daylight time
M.Ed.	Master of Education
memo	memorandum—**not** an abbreviation, but a shortened word
Messrs.	Misters (See ¶ 3009 for correct usage.)
mfg.	manufacturing
mfr(s).	manufacturer(s)
mg	milligram(s)
mgr.	manager
MGM	Metro-Goldwyn-Mayer
MI	myocardial infarction (m)
mi	mile
MICR	magnetic ink character recognition (IP)
min	minute(s)
min.	minimum
MIS	management information systems (IP)
misc.	miscellaneous
mkt.	market
ml	milliliter(s)
mm	millimeter(s)
Mmes.	plural of Madam (Best to avoid; see ¶ 3009.)
mo	month(s)
MO	mail order; money order
M.O.	*modus operandi,* the way in which something is done (f)
modem	modulator-demodulator (IP) (ac)
mpg	miles per gallon
mph	miles per hour
Mr.	Mister

Mrs.	Mistress
Ms.	Title for woman not identifying marital status
M.S.	Master of Science
Mses. *or* **Mss.**	plural of Ms. (Do **not** use; see ¶ 3009.)
MST	mountain standard time
n/30	net in 30 days
N/A *or* **NA**	not applicable
NAACP	National Association for the Advancement of Colored People
NAM	National Association of Manufacturers (ac)
NANA	North American Newspaper Alliance (ac)
NAS	National Academy of Sciences
NASA	National Aeronautics and Space Administration (ac)
NASD	National Association Securities Dealers
natl.	national
NATO	North Atlantic Treaty Organization (ac)
NBC	National Broadcasting Company
NBS	National Bureau of Standards
NCR	no carbon (paper) required
NEA	National Education Association
neg	negative
NIMH	National Institute of Mental Health
NLRB	National Labor Relations Board
NMA	National Microfilm Association
No. (Nos.)	number (numbers)
nol. pros.	*nolle prosequi,* Latin meaning "unwilling to prosecute" (f)
non seq.	*non sequitur,* Latin meaning "it does not follow" (f)
NOW	National Organization for Women (ac)
NRC	Nuclear Regulatory Commission
NSC	National Security Council
NSF	National Science Foundation
nt. wt.	net weight
NYD	not yet diagnosed (m)
NYSE	New York Stock Exchange
OAS	Organization of American States
OB/GYN	obstetrics/gynecology (m)
OCP	optical character printing (IP)
OCR	optical character reader (IP)
	optical character recognition (IP)
o.d. *or* **OD**	overdraft
OEM	original equipment manufacturer (IP)
OK	okay; all right
om	every morning (m)
	order of merit
OMB	Office of Management and Budget
on	every night (m)
op. cit.	*opere citato*, Latin meaning "in the work cited" (f)
OP Code	operation code (IP)
OPEC	Organization of Petroleum Exporting Countries
opt.	optional
OR	operating room (m)
org.	organization

MORE

CONTINUED

orig.	original
o/s *or* **OS**	out of stock
OTC	over-the-counter
oz	ounce(s)
p. (pp.)	page (pages)
PA	public address
	Physician's Assistant (m)
PABX	private automatic branch telephone exchange (IP)
PAC	political action committee
PAP smear	Papanicolaou Smear (m)
par.	paragraph
payt.	payment
PBS	Public Broadcasting Service
PBX	private branch exchange (IP)
pc	photocopy
PC or pc	personal computer
pd.	paid
PDT	Pacific daylight time
P/E	price/earnings ratio
PERT	Program Evaluation and Review Technique (ac)
PHA	Public Housing Administration
Ph.D.	Doctor of Philosophy
PHS	Public Health Service
pk.	peck
pkg.	package(s)
PL	programming language (IP)
P & L *or* **P/L**	profit and loss
p.m.	*post meridiem* (after noon)
PO	purchase order
P.O.	Post Office
p.o.e. *or* **POE**	port of entry
pp. *or* **PP**	parcel post
ppd.	prepaid
PR	public relations
pr.	pair(s)
pres.	president
prn	*pro re nata,* Latin meaning "as needed" (m)
prof.	professor
PROM	programmable read-only memory (IP)
pro tem	*pro tempore* (for the time being) (f)
prox.	*proximo* (in the next month) (f)
P.S. *or* **PS**	*postscriptum* (postscript) (f)
psi	pounds per square inch
PST	Pacific standard time
pstg.	postage
pt	pint(s)
pt.	part
	point(s)
	port
PTA	Parent-Teacher Association
PUSH	People United to Save Humanity (ac)
QCB	que control block (IP)

Q.E.D.	*quod erat demonstrandum* (which was to be demonstrated) (f)
qh	every hour (m)
qid	four times a day (m)
qr	quire
qt	quart(s)
qtr.	quarter(ly)
qty.	quantity
q.v.	*quod vide* (which see) (f)
R & D	research and development
radar	radio detecting and ranging (ac)
RAM	random access memory (ac) (IP)
RBC	red blood cells (m) red blood cell count (m)
RCA	Radio Corporation of America
re *or* **in re**	regarding, in the matter of (f)
recd.	received
ref.	reference
reg.	registered
rep.	representative
req.	requisition require
reqd.	required
ret.	retired
retd.	returned
rev.	revised
RFD	rural free delivery
rm	ream(s) room
R.N. *or* **RN**	Registered Nurse (m)
ROM	read-only memory (ac) (IP)
ROTC	Reserve Officers' Training Corps
RPG	report program generator (IP)
rpm	revolutions per minute
RR *or* **R.R.**	railroad rural route
r.s.v.p. *or* **RSVP**	*repondez s'il vous plait* (please reply) (f)
rte.	route
/s/	signed (before a copied signature)
SADD	Students Against Drunk Driving (ac)
SALAD	Spanish American League Against Discrimination
SASE	self-addressed, stamped envelope
SAT	Scholastic Aptitude Test
SBA	Small Business Administration
scuba	self-contained underwater breathing apparatus (ac)
SEC	Securities and Exchange Commission
sec	second
sec. *or* **secy.**	secretary
sect.	section
sen.	senator
shpt.	shipment
shtg.	shortage

MORE

SIDS	sudden infant death syndrome (m)
SO	Shipping Order
sonar	sound navigation ranging (ac)
SOP	standard operating procedure
SOS	Save our ship (distress call)
SPCA	Society for the Prevention of Cruelty to Animals
sp.	spelling special
spec.	specification
sq in	square inch
sq m	square meter
Sr.	senior
SRO	standing room only
SSA	Social Security Administration
SSS	Selective Service System
St.	saint street
stat	*statim* (immediately) (f) (m)
stat(s).	statistic(s)
std.	standard
steno	stenographer—**not** an abbreviation, but a shortened word
stge.	storage
stmt.	statement
sub.	substitute
subj.	subject
supra	above (f)—**not** an abbreviation, do not use a period
supt.	superintendent
TB	tuberculosis (m)
tbs. *or* **tbsp.**	tablespoon
tech.	technical
tel.	telegram telegraph telephone
temp	temperature (m)
Th.D.	Doctor of Theology
tkt.	ticket
TLC	tender, loving care
TM	trademark
treas.	treasurer
tsp.	teaspoon(s)
TTL	transistor-transistor logic (IP)
TV	television
TVA	Tennessee Valley Authority
typo	typographical or keyboarding error
uc *or* **Uc**	uppercase
UFO	unidentified flying object
UHF	ultrahigh frequency
ult.	*ultimo* (in the last month) (f)
UN	United Nations
UNESCO	United Nations Educational, Scientific,and Cultural Organization (ac)

UNICEF	United Nations Children's Fund (ac) (previously, *U*nited *N*ations *I*nternational *C*hildren's *E*mergency *F*und)
univ.	university
UPC	universal product code
UPI	United Press International
UPS	United Parcel Service (ac)
USA or U.S.A.	United States of America
USA	United States Army
USAF	United States Air Force
USCG	United States Coast Guard
USDA	United States Department of Agriculture
USES	United States Employment Service
USIA	United States Information Agency
USMC	United States Marine Corps
USN	United States Navy
VA	Veterans Administration
val.	value
var.	variable variety
VCR	videocassette recorder
VD	venereal disease (m)
VDT	video display terminal (IP)
ver.	verse version
VHF	very high frequency
via	by way of (f)—**not** an abbreviation, do not use a period
VIP	very important person
VISTA	Volunteers in Service to America (ac)
viz.	*videlicet* (namely) (f)
vol.	volume
V.P.	vice president
vs. *or* **v.**	*versus* (as opposed to) (f)
WATS	Wide-Area Telecommunications Service (ac)
WBC	white blood cells (m) white blood cells count (m)
WCC	World Council of Churches
wd.	word
WDW	Walt Disney World
WHO	World Health Organization (ac)
whsle.	wholesale
wk.	week(s)
wkly.	weekly
w/o	without
WP	word processing (IP)
wpm	words per minute (IP)
wt.	weight
yd	yard(s)
YMCA	Young Men's Christian Association
YMHA	Young Men's Hebrew Association
YWCA	Young Women's Christian Association
YWHA	Young Women's Hebrew Association
yr	year(s)
zip (code)	zone improvement plan (ac)

3

3100 CAPITALIZATION

CAPITALIZATION

3101 **Definition of capitalization.** **Capitalization** is the practice of using capital (uppercase) letters for emphasis, importance, and identification. Capitalized words demand more attention, and thus become more important within the context of the surrounding words.

There is growing agreement, however, that capitalization should be minimized in business writing. Too many capitalized words call attention to none.

3102 **First word in a sentence.** **Always** capitalize the first word in a sentence. This indicates to the reader where a new sentence begins.

Some of the cookies are now on sale.

The auditor needs your assistance immediately!

Students often need encouragement during finals week.

3103 **First word in a quoted sentence.** **Always** capitalize the first word of a quoted sentence.

Dr. McCabe announced, "We shall be married in June!"

Evelyn said quickly, "Please take my seat."

3104 **First word in an expression used as a sentence.** **Always** capitalize the first word of expressions used as sentences.

Wow!	Make that basket.
Unbelievable!	Come here!
Incredible!	Why not?

3105 **First word of a question within a sentence.** **Always** capitalize the first word of a formal, independent question within a sentence.

The question remains, Why was the scheduling not completed?

But: She thought, what for?

3106 **Names of specific persons, places, or things.** **Always** capitalize the exact names of specific persons, places, or things.

Will Dr. Tessa Tagle deliver the keynote address?

He had his car serviced at Benton's Auto Mart.

Yes, Reyes Syndrome is a concern for parents of young children.

3107 **Nicknames and created names.** Nicknames or created names that represent particular persons, places, or things are also capitalized.

Willie	the Sunshine State	the Deep South
Susie Q	Big Brother	Magic City

3108 **Common nicknames and created names.** When nicknames or created names become common, however, they are no longer capitalized as their usage applies to general categories of people, places, or things.

india ink	french fries	manila envelope
china pattern	plaster of paris	romaine lettuce

It is important to note that since capitalization is for the purpose of emphasizing certain words, excessive use of capitalization will reduce the value of this important tool.

3109 **Abbreviations, general rule.** The capitalization of abbreviations generally follows the capitalization of the words being abbreviated.

United States of America	U.S.A. *or* USA
International Telephone & Telegraph	ITT
account	acct.

3110 **Abbreviations of proper nouns.** Abbreviations of proper nouns are generally capitalized, following the same rules as those used for unabbreviated proper nouns.

North Atlantic Treaty Organization	NATO
Veterans Administration	VA

3111 **Abbreviations of common nouns.** Abbreviations of common nouns are usually not capitalized.

miles per hour	mph
each	ea.
amount	amt.

Exceptions:

eastern standard time	EST
anno Domini	A.D.
collect on delivery	c.o.d. or COD

See ¶ 3000–31 for additional information regarding abbreviations.

3112 **Adjectives.** Capitalize adjectives that are derived from proper nouns.

Jamaica	(noun)	Jamaican	(adjective)
Canada	(noun)	Canadian	(adjective)
Boston	(noun)	Bostonian	(adjective)
France	(noun)	French	(adjective)

3113 **Advertising.** In advertising copy, some words may be capitalized for special emphasis.

Don't miss our *Going-Out-of-Business Sale!*

Highest ratings are achieved for *Sabado Gigante!*

3114 **Armed forces.** Capitalize the names of the specific branches of the armed forces.

United States Air Force
United States Army
United States Coast Guard
United States Marine Corps
United States Navy

3115 **Awards and medals.** Capitalize the titles of awards and medals.

the *Golden Globe* award
a *Pulitzer Prize* winner
the *Purple Heart*
an *Emmy Award*
the *Nobel Prize*

3116 **Brand names and trademarks.** Capitalize the names of specific brand names and registered trademarks.

```
Sony Walkman          Doublemint chewing gum
Coca-Cola             Lincoln Continental
Kleenex               Xerox
```

Because of common usage, certain brand names are no longer capitalized.

```
He recommended I take some milk of magnesia.
Do you have any aspirin?
```

3117 **Business letters.** Within a business letter, the following rules of capitalization always apply:

- **Date.** Capitalize the first letter of the month.

```
December 18, 19--
```

- **Inside address.** Capitalize the first letter of personal or professional titles preceding names; professional titles on a line by themselves; names of individuals; names of companies or organizations; names of streets, avenues, and cities; and both letters of the two-letter state abbreviation.

Note: When capitalizing several words in a title, do not capitalize articles *(the, a, an)*, short prepositions (four or fewer letters), or short conjunctions *(and, as, nor, or, but)*.

```
Ms. Irene Canel-Petersen
Director of Research
The Duffy Manufacturing Company
2834 Avenida del Sol
Barceloneta, PR 00617-8709

Dr. Lourdes Rabade
Public Relations Division
Creative Group
2001 West 68th Street
Hialeah, FL 33016-5421
```

- **Salutation.** Capitalize the first word in a business letter salutation, as well as the title and last name.

```
Dear Dr. Alexiou:            Dear Ms. Thomas-Gibson
(Mixed Punctuation)          (Open Punctuation)

Ladies and Gentlemen:
(Mixed Punctuation)
```

- **Headings.** Capitalize the first letter in attention and subject lines. (*Subject* may also be keyed in all capitals.)

```
Attention       Technician White
Subject:        Welch, Reina
SUBJECT:        Welch, Reina
```

MORE

3

CONTINUED

- **Within the body of the letter.** While keying ordinary text within the body of the letter, follow capitalization rules that apply to ordinary text.

- **Complimentary close.** Capitalize **only** the first word in a complimentary close.

Sincerely,	Yours truly,	Sincerely yours
(Mixed Punctuation)	(Mixed Punctuation)	(Open Punctuation)

3118 **Business organizations and institutions.** Always follow the preference indicated by an organization for the capitalization of its name. The official letterhead is always a good guide.

3

Capitalize the specific names of associations, churches, clubs, colleges and universities (including divisions within a college or university), companies, conventions, fraternities and sororities, hospitals, independent committees and boards, institutions, libraries, schools, synagogues, and political parties.

Mt. Sinai Medical Center
Temple Beth El
Coppolechia Memorial Library
Michigan State University
Wayne County Realtors Association
Department of Duplicating
American Secretarial Association
Thornton Jewelry Designers
Variety Children's Association
Psychology Department
Democratic National Committee
Future Farmers of America

When generic terms are used alone or in place of the title, they are not capitalized.

The *company* picnic was an outstanding success!

Our *association* caters to the needs of all its members.

3119 **Celestial bodies.** The proper names of specific planets, stars, constellations, and other celestial bodies are capitalized. The more common terms earth, moon, and sun are not generally capitalized, unless written with the proper names of other bodies in the Solar System.

Venus	the Big Dipper	Mars
Saturn	Jupiter	Uranus
Ursa Minor	Mercury	Pluto

Becky was studying *Jupiter, Mercury,* and the *Earth.*

But: We looked up at the full *moon* for an hour.

3120 **Compass points and directions.** Follow these rules for capitalization of compass points and directions:

- **North, south, east, and west.** Capitalize *north, south, east,* and *west* **only** when they refer to specific regions or are part of a proper name.

the antebellum *South* the *Midwest* the *South Pole*

Do not capitalize such words when they indicate only a general direction, rather than a specific region.

It was in the *eastern* part of Spain that we got lost.

He lives somewhere on the *west* side of town.

- **Easterner, Westerner, Southerner, and Northerner. Always** capitalize words such as *Easterner, Westerner, Southerner,* and *Northerner.*

Marcia was a *Northerner* through and through!

- **Eastern, western, southern, and northern.** Capitalize words such as *eastern, western, southern,* and *northern* **only** when they refer to the region's residents, customs, or political or cultural activities. When such words precede a proper name, capitalize only if they are part of the name itself.

Suzanne was always noted for her *Southern* hospitality.

The *Western* states voted as expected.

She was able to identify the *Northern* Cross. (constellation)

But: The winter storm has blanketed the *eastern* states.

Mountain flowers are the prettiest in *northern* Colorado.

Summer sunsets are beautiful in *southern* Florida.

3121 **Direct address.** Capitalize any title used in direct address.

Please give me a call, *Doctor,* when the results are available.

But: The *doctor* is not in the hospital at this moment.

Do not capitalize terms such as *miss, sir,* or *madam* when used as a direct address.

Yes sir, I will check it out immediately.

3122 **Educational courses and degrees.** Capitalize the titles of specific educational courses, but do not capitalize references to general academic subject areas (except languages).

Specific course: All students are required to take Principles of Business before graduation.

A new course, Advanced Sports Health Analysis, will be added.

MORE

3

CONTINUED

General subject area: Nelson wants to take a course in history.
But: Sharon is studying Spanish.

When used with the name of an individual, an academic degree is capitalized. When used with the word *degree,* however, academic degrees are usually not capitalized.

With name: Victoria Sigler, *Juris Doctor,* is an excellent attorney.

With degree: Most colleges offer both *bachelor of science* and *bachelor of arts degrees*.

3123 **Geographic terms.** Capitalize the proper names of continents, countries, states, cities, towns, streets, bodies of water, and mountains.

Mississippi River
Alabama
Livonia
Rocky Mountains
Canada
Denver
Atlantic Ocean
Snake River

When similar terms are used without a proper noun, however, they are not capitalized.

We went *white-water* rafting down the fastest part of the river.

Which *state* did Barbara come from?

The baby loved swimming in the *ocean,* regardless of the temperature of the water.

3124 **Government.** Follow these rules in capitalization of government names.

- **Government bodies.** Capitalize the names of countries and international organizations, as well as the national, state, county, city, and local bodies, and agencies within them.

the United Nations
Ft. Collins School District
the Clinton Administration
the Cabinet
Germany
Department of Education
the Utah Legislature
the United Auto Workers

- **Short forms of international and national bodies.** Also capitalize the short forms of international and national bodies and their major divisions, when the reference is clear.

the *Court* (United States Supreme Court)
the *Agency* (Central Intelligence Agency)
the *House* (House of Representatives)
the *State* Department (Department of State)
the *Bureau* (Federal Bureau of Investigation)

- **Federal.** Federal should be capitalized if it is part of a proper name of a federal agency, act, or law. References to government or federal government are not capitalized unless they are part of a specific title.

Federal Bureau of Investigation
Federal Reserve Board

But:
All of this is governed by *federal,* state, and local laws.

We need to get help from the *government* officials on this project.

- **Titles of government officials.** Titles of international, national, and state government officials are capitalized when they immediately precede a specific individual's name, as part of the name. (Ambassador, Attorney General, Chief Justice, Chief of Staff, Governor, King, Lieutenant Governor, President, Prime Minister, Prince, Princess, Queen, Secretary-General of the United Nations, Secretary of State, Vice President)

State Senator Carrie Meek called me today about the HMO Bill.

While in office, *President John F. Kennedy* was responsible for starting the Peace Corps.

These titles are not capitalized, however, when used to refer to an entire class of officials.

Candidates for *treasurer* must have budgetary experience.

- **Title in place of a personal name.** A title used in place of a personal name is capitalized **only** for toasts, in direct address, or in formal introductions—with rare exceptions.

However, *Professor,* you told me to give you the paper today.

Ladies and gentlemen, the *President* of the United States.

- **Titles following a personal name.** Titles following a personal name, or used alone instead of a name, are generally lowercased.

Dora Corba, *administrative assistant,* took charge.

The *vice president* began the meeting on time.

However, some authors capitalize the titles of very high-ranking international (King, Queen, the Pope), national (President, Chief Justice), and state officials (Governor) when titles follow or replace the personal name, out of respect for the office.

The *Queen* will visit the hospital patients this afternoon.

The *Chief Justice* wrote the majority opinion.

MORE

CONTINUED

- **Laws, treaties, bills, and acts.** Laws, treaties, bills, and acts that have been formally adopted are capitalized when written in full, but are not capitalized when the shortened forms are used in place of the full name.

Full Title	Short Form
Public Law 88-6578	the law
the Panama Canal Treaty	the treaty
Senate Bill 9758	the bill
Exception:	
The Constitution of the United States of America	the Constitution

Descriptive references to pending legislation, however, should **not** be capitalized.

We shall canvass the neighborhood on behalf of the *education reform bill*, which is now designated as the Educational Reform Act.

3

- **-Elect, former, late.** Do not capitalize words such as -elect, former, or late when they are used with titles and/or names.

President-*elect* Robinson chaired the meeting.

The *late* Russell Sigler was remembered through a scholarship fund in his name.

3125 **Hyphenation and capitalization.** Follow these rules for hyphenation and capitalization.

- **Hyphenation and capitalization within a sentence.** Capitalize hyphenated words within a sentence in the same way you would capitalize those words if they stood alone.

It was *mid-April* before her condition began to improve.

The *Spanish-speaking* students are helping me learn their language.

It was David Harris' *thirty-eighth* annual Treasure Hunt.

- **Hyphenation and capitalization beginning a sentence.** At the beginning of a sentence, however, remember to capitalize the first letter of the hyphenated word.

Mothers-in-law take too much abuse.

Up-to-date equipment is a must for accurate diagnosis.

- **Capitalization of hyphenated titles.** Capitalize each word of hyphenated titles except articles *(the, a, an)*, short prepositions *(four or fewer letters)*, short conjunctions *(and, as, but, nor, or)*, and second elements not of equal force with the first.

Miami-Dade Community College

Slow-and-Easy Rowing Machine

President-elect Brookner

3126 **Numbers and letters with nouns.** Nouns followed by letters or numbers should be capitalized, with the exception of *line, note, page, size, step,* and *verse*. Capitalizing the noun *paragraph* is optional.

Appendix C	line 17
Article VI	page 116
Bulletin 88	size 16
Chapter XVIII	note 3
Column 2	verse 6
Diagram 9	
Exhibit D	
Figure 79	
Paragraph 9	
Invoice 33-959	
Lesson 44	
Room 1515	

In-text Cross References:

See appendix C, chapter 18, or paragraph 9 on page 2.

3127 **Outlines.** The first word of each item in a list or outline should begin with a capital letter.

I. Completing items
II. Skipping over any question demanding excess time
III. Going back after completion
IV. Checking answers
    A. Using *B* as most common
    B. Guessing
    C. Marking on test book
    D. Erasing wrong answers

3128 **Names of individuals.** Names of individuals should be capitalized, spelled, and spaced exactly as the person does. A name containing a prefix such as *d', da, de, del, della, di, du, l', la, le, los, mac, mc, o', van,* or *von* can vary in capitalization and spacing. Follow the individual's preferences.

Zoila de Zayas	Patrick O'Connor
Juan De Varona	Gloria de los Reyes
Leah A. La Plante	Robert F. Leblanc
Christina Von Bampus	Raul de la Cruz

With names beginning with the prefix O', the O and letter immediately following the apostrophe are **always** capitalized.

Maureen O'Hara	Ivonne O'Donnell
Marie O'Connell	

When used alone, capitalize the first word of a surname not normally capitalized to avoid confusion with other words in a sentence.

Everyone voted for *De la Cruz* to lead the group.

MORE

When writing surnames in all capitals, capitalize all letters when there are spaces between the prefix(s) to the names.

DE LA CRUZ

But, capitalize entirely only the surname when no spaces follow the prefix.

MacMERRIAN

3129 **Titles of Relatives.** Titles of relatives are capitalized when they precede a name, or when they are used in place of a name (such as in direct address). They are not capitalized, however, when they follow a possessive pronoun or when they simply describe a family relationship.

I said, "Please come to my room, *Mother*."

Ted and *Uncle Ken* work in the assembly department.

Aunt Leota and *Aunt Sammy* visited me when I was in the Navy.

But:

My *cousin* enrolled in a dietary technician program.

I have sixteen *aunts* and *uncles*.

3130 **Titles preceding names.** Capitalize all formal titles when they precede a name.

Ms. Barbara Mateo
the Reverend Gene Whitehouse
Judge Margarita Esquiroz
President Robert McCabe

Note: The word *the* **must** precede *reverend* when used with a name. Be aware that *the Reverend So-and-so* is a use limited to writing and introductions. One never speaks of *the Reverend So-and-so*.

3131 **Titles following names.** Do **not** capitalize such titles when they **follow** the name.

Robert McCabe, *president*
Beverly Creely, *professor*

3132 **Titles with names set off by commas.** Do **not** capitalize such titles when the personal name that follows is set off by commas (appositive).

The *vice president*, Yvonne Santa Maria, will speak later.

But: *Vice President* Yvonne Santa Maria will speak later.

3133 **Occupational titles.** Do **not** capitalize occupational titles when they precede or follow personal names.

The introduction was made by *surgeon* Naim Nichar.

We had dinner at the home of Eileen Cunningham, *attorney*.

But, capitalize when the occupational title is a *specific* job title.

Senior Editor Richard Schinoff is working with me on my book.

3134 **Titles in place of personal names.** Generally, do not capitalize official titles when they follow a personal name or are used in place of a personal name. See ¶ 3124 for exceptions.

Annie Betancourt, *president,* will preside at the meeting.

Calling the group together was Richard Esper, *dean.*

Note: Some companies capitalize all or some of the titles of company officials. Always follow the procedures preferred by your employer, and respect the preferences of others regarding their own titles.

3135 **Doctoral degree.** With the doctoral degree, use *Dr.* before the name or the academic abbreviation following the name, but **not both.**

Dr. William McNae *or* William McNae, *D.O.*

Not: Dr. William McNae, D.O.

3

3136 **Specific places, things, or ideas.** Capitalize the entire titles of specific places, things, or ideas. (Do not capitalize articles, short prepositions, or short conjunctions used with these titles, however, unless they are the first word of the title.) Do not capitalize the short forms used in place of the full title.

Woodward Medical Center	the medical center
Jefferson Department Store	the store
Equal Rights Amendment	the amendment
Penobscot Building	the building
The Denver Post	the newspaper

But: the Post

3137 **City and state.** Capitalize *city* when it is part of a proper name, or part of a created name.

Panama City
the Automotive City

But: the city of Cincinnati

Capitalize *state* only when it follows a state name, or is part of a created name.

Colorado State
the Sunshine State

But: the state of Colorado

3138 **Common words part of proper name.** Capitalize words such as *the, upper, lower, west, east, north,* and *south* only when they are part of a proper name. (See ¶ 3120 for exceptions.)

The Washington Post West Virginia
Upper Peninsula

3139 **Short forms with clear association.** A few short forms are capitalized because they are easily identified with a legendary or popular place.

We want to take our next vacation and tour the *Canal.*
(the Panama Canal)

I was in the *Bay Area* last fall.
(the San Francisco Bay Area)

We have reservations right in the *Quarter.*
(the French Quarter)

3140 **Pronouns.** **Always** capitalize the pronoun *I*.

You know that *I* want to enter this contest.

All other pronouns are **not** capitalized unless they begin a sentence.

It was *my* computer program that was used.

Her aunt was the one wearing the black hat.

3

3141 **Principal words in publication titles.** Capitalize the principal words (and the first word after a colon or dash) in titles of publications (books, magazines, journals, pamphlets, newspapers) and other artistic works (movies, plays, songs, paintings, sculptures, poems). Titles of complete published works or complete artistic works (motion pictures, long musical compositions) are underscored, italicized, or written in all capital letters.

- **book** I find the *Physican's Desk Reference* a helpful aid.

  I find the PHYSICIAN'S DESK REFERENCE a helpful aid.
- **magazine** Your first copy of *The Balance Sheet* arrived today.

  Your first copy of THE BALANCE SHEET arrived today.
- **magazine article** Her article, "How to Get Ahead," appeared in *Lear Magazine.*

  Her article, "How to Get Ahead," appeared in LEAR MAGAZINE.
- **newspaper** The *Newark Star Ledger* won the award.

  The NEWARK STAR LEDGER won the award.
- **symphony—referred to by a special, given, descriptive title:**
  We have tickets for tonight's performance of the *Emperor Concerto* by Beethoven.

But: A classical composition referred to by type of piece (e.g., symphony) and number does not have its title set in italics or all capital letters, nor is it underscored.

We have tickets for tonight's performance of Beethoven's Symphony no. 9 in D Minor.

3142 **Titles of poems, songs, and television and radio programs.** The titles of short poems, songs, and television/radio programs are enclosed in quotation marks.

All of the students watched "General Hospital" every afternoon.

3143 **Capitalize the first word of each line within a poem.**

Across a Crowded Room*

Your face: My eyes wander around your face.
It's power: I shake and I'm amazed at its power.
What it does to me:
I feel strong and weak and sick and well.
I want to scream!
I want to sing:
"Some enchanted evening you will see a stranger..."
Your face: the magnificent power of your face.
I haven't spoken one word to you.
Yet I would walk blindfolded through Times Square,
Sleep all night in Central Park,
Fly to Siberia in the dead of winter.
If I could be sure that at the end
The smile on your face
Would be for me.

—*Larry Apple*

* This poem was created especially for "The Biggest Book in the World: A Celebration of Words and Images by artists from New York and South Florida" as part of the Miami Book Fair International.

3144 **Supreme being, persons revered.** Capitalize references to a supreme being, or to persons revered.

our Lord God
Allah
Buddha
Saint Luke

3145 **Personal pronouns in reference to supreme being.** Personal pronouns used in reference to a supreme being are not capitalized, though they once were.

We can count on *his* guidance.

3146 **Races, peoples, tribes, and languages.** Capitalize all names of races, peoples, tribes, and languages.

Hispanics
Zuñi tribe
Europeans
African-Americans
French
Orientals

Do not capitalize the terms *blacks, whites,* or *people of color.*

The *blacks* in the class scored the highest on the test.

The percentage of *people of color* is in column four.

3147 **Days and months.** Capitalize names of days and months.

Monday
Wednesday
December
June

3148 **Holidays and religious days.** Capitalize names of holidays and religious days.

Martin Luther King Day
Mother's Day
Passover
New Year's Eve

3149 **Historical events.** Capitalize the names of historical events and nicknames used for historical periods.

World War I
the Great Depression

3150 **Decades and centuries.** Do not capitalize numerical designations for decades and centuries unless they are part of a proper name or nickname.

in the nineteen-sixties
in the forties

But: the Seventeenth Dynasty
the Roaring Twenties

3151 **Seasons.** Do not capitalize seasons of the year unless they are part of a specific title or are personified.

spring fever
summer sunshine
fall colors

But:
Spring and Summer Sale
Oh beautiful Spring, I enjoy your days. (personification)

3152 **Titles.**

Business letters (See ¶ 3117)

Direct address (See ¶ 3121)

Educational courses and degrees (See ¶ 3122)

Government (See ¶ 3124)

Hyphenated (See ¶ 3125)

Occupational (See ¶ 3133)

Personal & professional (See ¶ 3130-31 and ¶ 3134-35)

Publications (See ¶ 3141)

Races (See ¶ 3146)

Relatives (See ¶ 3129)

Supreme being (See ¶ 3144-45)

3

COMPOUNDS

3201 **Definition of a compound.** A compound is an expression in which two or more words are combined to express a single concept. A compound may be written open *(eye chart)*, hyphenated *(eyeball-to-eyeball)*, or written solid *(eyeglasses)*.

Although not strictly compounds, a word may have additions to it; these include a prefix (*quasi*-judicial, *anti*climax), a suffix (president-*elect,* book-let), or both (*post*operative*ly*), (*para*journal*ism*).

Combination forms may be more accurately called compounds than may words with prefixes or suffixes. These combinations include a combining

MORE

form: a word element similar to a prefix or suffix (bell-*like,* child*less*). Combining forms are used to form temporary compounds and derivatives.

A compound may consist of a phrase used as an adjective: a *spur-of-the-moment* decision or an *Alice-in-Wonderland* attitude.

3202 **Compounds in general.** The writer who is in doubt about a compound form usually has one question in mind, should it be written open, be hyphenated, or be written solid? (e.g., basket ball, basket-ball, or basketball)

When it became apparent that the name of the game basket ball represents a single concept (a game) and not two separate concepts (basket and ball), writers began hyphenating basket-ball. Gradually, as the single concept of basket-ball became more firmly fixed in the minds of writers and embedded in the language itself, the hyphen was dropped—joining *basket* and *ball* to form the compound word *basketball*. This is typical of the manner in which compounds find their way into the language.

3

3203 **The need for compound words.** One does not grasp an entire sentence in a single glance. Rather, the sentence unfolds one word, or a few words, at a time. Reading the sentence *The patient needs constant care* requires the comprehension of three concepts:

```
the patient          needs              constant care
```

Suppose, however, that the sentence reads, *"The patient needs around the clock care."* Or, more properly, *"The patient needs **around-the-clock** care."* The hyphens in the second version join the words *around, the,* and *clock;* they identify *around-the-clock* as a single-concept compound adjective; they make it unnecessary for the reader to jump from *around* to *the* to *clock* searching for the meaning of the sentence. The hyphens identify the single concept—and make it easier to perceive. Similarly, *air-condition* is easier to grasp than *air condition; waterfront,* than *water front.*

3204 **Standard compound forms.** Standard compound forms are those found in the dictionary and on word lists. They are sometimes called permanent compounds. Actually, they are not permanent for two reasons. First,the list of standard compound forms is always evolving (see ¶ 3202 and ¶ 3205). Second, the word elements constituting a standard hyphenated compound adjective are most usually not hyphenated when the same elements are used other than as a compound adjective (¶ 3218-19).

A compound word may have more than one standard form-—and more than one meaning.

```
high hat (noun): A head covering with a tall crown.
                 (He wore his high hat to the fancy dress
                 ball.)

high hat (noun): A foot-operated cymbal.
                 (She played the high hat with a rushing beat.)
```

high-hat (adjective):	Supercilious, snobbish.
	(They think Chauncey has a high-hat attitude.)
high-hat (verb):	To treat another or act in a supercilious or snobbish manner.
	(They promised not to high-hat the new members.)

3205 **Creating new (temporary) compounds.** Creating new compounds is part of the evolutionary process that constantly renews the language. In addition to the standard compounds listed in dictionaries and style manuals, the rules and other information in ¶ 3201-41 facilitate the creation of compounds.

New compounds encourage creative writing and improve readability. A news reporter might write about a "sociophysical" response in a new study; a science fiction writer, about a "pseudogalaxy" that is wholly imaginary. Those who coin words to name and sell new products are yet another source of new compounds. The following compounds are brand names of household appliances:

Electrolux	Frigidaire	Panasonic
Magnavox	Vacuflo	

3206 **Compound nouns.** Compound nouns listed in the dictionary can safely be written as they are shown. Be sure the form is used as a noun. Compare these nouns to the words in ¶ 3207 and ¶ 3208.

castoff	cold shoulder	countersink
cleanup	short circuit	doubleheader
runaway	soft pedal	proofreader

3207 **Compound verbs.** Compound verbs listed in the dictionary can safely be written as they are shown. Be sure the form is used as a verb. Compare these verbs to the words in ¶ 3206 and ¶ 3208.

cast off	cold-shoulder (Informal)	countersink
clean up	short-circuit	postdate
run away	soft-pedal (Informal)	proofread

3208 **Distinguishing between compound nouns and compound verbs.** Notice the relationships between examples in the first column of ¶ 3206 and corresponding examples in ¶ 3207. There is a corresponding *compound verb (verb phrase, verb with particle)* for each of these *compound nouns*. The most common relationship between compound verbs and compound nouns is noun written solid, verb written open.

castoff (noun)	The coat he wore was a castoff.
cast off (verb)	Cast off the lines fore and aft.
cleanup (noun)	The committee has scheduled a cleanup.
clean up (verb)	It is time to clean up that mess.

MORE

runaway (noun)	The runaway was found later the same day.
run away (verb)	The colt may run away if the fence is not repaired.

In a few cases (second column in ¶ 3206 and ¶ 3207) the noun is written open and the verb is hyphenated.

cold shoulder (noun)	He gave her the cold shoulder.
cold-shoulder (verb)	She will cold-shoulder him again. (Informal)
short circuit (noun)	A short circuit was responsible for the fire.
short-circuit (verb)	They will short-circuit the electrical system.
soft pedal (noun)	Use the soft pedal for this passage.
soft-pedal (verb)	Please soft-pedal the report if possible. (Informal)

Other noun-verb relationships are possible.

countersink (noun)	This tool is called a countersink.
countersink (verb)	Countersink the screw so that it is flush with the surface.
proofreader (noun)	Wait for final approval from the proofreader.
proofread (verb)	Please proofread this material.
doubleheader (noun)	No verb "doublehead" is in standard use.
postdate (verb)	No noun "postdater" is in standard use.

3209 **Compound noun serving as an adjective.** Compound nouns are frequently used as adjectives. Generally, their forms (open, hyphenated, or solid) remain the same regardless of whether they are used as nouns or adjectives. A few nouns that are normally written open (blue chip) are hyphenated (blue-chip) when used as adjectives because hyphenation improves their readability in the adjective position (immediately preceding the noun).

Adjectives	Nouns
a data processing class	a class in data processing
a blue-chip opportunity	a stock that is a blue chip
a dinner-dance invitation (Informal)	an invitation to a dinner-dance (Informal)
the play-off excitement	the excitement of the play-off
the classroom teacher	the teacher in the classroom
an eyewitness account	the account of an eyewitness

3210 **Independent adjectives preceding a noun.** A hyphen is not used between adjectives that modify a noun independently. Test for this form by inserting *and* between the adjectives and transposing them: if *and* can be inserted and the adjectives can be transposed, the adjectives modify the noun independently—and a comma is used in place of *and*.

tired and hungry stranger tired, hungry stranger	swift and deep river swift, deep river
hungry and tired stranger hungry, tired stranger	deep and swift river deep, swift river

After the noun, the word *and* is used instead of a comma.

a stranger who is tired and hungry	a river that is swift and deep

3211 **Word order before a noun.** Idiom dictates the order of most adjectives before a noun. The approximate order is

1. Individual attributes: nice/nasty; honest/dishonest; handsome/beautiful/ugly; etc.
2. Categorical description: size, age, color, gender, ethnicity, breed, composition, nationality, brand.
3. The noun that names the thing described.

The following qualifications make the approximate order more useful:

1. Not all categories are applicable to a single thing.

the old gray mare	a little black spider
a big old hound dog	the little red hen
a red brick barn	massive granite mountains

2. The order will vary slightly from thing to thing.

   a brand new English Ford
   an old miniature poodle

3. Commas separate multiple individual attributes.

   the nice, honest, beautiful child
   the tired, hungry, thirsty, Persian cat

4. Avoid redundancy. Words such as mother, father, daughter, son, boy, girl, mare, and stallion may make the gender category redundant. Newly hatched, baby, foal, and the like, may make the age category redundant.

Not:	My mother is an elderly woman.	the young, newly hatched chicks
But:	My mother is elderly.	the newly hatched chicks

MORE

5. Personal opinions regarding idioms vary. Strive for word order that most readers will find logical and readable. Limit the number of adjectives preceding a noun. The first example used here is too long. Compare it to the second example in item 3 on page 153.

Not: the tired, hungry, thirsty, big, old, gray Persian cat

But: The big, old, gray Persian cat is a stray; he is tired, hungry, and thirsty.

3212 **Adjective + noun combinations.** An adjective and the following noun may be so closely related that they constitute a standard compound written open (Persian cat, high chair). Similar combinations may be so closely related as to be virtually inseparable when used in the same expression (military plane). Notice the results of applying the comma and transposition tests described in ¶ 3210.

	old high chair		sleek military plane
Not:	old, high chair	**Not:**	sleek, military plane
Not:	high old chair	**Not:**	military sleek plane

The adjective and the noun to which it is related in this manner are not separated in any reconstruction of the sentence.

	a high chair that is old		a military plane that is sleek
Not:	a chair that is high and old	**Not:**	a plane that is sleek and military

3213 **How to check a compound form.** The large numbers at the left of the chart on page 155 correspond to those in the following explanation.

1. The first step in checking an unfamiliar compound is to determine whether or not the words in question can be combined to form a standard compound: one that is listed in the dictionary. If so, it may be written just as it appears in the dictionary—if the compound is used as the part of speech specified in the listing and the dictionary is an up-to-date and acceptable reference. Be careful not to confuse compound nouns and verb phrases (¶ 3206-08). Be especially careful in writing hyphenated compound adjectives after the noun (¶ 3218-19).

2. If the words in question do not constitute a standard compound, you may be able to use them to form an improvised (temporary) compound. An improvised compound should conform to an applicable rule or to an acceptable pattern such as those illustrated in ¶ 3217-19. An improvised compound should improve the readability of the sentence.

3. Compounds *other than hyphenated compound adjectives* (nouns, verbs, unhyphenated adjectives, etc.) are written as they are listed in the dictionary.

4. A hyphenated compound adjective form—standard or improvised—may be used directly before the noun it modifies. This is called the **attributive position.** If the form occurs after the noun, see item 5.

5. With a few exceptions, a hyphenated compound adjective form—standard or improvised—occurring after the noun is hyphenated if it functions as an adjective. If the form does not function as an adjective, it is written open. See ¶ 3219.

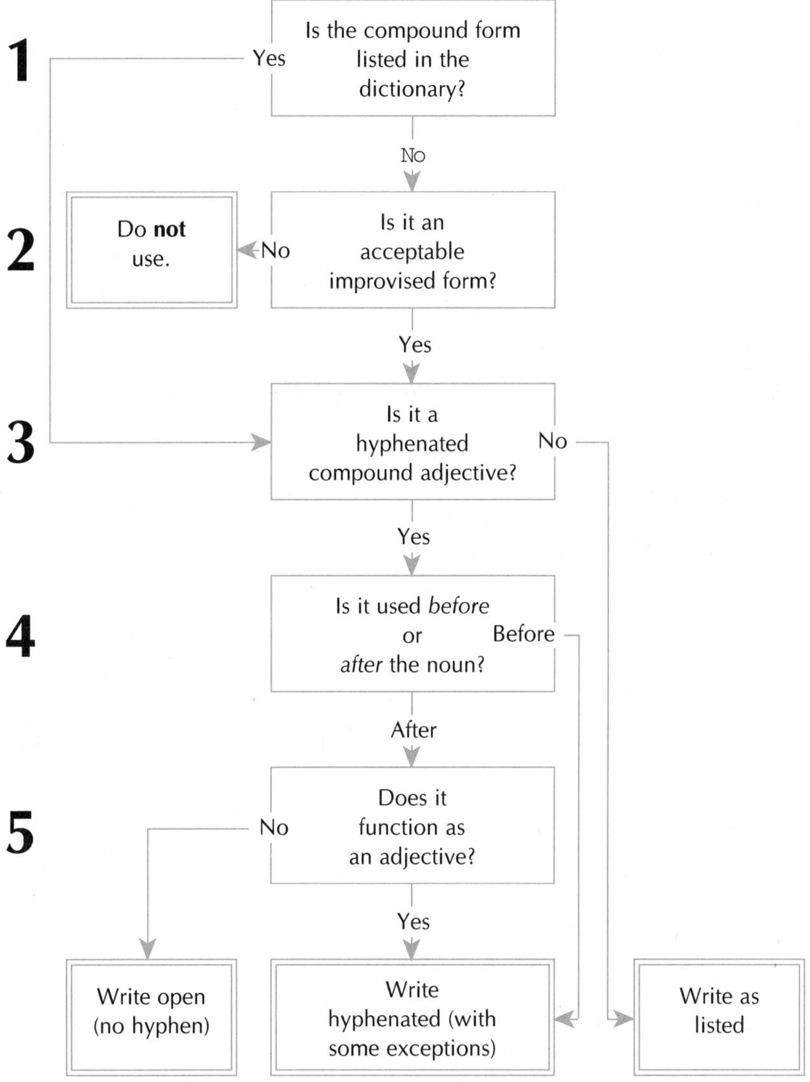

3214 **Looking up a compound.** A good dictionary is the best initial source to see how to write a compound. This manual relies on *Merriam-Webster's Collegiate Dictionary, Tenth Edition*.

Some style manuals, particularly *The Chicago Manual of Style, Fourteenth Edition,* are excellent sources of information on compounds.

The dictionary is the nearest thing there is to the final word on standard compound forms (¶ 3204). Standard compound forms must be used exactly as they are listed; i.e., as the part of speech specified in the listing. Be sure that any form listed as a standard compound adjective actually functions as a compound adjective in the sentence you are writing (¶ 3218-19).

3215 **Standard compound adjective *preceding* the noun it modifies.** A standard compound adjective occurring before the noun it modifies is written as listed in the dictionary.

a blue-ribbon committee	a full-time job
around-the-clock surveillance	mind-boggling consequences
a short-term loan	a soft-spoken person

Most dictionaries list *middle-class* as a compound adjective. Normal word order places a compound adjective before the noun it modifies.

They met to continue their discussion of middle-class values.

As a compound noun, *middle class* is written open without a hyphen and with a space between the words.

The values under discussion are those of the middle class.

The words *middle class* may function as the object of a preposition or the object of a verb.

The values *of* the middle class are under discussion.

We shall *study* the middle class.

But: We shall study middle-class values.

3216 **Improvised (coined, temporary) compounds.** If the compound word in which you are interested is not listed as a *standard* compound form, it may be permissible to **coin** (create) an *improvised* or *temporary* compound word. Many improvised compounds eventually become standard forms (*flatfoot, flypaper,* etc.).

The structure of English encourages improvisation of compound adjectives. Typically, two or more words are joined by a hyphen to serve as a single-concept compound adjective. Such an *improvised* or *temporary* compound adjective is created because of the use of the words in the current sentence, not because of any permanent relationship between the words themselves. The use of intensifiers (e.g., *very*) will not allow the use of a hyphen with compounds created with *well, ill, better, best, little, lesser.*

a better-than-even chance	a chance that is better than even
a well-designed product	a product that is well designed

But: a very well designed product

3217 **Quick reference for improvising temporary compound adjectives.** The following chart outlines prevalent patterns for improvising compound adjectives. See ¶ 3218-19 for information regarding hyphenation of improvised compound adjectives after the noun.

Patterns for Improvised Compound Adjectives Used Before the Noun They Modify

Hyphenate: (–)
Do **not** hyphenate: (≠)

Pattern		Example	
adjective — noun	**noun**	short-term loan	(–)
adjective — noun + ed	**noun**	heavy-handed tyrant	(–)
adjective — past participle	**noun**	long-remembered promise	(–)
adverb (ly) adjective	**noun**	suddenly apparent danger	(≠)
adverb (ly) participle	**noun**	carefully sheltered assets	(≠)
adverb (~~ly~~) adjective	**noun**	ever-fruitful method	(–)
adverb (~~ly~~) — participle	**noun**	well-made product	(–)
noun — adjective	**noun**	age-old maxim	(–)
object — present participle	**noun**	law-abiding citizen	(–)
past participle — adjective	**noun**	written-solid compound	(–)
past participle — adverb	**noun**	drawn-out meeting	(–)
past participle —preposition	**noun**	passed-over applicant	(–)

3218 **Compound adjective *after* the noun.** A compound adjective form, when used after the noun, may not function as an adjective. It may escape its status as a compound adjective to function in the predicate, function in or as a prepositional phrase, or to function in another capacity. Some compound adjectives are hyphenated only when they appear before the nouns they modify—see the charts in ¶ 3217 and ¶ 3219.

The committee awarded a *blue ribbon* to the winner. (object of verb)
The couple walked *over the hill* and down the road. (prepositional phrase)
The loan is for a *short term*. (object of preposition)
Alizia works *full-time*. (compound adverb)
The consequences are *mind-boggling*. (compound adjective)
She is exceptionally *soft-spoken*. (compound adjective)

3219 **Patterns for compound adjective forms occurring after the noun.** This chart defines patterns for the use of the compound adjective form after the noun. Some standard compounds do not conform to the patterns—and it is possible to improvise compounds that conform to the patterns only to fail the parts-of-speech test described in ¶ 3218. Nevertheless, forms that are consistent with this chart and improve the readability of the sentence are generally acceptable.

Hyphenated Compound Adjectives

Before the Noun		After the Noun Hyphenate: (-) Do **not** hyphenate: (-̸)	
adjective — noun short — term	**noun** loan	a loan for a short term	(-̸)
adjective — noun + ed heavy — handed	**noun** tyrant	a tyrant that is heavy-handed	(-)
adjective — past participle long — remembered	**noun** promise	a promise long remembered	(-̸)
adverb (~~ly~~) — participle well — made	**noun** product	a product that is well made	(-̸)
noun — adjective age —old	**noun** maxim	a maxim that is age-old	(-)
object — present participle law —abiding dust—catching	**noun** citizen object	a citizen who is law-abiding* an object that is dust catching	(-) (-̸)
past participle — adjective written — solid	**noun** compound	a compound written solid	(-̸)
past participle — adverb drawn — out	**noun** meeting	a meeting that was drawn out	(-̸)
past participle — preposition passed — over	**noun** applicant	the applicant who was passed over	(-̸)

* Only a few permanent, object - present participle compounds are hyphenated *after* the noun.

3220 **Conservative use of hyphens.** Hyphens are used to improve readability or eliminate ambiguity. They are not used in ordinary sentence structure between words that appear in regular order.

`high school`   `life insurance`   `real estate`

If you have looked up a compound form and tried to apply the rules and patterns and still cannot decide whether or not to hyphenate, it is probably better to write the form open—unhyphenated.

3221 **Two-element pronoun is written solid.** Write solid all two-element pronouns (everyone) except *no one,* which is written open.

anybody	everything	nobody	ourselves	themselves
anyone	herself	no one	somebody	thyself
anything	himself	nothing	someone	yourself
everybody	itself	oneself	something	yourselves
everyone	myself			

3222 **Verb + adverb is written solid.** The combination of a short verb and an adverb is written solid *except for those cases in which a hyphen is used to improve readability*. Notable exceptions are combinations ending with *-in* and *-on*.

blowout	hangover	payoff	run-in	run-on
breakdown	holdup	runaway	trade-in	slip-on

3223 **Adverb ending in *-ly*.** A two-word compound adjective beginning with an adverb ending in *-ly* is not hyphenated.

newly constructed building   highly believable story

3224 **Derivatives of compound forms.** The derivatives of a compound retain the form of the original compound.

Adjectives	Adverbs	Nouns
heavy-handed	heavy-handedly	heavy-handedness
underhanded	underhandedly	underhandedness

3225 **Comparatives and superlatives.** A two-word modifier beginning with a comparative or superlative is written open.

higher priced merchandise
smaller sized shoes
bigger-than-life
holier-than-thou

But: lowercase letters
lower-class (adjective)
mocker-up (noun)
upper-class (adjective)

3226 **Hyphen *after* a combining form or prefix.** Generally, a hyphen is not used after a combining form or prefix; these forms are usually written solid. A hyphen almost always is used, however, (1) after *ex, quasi,* and *self,* (2) to avoid doubling a vowel, (3) to avoid tripling a consonant, (4) to join the combining form or prefix to a proper noun, (5) to join the combining form or prefix to a word already hyphenated, or (6) to distinguish between homonyms.

*anti*biotic	*hyper*active	*multi*media	*step*daughter
*by*law	*inter*action	*non*conformist	*trans*oceanic
ex-president*	*quasi*-judicial	*self*-control	*self*-starting
semi-independent	*bell*-like	*pro*-American	*anti*-write-in

* See ¶ 1301 regarding the use of *ex-*.

But: selfhood selfish selfless selfsame

The avoidance of double vowels and triple consonants is not practiced in the case of short prefixes such as *co, de, pre, re,* and *un*.

cooperative deemphasizes preeminent
reemployment unnoticed

But: co-op (to avoid confusion with *coop*)
re-cover (to avoid confusion with *recover*)
re-sort (to avoid confusion with *resort*)
un-ionized (to avoid confusion with *unionized*)

3

3227 **Hyphen *before* a combining form or suffix.** Generally, a hyphen is not used before a combining form or suffix. A hyphen is used, however, (1) before *elect* or *designate,* or (2) to avoid tripling a consonant.

amend*able* art*ful* list*less* absentminded*ness*
oper*ate* photo*graphy* outer*most* southwest*ward*

president-*elect* ambassador-*designate*
bell-*like* shell-*like*

3228 **Phrases as compound adjectives.** A phrase used as a compound adjective is hyphenated when it occurs before the noun.

a coat-of-arms dispute a mother-of-pearl bracelet
the pay-as-you-go plan an over-the-counter medicine

After the noun, omit the hyphens **only** if the phrase is literal.

a dispute over a coat of arms
a plan to pay as you go
Lucy is the mother of Pearl.
The shelf is over the counter.

3229 **Foreign phrases as compound adjectives.** Do not hyphenate a foreign phrase used as an adjective unless it was hyphenated in the original language.

ad hoc antebellum per capita **But:** laissez-faire
à la carte bona fide per diem

3230 **Compound forms that eliminate ambiguity.** Compound forms are sometimes used to avoid ambiguity.

goldbrick (false gold, swindle, lout) gold brick (literally)
lowball (deceptively low price) low ball (literally)
co-op (cooperative) coop (pen)
re-treat (treat again) retreat (fall back)
re-cover (cover again) recover (recuperate)

3231 **Hyphenation indicating extremes, ranges, balance, or duality.** The hyphen is used in certain compound forms to indicate a balance between extremes (true-false), repeated or rhyming words (razzle-dazzle), ranges (high-low), or dual functions (secretary-treasurer).

artsy-craftsy	boo-boo	cha-cha	dilly-dally

3232 **Hyphenating proper nouns.** Proper nouns retain their form (open, hyphenated, or solid) when hyphenated to indicate duality.

Anglo-Saxon history	the Northbrook-Oak Brook Road
Canadian-Latin American trade	San Francisco-Oakland traffic

3233 **Titles of relatives.** Compound titles of relatives beginning with grand or step are written solid.

granddaughter	grandaunt	stepdaughter	stepbrother
grandfather	grandnephew	stepfather	stepsister
grandmother	grandniece	stepmother	
grandson	granduncle	stepson	

Those beginning with *great* or ending with *-in-law* are hyphenated.

great-granddaughter	great-aunt	daughter-in-law
great-grandfather	great-nephew	father-in-law
great-grandmother	great-niece	mother-in-law
great-grandson	great-uncle	son-in-law

Note: grandaunt = great-aunt; grandniece = great-niece; grandnephew = great-nephew; granduncle = great-uncle

Those beginning with *half* are written open.

half brother	half sister

3234 **Titles of office.** Generally, titles of office are not hyphenated.

surgeon general		deputy district attorney
under secretary	**But:**	under-secretaryship
vice president		vice-regent

Dual titles indicating that one person fills two offices are hyphenated.

secretary-treasurer	treasurer-agent

Hyphenate a title containing *ex, elect,* or *designate*. (ex- for "former" is not standard. See ¶ 1301.)

ex-Senator Langley (avoid)	president-elect
ambassador-designate	

3235 **Points of the compass.** Write solid those points of the compass consisting of two words *(northeast)*. Where three words are required, hyphenate between the first and second; write the second and third solid *(north-northeast):*

north	east	south	west
north-northeast	east-southeast	south-southwest	west-northwest
northeast	southeast	southwest	northwest
east-northeast	south-southeast	west-southwest	north-northwest

3236 **Colors.** Write words describing colors open when the first word modifies the second. Hyphenate when the words are of equal importance.

Open		Hyphenated
silver gray	silver gray material	blue-green paint
bluish green	bluish green paint	red-green color blindness

3237 **Individual numbers and letters in compounds.** Hyphenate *number-noun* combinations before the noun (whether the number is written in figures or spelled out). Hyphenate spelled-out numbers from twenty-one through ninety-nine and twenty-first through ninety-ninth. Hyphenate or write open a compound having a single letter as its first element (A-frame, S-curve); the hyphen is preferred.

Hyphenate		Preferred		Acceptable
5-yard penalty		A-frame		
99-year lease		f-stop	or	f stop
one-horse town		f-number	or	f number
one-stop shopping		H-bomb	or	H bomb
one-two punch		I-beam	or	I beam
two-dollar bet		T-shaped	or	T shaped
two-faced behavior		T-square	or	T square
two-headed monster		U-turn	or	U turn
twenty-one		U-boat	or	U boat
twenty-first		V-necked	or	V necked
ninety-nine		Z-brace	or	Z brace
ninety-ninth	**But:**	X-ray (verb or adjective)		
		X ray (noun)		

3238 **Hyphens in fractions.** Use a hyphen between the numerator and denominator of a fraction that is spelled out.

three-fourths three-thousandths of an inch

Omit the hyphen if either the numerator or denominator is hyphenated.

thirty-three thousandths twenty-seven thirty-seconds

See ¶ 3330-31.

3239 **Hyphens in a series.** A form in which two or more compound words share a common word element is shortened by omitting the shared common element from each compound word except the last.

2-, 3-, and 4-blade propellers
long- and short-term interest rates*
first-, second-, and third-string players

*If the suspended hyphen is not followed by a punctuation mark, it is followed by a space.

3240 **Transposed listings.** On lists, inventories, taxonomies and the like, each item is usually a single concept, but an item may have several modifiers. For clarity, write the singular form of the noun first, then list the modifiers in order and separated by commas.

```
beaker, glass, 8-, 16-, and 32-ounce
```

Not: `8-, 16-, and 32-ounce glass beakers`

```
tube, glass, 1/4-, 3/8-, and 1/2-inch
```

Not: `1/4-, 3/8-, and 1/2-inch glass tubes`

3241 **Compound units of measure.** Most compound technical units of measure require hyphens.

```
light-year          passenger-mile          foot-pound
```

3300 NUMBERS

(continued)

NUMBERS

Style and Consistency in Writing Numbers

3301 **Quick reference for writing numbers.** The following chart summarizes basic styles for writing numbers. Variations, exceptions, and special applications are discussed in ¶ 3302-3395.

	Ordinary Text	Technical Material	Ornate Text	Formal Text
Numbers 1-10	Write in words See ¶ 3302-1	Write in figures See ¶ 3302-2	Write in words See ¶ 3302-3	Write in words See ¶ 3302-4
Numbers 11-20	Write in figures See ¶ 3302-1	Write in figures See ¶ 3302-2	Write in words See ¶ 3302-3	Write in words See ¶ 3302-4

	Ordinary Text	Technical Material	Ornate Text	Formal Text
Numbers 21-99	Write in figures See ¶ 3302-1	Write in figures See ¶ 3302-2	Write in words See ¶ 3302-3 Hyphenate See ¶ 3307	Write in words See ¶ 3302-4 Hyphenate See ¶ 3307
Numbers 100+	Write in figures See ¶ 3302-1	Write in figures See ¶ 3302-2	Write in words See ¶ 3302-3	Write in words See ¶ 3302-4
For Consis-tency	Convert words to figures See ¶ 3303-1	Write in figures See ¶ 3303-2	Write in words See ¶ 3303-3	Write in words See ¶ 3303-4

3302 **Conventional styles.** In most documents, each passage clearly represents one of four major writing styles: ordinary text, technical material, ornate text, or formal text.

3

The initial passages of an annual corporate report, for example, may be written in *ornate text,* calculated to portray the events of the year as attractively as possible. In subsequent passages of the report, however, *ordinary text* may be required to explain matters of a more intricate nature. Other passages may contain *technical material* such as financial statements, tables, charts, and the like.

A *typical* business report is written in ordinary text—and includes some technical material. Ornate and formal text are for special purposes such as impressive promotional campaigns (ornate text) and invitations to formal events (formal text).

1. **Ordinary text** is the written matter, mostly words, used in business correspondence, nontechnical books, textual sections of newspapers and magazines, and so on.

   In ordinary text, numbers from 1 through 10 are spelled out; numbers 11 and above are written in figures. However, there are exceptions. For instance, all numbers used before the word *percent* are written as figures, unless they begin a sentence.

`Put ten books on the first shelf and four on the second.`

`Put 11 books on the first shelf and 4 on the second.`
(Four written as a figure for consistency.)

`Put 11 books on the 1st shelf and 4 on the 23rd shelf.`

But: `I placed 5 percent of the work on Jack's desk.`

   See ¶ 3303 on consistency and ¶ 3312 on ordinal numbers.

2. **Technical material** is specialized information that requires the intensive use of numbers, symbols, abbreviations, or graphics. It is the functional, utilitarian writing found in memos, notes, explanations, instructions,

MORE

specifications, financial statements, statistical reports, scientific matter, and the like. In technical material, all numbers are written in figures.

```
The paved area will be 48' 7" x 36' 9".
```

3. **Ornate text** is written matter, mostly words, calculated to convey or create an impression of elegance, luxury, good taste, sophistication, and the like. It characterizes certain slick-paper publications appealing to the elite and those interested in the elite, some advertisements for luxury goods, and the correspondence of some high-level corporate executives. Ornate text transforms a seaside house into a villa, a porch into a lanai (Hawaiian for *porch*), and an office into a suite.

   In ornate text, numbers are written in figures only when spelling them out would be awkward or would detract from the impression the writer hopes to create or convey. Many documents written in ornate text contain passages, sections, illustrations, or enclosures that are written in ordinary text or consist of technical material.

```
The price of luxury is only forty-two thousand, five hundred
dollars.
```

4. **Formal text** is found in *invitations* to formal events (weddings, receptions, etc.), the *proclamations* of presidents, governors, and other ranking executive officers, the *resolutions* of Congress, legislatures, and boards, and in similar formal documents.

   In formal text, all numbers are spelled out and the language used is very formal.

```
A reception will follow at half past eight o'clock in the
evening.
```

3303 **Consistency in writing numbers.** In a given context, numbers in the same category should be treated alike: spelled out or written in figures. The **context** of a number is the environment in which it occurs: a single sentence, a paragraph, a passage consisting of several paragraphs, a chapter, or the entire document. The context of a category of numbers starts with the first occurrence of a number in the category and ends with the last such occurrence.

If a single sentence refers to 23 bass and 17 trout, and that is the only place in which a number of fish is mentioned, that sentence is the context of the category *fish*. If a single paragraph deals with fish, that paragraph is the context of the category *fish*. The same is true of longer passages, chapters, sections, and the entire document. The context of the category *fish* begins with the first reference to a number of fish and ends with the last such reference.

Most problems of consistency and context arise in ordinary text; technical material, ornate text, and formal text—each has a special orientation that makes the right choices easier. In technical material, all numbers are written in figures. In ornate text, numbers are spelled out unless the writer has a compelling reason for writing them in figures. In formal text, all numbers are spelled out. See ¶ 3301.

1. **Consistency in ordinary text.** In ordinary text, spelled-out and written-in-figures numbers are mixed, but the numbers in a given category (fish, for example) in a given context (chapter, for example) are consistently spelled out or consistently written in figures.

   Suppose that the following references to fish occur in a chapter:

   `3 fish          1 fish          9 fish`

   The first reference to fish in the chapter is 3 fish; the last reference to fish is 9 fish. Since all the numbers in the category (fish) are 10 or below, the numbers in this category (fish) in this context (the chapter) will be spelled out.

`We caught three fish Monday, one Tuesday, and nine Wednesday.`

   Now suppose that the first reference to fish in the chapter is 3 fish, the second is 1 fish, and the last is 12 fish. Since one number is above 10, all numbers in this category (fish) in this context (the chapter) will be written in figures.

`We caught 3 fish Monday, 1 Tuesday, and 12 Wednesday.`

   Before processing a document, analyze the copy, taking note of the category to which each number belongs. If a number in a category appears in ordinary text and there are no numbers above 10 in the category, all numbers in the category should be spelled out. If a category contains one number (or more) above 10, all numbers in that category should be written in figures.

   For example, an article on a real estate sales contest in which 8 *salespersons* sold 9 *pieces of property* in a period of 30 *days* for total *sales* of $987,493 should refer to the numbers in each category consistently:

Category	Largest Number In Category	Write Numbers In
Salespersons	Eight	Words
Pieces of Property	Nine	Words
Days	30	Figures
Sales (Dollars)	987,493	Figures

If all the numbers were to appear in a single sentence, they would be written as follows:

`Eight salespersons sold nine pieces of property in 30 days for $987,493.`

MORE

2. **Consistency in technical material.** Technical material is characterized by the intensive use of numbers, symbols, abbreviations, charts, tables, and other graphics. Technical material may or may not be scientific material. Once a passage (context) has been identified as technical, all numbers in that passage are written in figures.

   Many technical documents, however, contain passages (contexts) of ordinary text. Within these passages, the conventions for ordinary text apply.

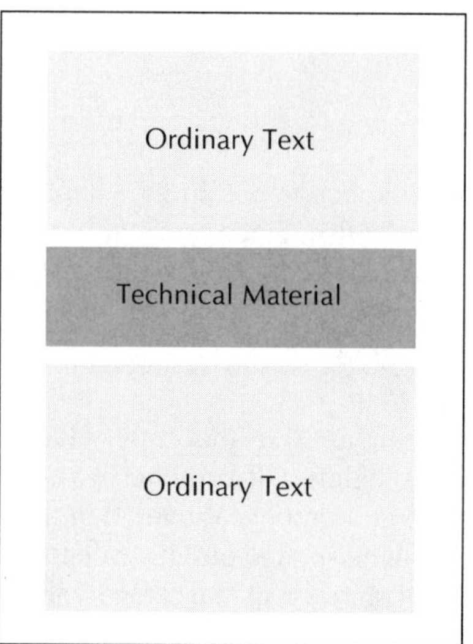

Brief Passage of Technical Material in a Context of Ordinary Text

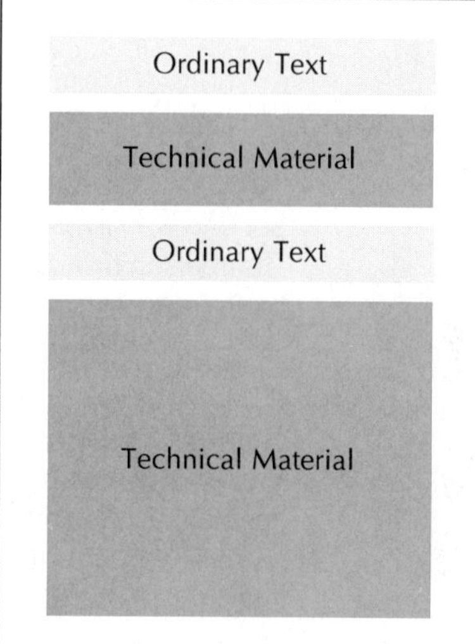

Brief Passages of Ordinary Text in a Context of Technical Material

3. **Consistency in ornate text.** In ornate text, all numbers are written in words except those that are awkward when spelled out. Ornate style should **not** be used in envelope addresses (see ¶ 3316-23).

   Exquisite Apparel Limited
   Suite One Hundred Seven
   Four Hundred Wendway Walk
   Dayton, OH 45406

4. **Consistency in formal text.** In formal text, all numbers are spelled out—even when doing so may seem awkward. Formal style should **not** be used for envelope addresses (see ¶ 3316-23).

   at half past the hour
   of nine o'clock
   on the evening
   of Saturday, the twenty-fourth of June
   one thousand, nine hundred and ninety-five

3304 **Abbreviations and symbols.** Abbreviations and symbols are used extensively in technical material, to a limited degree in ordinary text, and not at all in formal and ornate text. Figures, rather than words, are used with abbreviations and symbols.

35¢	88%	5' 2"	No. 17
@ 50¢ ea	.7%	5 ft 2 in	#18
$143.68	7 1/4%	23 lb	19.5#
$5	+12	11 oz	5:30 a.m.
$3 million	-17	23 lb 11 oz	6:30 p.m.

See ¶ 3000-31 on abbreviations.

1. **Contractions.** In informal contexts and technical material, an apostrophe may be used to replace the first two figures in the number representing a year if the resulting contraction will be understood by those who read it.

   the class of '89   the '37 flood   April of '75

2. **Number symbol (#).** The number symbol is used, primarily in technical material, for special purposes such as indicating a blank in which a number is to be entered (#________________), or indicating in a manuscript the format for a number that is to be filled in later (###.##). Similarly, the abbreviation *No.* may be used to indicate that a number is to be used (No.________________).

3. **Pound symbol (#) to indicate pounds.** In *technical material only* the pound symbol is used following a number written in figures to indicate pounds (23# = 23 lb = 23 pounds).

4. **The abbreviation *No.*** The abbreviation *No.* (used in technical matter) may be used before a number stated in figures to indicate that it is a *serial* number. If the number is preceded by a noun that identifies it (Model, Volume, Invoice, P.O. box, etc.) the abbreviation *No.* should be used only if there is a special need to emphasize the fact that the number is a *serial* number.

No. 402222111	Serial No. 35822220
Policy No. 3115-531-4309	License No. 4052470
Permit No. 49587	Account No. 85746-A

But: Model 29	P.O. Box 33949	Error Code 137
Not: Model No. 29	P.O. Box No. 33949	Error Code No. 137

5. **The word *number*.** The word *number* may be used at the beginning of a sentence to avoid beginning the sentence with figures. The expression *number* or *the number* or *the numbers* is also used to refer to numbers or figures in the nonsymbolic sense—as graphic representations. (See ¶ 3311.)

Number 113418 has been drawn by the Lottery Committee.

The sign painter will move the numbers 8 and 37 a little to the right.

3305 **Adjacent numbers.** Within a sentence, adjacent but independent numbers are separated by a comma if both are spelled out or both are written in figures. It is better to rewrite the sentence to avoid the conjunction of the numbers.

Acceptable: When I make six, seven will become my goal.

Acceptable: By 2003, 112 new installations are expected to be in operation.

Better: The year 2003 should see 112 new installations in operation.

Adjacent numbers preceding a noun. When adjacent numbers occur in the attributive position (immediately before a noun), spell one out and express the other in figures. Spell out the number that requires fewer letters. If both require the same number of letters, spell out the first number and express the second in figures.

They had lashed the three 32-foot boats together.

Four of the five 2003 calendars have been sold.

The report indicates that 2447 five-in-one sets have been delivered.

3306 **Number beginning a sentence.** Spell out a number that occurs at the beginning of a sentence. If the number requires more than two words, reword the sentence so the number appears *within* the sentence and can, therefore, be written in figures.

Not: 137 horses were treated by the veterinarian.

Nor: One hundred thirty-seven horses were treated by the veterinarian.

But: The veterinarian treated 137 horses.

3307 **Hyphens in numbers.** Hyphens are used to divide some long numbers (usually serial numbers) into manageable groups of figures. All numbers should be copied exactly as they are written, including hyphens, spaces, commas, and so on.

Telephone Number:	813-555-1234	*or*	(813) 555-1234
Social Security Number:	402-22-2111		

Numbers written as compounds. Hyphens are used (1) in spelled-out numbers from *twenty-one* (or *twenty-first*) through *ninety-nine* (or *ninety-ninth*) and (2) in compound modifiers that occur in the attributive position (immediately before the noun).

(1) forty-three dollars   our twenty-ninth anniversary

(2) a 43-foot *trawler*

3308 **Large numbers.** The American and British number systems differ.

Number	American	British*
1,000,000,000	billion	milliard**
1,000,000,000,000	trillion	billion (million ^{2})
1,000,000,000,000,000	quadrillion	—
1,000,000,000,000,000,000	quintillion	trillion (million^3)
1,000,000,000,000,000,000,000	sextillion	—
1,000,000,000,000,000,000,000,000	septillion	quadrilion (million^4)

* The logic in the British system is that the prefixes (bi-, tri-, quadri-, etc.) relate to the powers of a million.
** *Milliard* is rarely used today. *A thousand million* is preferred British usage.

3309 **Figure-word patterns.** Figure-word patterns are preferred for writing numbers with the words million, trillion, quadrillion, and so on. In this format, the amount written in figures:

- must include a whole number.
- may include a decimal of no more than three digits.
- may include a fraction equivalent to a three-digit decimal instead of the decimal itself.

$3 million	5 1/2 million	$10.1 billion
$30.7 million	7 3/4 million	$9.125 million

Not: $7.3472 million 7 15/49 million

In a mixed number, space between the whole number and the fraction—unless your equipment allows stacked fractions, which are written solid.

5 1/2 billion 3 3/4 million

But: $6\frac{3}{4}$ million

3310 **Round numbers.** These general rules apply to round numbers.

1. **Ordinary text.** Write all numbers above 10 in figures; therefore, write round numbers in figures. (See ¶ 3309 on figure-word patterns.)
2. **Technical material.** Write all numbers in figures; therefore, write round numbers in figures.
3. **Ornate text.** Spell out all numbers except those that, when spelled out, are unacceptably awkward; therefore, spell out round numbers.
4. **Formal text.** Spell out all numbers; therefore, spell out round numbers.

3311 **Nonsymbolic use of numbers.** Numbers referred to as graphic figures rather than for their symbolic value are written in figures.

Write a 9 in the blank. Paint 65 on the speed limit sign.

3312 **Ordinal numbers.** An **ordinal number** designates the place of an item in an ordered sequence (1st, 15th, 23d, 110th, etc.). In ordinary text, ordinal numbers 10th and below are spelled out; those above 10th are written in figures. Figures replace spelled-out forms when necessary to achieve consistency in the same context.

Different contexts	first	tenth	11th	103d	150th
Same context	1st	10th	11th	103d	150th

In technical material, all ordinal numbers are written in figures.

1st 10th 11th 103d 150th

In ornate and formal text, all ordinal numbers are spelled out.

one hundred twenty-third ninety-nine hundred twenty-fifth

See ¶ 3364 for discussion of ordinal numbers following surnames (Winston Wallace III, etc.).

3

3313 **Plural forms of numbers.** To form the plural of a number written in figures, add *s*. Ordinal numbers written in figures are pluralized in the same manner.

Some of the 2s look like Zs.

The 1990s are, in some respects, similar to the 1930s.

The ruler is divided into 12ths of an inch.

To form the plural of a number written in words, follow the conventions for creating regular plurals as illustrated in the following. Spelled-out ordinal numbers also have regular plural forms.

They lined up by twos and threes.

She is always at sixes and sevens.

He was dressed to the nines.

One pianist practices thirds with her right hand.

The other practices tenths with his left.

3314 **Writing numbers in figures.** Whole numbers of four or more digits are divided into thousands, millions, billions, trillions, and so on, by using commas. Do **not** space before or after a comma used in a number.

four thousand	4,000		
fifty thousand	50,000		
two hundred fifty thousand	250,000		
four million, two hundred fifty thousand	4,250,000	*or*	4.25 million
three billion	3,000,000,000	*or*	3 billion (spell out in ordinary text)
sixteen trillion	16,000,000,000,000	*or*	16 trillion (spell out in ordinary text)

The comma is frequently omitted in writing four-digit numbers. This is the preferred form—unless a comma is required for consistency with other (larger) numbers containing commas.

Context 1:	3847	9873	2746	8725
Context 2:	3,847	9,873	2,746	18,725

Use spaces instead of commas in writing metric quantities. In writing four-digit metric quantities, do **not** leave such a space unless the number appears in a column with at least one number of five digits or more.

2 345 635	384
788 987	8344
3 893	94
8 345 174	2765

3315 **Writing numbers in words.** Compound numbers from 21-99 are hyphenated when spelled out.

Cardinal:	twenty-one	fifty-three	ninety-nine
Ordinal:	twenty-first	fifty-third	ninety-ninth

If a number in this range is part of a larger number, do not use additional hyphens.

Cardinal:	one hundred twenty-one	fifteen hundred fifty-three
Ordinal:	one hundred twenty-first	fifteen hundred fifty-third

However, if two numbers in this range occur in a larger number, hyphenate both of them.

Cardinal: ninety-nine hundred twenty-one
twenty-three hundred forty-seven

Ordinal: ninety-nine hundred twenty-first
twenty-three hundred forty-seventh

Addresses

3316 **Inside address and envelope address.** The **inside address** should be written as it is found in the letterhead or return address of the addressee. Convention suggests figures in ordinary text—except for house or building number one, and street numbers one through ten, which are spelled out. (See ¶ 3317-23.)

The corresponding *envelope* address should comply with U.S. Postal Service guidelines for machine-readable addresses in order to be compatible with the Postal Service's OCR equipment. In envelope addresses, all numbers are written in figures. (See ¶ 3317-23.)

MORE

Inside Address	Envelope Address
Ms. Abbigail Demeter President, Apex Industries Room 327 One Canal Street Loveland, CO 80537	MS ABBIGAIL DEMETER PRESIDENT APEX INDUSTRIES 1 CANAL ST RM 327 LOVELAND CO 80537
Mr. Jerome Guerensa 2 Albermarle Street Pittsfield, MA 01203-1241	MR JEROME GUERENSA 2 ALBERMARLE ST PITTSFIELD MA 01203-1241
Ace High Card Co. 398 East Second Street Detroit, MI 48213	ACE HIGH CARD CO 398 E 2D ST DETROIT MI 48213
Mr. W. Harmon Wilson 122 West 11th street Hayden Lake, ID 83835	MR W HARMON WILSON 122 W 11TH ST HAYDEN LAKE ID 83835

Note: Most word processors can capture the inside address and print it on the envelope, thus eliminating rekeying of the address. (See ¶ 5649.)

3317 **Apartment, suite, and office numbers.** Apartment, suite, and office numbers are important to local mail delivery. They are written in figures in both the inside and envelope addresses.

Inside Address	Envelope Address
Ms. B. J. Bandolier Cintron Insurance Company Suite 222 1107 Palm Drive San Jose, CA 95131-4322	MS B J BANDOLIER CINTRON INSURANCE COMPANY 1107 PALM DR SUITE 222 SAN JOSE CA 95131-4322

3318 **House and building numbers.** In ordinary text, the numbers of houses and buildings are written in figures—except for house or building number one, which is spelled out. In envelope addresses intended for optical scanning, all numbers are written in figures.

Inside Address	Envelope Address
Serious Software, Inc. One East Park Avenue Richmond, MO 64085	SERIOUS SOFTWARE INC 1 E PARK AVE RICHMOND MO 64085
Ms. Susan Zoltoff 2 Page Road Kaysville, UT 43037	MS SUSAN ZOLTOFF 2 PAGE RD KAYSVILLE UT 43037

3319 **Street numbers.** In ordinary text, the numbers of streets, avenues, boulevards, etc. are written in figures—except for numbers 10 and below which are spelled out. Ordinals are used in both cases (Seventh, Ninth, 22d, 123d, etc.). The numbers of U.S., state, and county highways and interstate expressways are written in figures. (See ¶ 3320.)

Inside Address	**Envelope Address**
Mr. Andrew Haberman President, Apex Industries 1107 Tenth Avenue Northeast Salem, OR 97302-3847	MR ANDREW HABERMAN PRESIDENT APEX INDUSTRIES 1107 10TH AVE NE SALEM OR 97302-3847
Ms. Estrella Ingersol 332 11th Street East Ann Arbor, MI 48106	MS ESTRELLA INGERSOL 332 11TH ST E ANN ARBOR MI 48106

3320 **Highway numbers.** Use figures and abbreviations (without periods or spaces) to identify federal, state, and county highways; a capital I and hyphen for interstate expressways.

I-75 (interstate expressway)	US 41 (federal highway)
CR 951 (county road)	SR 19 (state route)

See ¶ 3319.

3321 **Machine-readable (OCR) addresses.** Most envelope addresses are read by OCR (optical character recognition) equipment. The guidelines for envelope addresses published by the U.S. Postal Service are based on the requirements of OCR equipment.

Sender-assigned ID number:	004576-4736BC
Information, attention, routing:	ATTN MR ASHLEY IMROOD PRES
Recipient	IMROOD MACHINE WORKS
Complete delivery address:	PO BOX 3223 OAKLEY STA
City/State/Zip:	CINCINNATI OH 45227-3223

3322 **Zip codes.** Zip codes are always written in figures. Be sure to include the building or block number (the four low-order digits). Your local post office will supply your building or block number if you do not know it.

DENVER CO 80212-2144	RICHMOND MO 64085-2959
CRANFORD NJ 07016-3825	

3323 **Addresses in ornate and formal text.** Ornate style is not used in envelope addresses and is not used in inside addresses unless it is to follow the wishes of the addressee (as expressed in the addressee's letterhead or return address) or to complement ornate text used in the letter itself.

See ¶ 3321 on machine-readable (OCR) addresses.

Decimals

3324 **Decimal fractions.** A **decimal** is a number expressed in base 10, especially a decimal fraction. A **decimal fraction** is a fraction or mixed number in which the denominator is a power of 10, usually expressed with a decimal point.

Decimals:	3	.75	3.75	19.57
Decimal Fractions:	.25	.75	3.75	19.57

3325 **Numbers containing decimal points.** In ordinary text and technical material, any number containing a decimal point is written in figures.

The three averages were .357, .382, and .389.

Numbers containing decimal points are rarely used in ornate or formal text and then only for special purposes. For example, an advertisement written in ornate text might refer to "a mere tenth of an inch." When they are so used, both numbers and units of measure are spelled out.

3

3326 **Commas with decimal points.** Follow the general rule regarding commas in numbers for digits preceding the decimal point; do not use commas following the decimal point.

37,482.125475847   .00075

See ¶ 3314.

3327 **Spacing with decimal points.** Do **not** space before or after a decimal point or a comma used in a number.

375,485.28374655   .003   2.7

See ¶ 3314.

3328 **Zero before a decimal point.** Use a zero before a decimal point only if the zero is necessary to call attention to the decimal point. That is not the case when a zero follows the decimal point immediately (.025), when the context contains numerous other decimal fractions, or when the format is well known (caliber of firearms, batting averages, etc.).

Appearing alone:	.05	0.1	0.225	0.385
With other decimal fractions:	.05	.1	.225	.385

3329 **Zero after a decimal point.** Add a zero or zeros to the right of a decimal point only to (1) right-justify a column of figures, (2) indicate that a calculation has been carried to another decimal place, or (3) for consistency among numbers in a set.

```
(1)   243.847     (2) 37.760 (correct to three decimal places)
        4.700
         .890     (3) .395     .370     .337     .500
```

Fractions

3330 **Fractions: Spelled out or written in figures.** In ordinary, ornate, and formal text, a fraction is written in words unless it is part of a mixed number, is awkward when written in words, or pertains to calculation or precise measurement. Fractions are seldom used in ornate and formal text. In technical material, fractions are written in figures.

Accordingly, most common fractions are spelled out (one-half, one-fourth, two-thirds, etc.) except in technical material. Most uncommon fractions are written in figures because they pertain to precise measurement or calculation (7/16, 15/32, 19/64, etc.).

At least three-fifths of those present agreed with the speaker.

Mixed number:	2 1/2 turns counterclockwise
Awkward in words:	divided into 7/8-acre tracts (*Seven-eighth acre tracts* is awkward.)
Measurement:	1/2 cup the 3/4-mile marker 1 5/16 inch
Calculation:	multiply by 1/8

3331 **Hyphenating spelled-out fractions.** The numerator and denominator of a fraction that is spelled out are joined by a hyphen unless either the numerator or denominator already contains a hyphen.

two-thirds	seven thirty-seconds	twenty-seven thirty-seconds
Compare:	forty-three hundredths	forty three-hundredths

3332 **Keyboarding fractions.** Some type fonts and the character sets of some computers include a few *single-character* common fractions ($\frac{1}{2}$ as a single character, or $\frac{1}{4}$ as a single character, for example). If you wish to print an isolated fraction or mixed number, the use of these common fractions is acceptable.

Many character sets, keyboards, computers, printers, and type fonts do not include fractions. A fraction is entered by keying the numerator, keying a diagonal, then keying the denominator—thus using three or more characters to enter a single fraction; the result is called a **multicharacter fraction.**

Do not mix single-character fractions and multicharacter fractions in the same context. Use all multicharacter fractions when necessary to avoid mixing styles.

3333 **Fractions are not ordinal numbers.** Certain ordinal numbers can be confused with similar spelled-out fractions. The fractions end with the letter *s*; the ordinal numbers do not. The fractions are hyphenated; the ordinal numbers are not.

four-thousandths of an inch; the four thousandth person

Fractions:	.03, or 3/100 three-hundredths	.004, or 4/1000 four-thousandths	.000007, or 7/1,000,000 seven-millionths
Ordinal Numbers:	three hundredth	four thousandth	seven millionth

3334 **Denominators are not ordinal numbers.** Do **not** use an ordinal suffix, *of* phrase, or similar addition to the denominator of a fraction that is written in figures.

Not:	7/32ds	9/64ths	5/8 of an inch	1/2 an inch
But:	7/32	9/64	5/8 inch	1/2 inch

3335 ***Of* phrase with spelled-out fraction.** An *of* phrase or similar construction may be used with a fraction that is spelled out.

	one-quarter of an ounce	half an hour
Not:	1/4 of an ounce	1/2 an hour

3336 **Mixed numbers.** A **mixed number** consists of a whole number (integer) and a fraction or decimal fraction (2 1/2, 2.5, 2 3/4, 2.75, etc.). Write a mixed number in figures unless it occurs at the beginning of a sentence or appears in ornate or formal text.

If possible, reword any sentence that begins with a number written in figures. Reword—or use enclosures, illustrations, or the like—to avoid the use of figures in ornate or formal text.

Not: 2 1/2 acres of bottomland will be sold at the auction.

Not: 2.5 acres of bottomland will be sold at the auction.

But: The auction will include 2 1/2 acres of bottomland.

or: The auction will include 2.5 acres of bottomland.

In a mixed number, space between the whole number and the fraction.

6 7/8 3 3/4 million

Measurements

3337 **Conventions for writing measurements.** Use these patterns for writing measurements in ordinary text and technical material.

Ordinary Text	¶	Technical Material	¶
6 pounds 12 ounces	3338	6 lb 12 oz	3345
17 feet 4 inches	3339	17′ 4″	3346
5 feet 2 inches	3340	5 ft 2 in or 5′ 2″	3446
an eight-foot scantling	3341	an 8-foot scantling, *or* an 8' scantling	3347
a five-foot-nine-inch person	3341	a 5' 9" person	3346
nine by twelve feet	3342	9 ft x 12 ft *or* a 9' x 12' rug	3349
30 inches wide, 48 inches high x 18 inches deep	3344	30" w, 48" h, 18" d, or 30" wide x 48" high x 18" deep	3350

3338 **Measurements in ordinary text.** In ordinary text, measurements such as weight, volume, count, dimensions (length, width, depth, etc.) are expressed in figures—except for occasional isolated measurements that are easily expressed in words.

The machines weigh 2375, 579, and 1483 pounds respectively.

The drill press weighs more than three hundred pounds.

3339 **Units of measure.** In ordinary text, units of measure are spelled out. A concentration of measurements in ordinary text is treated as an inserted passage of technical material. Such passages may consist of sentences, tables, charts, diagrams, and the like. See ¶ 3303 on consistency.

6 pounds 12 ounces   17 feet 4 inches

3340 **Symbols and abbreviations for units of measure.** Symbols and abbreviations for units of measure are **not** used in ordinary text.

Not: 30" w, 48" h, 18" d	**But:** 30 inches wide, 48 inches high, 18 inches deep
23' x 19'	23 feet by 19 feet

3341 **Hyphens in measurements.** In ordinary text, hyphenate a measurement that is a compound adjective immediately preceding the noun. See ¶ 3342 and ¶ 3216-19 on compound adjectives before and after the noun.

an eight-foot wall	an 8-foot wall
a five-foot-nine-inch statue	a 5-foot-9-inch statue

3342 **The word *by* in dimensions.** In ordinary text, use the word *by* to indicate dimensions. See ¶ 3348 on *x* in technical material and ¶ 3216-19 on compound adjectives before and after the noun. Follow the general rules for spelling out numbers, unless the result would be too cumbersome.

a three-by-five card
a 6-foot-by-32-foot hallway
a hallway that is 6 feet by 32 feet

3343 **Units of measure in ordinary text may be understood.** In ordinary text, some or all units of measure may be omitted when the result is unambiguous.

a 12-by-12 rug	a 10-by-50-foot driveway
8 1/2-by-11 paper	6-, 12-, and 18-inch drills
a three-by-five file card	

3344 **Complex measurements in ordinary text.** If a passage in ordinary text contains complex measurements, or deals intensively or extensively with measurements, or otherwise becomes cumbersome because of spelled-out numbers and units of measure, it is permissible to lapse into technical style, writing all numbers in figures and using abbreviations and symbols. Do not shift styles unnecessarily; mark such shifts by paragraphing when feasible.

See ¶ 3303.

30 inches wide, 48 inches high, 18 inches deep	30" wide x 48" high x 18" deep

3345 **Measurements in technical material.** In technical material, measurements (and other numbers as well) are expressed in figures. If the measurements are simple, brief, and isolated in a textual context, units of measure (pounds, feet, etc.) are spelled out.

```
The drill press weighs more than 300 pounds.
The room is a little less than 30 feet long.
```

See ¶ 3346 for measurements that are clustered rather than isolated.

3346 **Clustered or concentrated measurements.** When measurements are clustered or concentrated in technical material, abbreviations or symbols are used for units of measure—not only in tables, drawings, and the like, but in sentences as well.

```
6 lb 12 oz        5 ft 2 in       17' 4"          5' 2"
The base will be 2' 3 1/2" x 4' 7 1/4".
```

3

3347 **Hyphens in technical material.** In technical material, hyphenate a compound adjective in the attributive position (before the noun) if an abbreviation is used; do not hyphenate if a symbol is used.

an 8-ft scantling

But: an 8' scantling

3348 ***x* in technical material.** Use an *x* for the word *by* when writing dimensions in technical material.

9 ft x 12 ft *or* 9' x 12'

3349 **Repeating units of measure.** In technical material, units of measure are not understood or suspended as they may be in ordinary text. (See ¶ 3343.)

Not:	**But:**
3 x 5 ft	3 ft x 5 ft
3 x 5′	3′ x 5′
6-, 12- and 18-in drills	6-in, 12-in, and 18-in drills
6-, 12-, and 18″ drills	6″, 12″, and 18″ drills

3350 **Complex measurements in technical material.** Technical material may consist of page after page of detailed information—each crammed with numbers, abbreviations, and symbols. The layout of each page should be designed carefully to simplify the information—to facilitate reading and comprehension. Recent generations of word processors, computers, and software have made tables, charts, diagrams, illustrations, and other graphics easier to use effectively. In technical material, graphics are generally preferable to text as a means of explanation. (See ¶ 3301, 3303, 3337.)

3351 **Measurements in ornate and formal text.** Measurements are rarely necessary in ornate or formal text. When they are, spell them out if feasible. If not, put them in enclosures, illustrations, or sections of the document itself that are clearly technical in nature.

Metrics

3352 **Metric units.**

Basic Metric Units		
Quantity	**Unit**	**Symbol**
length	meter	m
mass	kilogram	kg
time	second	s
temperature	kelvin	K
	degree Celsius	C
electric current	ampere	A
luminous intensity	candela	cd
amount of substance	mole	mol
Supplementary Metric Units		
Quantity	**Unit**	**Symbol**
plane angle	radian	rad
solid angle	steradian	sr

3353 **Derived metric units.**

Quantity	Unit	Symbol	Formula
acceleration	meter per second squared	m/s^2	—
area	square meter	m^2	—
density	kilogram per cubic meter	kg/m^3	—
electric charge	coulomb	C	A · s
electric field strength	volt per meter	V/m	—
electric resistance	ohm	Ω	V/A
energy	joule	J	N · m
force	newton	N	$kg \cdot m/s^2$
frequency	hertz	Hz	s^{-1}
illumination	lux	lx	lm/m^2
power	watt	W	J/s
pressure	newton per square meter	N/m^2	—
quantity of heat	joule	J	N · m
velocity	meter per second	m/s	—
voltage	volt	V	W/A
volume	cubic meter	m^3	—
work	joule	J	N · m

3354 **Metric prefixes.**

Value	Power of 10	Prefix	Symbol
1 000 000 000 000	10^{12}	tera (ter´ a)	T
1 000 000 000	10^{9}	giga (jig´ a)	G
1 000 000	10^{6}	mega (meg´ a)	M
1 000	10^{3}	kilo (kil´ o)	k
100	10^{2}	hecto (hek´ to)	h
10	10^{1}	deka (dek´ a)	da
0.1	10^{-1}	deci (des´ i)	d
0.01	10^{-2}	centi (sen´ ti)	c
0.001	10^{-3}	milli (mil´ i)	m
0.000 001	10^{-6}	micro (mī´ kro)	µ
0.000 000 001	10^{-9}	nano (nan´ o)	n
0.000 000 000 001	10^{-12}	pico (pe´ ko)	p

3355 Metric units of area, capacity, length, etc.

Area

100 square millimeters	(mm^2)	-------------	1 square centimeter	(cm^2)
100 square centimeters	(cm^2)	-------------	1 square decimeter	(dm^2)
100 square decimeters	(dm^2)	-------------	1 square meter	(m^2)
100 square meters	(m^2)	-------------	1 square dekameter	(dam^2)
100 square dekameters	(dam^2)	-------------	1 square hectometer	(km^2)
100 square hectometers	(hm^2)	-------------	1 square kilometer	(km^2)

Capacity

10 milliliters	(ml)	-------------	1 centiliter	(cl)
10 centiliters	(cl)	-------------	1 deciliter	(dl)
10 deciliters	(dl)	-------------	1 liter	(L)
10 liters	(L)	-------------	1 dekaliter	(dal)
10 dekaliters	(dal)	-------------	1 hectoliter	(hl)
10 hectoliters	(hl)	-------------	1 kiloliter	(kl)
1 cubic decimeter	(dm3)	-------------	1 liter	(L)

Length

10 millimeters	(mm)	-------------	1 centimeter	(cm)
10 centimeters	(cm)	-------------	1 decimeter	(dm)
10 decimeters	(dm)	-------------	1 meter	(m)
10 meters	(m)	-------------	1 dekameter	(dam)
10 dekameters	(dam)	-------------	1 hectometer	(hm)
10 hectometers	(hm)	-------------	1 kilometer	(km)

Mass and Weight

10 milligrams	(mg)	-------------	1 centigram	(cg)
10 centigrams	(cg)	-------------	1 decigram	(dg)
10 decigrams	(dg)	-------------	1 gram	(g)
10 grams	(g)	-------------	1 dekagram	(dag)
10 dekagrams	(dag)	-------------	1 hectogram	(hg)
10 hectograms	(hg)	-------------	1 kilogram	(kg)
1 cubic decimeter	(dm3)	-------------	1 liter (L) = 1 kilogram	(kg)

Volume

1000 cubic millimeters	(mm^3)	-------------	1 cubic centimeter	(cm^3)
1000 cubic centimeters	(cm^3)	-------------	1 cubic decimeter	(dm^3)
1000 cubic decimeters	(dm^3)	-------------	1 cubic meter	(m^3)

3356 Metric <> English conversion.

Metric-English Conversion		English-Metric Conversion	
Approximate Values		**Approximate Values**	
1 mm -------------	0.04 inch	1 inch -------------	25.4 mm
1 cm -------------	0.4 inch	1 inch -------------	2.54 cm
1 m -------------	39.37 inches	1 foot -------------	0.305 m
1 km -------------	0.6 mile	1 yard -------------	0.91 m
		1 mile -------------	1.61 km

Metric-English Conversion Approximate Values		English-Metric Conversion Approximate Values	
1 cm^2	0.16 square inch	1 square inch	6.5 cm^2
1 m^2	10.8 square feet	1 square foot	0.09 m^2
1 m^2	1.2 square yards	1 square yard	0.8 m^2
1 hectare	2.5 acres	1 acre	0.4 hectare
1 cm^3	0.06 cubic inch	1 cubic inch	16.4 cm^3
1 m^3	35.3 cubic feet	1 cubic foot	0.03 cm^3
1 m^3	1.3 cubic yards	1 cubic yard	0.8 m^3
1 ml	0.034 ounce		
1 cl	0.34 ounce		
1 L	2.1 pints	1 pint	0.47 L
1 L	1.06 quarts	1 quart	0.95 L
1 L	0.26 gallon	1 gallon	3.79 L
1 g	0.035 ounce	1 ounce	28.35 g
1 kg	2.2 pounds	1 pound	0.45 kg
1 metric ton	1.1 U.S. ton	1 U.S. ton	0.9 metric ton

Money

3357 **Basic conventions for writing money amounts.** Conventions for writing money amounts vary with the context within which the money amounts appear. In all cases, use the word *dollars* with amounts that are spelled out; the *dollar sign* ($) with amounts that are written in figures. (See ¶ 3363 for amounts under one dollar.)

1. **Ordinary text.** In ordinary text, whole-dollar amounts of $10 and less are spelled out; other amounts are written in figures. Even dollar amounts are not followed by decimals or zeros.

ten dollars	nine dollars	five dollars	one dollar
$12.39	$20	nearly $50	over $1000

   See ¶ 3361 on isolated money amounts.

2. **Money amounts in technical material.** In technical material, money amounts are written in figures and symbols are used.

   $12 $123.47 $1   2¢   37¢

3. **Money amounts in ornate text.** In ornate text, money amounts are spelled out unless they are so long as to be awkward rather than elegant.

   The price is only twelve thousand, eight hundred ninety-two dollars.

MORE

4. **Money amounts in formal text.** Although money amounts rarely appear in formal text, those that do should be spelled out—even if they are somewhat awkward.

```
The reception will commemorate completion
of the
twelve-million-dollar addition
to the main building
```

3358 **Money amounts in negotiable instruments.** In negotiable instruments (checks, drafts, notes, bonds, etc.) numbers, especially amounts of money, are spelled out **and** written in figures to increase clarity and certainty. (See ¶ 3315 on writing numbers in words.)

$97.83	=	Ninety-seven and 83/100 dollars
$9955.55	=	Ninety-Nine Hundred Fifty-Five and 55/100 dollars
$157,872.98	=	One hundred fifty-seven thousand, eight hundred seventy-two and 98/100 dollars

Capitalization is optional, but should be consistent within each document.

The word *and* should be used only once if at all.

Five hundred thirty-six *and* no/100 dollars

Not: Twenty-One Hundred *and* Fifty-Eight *and* 37/100 dollars

But: Twenty-One Hundred Fifty-Eight *and* 37/100 dollars
Twenty-One Hundred Fifty-Eight & 37/100 dollars
Twenty-One Hundred Fifty-Eight dollars

3359 **Money amounts in law documents.** In many law documents, such as wills and contracts, money amounts and other numbers are spelled out **and** written in figures as they are in negotiable instruments. (See ¶ 3358.)

3360 **Indefinite money amounts.** In all written material, indefinite amounts of money are spelled out.

several hundred dollars   many thousands of dollars

3361 **Isolated money amounts.** In ordinary text, an isolated money amount is spelled out unless the result is awkward or too lengthy.

The amount in question was twenty-three dollars.

3362 **Decimal and zeros following a money amount.** When writing an even amount of money in figures (ordinary text and technical material) **do not** add a decimal point **or** zeros.

The rates are $3.85 per week and $16 per month.

3363 **Cents.** In ordinary text, spell out amounts of ten cents and less; write amounts of 11 cents through 99 cents in figures. Use the word *cents* instead of the symbol ¢.

one cent two cents ten cents 50 cents 99 cents

For consistency within any given context in ordinary text, figures replace spelled-out numbers and $ replaces *cents*.

Isolated: nine cents 50 cents $1.21

Same context: 9 cents and 50 cents

Same context: $ .09, $ .40, and $1.21 — Use this form only to achieve consistency with amounts of $1 or more in the same context.

In technical material, use figures and ¢ to express isolated amounts of 99 cents and less. Replace ¢ with $ in order to achieve consistency within a given context. See the example immediately preceding.

Isolated: 9¢ 50¢ 99¢

In ornate and formal text, spell out all amounts expressed as cents and use the word *cents*. Do not use figures, $, or ¢.

nineteen cents twenty cents twenty-one cents
ninety-nine cents

Names

3364 **Name followed by roman numeral or *Jr.*** Traditionally, a male child who is given the same name as that of his father or grandfather adds Jr. to the name—unless a *Jr.* already exists. In that case, the child adds *III* to the name. If the child is named for an uncle or other nonlineal male relative, he adds *II* to the name. If other male children in the family are given the same name, they may be designated as *III, IV, V,* and so on.

The tradition was once that, upon the death of the senior person bearing the name, each namesake advanced one step in seniority (Jr. became Sr., III became Jr., etc.). More recently, the practice has been to retain permanently the surname suffix adopted at birth.

The suffix *Sr.* or *Jr.* is preceded by a comma; roman numerals (III, IV, etc.) are not. The roman numerals are pronounced as ordinals: *the third, the fourth,* etc.

Grandfather: Walter Izand Entner
Father: Walter Izand Entner, Jr.
Son: Walter Izand Entner III
Nephew: Walter Izand Entner II

Numbers in Order

3365 **Ranges.** In ordinary text, the numbers in a range that contains no number above 10 are spelled out. The numbers in a range that contains a number above 10 are written in figures. Do not mix words and figures in the same range or set of ranges.

```
Their ages range from three through seven.
The range of their ages is 9-13.
```

Not: `The range of their ages is three through 12.`

Abbreviating the higher number in a range. The higher number in a range may be abbreviated if both numbers have at least three digits and neither number ends in *00*. To abbreviate the 109 in 101-109, retain only the part of the higher number that differs from the lower number (101-9). For 101-199, *two* digits are retained in the higher number because *two* digits differ (101-99). Do **not** change more than two digits.

100-105	→	100-105		1005-1008	→	1005-8
105-108	→	105-8		125-145	→	125-45
1000-1005	→	1000-1005		1522-1568	→	1522-68
			But:	1598-1601	→	1598-1601

3366 **Numbers in series.** In a series or a list of selected numbers, use a comma after each number except the last and a space after each comma. The same rules for spelled-out numbers or figures apply except where too many spelled-out numbers would make a sentence confusing.

```
The numbers are 12, 26, and 48.
```

But: `The series is 2, 4, 8, 16, 32, and 64.`

```
The series is two, four, and six.
```

3367 **Serial numbers.** In all styles, serial numbers of all kinds are written in figures. Serial numbers do not usually include commas, but may include letters of the alphabet, spaces, or other characters.

Policy number:	FDN 334 384756
Social Security number:	402-24-7093
Military serial number:	35822220
Telephone number:	513-555-6121

3368 **Statistics: Voting, scores, etc.** In ordinary text and technical material: voting results, the scores of sporting events, and other statistics are written in figures. Normally, statistics do not occur in ornate or formal text. It is not unusual, however, for ornate text or formal text to contain distinct *passages* of statistics (technical material)—or to include such material in enclosures.

104-92 15-6 9 to 5

Percentages

3369 **Percentage.** How a percentage is written in a specific sentence may depend on whether that sentence appears in technical material, ornate text, formal text, or ordinary text.

In technical material, percentages are written in figures; the symbol % is used.

`Fewer than 23% of the surveys were returned.`

In ornate and formal text, percentages are spelled out; the word *percent* is used.

`Yes, ninety-four percent of the answers were correct.`

In ordinary text, percentages are written in figures; the word *percent* is used.

`Among those present, 17 percent planned to respond.`

3

1. **Percentage with fraction or decimal fraction.** With any percentage that includes a fraction or decimal fraction, it is preferable to use the decimal fraction.

   Preferred: Only 5.5 percent failed to return the survey.

   Acceptable: Only 5 1/2 percent failed to return the survey.

2. **Fraction of percent.** Write fractions of 1 percent as spelled-out fractions if followed by *of;* in all other cases use figures and decimal fractions.

   Preferred: In September, .5 percent failed to complete registration.

   Acceptable: In September, one-half of 1 percent failed to complete registration.

   Not: In September, 1/2 percent failed to complete registration.

   Preferred: In the final report, .656 percent were disqualified.

   Not: In the final report, twenty-one thirty-seconds percent were disqualified.

   Not: In the final report, 21/32 percent were disqualified.

3. **Percentage beginning a sentence.** Do **not** begin a sentence with a percentage written in figures (or any other number written in figures). Reword the sentence if feasible. If not, spell out the percent.

   Not: 57 percent of those present supported the resolution.

   Preferred: The resolution was supported by 57 percent of those present.

   Acceptable: Fifty-seven percent of those who were present supported the resolution.

MORE

4. **Consistency in writing percentages.** Convert *words* to *figures* and *fractions* to *decimal fractions* when necessary for consistency within a context.

Not: In the last group, 81.3 percent passed, 11 7/8 percent transferred, and six percent failed.

But: In the last group, 81.3 percent passed, 11.875 percent transferred, .825 percent were ill, and 6 percent failed.

3

Proportions and Ratios

3370 **Proportions and ratios.** In ordinary text, proportions and ratios are generally written in figures.

a 3-to-1 proportion   a ratio of 3 to 1   a 3-to-1 ratio

But, isolated proportions and ratios are spelled out.

a three-to-one ratio   a ratio of three to one

In technical material, all proportions and ratios are written in figures.

a ratio of 27:1   4 parts water to 1 part pigment

In ornate and formal text, proportions and ratios are spelled out. Proportions and ratios occur infrequently in ornate text and are rarely seen in formal text.

a proportion of four to one   a four-to-one ratio

Roman Numerals

3371 **Roman numerals.** Roman numerals are frequently used to identify the main sections of outlines. They are also used in lowercase form (xiv, for example) to number pages in the front sections of books. Roman numerals are used in the title and credits sections of motion pictures, on buildings, and in other applications in which the writer or designer wishes to convey an image of historical significance. In ornate and formal text, roman numerals are frequently substituted for arabic figures in order to convey a similar image. References to parts of a book are always set in arabic numerals, **not** roman numerals.

3372 **Conversion table, roman numerals ↔ arabic numerals.** The following table shows equivalent values of selected roman numerals and arabic numerals.

1	I	11	XI	30	XXX	400	CD
2	II	12	XII	40	XL	500	D
3	III	13	XIII	50	L	600	DC
4	IV	14	XIV	60	LX	700	DCC
5	V	15	XV	70	LXX	800	DCCC
6	VI	16	XVI	80	LXXX	900	CM
7	VII	17	XVII	90	XC	1,000	M
8	VIII	18	XVIII	100	C	2,000	MM
9	IX	19	XIX	200	CC		
10	X	20	XX	300	CCC	5,000	$\overline{V}$*
						10,000	$\overline{X}$*
						100,000	$\overline{C}$*
						1,000,000	$\overline{M}$*

* A line over a numeral multiplies its value by 1,000.

3373 **Writing other numbers in roman numerals.** Numbers not shown in the preceding table may be written by using prefixes and suffixes. Prefixing a numeral is the equivalent of subtracting the value of the prefixed numeral; suffixing a numeral is the equivalent of adding the value of the suffixed numeral.

```
49 = 40 (X less than L) plus 9 (I less than X) = XLIX
64 = 60 (L plus X) plus 4 (I less than V) = LXIV
```

Temperature

3374 **Temperature: Celsius ↔ Fahrenheit.**

Celsius		Fahrenheit
0°C	freezing point of water	32°F
10°C	a spring day	50°F
20°C	recommended indoor temperature	68°F
30°C	a summer day	86°F
37°C	body temperature	98.6°F
100°C	boiling point of water	212°F

Converting from Fahrenheit to Celsius

$$C = \frac{5}{9}(F - 32)$$

Converting from Celsius to Fahrenheit

$$F = \frac{9}{5}C + 32$$

Time, Age, Dates

3375 **Clock time.** In ordinary text, write exact times of day in figures and use the abbreviations *a.m.* and *p.m.* In technical material, write all times using *a.m.* and *p.m.* Do **not** use the words *o'clock, morning,* and *evening* with *a.m.* or *p.m.*

9:45 a.m. 12:04 p.m. 6:30 p.m. 12:45 a.m.

3376 **On-the-hour times.** Write on-the-hour times without zeros (9 a.m.) unless they occur in tables or columns with times that are not on the hour.

They will start at noon and stop at midnight.

They will start at 5 p.m. and stop at 12 midnight.

The departure times are 4:35 a.m., 5:55 a.m., 7 a.m., and 9:20 a.m.

These are the departure times: 4:35 a.m.
5:55 a.m.
7:00 a.m.
9:20 a.m.

3
3377 **Conventional formats for time.** Use these conventional formats for stating clock time and dates.

Conventional Formats	NOT Acceptable
5:30 a.m.	5:30 this a.m.
5:30 a.m. today	5:30 today a.m.
5:30 this morning	5:30 a.m. this morning
this morning	this a.m.
11:30 p.m. until 12 p.m.	11:30 p.m. until midnight
noon until midnight	(12 noon until 12 midnight)
12:00 n. until 12 p.m. (technical)	12 n. until midnight

3378 **Noon and midnight.** The words *noon* and *midnight* may be used alone to designate 12 a.m. and 12 p.m., respectively; they are **not** used with *a.m.* or *p.m.* In technical writing, 12 n. and 12 p.m. are used for consistency with other times. (See ¶ 3377).

3379 **Clock time in ornate and formal text.** In formal text, times of day are spelled out and the word *o'clock* is often used. Either this pattern or the one prescribed for ordinary text may be used in ornate text, depending upon the purpose of the writer. (See ¶ 3376-78.)

Formal text: half after seven o'clock in the evening

	Typical Formats
Formal text:	at eight o'clock in the evening on the twenty-fourth day of May
Ornate text:	at eight o'clock in the evening on the twenty-fourth of May
Ordinary text:	at 8 p.m. on May 23
Technical writing:	at 8 p.m. on May 23; at 8:00p My 23

When spelling out a time of day, use a hyphen between the elements of a two-word expression; use a hyphen between the second and third words in a three-word expression.

seven-thirty   seven thirty-five   twelve forty-five

3380 **Ages.** In ordinary text, expressions of age are governed by the general rule that numbers ten and below are spelled out and those above ten are expressed in figures.

Their daughter is ten, but they have a son who is older.

If ages in the ten-and-below bracket and ages above that bracket appear in the same context, write all ages in that context in figures. The context may be a sentence, a paragraph in which ages are expressed several times, or an entire article or book in which ages are expressed frequently, repeatedly, or periodically.

Their daughter is 12 and their son is 9.

See ¶ 3303.

3381 **Precise expressions of age.** In ordinary text, expressions of age more precise than the number of years are written in figures. Commas are not used.

Margarita is 27 days and 11 hours old.

Matsushita is 24 years 7 months and 12 days old.

One twin is 2 1/2 minutes older than the other.

3382 **Commas in statements of age.** In ordinary text, commas are used to set off the age of a person stated immediately after the person's name, but not to separate the elements of a precise statement of age.

Wanda Walker was born 22 years 3 months and 7 hours ago.

Suenora Agnos, aged seven, was playing nearby.

Emily's mother, aged 100, is in good health.

Theodore Arflind, 44, was not at home at the time.

3383 **Ages in technical material.** In technical material, ages are written in figures. Technical material includes statistical information, rules, regulations, and the like. (See ¶ 3303.)

The earnings rule applies to those over 62 who are receiving social security retirement benefits.

Children younger than 5 are not permitted in the pool.

3384 **Ages in ornate and formal text.** In invitations, announcements, and other formal text—and in ornate text—ages are spelled out.

Mrs. Clangford attained the age of one hundred and five on the twenty-fourth of January!

3385 **Anniversaries and birthdays.** In ordinary text, the general rule for writing numbers applies to anniversaries and birthdays: spell out anniversaries or birthdays 1–10; write all others in figures. Use ordinal numbers.

```
the third anniversary          their 50th anniversary
the 125th anniversary of the founding of the firm
```

Should a reference to an anniversary or birthday occur in technical material, apply the general rule: write all numbers in technical material in figures. Write ordinal numbers in figures.

```
our 25th anniversary           her 21st birthday
```

3386 **Anniversaries and birthdays in ornate and formal text.** References to anniversaries and birthdays are often written in ornate or formal style. Spell out all numbers; hyphenate compounds from 21 through 99; use ordinal numbers.

```
our twenty-fifth anniversary   their fiftieth anniversary
the one hundred twenty-fifth anniversary of the founding of the
firm
```

3

3387 **Dates.** In ordinary text, spell out the month and write the day and year in figures.

```
September 12, 1999             January 24, 2002
```

3388 **Dates in other nations and in the U.S. military.** In many other nations, and in the U.S. military services, dates are expressed in the format *day month year* in which *day* is the day of the month written in figures, *month* the month spelled out, and *year* all four figures of the year. A comma is not used.

```
12 September 1999              24 January 2002
```

3389 **Dates in technical material.** Several abbreviated formats are used for dates in technical material. Some computer applications require a rigidly fixed format, including high-order zeros, as shown in the second line of examples. Care should be exercised in the use of these forms since the style used in the U.S. is *month-day-year* and the style used in some other nations is *day-month-year*. In the first example, January 2, 1996 could be mistaken for 1 February 1996.

```
1-2-96        2-9-1996        3/27/03        4/4/2003
01-02-96      02-09-1996      03/27/03       04/04/2003
```

3390 **Dates expressed in ordinal numbers.** In ordinary text, use ordinal numbers if the day precedes the month.

```
The exposition opens on the 23d of October and closes on the
28th of October.
```

Cardinal numbers should be used for dates in ordinary text if the number representing the year is written in figures.

```
The ceremony scheduled for May 3, 1999, has been postponed.
```

3391 **Dates in ornate text.** In ornate text, days of the month are written in ordinal numbers and spelled out *unless they are too long or awkward in their spelled-out form*. Those who write in ornate style do so for a special purpose. They use a variety of formats to achieve what they construe as elegance.

```
May twenty-second, two thousand one
May 22, 23, and 24, 2001
```

3392 **Dates in formal text.** In formal text, days of the month are written in ordinal numbers and spelled out. Those who write in formal style do so for a special purpose. They use a variety of formats to make their efforts appear formal.

```
the thirty-first day of May, nineteen hundred ninety-nine
May twenty-second, twenty-third, and twenty-fourth,
two thousand one
```

3

3393 **Centuries and decades.** Centuries and decades are spelled out.

```
the twentieth century          the thirties
```

If decades are identified by the century, they are always written in figures.

```
the early 1940s                the early 1960s
```

The **names** of decades are capitalized.

```
the Golden Age of Greece       the Roaring Twenties
the Dark Ages                  the Gay Nineties
the Renaissance                the Fabulous Fifties
```

3394 **B.C. and A.D.** The abbreviations *B.C.* and *A.D.* are written after the number that identifies the year. **B.C.** means *before Christ*; **A.D.** is Latin for *in the year of our Lord*. Either may be written with or without periods.

All styles:	2225 A.D.	284 B.C.	14,500 B.C.
Or:	2225 AD	284 BC	14,500 BC

In ornate or formal text, the abbreviation may be written *before* the number with periods.

Ornate or formal:	A.D. 2225	B.C. 284	B.C. 14,500

Vessels and Vehicles

3395 **Vessels and vehicles.** Ships, boats, aircraft, spacecraft, and vehicles are sometimes named after their predecessors and given numbers to distinguish them from those namesakes. Roman numerals without commas are used for this purpose.

```
Enterprise IV                  Lucy III
```

3

3400 PLURALS

PLURALS

3401 **Quick reference for writing plurals.** The following chart outlines brief rules for forming plurals. Each brief rule includes reference to a paragraph that states the rule in full and provides additional examples. This combination is especially useful in the case of **regular plurals**—those formed by adding *s* or *es*—since most regular plurals are not listed in the dictionary. The dictionary does list **irregular plurals** and others that are likely to be troublesome.

Singular Nouns Ending in	¶	Singular	Change	Add	Plural
most letters	3402	boat		s	boats
ch	3403	porch		es	porches
f	[1] 3404	leaf	*f* to *ve*	s	leaves
fe	[1] 3404	life	*fe* to *ve*	s	lives
vowel + o	3405	radio		s	radios
consonant + o	3406	auto potato cargo		some *s* some *es* some either	autos potatoes cargos/ cargoes
s sound	3403	alias		es	aliases
s, but not s sound	3407	chamois			chamois
sh	3403	wish		es	wishes
x	3403	fax		es	faxes
vowel + y	[2] 3408	attorney		s	attorneys
consonant + y	3409	agency	*y* to *i*	es	agencies
z	3403	waltz		es	waltzes

[1] See ¶ 3404 for exceptions [2] See ¶ 3408 for exceptions.

3402 **General rules for pluralizing nouns.** Pluralize most nouns by adding *s* to the singular. (See ¶ 3401 for exceptions.)

bases	books	flowers	thoughts

the Hinkles (Add *s* to pluralize most proper nouns. See ¶ 3415-16.)

3403 **Nouns ending in *ch, s, sh, x,* and *z*.** Pluralize nouns ending in *ch, s, sh, x,* and *z* by adding *es*. (See ¶ 3407 for exceptions.)

benches	aliases	brushes	boxes	klutzes
winches	passes	crashes	duplexes	topazes

the Alvarezes (Add *es* to pluralize proper nouns ending in *ch, s, sh, x,* and *z*. See ¶ 3415-16.)

3404 **Nouns ending in *f* and *fe*.** Some common nouns ending in *f* and *fe* are pluralized by changing the ending to *ve* and adding *s*. The dictionary lists these plurals, but does not list plurals that are formed by simply adding *s*.

knife	knives	**But:**	belief	beliefs
leaf	leaves		chief	chiefs
life	lives		proof	proofs
thief	thieves		safe	safes
wife	wives		serif	serifs

But: the Wolfs (proper noun)

Not: the Wolves (Do not change the internal spelling of a proper noun to pluralize it. See ¶ 3415-16.)

3405 **Nouns ending in a *vowel plus o*.** Pluralize nouns ending in a *vowel plus o* by adding *s*.

bugaboos	duos	ratios	shampoos	trios
cameos	folios	rodeos	stereos	videos
curios	radios	scenarios	studios	zoos

the Camareos (Add *s* to pluralize a proper noun ending in a *vowel plus o*. See ¶ 3415-16.)

3406 **Nouns ending in a *consonant plus o*.** Some singular nouns ending in *consonant plus o* require an *s* ending when pluralized. Others require an *es* ending. A few may be spelled with either an *s* or *es* ending.

alter egos	cellos	fiascos*, fiascoes	pimentos
autos	sopranos	gazebos	potatoes
cargos, cargoes*	didos*, didoes	grottos, grottoes*	tomatoes

* = Preferred

the Zozzaros (Add *s* to pluralize a proper noun ending in a *consonant plus o*. See ¶ 3415-16.)

3407 **Nouns ending in silent *s*.** Singular nouns ending in *s* but not in the *s sound* are spelled identically in their singular and plural forms.

bourgeois	chamois	chassis	corps	patois

the Dubois (The singular form of a proper noun ending in silent *s* also serves as the plural form. See ¶ 3415-16.)

3408 **Nouns ending in a *vowel plus y*.** Pluralize a singular noun ending in a *vowel plus y* by adding *s*.

buy*s*	jockey*s*	**But:**	colloquy	colloqu*ies*
byway*s*	joy*s*		obloquy	obloqu*ies*
donkey*s*	key*s*		obsequy	obsequ*ies*
highway*s*	ploy*s*		soliloquy	soliloqu*ies*

the Lackey*s* (Add *s* to pluralize a proper noun ending in a *vowel plus y*. See ¶ 3415-16.)

3409 **Nouns ending in a *consonant plus y*.** Pluralize a singular common noun ending in a *consonant plus y* by changing the *y* to *i* and adding *es*.

agency	agenc*ies*	copy	cop*ies*	comedy	comed*ies*
baby	bab*ies*	enemy	enem*ies*	spy	sp*ies*

the Abernathy*s* (Add *s* to pluralize a proper noun ending in a *consonant plus y*. See ¶ 3515-16.)

3410 **Irregular plurals.** Some singular common nouns are pluralized by altering the word itself or by adding a suffix other than *s* or *es*. All irregular plurals are listed in the dictionary.

child	children	mouse	mice	man	men
foot	feet	ox	oxen	woman	women
goose	geese	tooth	teeth		

3411 **Collective nouns.** A **collective noun** is singular in form but denotes a group: *couple, government, majority, orchestra, pair, team,* etc. If the writer is referring to a group *acting as a unit,* a singular verb is used. (See ¶ 1021.)

The *couple is* planning *its* trip abroad.

The *government is* prepared to deal with *its* critics.

Test for this construction by adding *as a unit*.

The couple (*as a unit*) is planning its trip abroad.

The government (*as a unit*) is prepared to deal with its critics.

If the collective noun refers to individual members or parts of the group rather than to the group as a unit, a plural verb is used.

The *couple* are planning *their* trips abroad.

The *government* are undecided on how to deal with *their* critics.

Test for this construction by adding *members of the* or *parts of the*.

The (*members of the*) couple are planning their trips abroad.

The (*members of the*) government are undecided on how to deal with their critics.

Avoid inconsistency between verb and pronoun.

The couple *is* planning *its* (**not** *their*) trip abroad.

The government *is* prepared to deal with *its* (**not** *their*)critics.

The couple *are* planning *their* (**not** *its*) trips abroad.

The government *are* undecided on how to deal with *their* (**not** *its*) critics.

3412 **Plural in form—singular in meaning.** A noun that is plural in form but singular in meaning takes a singular verb. Such nouns are identified in their dictionary listings. (See ¶ 1019.)

Economics *is* primarily the study of scarcity.

Electronics *is* a challenging field.

Measles *is* a contagious disease.

News *is* reported by the media.

Physics *is* often associated with chemistry.

Some plural-in-form nouns can be either singular or plural in meaning. (See ¶ 1017 and 1019.)

The first series *is* scheduled for next Wednesday.

Both series *are* scheduled for next Wednesday.

This deer *eats* corn. That sheep *eats* grass.

Most deer *eat* corn. All sheep *eat* grass.

Politics *is* the field for her.	(practice of the field of politics)
Her politics *are* above reproach.	(individual political actions, practices, or policies)
Statistics *is* a branch of mathematics.	(a field of endeavor)
Statistics *are* sometimes difficult to interpret.	(individual units of statistical information)

Athletics *is* the field of exercises, sports, and games.

Athletics *are* exercises, sports, or games.

3413 **Foreign language plurals.** Some foreign language expressions retain their foreign plural forms; others are given English plural forms. The dictionary provides both, when they exist, and indicates the preferable form.

Singular	Foreign Language Plural Used in English	English Plural
alumna [1]	alumnae [1]	alumnae [1]
alumnus [2]	alumni [3]	alumni [3]
criterion	criteria	criteria
curriculum	curricula	curriculums
datum [4]	data [4]	data [4]
matrix	matrices	matrices
medium	media	mediums or media
phenomenon	phenomena	phenomena

[1] Feminine.
[2] Masculine.
[3] Masculine and feminine.
[4] *Data* is frequently treated as a singular mass noun analogous to *water* (data is gathered). (See ¶ 3414.)

MORE

The alumna is a young woman; the alumnae are young women.

The alumnus is a young man; the alumni are young women and young men.

The criterion has been met; the criteria are demanding.

Most data is important; massive amounts of data are formidable.

The matrix is ready; the matrices are ready.

The newspaper is a medium; newspapers, radio, and TV are media.

They recorded a phenomenon; they witnessed several phenomena.

3414 **Count nouns and mass nouns.** **Count nouns** represent things that are conceptualized as individual (counted) items: autos, eggs, trees, etc. **Mass nouns** represent things that are conceptualized as homogeneous (measured) substances: air, sand, water, etc.

Certain antecedent expressions are used with count nouns (*a, an, few, fewer, many,* etc.); others are used with mass nouns (*little, less, much, a great deal of,* etc.); others are used with both count nouns and mass nouns (*all, some, more, most,* etc.).

Most of the problems involving count nouns and mass nouns are related to their use with *fewer* and *less.*

Fewer is used with plural count nouns (autos, eggs, trees, etc.), including the units used to measure mass nouns (*cubic feet, tons, gallons,* etc.).

fewer — autos / eggs / trees

fewer — cubic feet of air / tons of sand / gallons of water

But: less — air / sand / water

And: less than — 30 cubic feet of air / 8 tons of sand / 20 gallons of water

Less is used with singular mass nouns (air, sand, water, etc.), and with nonmaterial things that cannot be measured (anger, hate, love, etc.).

less — air / sand / water

less — anger / hate / love

Not: less — autos / eggs / trees

Less than may refer to a fixed amount, aggregate, total, balance, etc. It is used when the emphasis is on the fixed amount rather than the individual units of measure.

less than — 30 cubic feet of air / 8 tons of sand / 20 gallons of water

a — balance / sum / total — **of less than** — a hundred dollars / $198.37 / 200 units

3415 **Plurals of given names and surnames.** Generally, given names and surnames are pluralized by adding *s*. (See ¶ 3416 for exceptions.)

one William or Bill	two Williams or Bills
one Maria or Millicent	two Marias or Millicents
Mr. and Mrs. Waldorf	the Waldorfs
Alice and Bill Chandler	the Chandlers
Cergio and Maria Alevaro	the Alevaros

A suffix of *s* is added to pluralize the name, but the spelling of the name itself remains unchanged.

one Billie, one Billy	two Billies, two Billys	
Celia and Bill Anthony	the Anthonys	**Not:** the Anthonies
Alfred and Yvrose DeWolf	the DeWolfs	**Not:** the DeWolves

3

3416 **Plurals of names ending in *ch, s, sh, x,* and *z*.** Pluralize names ending in *ch, s, sh, x,* and *z* by adding *es* to the singular.

Butches	Mavises	Rushes	Maxes	Fritzes
the Finches	the Weisses	the Marshes	the Foxes	the Blatzes

If the addition of *es* makes a name difficult to pronounce, omit the *es* and use the singular form as the plural.

Not:	the Cisneroses	the Walterses	the Isaacses	the Heureuxes
But:	the Cisneros	the Walters	the Isaacs	the Heureux

3417 **Pluralizing compound nouns.** Generally, create the plural form of a compound noun by pluralizing its final element. (See ¶ 3418 for exceptions.)

big brother	big brothers	layout	layouts
bull's-eye	bull's-eyes	meat loaf	meat loaves
come-on	come-ons	merry-go-round	merry-go-rounds
cough drop	cough drops	polar bear	polar bears
cure-all	cure-alls	rip-off	rip-offs
dinner-dance	dinner-dances	roll bar	roll bars
follow-through	follow-throughs	set-aside	set-asides
follow-up	follow-ups	sick bay	sick bays
get-together	get-togethers	standby	standbys
hangover	hangovers	takeoff	takeoffs
higher-up	higher-ups	trademark	trademarks
kickback	kickbacks	walk-in	walk-ins

3418 **Irregular plural compounds.** Most irregular plural compounds exist because the dominant word is not in the final position **and** pluralizing the final element would make the compound awkward (*ambassador-at-larges* as opposed to *ambassadors-at-large*). The dictionary lists *irregular* plural compounds.

ambassador-at-large	ambassador*s*-at-large
father-in-law	father*s*-in-law
attorney-at-law	attorney*s*-at-law
hanger-on	hanger*s*-on
carrying-on	carrying*s*-on
leave of absence	leave*s* of absence
diner-out	diner*s*-out
passerby	passer*s*by
falling-out	falling*s*-out
sergeant at arms	sergeant*s* at arms

3500 POSSESSIVES

POSSESSIVES

3501 **Possessive forms.** Possessive forms consist of three parts: the possessor, the indicator of possession, and the object possessed.

	Possessor	Indicator of Possession	Object Possessed
(Singular)	Andrea Jones	's	stereo
(Plural ending in *s*)	the Joneses	'	telephone
	the Fawcetts	'	van
(Plural not ending in *s*)	the men	's	books

The indicator of possession is either an *apostrophe* or an *apostrophe s,* not *s apostrophe*. In the example, the *es* in Joneses and the *s* in Fawcetts are each part of the plural form of the name, not part of the indicator of possession. (See ¶ 3502.)

3502 **Plural possessives.** To create a plural possessive, first form the plural, then add the indicator of possession. (See ¶ 3401-18 on creating plurals.)

the *woman*'s chair	the *women*'s chairs
the *boss*'s desk	the *bosses*' desks
the *lawyer*'s hand	the *lawyers*' debates

3503 **Kinds of possession.** There are four major kinds of possession.

• **Owning:**	the accountant's	calculator	(singular)
	the farmers'	tractors	(plural)
• **Having:**	the renter's	apartment	(singular)
	the givers'	time	(plural)
• **Creating:**	the artist's	paintings	(singular)
	the authors'	book	(plural)
• **Measuring:**	a week's	work	(singular)
	a stone's	throw	(singular)
	five dollars'	worth	(plural)

3504 **Indicating possessive relationships.** There are three ways to indicate possessive relationships.

- **An apostrophe.**

Henry's paper   Florida's name   Margarita's family

- **A prepositional phrase.**

the parts [for / of / in] the automobile   the breeze from the ocean

- **A noun used as a modifier in the attributive position** (just before the noun that is modified).

the automobile parts   the ocean breeze

3505 **Quick reference for creating possessives.** Refer to this chart when you know that an *apostrophe* or *apostrophe s* is required to create a possessive, but you do not know which is required. If a plural form is needed, first form the plural (see ¶ 3401-18) and then add the indicator of possession: *apostrophe* or *apostrophe s*.

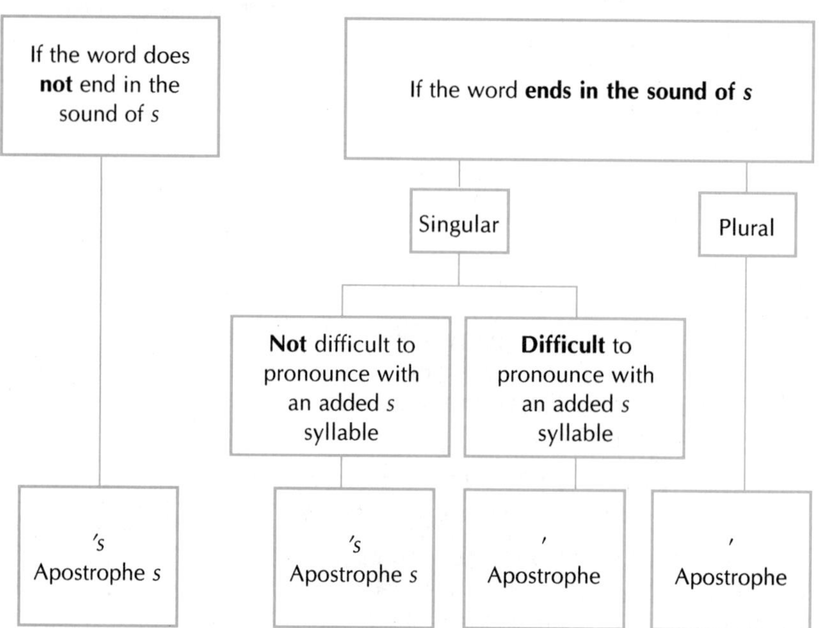

3506 **Possessive forms in brief.** Refer to this chart for a capsule explanation of each possessive form; refer to the paragraphs indicated for details.

SEE ¶	TO CREATE POSSESSIVE FORMS	ADD OR USE	EXAMPLES
3507	Nouns not ending in the sound of *s*.	'*s*	Marvin's bicycle the dog's tail
3508	Singular nouns ending in the sound of *s* (if adding *s* sound does not make pronunciation awkward).	'*s*	the prince's sword the princess's veil Ralph Ross's roses the spitz's tail
3508	Singular nouns ending in the sound of *s* (if adding *s* sound does make pronunciation awkward).	'	Ulysses' coat Jane Withers' pictures
3509	Plural nouns ending in the sound of *s*.	'	the members' votes the bosses' desks
3510 3511 3512	Appositives (noun or noun substitute beside another noun or noun substitute to explain or identify it).	Use *of* phrase	**Not:** Henry the plumber's shop **But:** the shop of Henry the plumber

SEE ¶	TO CREATE POSSESSIVE FORMS	ADD OR USE	EXAMPLES
3513	Compound nouns	′ or ′*s* added to final word element	the ne′er-do-wells′ gathering her brother-in-law′s money
3514	Gerunds (*ing* form of a verb that functions as a noun).	′ or ′*s* added to gerund′s modifier	Wilma′s walking Stanley′s driving
3515	Understood nouns.	′ or ′*s* added to understood noun′s modifier	at the Barnabys′ (home) to the doctor′s (office)
3516	For possessive forms of nouns other than those representing people, animals, organizations, geographic locations, time, value, distance, and celestial bodies.	Prepositional phrase or noun as modifier	the transistors in the TV the handle of the hammer the TV transistors the hammer handle
3517	Expressions suggesting personification	′ or ′*s*	Age′s resignation the Four Winds′ names
3518	Personal pronouns and the relative pronoun *who.*	Special forms	**Pronoun** — **Possessive Form** he — his who — whose
3519	Indefinite pronouns with regular possessive forms.	′ or ′*s*	someone′s contribution the others′ collection
3520	Indefinite pronouns without regular possessive forms.	Prepositional phrase	the problems of a few the achievements of some (**Not** a few′s or some′s)
3521	Abbreviations, singular.	′*s*	the MBA′s analysis
3522	Abbreviations, plural.	′	the MBAs′ desks
3523	Personal names ending with abbreviations or numbers.	′ or ′*s*	James Thannes, Jr.′s book the Roy Wallace IIIs′ children
3524	Joint possession, all possessors identified by name	′ or ′*s* to final name	Wilton and Smedley′s office Melanie and May′s cat Plato and Epictetus′ idea
3525	Joint possession, possessor identified by pronoun.	possessive forms of nouns and pronouns	Barry′s and her farm His and Celia′s station wagon

MORE

CONTINUED

SEE ¶	TO CREATE POSSESSIVE FORMS	ADD OR USE	EXAMPLES
3526	Separate possession.	possessive forms of nouns and pronouns	Elsa's and John's teeth His and her books
3527	Organizational names ending with an abbreviation, prepositional phrase, or number (See ¶ 3530.).	' or *'s*	National Music Assn.'s offices Association of CEOs' offices Association of Musicians' bus Society of 55's newspaper
3528	Organizational names containing a possessive form. (See ¶ 3530.)	' or *'s*	National Yeoman's Association National Women's Association
3529	Organizational names containing a word that could be a possessive form or a plural. (Presume that it is plural. See ¶ 3530.)	No apostrophe	Air Line Pilots Association National Consumers League
3530	Regardless of conventions in ¶ 3527, 3528, and 3529, write the name as it is used by the organization itself	As preferred by the organization	National Science Teachers Association United Seamen's Service
3531	Avoid nested possessives.	Use *of* phrase, *belonging to, used by,* etc.	**Not:** Jess's mother's cousin's car **But:** the car belonging to a cousin of Jess's mother
3532	Use idiomatic possessive forms.	Independent conventions apply.	Mother's Day / donkey's years Presidents' Day / cats' cages Veterans Day / dog days
3533	Do **not** confuse contractions with possessive pronouns.	Use the ' in contractions, not pronouns.	*it's* (it is) contraction *its* (belonging to it) pronoun *they're* (they are) contraction *their* (belonging to them) pronoun

3507 **Nouns not ending in the sound of *s*.** Form the possessive of a noun not ending in the sound of *s* by adding an *apostrophe s*.

Singular:	Benedict's	eggs	the sailor's	cap
	Melba's	toast	the actor's	part
	the woman's	story	the blacksmith's	forge
Plural:	the women's	books	the children's	toys

3508 **Singular nouns ending in the sound of *s*.** Form the possessive of a singular noun ending in the sound of *s* in one of two ways:

- If adding an *apostrophe s* does not make the singular noun difficult to pronounce, do so.

Bill Burgess's	bat	the boss's	desk
Congress's	debate	the witness's	testimony

- If adding an *apostrophe s* makes the singular noun difficult to pronounce, add an *apostrophe only*.

Sophocles'	tragedies	Ulysses'	return
Grand Forks'	sidewalks	Massachusetts'	capitol

3509 **Plural nouns ending in the sound of *s*.** Form the possessive of a plural noun ending in the sound of *s* by adding an *apostrophe*.

the witnesses'	testimony	the passengers'	safety
the Hendersons'	mail	five dollars'	worth

3

3510 **Appositives defined.** An **appositive** is a noun that occurs near another noun (or words functioning as a noun), which refers to the same entity. Typically, the noun names the entity; the appositive identifies or explains it. The noun and the appositive can usually be transposed.

Apposition		
Proper noun	**Appositive**	**Rest of Sentence**
Vanderbilt	the author	was present.

Apposition		
Noun	**Appositive**	**Rest of Sentence**
The author	Vanderbilt	was present.

See ¶ 2274 for the use of commas with appositives.

3511 **Possessive forms of appositives.** The indicator of possession is applied to the essential appositive. (See ¶ 2274 for essential appositives.)

Vanderbilt the author's pen has signed many autographs.

The author Vanderbilt's pen has signed many autographs.

Better: The pen of Vanderbilt the author has signed many autographs.

See ¶ 3512 on awkward and misleading possessive appositives.

3512 **Awkward and misleading possessive appositives.** Possessive appositives can be awkward or misleading. *Of* phrases, *used by, owned by, belonging to,* and the like can be used to avoid awkwardness or lack of clarity.

Not: Herb the actor's performance
But: the performance of Herb the actor

Not: Indianapolis, Indiana's center
But: the center of Indianapolis, Indiana

See ¶ 2274 for the use of commas with appositives.

See ¶ 3510-11 for more about appositives.

3

3513 **Compound nouns.** A **compound noun** consists of two or more words combined or used together to serve as a single noun. To create a possessive compound noun, apply an *apostrophe* or an *apostrophe s* to the final word element.

my brother-in-law's	influence
the castaways'	signals
the Johnny-come-latelies'	attitudes
the go-between's	concessions

See ¶ 3201-41 on compounds.

3514 **Gerunds.** A **gerund** is the *-ing* form of a verb serving as a noun. To create the possessive form of a gerund, apply an *apostrophe* or *apostrophe s* to the noun or indefinite pronoun modifying the gerund.

the children's playing   Walter's walking   everyone's talking

3515 **Understood (omitted) nouns.** To create the possessive form of an understood noun, apply an *apostrophe* or *apostrophe s* to the noun modifying the understood (omitted) noun.

Singular: left it at the attorney's (office)
Plural: arriving at the Whartons' (house)

3516 **When to use possessive forms of nouns.** Generally, possessive forms are restricted to nouns representing the following:

animals	distance	organizations	time
celestial bodies	geographic locations	people	value

Possession by inanimate beings other than those listed above is indicated by using a prepositional phrase or by using the noun as a modifier.

Not: the automobile's parts

But: parts { of / for / in } the automobile (A prepositional phrase.)

Or: the automobile parts (The noun as a modifier.)

3517 **Personification.** Expressions suggesting **personification** (giving human qualities to things, places, or ideas) may be stated in possessive form.

Reason's appeal   Principle's discipline   Youth's impatience

See ¶ 3151 for capitalization and personification.

3518 **Personal pronouns and the relative pronoun *who*.** Certain pronouns have irregular possessive forms that do not require the apostrophe.

Pronoun	Possessive	Pronoun	Possessive
I	my, mine	we	our, ours
you	your, yours	they	their, theirs
she	her, hers	it	its
he	his	who	whose

3519 **Indefinite pronouns with regular possessive forms.** Some indefinite pronouns have regular possessive forms requiring use of the apostrophe.

Indefinite Pronoun	Possessive Form	
another	another's	feelings
anybody	anybody's	guess
anyone	anyone's	opinion
either	either's	work
everybody	everybody's	friend
everyone	everyone's	reaction
neither	neither's	effort
no one	no one's	advice
nobody	nobody's	friend
one	one's	health
other	other's	need
others	others'	property
somebody	somebody's	purse
someone	someone's	shoes

3520 **Indefinite pronouns without regular possessive forms.** Some indefinite pronouns have no regular possessive forms. In such cases, brief idiomatic expressions (generally prepositional phrases) are used in lieu of possessive forms.

Pronoun	Possession	Pronoun	Possession
all	of all	many	owned by many
any	of any	none	of none
each	belonging to each	others	of others
few	of few of a few	some	held by some

3521 **Singular possessive abbreviations.** Singular possessive forms of abbreviations are created by adding an *apostrophe s* to the singular form of the abbreviation—regardless of whether the abbreviation is spelled out in speech (FAA) or used as a word in speech (NASA).

the CEO's office   the MBA's report   the CPA's hat

3522 **Plural possessive abbreviations.** Plural possessive forms of abbreviations are created by adding an *apostrophe* to the plural form of the abbreviation—regardless of whether the abbreviation is spelled out in speech (CPA) or used as a word in speech (AMVET).

the CEOs' offices   the MBAs' positions   the CPAs' meetings

3523 **Abbreviations or numbers following personal names.** Possessive forms of personal names ending with abbreviations or numbers follow these patterns:

Singular Add Apostrophe *s*	Plural Add Apostrophe
Hakimar Knodlas Jr.'s essay.	the Hakimar Knodlas Jrs.' children.
Edward Thompson III's car	the Edward Thompson IIIs' home

3

3524 **Joint possession: Nouns.** If *nouns* are used to identify all possessors, joint possession is indicated by using the possessive form of the *final noun* only.

John and Mary's furniture
John and the Joneses' partnership
the Smiths and Mary's understanding
the Smiths and the Joneses' common driveway
the partners and employees' lounge

See ¶ 3525 on mixing nouns and pronouns in joint and separate possession.

3525 **Joint possession: Nouns and pronouns used together.** If a possessive pronoun is used to identify one possessor, joint possession is indicated by using the possessive forms of all nouns and pronouns identifying possessors. Do **not** use this form if it creates ambiguity, as it *may* in the first five examples and *does* in the **last** two examples.

his and Mary's trip
his and the Joneses' effort
John's and her meeting
John's and their resolution
the Smiths' and her foray
the Smiths' and their voyage
the partners' and their lounge

	Avoid if Ambiguous	**Preferred**
Joint Possession	Emile's and his home	Emile and Mario's home
	his and Emile's home	Mario and Emile's home
	the partners' and their lounge	the partners and employees' lounge
	their and the partners' lounge	the employees and partners' lounge

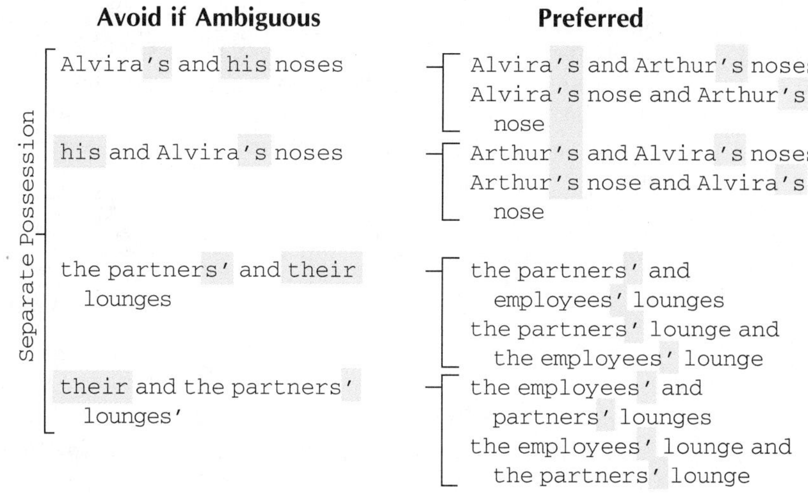

	Avoid if Ambiguous	Preferred
Separate Possession	Alvira's and his noses	Alvira's and Arthur's noses Alvira's nose and Arthur's nose
	his and Alvira's noses	Arthur's and Alvira's noses Arthur's nose and Alvira's nose
	the partners' and their lounges	the partners' and employees' lounges the partners' lounge and the employees' lounge
	their and the partners' lounges'	the employees' and partners' lounges the employees' lounge and the partners' lounge

3

3526 **Separate possession.** To indicate separate possession, use the possessive form of the noun or pronoun that identifies each possessor.

John's	and Mary's	ears
John's	and the Joneses'	boats
the Smiths'	and Mary's	musical instruments
the Smiths'	and the Joneses'	front porches
his	and Mary's	front row seats
John's	and her	opposing opinions
the partners'	and employees'	lounges

See ¶ 3525 on mixing nouns and pronouns in joint and separate possession.

3527 **Organizational names ending with an abbreviation, a prepositional phrase, or a number.** The possessive form of an organizational name that ends with an abbreviation, a prepositional phrase, or a number is created by adding an *apostrophe* or an *apostrophe s* to the final character or word element. (See the quick reference in ¶ 3505. Also see ¶ 3530 on using the organization's adopted style for writing its name.)

South-Western Publishing Co.'s	book
National Association of the Deaf's	membership
Engine Number 9's	advertisement
American Institute of Architects'	convention

3528 **Organizational names containing possessives.** Organizational names containing possessives should be written as preferred by those who represent the organization. Look at return addresses, letterheads, directory listings, and the like to determine what that preference is. (See ¶ 3530 on using the organization's adopted style.)

International Juggler's	Association
Children's	Book Council
Lands'	End clothing
American Nurses'	Association

3529 **Organizational names containing regular plural forms.** Some organizational names contain regular (ending in *s*) plurals that, with the addition of an apostrophe, would be possessives. Presume that they are **not** meant to be possessives and write them as they appear—without the apostrophe. (See ¶ 3530 on using an organization's adopted style for writing its name.)

American Sportscasters Association	National Consumers League
Boys and Girls Clubs of America	Songwriters Guild of America

3530 **Organization's adopted style for its name.** Paragraphs 3527-29 reflect prevailing practices. Some organizations choose not to follow the prevailing practices: South-Western Publishing Co. (not *Southwestern* and not *Company*) and Delta Air Lines (not *Airlines*) for example. Whether or not they choose to follow prevailing practices, most organizations adopt standard styles for writing their names. One should observe the preference of the organization itself in this matter.

3

3531 **Avoid nested possessives.** The use of multiple possessives in the same sentence can be both awkward and confusing. Substitute *belonging to, owned by, of* phrases, *nouns as modifiers,* and the like, for possessives, or reword the entire thought to avoid possessives altogether.

Not: Debbie Jarvis's sorority's kittens' bed

But: the bed of the kittens belonging to Debbie Jarvis's sorority.

Or: the kittens' bed in Debbie Jarvis's sorority

Or: Debbie Jarvis belongs to a sorority that has some kittens. This is their bed.

3532 **Singular/plural possessives.** There are some cases in which seemingly plural words are treated as singular.

Mother's Day	traveler's checks
Father's Day	painter's colic

donkey's years (a long time)
farmer's lung (a disease)

3533 **Pronoun contractions versus possessive pronouns.** The apostrophe is used in pronoun contractions to indicate the omission of letters. (See ¶ 2002 on placement of the apostrophe.) The apostrophe is not used in or following possessive pronouns.

Pronoun Contractions		*vs*	**Possessive Pronouns**	
it's	(it is)		its	(belonging to it)
they're	(they are)		their	(belonging to them)
who's	(who is)		whose	(belonging to whom)
you're	(you are)		your	(belonging to you)

3

SPELLING

3601 **Pronunciation.** The most effective way to improve spelling is to improve pronunciation. Even though many words are not spelled as they are pronounced and most spelling rules have numerous exceptions, correct pronunciation will usually provide at least the framework of letters that makes it possible to look the word up in the dictionary.

Correct pronunciation can eliminate spelling errors caused by *adding* syllables (ath*e*letic instead of athletic, hind*e*rance instead of hindrance, etc.). It can eliminate spelling errors caused by *dropping* syllables (probbly instead of prob*a*bly, reconize instead of reco*g*nize). It helps one avoid the transposition of letters (irreve*l*ant instead of irre*l*evant). Finally, correct pronunciation helps eliminate simple phonetic errors (*b*retzel instead of *p*retzel, zink instead of *s*ink).

3602 **Dictionary use.** Another effective aid to correct spelling is a good dictionary. Spelling in *Reference Manual for the Office* is based on *Merriam-Webster's Collegiate Dictionary, Tenth Edition.*

3603 **Computerized spell checkers, dictionaries, and thesauruses.** Spell checkers (to check spelling and certain other errors), thesauruses (to assist in word choice by identifying related and substitute words), and dictionaries (to spell and define words) are available for computers. Some are included in word processing programs where they pop-up when called for; others are separate TSR (transfer and stay resident) programs that operate similarly when they are loaded with a word processing program.

3604 **Rules for spelling.** Some spelling rules apply to only a few words and have numerous exceptions. The more useful rules apply to larger numbers of words and have fewer exceptions. Some of the more useful rules are discussed in ¶ 3605-10.

3605 **Word roots.** Many English words are derived from Latin or Greek roots. The **root** is the *central part* of the word, the core of meaning. Familiarity with the structure of words—prefixes, roots, and suffixes—helps one recognize and remember spelling patterns.

Latin or Greek Root	English Root	Meaning	English Words
corpus (L)	corp	body	corpse, corsage, corporation
credere (L)	cred	believe	credit, credible, credence
nomen (L)	nomin	name	nominate, nominal, nominee
novus (L)	nov	new	novel, innovate, novice

3606 **Prefixes.** A **prefix** is a syllable (or syllables) placed *before* the root to qualify the meaning of the root.

Prefix	Meaning	Example
de	down from	decry, debase, decline
dis	opposite, not	discredit, disable, disagree
re	again, back	repeat, rebuild, return

3607 **Suffixes.** A **suffix** is a syllable (or syllables) placed *after* the root to qualify the meaning of the root.

Suffix	Meaning	Examples
able, ible	capable of, fit for, worthy	workable invisible incurable
dom	condition of being, jurisdiction	wisdom kingdom freedom
ward	in the direction of	northward seaward inward

3608 **Final e before a suffix.**

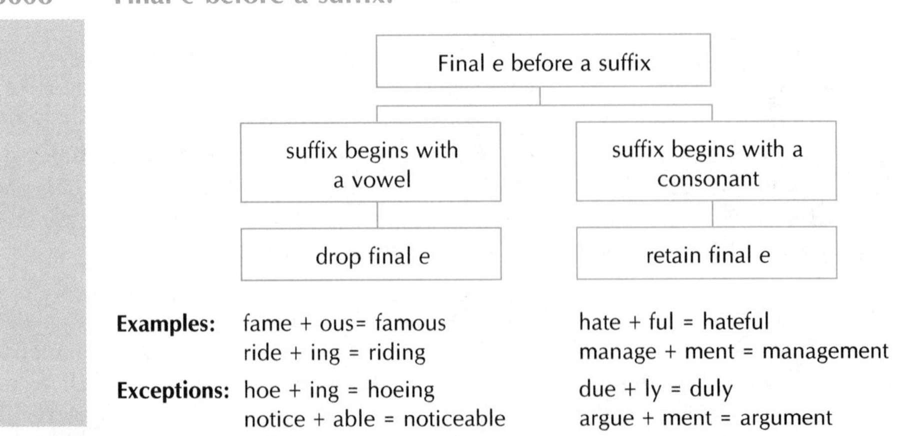

3609 **Doubling the final consonant when adding a suffix.**

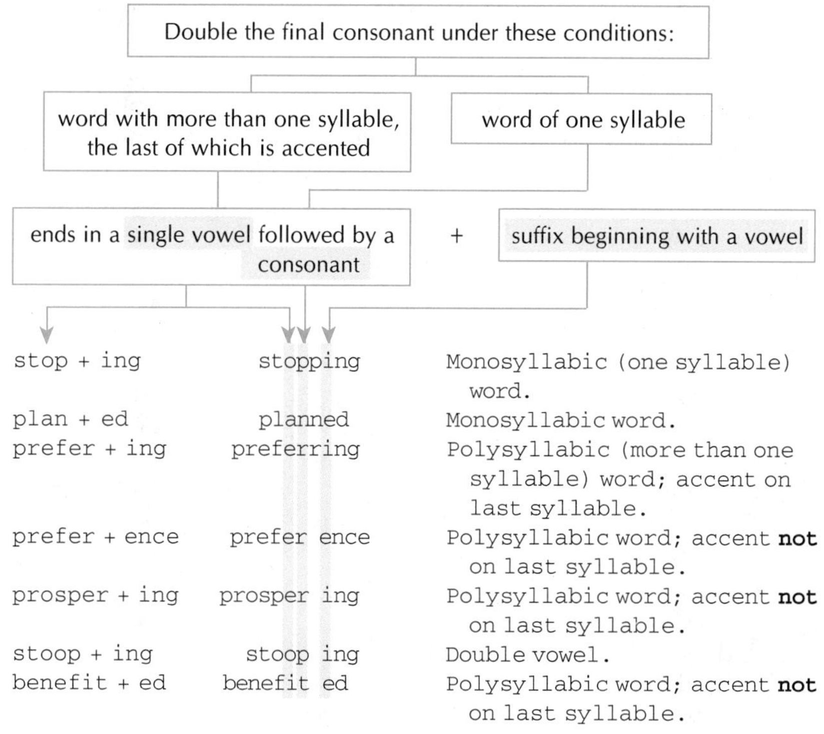

Double the final consonant under these conditions:
word with more than one syllable, the last of which is accented
word of one syllable
ends in a single vowel followed by a consonant
+
suffix beginning with a vowel
stop + ing
stopping
Monosyllabic (one syllable) word.
plan + ed
planned
Monosyllabic word.
prefer + ing
preferring
Polysyllabic (more than one syllable) word; accent on last syllable.
prefer + ence
prefer ence
Polysyllabic word; accent not on last syllable.
prosper + ing
prosper ing
Polysyllabic word; accent not on last syllable.
stoop + ing
stoop ing
Double vowel.
benefit + ed
benefit ed
Polysyllabic word; accent not on last syllable.

Exceptions: format (formatting, formatted); program (programming, programmed).

3610 ***ie* or *ei*.** Use *i* before e except directly following *c* if the combined vowels are sounded like long e.

Examples:

Sounded Like Long e		Not Sounded Like Long e	
believe	field	deign	neighbor
chief	niece	foreign	weight

Exceptions: either* neither* seize leisure financier

**either* and *neither* were originally pronounced with a long *i* sound (eye′ ther). Some persons still prefer that pronunciation.

3611 **Word list.** The following words are frequently misspelled. Some of the words **may** be spelled in more than one way. In those cases, the preferred (most common) spelling is listed.

A
abbreviation
abscond
absence
abundant
academic
academy
acceptable
access
accessible
accidentally
acclaim
accommodate
accompanied
accompanies
accompanying
accomplish
accurately
accuser
accusing
accustom

MORE

achieve
achievement
acknowledgment
acoustics
acquaintance
acquiesce
acquire
acquisition
across
actual
actuality
actually
address
adequate
adjacent
admission
admit
admittance
adolescence
adolescent
adrenaline
adsorb
advantage
advantageous
adventurous
adversity
advertisement
advice
advisable
advise
advisement
advisory
aegis
aerial
aerosol
aesthetic
affect
affectation
affective
affidavit
affirmative
affluence
affluent
against
aggravate
aggressive
aging
aisle
align
all right
alleged
alleviate
allocate
allocation
allot
allotment
allotted
allowed
allusion
alphabetize
already
aluminum
amalgamate
amateur
ambulatory
amenable
amiable
amicable
amortize
amphibious
amphitheater
amplifier
analogous
analysis
analyze
annually
anomalous
anticipated
anxiety
apologetically
apologize
apology
apparatus
apparent
applicable
applicant
application
applying
appoint
appointment
appreciation
approaches
appropriate
approximate
appurtenance
appurtenant
aptitude
arbitrary
arbitrate
arbitration
arbitrator
archaic
architect
architectural
arraign
arrogance
arrogant
arrogate
artificial
ascend
assess
assessment
assist
assistance
assistants
associate
association
athlete
athletic
attack
attempts
attendance
attitude
attorney
audience
authoritative
autumn
auxiliary

B

baccalaureate
bachelor
bailiff
bailiwick
balloon
ballot
bankruptcy
banquet
barbarian
bargain
barrel
basically
beautified
beginner

beginning
behavior
beneficial
beneficiary
benefit
benefited
biased
biscuit
bookkeeper
brilliance
brochure
buoyant
bureau
buses
business

C

cafeteria
calendar
calorie
campaign
canceled
cancellation
capability
capacitor
capacity
capital
capitalism
capitol
capricious
career
catalog
category
ceiling
cemetery
certificate
challenge
chandelier
changeable
changing
characteristic
chargeable
charisma
charismatic
chasm
chassis
chauffeur
chronic
chronological
cipher
circuit
circuitry
cite
clamorous
clientele
coincidence
collateral
column
commission
commitment
committee
companies
comparatively
compelled
compensation
competition
competitive
competitor
compliance
compliant
compulsion
concede
conceivable
conceive
concentrate
conception
condemn
connoisseur
connotation
conqueror
conscience
conscientious
conscious
consecutively
continuous
continuously
controlling
controversial
convenience
convenient
coolly
cooperate
cooperation
cooperative
coordinate
coordinating
coordination
coordinator
correlate
correspondence
correspondent
correspondents
council
counsel
counselor
counterfeit
courteous
courtesy
coverage
creditor
criteria
criterion
criticism
curiosity
currency
curriculum
cylinder

D

debtor
deception
decided
deductible
defendant
defense
deferred
definitely
definition
dependent
descendant
describe
description
desirability
desirable
desperate
destruction
detrimental
devastating
development
dictionary
difference
dilemma
diligence
disappear

MORE

CONTINUED

disappoint
disastrous
discipline
discrimination
discussion
disgusted
disillusioned
dismissal
dissatisfied
dissimilar
doctrinaire
dominant
dormitories
dossier
drudgery

E

ecstasy
effective
efficiency
efficient
eliminate
embarrass
emphasis
emphasize
employee
encourage
enforcement
engineering
enterprise
entertain
entertainment
entrepreneur
enumerate
envelop (v)
envelope (n)
environment
environmental
equipment
equipped
equivalent
escapade
escrow
especially
evaluate
evaluation
evidently
exaggerate
exceed
excellence
excellent
excitable
exercise
exhaust
exhaustible
exhibition
exhilaration
existence
existent
exonerate
exorbitant
expense
experience
explanation
extension
extraordinary
extremely

F

facsimile
fallacy
familiar
families
fantasy
fascinating
feasible
fictitious
fiery
finally
finance
financial
financially
financier
fiscal
fluorescent
forehead
foreign
foreigners
forfeit
forward
friend
friendliness
fulfill
fundamental
fundamentally
furniture
further

G

gaiety
gauge
genuine
ghost
glamorous
glamour
government
grammar
grammatically
grandeur
grateful
grievous
gruesome
guarantee (v)
guaranteed
guardian
guidance

H

handicapped
handkerchief
handled
happened
happiness
harass
height
hemorrhage
hesitancy
heterogeneous
hindrance
hopeless
hospitalization
humorist
hundred
hunger
hurriedly
hygiene
hypocrisy
hypocrite

I

ignorance
ignorant
imagination

imitation
immediately
immense
imminent
impasse
implement
implementation
implication
importance
important
incident
incidentally
increase
incredible
indefinite
independence
independent
indicate
indication
indispensable
individually
industrious
inevitable
influential
ingenious
ingredient
initiative
innocuous
innovation
innuendo
inoculate
insistence
installation
instrument
intelligent
intentionally
intercede
interfering
interim
interpret
interpretation
interrupt
involve
irrelevant
irresistible
irritable
itinerary

J
judgment

K
knowledge
knowledgeable

L
labeled
laboratory
laborer
laboriously
lavatory
ledger
legitimate
leisurely
lengthening
lessee
lessor
liable
liaison
library
license
lien
lieutenant
likable
liquefy
literature
liveliest
livelihood
liveliness
loneliness
luxury

M
magazine
magnificence
maintain
maintenance
manageable
management
maneuver
manufacturer
marriage
material
mathematics
medicine
medieval
melancholy
memento
messenger
methods
mileage
milieu
millennia
millionaire
miniature
minuscule
minute
minutiae
misapprehension
miscellaneous
mischief
mischievous
misspell
monitor
moral
morale
mortgage

N
necessary
negotiate
neither
nevertheless
notable
noticeable
nuclear
numerous

O
obliged
obsolescent
obstacle
occasion
occasionally
occupation
occupational
occurred
occurrence
offered
omission
omit
omitted

3

MORE

3

opinion
opponent
opportunity
opposite
optimism
optimistic
organization
original
outrageous

P

pamphlet
parallel
paralyzed
parliament
partially
particular
peculiar
perceive
performance
permanent
permissible
permitted
perseverance
persistent
personal
personnel
persuade
pertain
pertinent
phenomenal
phenomenon
philosophy
physically
physician
picnicking
plateau
plausible
politician
possess
possession
prairie
precede
precedence
preceding
preferable
prejudice
prerogative
presence
prestige
presumptuous
pretense
prevalent
primitive
principal
principle
privilege
probably
procedure
proceed
production
profession
programmed
programmer
prohibition
prominent
promissory
pronunciation
propaganda
psychiatric
psychiatrist
psychoanalysis
psychological
psychology
psychopathic
psychosomatic
pursuant

Q

qualitative
quantitative
questionnaire

R

receipt
receive
recognize
recommend
referred
referring
regrettable
reinforce
relevant
reminiscence
remittance
renaissance
rescind
reservoir
restaurant
résumé
revealed
rhapsody
rhetoric
rhetorical
rhythm
ridiculous

S

sacrilegious
satellite
satirize
scent
schedule
science
scientific
scissors
secession
secretary
sediment
sentiment
separation
sergeant
serviceable
siege
significance
significant
significantly
simile
simple
simultaneous
sincerely
sizable
skillful
soliloquy
sophomore
souvenir
specific
specifically
specifications
specify
statutory
strength
stretch
structural

subpoena	symmetry	tremendous
subsequent	synonymous	tyranny
subtlety		
subtly	**T**	**U**
success	tariff	unanimous
succession	technique	undoubtedly
sufficient	temperament	unforgettable
suing	temperature	unmanageable
superintendent	tenant	unnecessary
supersede	tendency	unwieldy
suppose	tentative	usable
suppress	theater	usage
surgeon	theories	using
surreptitious	therefore	utilization
surrounding	tragedy	
surveillance	traveled	**V-Z**
susceptible	traveler	weird
syllable		

3

3700 WORD DIVISION

WORD DIVISION

3701 **Avoid word division.** Word division should be avoided when possible. Divided words can be confusing to a reader and thus interrupt speedy comprehension of what is written. When words must be divided, try to maintain balanced margins. Divide between syllables at a point that least hinders reader comprehension.

MORE

- **Reading interrupted with word division:**

The Pediatric Care Unit needs medical secretaries who recognize the importance of accurate medical records and careful treatment of patients. These areas were stressed in my medical transcription training.

- **Reading clearer without word division:**

The Pediatric Care Unit needs medical secretaries who
recognize the importance of accurate medical records and
careful treatment of patients. These areas were stressed
in my medical transcription training.

Most word processing software provides some assistance with word division by indicating (when reformulating a paragraph) a word falling beyond the right margin. This process allows the writer to determine an appropriate place for word division or to decide not to divide the word. If word division is not indicated, the program adds additional spacing to the current line to balance the right margin and carries the word not divided to the beginning of the next line. This automatic balancing of each line reduces word division.

3702 **"Do nots" of word division.** One of the most common uses of the hyphen is to divide long words at the end of a line so that all lines of a printed document are balanced. Before reviewing how such words are divided, however, it is important to review some "do nots" of word division (¶ 3703-11).

3703 **Unnecessary division.** Do **not** divide words unless necessary. Avoid word division whenever possible.

3704 **One-syllable and other short words.** Do **not** divide one syllable or very short words (five or fewer letters) of more than one syllable. For example, do not divide the following words:

home	town	could	out	love
help	item	would	title	enter
stone	week	should	boat	ever

3705 **Confusing divisions.** Do **not** divide words if the divided word looks strange, or if the divided word would cause confusion or mislead the reader.

piz- zazz	picto- rial	ide- alistic	but- toning

3706 **Avoid stranded letters.** Do **not** divide a word if doing so leaves only one or two letters on the current line or if you carry only one or two letters to the next line.

enter	**Not:**	en- ter	stranger	**Not:**	strang- er
duress	**Not:**	du- ress	sickly	**Not:**	sick- ly

3707 **Words between pages.** Do **not** divide a word at the end of a page.

3708 **Consecutive lines with divided words.** Do **not** divide words on consecutive lines or have many divided words on the same page. Remember that each divided word may cause a break in the reader's concentration and thus limit understanding.

3709 **Contractions.** Do **not** divide contractions.

wouldn't	**Not:**	would- n't	haven't	**Not:**	have- n't

3710 **Abbreviations.** Do **not** divide abbreviations.

NAACP	**Not:**	NAA- CP	UNICEF	**Not:**	UNI- CEF

3

3711 **First and last lines of a paragraph.** Do **not** divide a word at the end of the last full line of a paragraph. **Avoid** dividing a word ending the first line of a paragraph.

3712 **Divide between syllables.** Divide words only between syllables. While words can be divided at most of the syllable breaks indicated in your dictionary, words divided according to the guidelines in ¶ 3713-28 are easier to comprehend. Refer to ¶ 3611 for commonly misspelled words; consult your dictionary for syllable identification of all other words.

3713 **Break in midword.** Divide at the syllable break that is as close as possible to the middle of the word. Since half the word will be on one line and half on the next line, the divided word will be easier to read. (/=syllable break)

opportunities	op/por/tu/ni/ties	opportu-nities
compensation	com/pen/sa/tion	compen-sation
requirement(s)	re/quire/ment(s)	require-ment(s)
interpret	in/ter/pret	inter-pret

3714 **Divide for clear meaning.** Divide at natural syllable breaks that help clarify meaning.

extracurricular	ex/tra/cur/ric/u/lar	extra-curricular
environmental	en/vi/ron/men/tal	environ-mental
development	de/vel/op/ment	develop-ment
introduction	in/tro/duc/tion	intro-duction

Caution: When the same word can be used as both a noun and a verb, the pronunciation (and thus the syllabication) may also change.

	As a Noun	**As a Verb**
progress	prog-ress	pro-gress
founder	founder (do not divide)	foun-der
project	proj-ect	pro-ject

3715 **Dividing hyphenated compound words.** Divide hyphenated compound words immediately after the hyphen. Hyphenated expressions of more than two words are divided after the hyphen closest to the middle of the expression.

full-length	full-	length
self-educated	self-	educated
jack-in-the-box	jack-in-	the-box

3716 **Dividing solid compound words.** Divide solid compound words between the word elements.

honeymoon	honey-	moon
checkbook	check-	book
firsthand	first-	hand

3

3717 **Dividing root word ending in double consonant.** When a root word ends in a double consonant, divide the word after the double consonant, prior to any added suffix.

falling	fall-	ing
recallable	recall-	able
businessperson	business-	person

However, sometimes the syllables change when the suffix is added and extra letters are eliminated (always consult your dictionary if you are unsure).

impress + sion	impression	
im/pres/sion	impres-	sion
secede + sion	secession	
se/ces/sion	seces-	sion

3718 **Dividing root word ending in vowel + consonant.** When a root word . . .

- ends in a vowel plus consonant
- and the final consonant is doubled when adding a suffix
- and the suffix creates a new syllable, divide the word between the doubled consonant.

omitted	omit-	ted
riddance	rid-	dance

3719 **Dividing root word with doubled letter.** When a root word . . .

- contains a doubled letter
- and has at least two syllables, divide between the doubled consonant.

letters	let-	ters
accommodate	accom-	modate

3720 **Titles of relatives.** Use the following guidelines for dividing titles of relatives.

- **Prefix *great.*** Words containing the prefix *great*- should be divided immediately after the hyphen.

great-grandfather	great-	grandfather
great-grandmother	great-	grandmother

- **Suffix *in-law.*** Words containing the suffix *in-law* should be divided at the hyphen preceding the suffix.

mother-in-law	mother-	in-law
brother-in-law	brother-	in-law

- **Solid compounds.** Solid compounds that describe family relationships should be divided between word elements.

stepson	step-	son
grandmother	grand-	mother
godfather	god-	father

3

3721 **Dividing names.** Every attempt should be made to keep full names together. However, where space is limited and in technical material, names may be divided between the first name (including middle initial) and surname. (/ = break point)

Maria Elena Diaz de Villegas	Maria Elena/ Diaz de Villegas
Dr. William A. McNae	Dr. William A./ McNae

3722 **Dividing titles with names.** When an extremely long title precedes a name, a break may occur immediately following the title. (/ = break point)

Administrative Assistant Winston Richter
Administrative Assistant/
Winston Richter

Executive Vice President Sue Skidmore
Executive Vice President/
Sue Skidmore

3723 **Dividing numbers (including dates and addresses).** Avoid dividing numbers whenever possible. When word division **must** be used. . .

- divide **long numbers** after a comma, leaving at least four numbers on the first line and carrying at least six numbers to the following line.

1,356,864,900	1,356,- 864,900

- divide **dates** following the comma, between the date and year, without a hyphen.

February 18, 1994	February 18, 1994

MORE

CONTINUED

- divide **street addresses** between street name and descriptor, without a hyphen.

2055 Belding Court	2055 Belding Court

or

between words of a two-word street name.

8625 North Bassett Way	8625 North Bassett Way

- divide **numbered or lettered lists** immediately before the number or letter, without a hyphen.

```
. . . bringing the gift certificate,
(2) Visit the store of your choice, (3) . . .
```

3

3724 **Dividing cities, states, and zip codes.** Break names of places between the city and state or between state and zip code. Two-word city or state names may be broken between the two words.

```
Fort Lauderdale,
      FL 33313-0123
Upper Saddle
      River, NJ 07458
Austin, Texas
      78705-7111
```

3725 **Dividing prefixes and suffixes.** Divide words immediately following any prefix or immediately before any suffix whenever possible or logical.

introduction	intro-	duction
photogenic	photo-	genic
activity	activ-	ity
extremism	extrem-	ism

Caution: Often when a prefix or suffix is added or changed, the syllabication of the root word changes.

consist	con-sist	**But:**	consistency	consis-tency
preventing	prevent-ing	**But:**	prevention	preven-tion

3726 **Dividing a sentence with a dash.** Divide sentences that contain a dash immediately following the dash.

```
When she arrives—and it will be late—
the meeting will begin.
```

3727 **Vowels as single letter syllables.** When a one-letter vowel syllable comes within a word, divide the word immediately after this vowel.

regulate	regu-	late
manipulate	manipu-	late
democratic	demo-	cratic

But, when a single-vowel syllable immediately precedes an ending two-letter syllable, divide before the vowel.

pacify	pac-	ify
humility	humil-	ity

Or when a single-vowel syllable *a* or *i* is followed by an ending syllable *-ble, -bly, -cle,* or *-cal,* divide before the vowel.

comical	com-	ical
operable	oper-	able
possibly	poss-	ibly
miracle	mir-	acle
probably	prob-	ably

3728 **Two vowels together.** Usually when two vowels come together within a word with each vowel sounded separately, divide the word between the vowels.

anxiety	anxi-	ety
continuation	continu-	ation
psychiatric	psychi-	atric
But: psychiatry	psychia-	try

But, when the two vowels represent one combined sound, divide the word to keep the vowels together.

faithless	faith-	less
housewarming	house-	warming
millionaire	million-	aire

CHAPTER 4

INFORMATION PROCESSING

THE INFORMATION AGE

4001 **Information processing.** **Information processing** is the gathering, refinement, and transmission of data or information. Although *data* and *information* may be used interchangeably, those who are careful with words use *data* when they wish to emphasize the raw material and *information* when they wish to emphasize the finished product. Data, through refinement, becomes information just as wheat, through refinement, becomes flour.

MORE

The purpose of information processing is to make the raw material—data—more useful: to convert data to information. For example, utility companies routinely gather raw data (take meter readings), refine or process the data (convert meter readings into utility bills), and transmit the resulting information (utility bills) to customers.

Information is knowledge. It is usually expressed in letters (AfDj), figures (3945), or special characters (@#$%). Information looks like this:

(1) `2# @ $3/# = $6`

(2) `two pounds at three dollars per pound equals six dollars`

(3) `Avante is 5'8" tall; she weighs 121 pounds.`

(4) `Travis is six feet one inch tall; he weighs 167 pounds.`

Lines (1) and (2) contain the same information; they differ in form only.

Processing is refining data to make it more useful. Lines (3) and (4) can be made more useful (and more understandable, in this case) by expressing all measurements of height and weight in figures—and arranging the information in tabular form.

Name	Height	Weight
Avante	5'8"	121
Travis	6'1"	167

Processing includes compiling data (gathering it from different sources), categorizing data (placing it in categories, such as height and weight), sorting data (alphabetically, numerically, by weight, by date, and so forth), ranking data (by dollar value, size, ability and the like), and other operations that refine data to make it more useful.

Processing may include calculation. For example, if *quantity* and *price* are among the data items, having the computer multiply them together to determine the *amount* will probably be part of processing. Processing may also include *formatting,* which is what we did when we chose a tabular arrangement for the height and weight information.

Now, suppose that Avante and Travis are members of the basketball team and that we wish to compile height and weight information for the team's five starters.

BASKETBALL TEAM

Name	Height	Weight
Avante	5'8"	121
Travis	6'1"	167
Charlie	6'6"	224
Gertie	6'0"	159
Abner	6'2"	219

Obviously, the information is now much clearer than it would be in sentence form. We could further process (refine) it by alphabetizing the name column, arranging the items by height or weight, and so forth.

4002 **Office work in the Information Age.** The current era is often described as the Information Age. Certainly, innovations in information processing have changed the way office work is done. New devices, methods, knowledge, and skills that characterize the Information Age are discussed in chapters 4-7. Chapter 4 concentrates on the devices used in the Information Age office.

4003 **Offices then and now.** The offices of fifty years ago were equipped with manual typewriters, hand calculators, mimeograph machines, spirit duplicators, carbon paper, and plug-and-socket telephone switchboards. Today, the office is a showcase of Information Age technology: computers, laser printers, xerographic copiers, automated telephone systems, and fax machines.

4004 **Microchips.** The development of microchip technology was indeed revolutionary. It made possible the mass production of inexpensive chips, some containing the equivalent of thousands of transistors, resistors, and capacitors. The electronic circuitry for a computer, clock radio, or TV set can be mass-produced by a process analogous to printing—in contrast to the old method of hand assembling components that, continuing the analogy, is comparable to writing thousands of copies of a book by hand—slow, laborious, and expensive.

In the manufacture of a microchip, the design of the circuitry is lithographed on a wafer of semiconductor material, usually polished silicon, about 1/4-inch square. The chip is then treated with acid, which etches the pattern of the circuitry into the silicon. Other chemical and physical processes may be applied repeatedly to create several layers of circuitry on the same chip. Finally, the chip is mounted inside a plastic case and equipped with connectors that allow it to be plugged into a circuit board.

The small size of the microchip makes smaller electronic devices possible; the ability to reproduce complex circuitry inexpensively makes these devices more affordable. The Information Age as we know it would not have been possible without the microchip.

4005 **Xerography.** The xerographic copier that made inexpensive high-quality, plain-paper dry copies available in most offices has done much to facilitate office work. Laser printers for computers combine laser technology with xerography.

Before xerography, copies were produced by carbon paper, wet-paper photocopiers, thermal copiers (special heat-transfer paper), spirit duplicators (the purple dye process), stencil duplicators, and offset duplicators.

The xerographic process consists of the following steps:

1. A photoconductor drum inside the copier is given a negative electrostatic (static electricity) charge of 2000-6000 volts.
2. The image of the copy is reflected to the drum. White areas are fully reflective; gray areas are partially reflective; black areas do not reflect at all.

MORE

3. Where white, nonimage areas reflect light to the drum, the negative charge is erased. Where black, image areas do not reflect light to the drum; the negative charge is retained. Areas that are neither black nor white reflect varying amounts of light.
4. Positively charged black toner is wiped across the drum.
5. The darkest areas retain the greatest charge and attract the most toner; the more toner, the blacker the image. This reproduces sharp, dense blacks, clear whites, and a full range of gray tones.
6. The negative charge on the drum is relaxed, but the image remains.
7. A heavy negative charge is applied to the copy paper before it passes between the drum and a roller. That charge attracts the image from the drum to the paper.
8. The paper passes between the fuser rollers where heat and pressure fix the image permanently to the paper.
9. The drum is erased, cleaned, and recharged for the next copy.

4006 **Lasers.** A **laser** is a concentrated beam of light (energy or radiation in the ultraviolet, visible, or infrared portions of the spectrum) that can be focused and directed very precisely. *Laser* is an acronym for **l**ight **a**mplification by **s**timulated **e**mission of **r**adiation. Lasers are used in micromachining small parts, in surveying, and in precision welding. Lasers are also used in several kinds of surgery.

Laser applications for the computer are primarily in printers, scanners, and bar-code readers. A typical laser printer produces a precise pattern of 300 dpi (dots per inch) or more.

4007 **Satellite communication.** The primary purpose of communication satellites is to relay information between points on the earth's surface via microwave. Earthbound microwave towers are limited in the distance they can cover because of the curvature of the earth.

Live TV transmissions, telephone calls, and other information are routinely relayed from continent to continent by satellite.

Satellites also provide surveillance for defense purposes and reference points for navigation. Navigation equipment can fix the position of a ship or aircraft precisely, using the positions of as many as four satellites to obtain a single confirmed fix.

4008 **Microwave communication.** The microwave band has enough frequency space to accommodate a variety of communication services—more than 100 times the frequency space of all the lower bands: AM, FM, TV, mobile radio, amateur radio, and citizens band radio combined. Microwave transmissions can be concentrated, and are, therefore, highly directional, making them suitable for cross-country transmission systems employing relay towers from 10 to 100 miles apart—and for satellite relay transmissions that traverse far greater distances.

4009 **Fiber optics.** **Fiber optics** are thin, transparent fibers of glass or plastic that transmit light internally. The light waves are used to carry information. They are thinner, lighter, and more efficient than metallic conductors.

Typically, many conductors are bundled in a single cable. In some devices, images are transmitted internally by fiber optic cables in which each pixel is transmitted by a separate conductor. A **pixel** (picture element) is one of the dots that make up an image on the screen.

4010 **Magnetic media.** The 5 ¼-inch floppy disks sold today seem identical to those sold 25 years ago. However, the original capacity of 180kb has been increased to 360kb, 720kb, and now 1.2mb. The newer 3 ½-inch floppy disk has a hard cassette-type case with an automatic shutter opening that protects the disk itself from foreign matter. The 3 ½-inch disk has a capacity of 1.4mb. The same cassette-type case is used for a Floptical™ disk that has a capacity of 21mb.

Similar increases in capacity have been developed for hard drives. Typical hard drive capacity has been increased from 10mb to well over 200mb; some hard drives have capacities exceeding 1GB (approximately 1000MB).

COMPUTER DESIGN

4101 **Computer defined.** A **computer** is a programmable electronic device for processing information. Typically, it receives data that is entered via keyboard, scanner, or other input device; processes that data; and outputs information to a printer, screen, or other output device. A computer

- *Enters* into memory data that is transmitted from a keyboard, scanner, or other input device.
- *Stores* data on disk and *retrieves* it as needed.
- *Calculates* information based on the input.
- *Formats* information: sorts, tabulates, etc.
- *Outputs* information to a printer, monitor, or other output device.

4102 **Mainframe.** Computers are classified by size or power. The largest and most powerful general-purpose computers are **mainframes.** They have enormous amounts of memory and storage, the ability to perform many functions simultaneously, and the capacity to serve many clients simultaneously. For example, the computer used by a credit card company to approve charge sales instantly via telephone line is a mainframe.

The CPU (central processing unit) of a mainframe may include several microchips and additional circuitry (see ¶ 4106).

4103 **Minicomputer.** A **minicomputer** is a midsized computer designed to serve a small company or a single department of about 100 users. A minicomputer system may include terminals and may be included in a LAN (local area network). A minicomputer is larger than a microcomputer and smaller than a mainframe. Its CPU contains more than one chip.

4104 **Microcomputer.** A **microcomputer** is a small computer; its CPU consists of a single microchip. It is may be a desktop, laptop, notebook, subnotebook, or handheld computer.

4105 **System case.** The **system case** is the cabinet in which the main circuitry and central components of the computer system are housed. It usually contains all the system components other than the keyboard, display, printer, and other input/output devices. The system case varies with the design of the computer: horizontal desktop, tower, laptop, notebook, or handheld.

4106 **CPU.** The **central processing unit** is the main device that controls other components in the system. In a microcomputer, the CPU is a single microchip (the microprocessor) and the circuitry that directly supports it (see illustration 4106.1). Main memory is sometimes considered part of the CPU. The system case contains the CPU—and much more (see ¶ 4105).

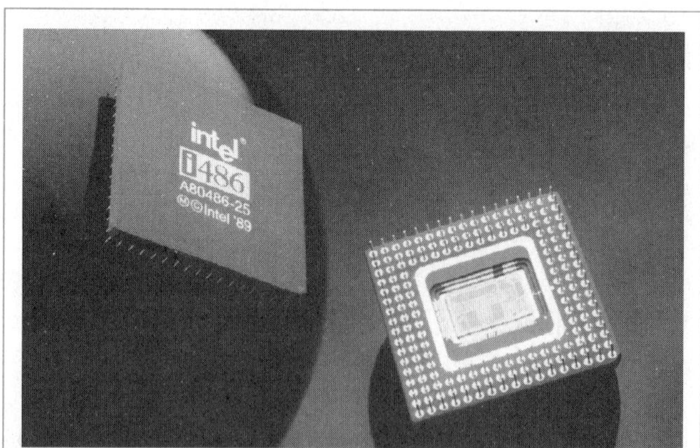

Illustration 4106.1 Intel486™ Microprocessor
(Photo courtesy of Intel Corporation)

Early personal computers (PCs) were identified by model name: PC, XT, AT. Currently, PCs are identified by the three low-order digits of numbers identifying their CPU chips: 286 for computers using the 80286 chip, 386 for computers using the 80386 chip, 486 for computers using the 80486 chip, and so on. A suffix indicates a specific variation of the chip: 386SX, 486DX, and so forth.

4107 **Motherboard.** The **motherboard,** or *system board,* is the circuit board on which the CPU, other microchips, circuitry, and major internal components are mounted. It is located inside the system box.

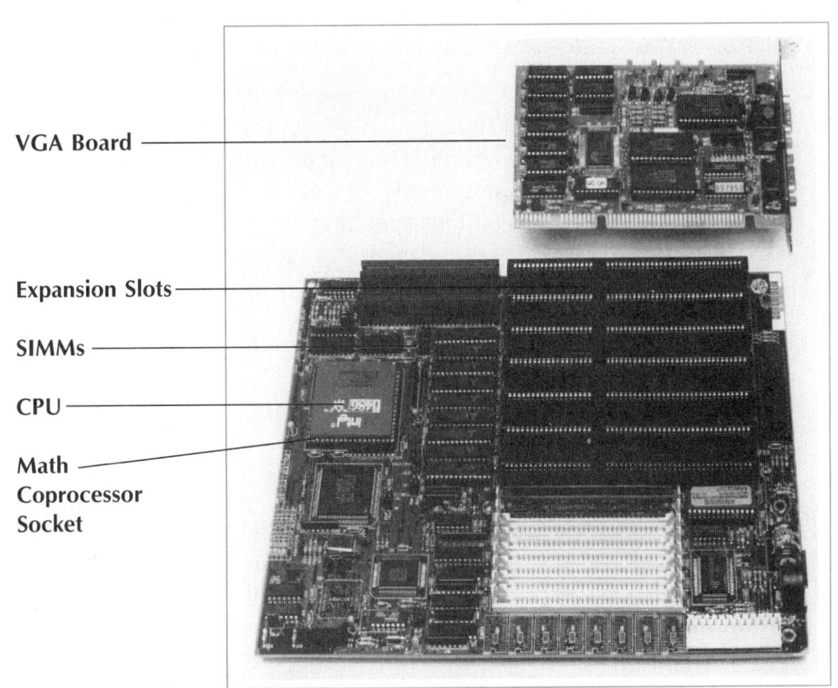

Illustration 4107.1 Motherboard
(Photo courtesy of Stephen McBrady/PhotoEdit)

The motherboard in illustration 4107.1 has eight expansion slots. Expansion slots are connected to the bus. Each slot provides the connections for a circuit board that controls a component of the system. Expansion boards can be purchased to add a component to the system, upgrade a component for better performance, or replace a component that has malfunctioned. The circuit board in the illustration is a VGA (video graphics adapter) board that controls a high-resolution monitor.

4108 **Bus.** The **bus** is the main line of the computer's circuitry. It is located on the motherboard and consists of parallel electrical conductors connecting the major components: CPU, memory, disk drives, and so on. The faster data can travel on the bus, the faster the computer can operate.

The bus may have 8, 16, or 32 channels. Just as an expressway with many lanes moves traffic faster, a bus with more channels moves data faster. Early PC buses had 8 channels; the newer ones have 32. A 32-bit bus is so named because it can move 32 bits of data in parallel.

BASIC COMPUTER CONCEPTS: GLOSSARY OF TERMS

Abort To cancel or terminate a program or operation before its completion. Many programs designate an abort key (frequently *<Escape>*) that allows the user to terminate various operations controlled by the program and another key (or menu choice) to terminate the program itself.

Access To locate and read data from or to write data to memory or storage. See, also, ¶ 4413-14 and 4535.

Access code See ¶ 4413-14.

Access privilege See ¶ 4535.

Access time The time required for a program or peripheral device to find a single byte of information and make it available to the system for processing.

Acoustic coupler See ¶ 4505.

Address A location in memory or storage.

Agents See ¶ 4534.

AI (Artificial Intelligence) A field of endeavor in which computer scientists attempt to develop computer systems that emulate human intelligence in areas such as problem solving and language translation.

Aliasing The rough-edge effect created by bitmapped graphics. Although bitmapped graphics can reproduce straight and smooth horizontal and vertical lines, diagonal lines and curves take on a jagged, step-like appearance caused by the dot pattern. The protruding dots are called **jaggies.** The effect is called **aliasing.**

Align *Justification,* see ¶ 5322. *Proofreader's marks,* see ¶ 5036.

Alternate <Alt> key Provides an alternate use for each function key and for some other keys. In a word processor, for example, *<F2>* might call the spell checker, *<Alt>+<F2>* the dictionary, and *<Ctrl>+<F2>* the thesaurus.

Analog A type of measurement, description, or representation based on continuous signals—as the moving hand of a clock represents the passage of time or the rise of mercury or alcohol in a thermometer represents an increase in temperature.

Contrast with *digital.*

Append To add at the end. Data can be appended to a file; a file can be appended to a database.

Application software See ¶ 4400.

Architecture Computer design that specifies the components of the system and their arrangement. **Open architecture** is a design that is made public, permitting any manufacturer to market components for the system. The original PC standards are examples of open architecture. Since many components, upgrades, adapters, and so on, plug into the bus via expansion slots, the design of buses and expansion slots is one of the most critical aspects of open architecture.

Proprietary architecture is a computer design that is not in the public domain. The manufacturer retains the right to use the design and may license or sell that right to others. Proprietary architecture limits the ability of competing manufacturers to develop upgrades, expansions, and the like, for the system.

Archive To use an archiving utility program to **compress** a file for inactive storage. Archived files require less space on the disk or other storage medium. Before an archived file can be used, the same archiving utility program must be used to **decompress** the file (i.e., return it to its original form).

Artwork See ¶ 5311-14.

ASCII characters (American Standard Code for Information Interchange) The first generally accepted character set for computers was the **ASCII** character set, which assigns the numbers 0-127 to commonly used symbols. After the original ASCII character set had been in use for several years, IBM assigned the numbers 128-254 to additional symbols—including a set of block-graphics characters

The de facto standard character set for the computer industry is the ASCII set plus IBM's extended character set plus two characters that are variously defined to make a total of 256 (2^8) characters (0 255). The entire set is referred to as the ASCII characters.

The 256-character limitation is dictated by the fact that most computer memory and storage is made up of bytes, each of which consist of eight bits. The largest binary number that can be stored in one position is 11111111, or 2^8, or 256 (0-255).

MORE

ASCII file A computer file that stores one ASCII character in each position of memory or storage. Suitable for the storage of text and other information that is not primarily numbers or programming code. ASCII files do contain numbers and can be used for calculation, but the calculation will be slow compared to the speeds possible using binary files. See, also, *binary file*.

0	BLANK (NULL)	19	‼	38	&	57	9	76	L	95	_
1	☺	20	¶	39	`	58	:	77	M	96	´
2	☻	21	§	40	(	59	;	78	N	97	a
3	♥	22	▬	41	)	60	<	79	O	98	b
4	♦	23	↨	42	*	61	=	80	P	99	c
5	♣	24	↑	43	+	62	>	81	Q	100	d
6	♠	25	↓	44	,	63	?	82	R	101	e
7	•	26	→	45	-	64	@	83	S	102	f
8	◘	27	←	46	.	65	A	84	T	103	g
9	○	28	∟	47	/	66	B	85	U	104	h
10	◙	29	↔	48	0	67	C	86	V	105	i
11	♂	30	▲	49	1	68	D	87	W	106	j
12	♀	31	▼	50	2	69	E	88	X	107	k
13	♪	32	BLANK (SPACE)	51	3	70	F	89	Y	108	l
14	♫	33	!	52	4	71	G	90	Z	109	m
15	☼	34	"	53	5	72	H	91	[	110	n
16	►	35	#	54	6	73	I	92	\	111	o
17	◄	36	$	55	7	74	J	93	]	112	p
18	↕	37	%	56	8	75	K	94	^	113	q

114	r	138	è	162	ó	186	║	210	╥	234	Ω
115	s	139	ï	163	ú	187	╗	211	╙	235	δ
116	t	140	î	164	ñ	188	╝	212	╘	236	∞
117	u	141	ì	165	Ñ	189	╜	213	╒	237	∅
118	v	142	Ä	166	ª	190	╛	214	╓	238	∈
119	w	143	Å	167	º	191	┐	215	╫	239	∩
120	x	144	É	168	¿	192	└	216	╪	240	≡
121	y	145	æ	169	⌐	193	┴	217	┘	241	±
122	z	146	Æ	170	¬	194	┬	218	┌	242	≥
123	{	147	ô	171	½	195	├	219	█	243	≤
124	¦	148	ö	172	¼	196	─	220	▄	244	⌠
125	}	149	ò	173	¡	197	┼	221	▌	245	⌡
126	~	150	û	174	«	198	╞	222	▐	246	÷
127	Δ	151	ù	175	»	199	╟	223	▀	247	≈
128	Ç	152	ÿ	176	░	200	╚	224	∝	248	°
129	ü	153	Ö	177	▒	201	╔	225	β	249	●
130	é	154	Ü	178	▓	202	╩	226	Γ	250	•
131	â	155	¢	179	│	203	╦	227	π	251	√
132	ä	156	£	180	┤	204	╠	228	Σ	252	^{n}
133	à	157	¥	181	╡	205	═	229	σ	253	^{2}
134	å	158	₧	182	╢	206	╬	230	μ	254	■
135	ç	159	ƒ	183	╖	207	╧	231	τ	255	BLANK 'FF'
136	ê	160	á	184	╕	208	╨	232	Φ		
137	ë	161	í	185	╣	209	╤	233	Θ		

Illustration 4200.1 ASCII Characters

Assembly language A programming language that uses codes to represent machine operations. Although the codes are somewhat easier for people to understand than is machine language, assembly language (like machine language) requires that every operation be programmed in tedious detail. See, also, *high-level programming language, low-level programming language,* and *machine language.*

Back up To copy data from one storage device to another for use in case the first device fails. See, also, *backup.*

Background task See ¶ 4325.

Backslash ASCII character 92: \. Used in DOS to indicate a path through the directory system of a disk to a file. See, also, *disk organization.*

Backup A secondary copy of stored data for use in case the primary copy becomes unusable. The primary and secondary copies usually reside on different devices or different media. See, also, *back up* and ¶ 4539.

Bar code A machine-readable printed pattern composed of vertical bars varying in width and spacing. Each bar code is translated by a **bar-code reader** into a number.

Bar codes are most commonly used for **UPC** (**U**niversal **P**rice **C**ode). In this application, each manufacturer and product has a discrete code. Retail stores program the price of each product into their computer systems. As the bar code is read at the check-out counter, the computer matches the product number to the price and enters the item on the cash register.

Books are identified similarly by a bar-coded **ISBN** (**I**nternational **S**tandard **B**ook **N**umber).

51695>

9 780945 575795

Illustration 4200.2 UPC ISBN

Base Each number system has a base. The decimal system is based on the number 10. For it, we use the figures 0, 1, 2, 3, 4, 5, 6, 7, 8, and 9. In counting, when we get past 9, we move left one column, place a 1 there, and a 0 in the right column. Notice how the numbered wheels on an odometer work.

BASIC (Beginner's All-purpose Symbolic Instruction Code)
A high-level programming language that is relatively easy to learn but somewhat limited in application. BASIC is furnished with many PCs and widely used in business and education applications. It is available for use with either an *interpreter* or *compiler*.

Batch file
A file used on a DOS system to execute a list of DOS commands as though the commands were entered from the keyboard. A batch file has a standard filename, always including the extension *.BAT*. During the *booting* process, a DOS system reads the *AUTOEXEC.BAT* file that provides certain instructions the system needs at that time.

Batch processing
The repetitive processing of groups of similar records. Batch processing is used for relatively simple operations in which the program acts on the records one at a time until the batch of records has been processed. For example, a list of transactions on one disk can be posted to accounts stored on another disk. Contrast with *interactive processing*.

Baud
See ¶ 4508.

BBS (bulletin board system)
An electronic message center. Many BBSs are operated by nonprofit user groups, local clubs, and hobbyists. Users employ communications software and modems to post and retrieve messages, upload and download public domain software, and so on.

The popularity of BBSs has diminished somewhat because of the danger of computer viruses. See, also, *download, public-domain software, shareware, upload,* and *virus*.

Benchmark
A test of system performance used to evaluate hardware and software. A benchmark usually is a measure of the time required to process a standard collection of test data.

Bernoulli box
A mass storage system employing removable magnetic disks. It was named for the Swiss scientist who discovered the principle of aerodynamic lift. That principle keeps a cushion of air between the disk surface and the read-write head. See, also, *removable hard disk*.

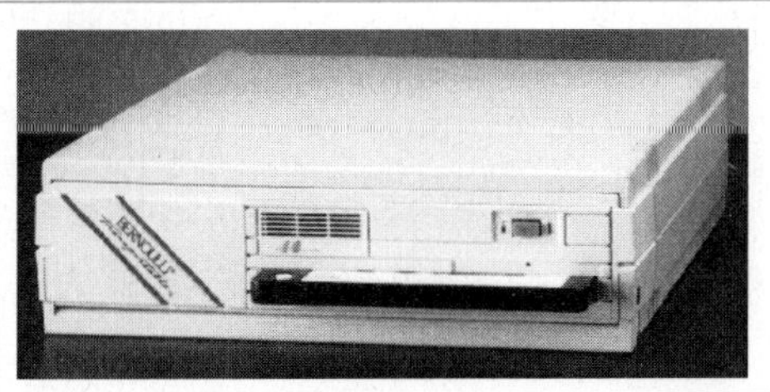

Illustration 4200.3 Bernoulli Box
(Photo courtesy of David Young-Wolfe/PhotoEdit)

MORE

Binary The number system used by computers and based on two numbers. The numbers 0 and 1 are used in binary arithmetic. In counting, when we get past 1, we move left one column, place a 1 there and a 0 in the right column. Binary 10=decimal 2. See, also, *number systems*.

Binary file A file written in binary code. Suitable for the storage of information that is primarily numbers. Numeric files are written in binary code because binary is easier for the computer to manipulate—even though users have difficulty in reading expressions such as 10110101. Similar machine efficiency dictates the use of binary files for programs. See, also, *binary*.

BIOS (Basic Input-Output System) Read-only code used for the automatic control of components (keyboard, monitor, disk drives, etc.) in a DOS system. BIOS is usually stored in a ROM clip called the ROM BIOS.

Bit (binary digit) The smallest unit in binary (base 2) code or arithmetic in which the computer records all data. A bit records a *1* as an *on,* magnetized, or high-current condition and records a *0* as an *off,* demagnetized, or low-current condition.

1	0
On	Off
Magnetized	Deagnetized
Current	No Current
High Current	Low Current

A bit records one of two conditions: 1 or 0

Bitmapped font See ¶ 5318.

Bitmapped images Images that are stored electronically as dots. Most computer printers create images by applying dots to paper. The finer the dots, the more accurate and pleasing the image.

Bitmapped images produce sraight and smooth horizontal and vertical lines. Diagonal lines and curves, however, take on a jagged, step-like appearance caused by the dot pattern. The protruding dots are called **jaggies.** As the illustration above indicates, more dots of smaller size minimize the problem—even make the jaggies invisible to the naked eye.

Artwork or fonts stored as bit maps cannot be enlarged or reduced without introducing distortions and emphasizing jaggies. For these reasons, vector (outline) graphics are generally considered superior to bitmapped graphics. Compare to *vector graphics*. See, also, *aliasing*.

Illustration 4200.4 120 dpi 300 dpi 1200 dpi
(Photo courtesy of New York Convention & Visitors Bureau)

Block graphics See ¶ 5314.

Block of text See ¶ 5216-20.

Boilerplate See *macros, macros* for *boilerplate,* and ¶ 5235.

Boldface See ¶ 5213 and 5324.

Boot Short for *bootstrap*. Boot is an automatic routine during which the system's ROM and a bootable disk containing the operating system clear memory, load the operating system, and prepare the system for use. See, also, ¶ 4301.

Boot up See *boot.*

Bootstrap See *boot.*

BPS (**b**its **p**er second) See ¶ 4508.

Bridges See ¶ 4545.

Buffer A block of memory reserved as a holding area for data that is waiting for a slower component of the system. Typically, the CPU races ahead, leaving a buffer full of data as work for the printer. See, also, *CPU.*

Bug A programming error or corrupted file that causes a computer system to behave erratically, make errors, or crash.

Bulletin board system See *BBS.*

Bus See ¶ 4108.

Business application See ¶ 4420.

MORE

Button — A small area on the screen sensitized to respond to the clicks of a mouse or other pointing device. Typically, a menu or dialog box contains a button for each option available to the user, who selects one or more by clicking on the appropriate button or buttons.

Byte — One position in computer memory or storage. Each byte is capable of storing one character. A character is a single letter (A-Z), number (0-9), or another of the 256 characters that make up the ASCII set. See *ASCII characters*.

A single byte (one position in memory or storage) consists of eight bits. Each bit can represent a 1 or a 0. The lowest number is 00000000; the highest number a single byte can represent is 11111111, or decimal 256. The letter *A* is represented by the binary number 01000001, decimal 65. Programs frequently state binary numbers in octal or hexadecimal to render them less cumbersome and somewhat easier for people to read. See *number system*.

C — A high-level programming language widely used by professional programmers. C is portable in the sense that it can be used on any system that has a C compiler. It is used effectively with the UNIX operating system.

4

Cache — A portion of memory or disk storage especially reserved for frequently used program code or data, keeping it ready for quick retrieval.

CAD (computer-aided design) — The use of a computer system and a CAD program to design devices ranging from machine parts to houses. Typically, a CAD system includes a graphics monitor, mouse, light pen, digitizer, and graphics plotter.

CADD (computer-aided design and drafting) — The use of a computer system and a CADD program to design products *and do the necessary drafting as well.*

CAM (computer-aided manufacturing) — The use of a computer system and a CAM program to control a manufacturing process.

Case-sensitive — The ability of a program or operation to distinguish between capital (uppercase) letters and lowercase letters. A case-sensitive alphabetic sort puts each capital letter before its corresponding lowercase letter. A non-case-sensitive alphabetic sort treats capital and lowercase letters the same.

CD-ROM (compact disk-read-only memory) — Mass storage technology employing an optical reader for compact disks. A single disk can store 250,000 pages of information on a disk identical to those used in compact disk music systems. The system is fast and inexpensive—but does not permit computer users to store their own data. Like music disks, CD-ROM computer disks can play back only what the disk manufacturer has recorded. CD-ROM disks are used for economical distribution of information that does not require frequent updating, such as encyclopedias, clip art, and so on.

CDs (compact disks) — Used for recording music; convert the sound waves of the music itself into *digital* data. When the disk is played, the digital data is converted back to analog data: a seemingly real representation of the original music. See, also, *digital.*

Cell — See ¶ 4405.

Character — A letter, number, punctuation mark, other symbol, or block-graphic that can be entered, stored, or displayed on the screen in a single position. See, also, *ASCII characters.*

Character mode — In **character mode,** also called **text mode,** a PC can reproduce only those characters that are included in the character set of the system itself. In most cases, this is the 256-character extended ASCII set. If the characters are to be printed, the character set of the printer may be a further limitation. See, also, *ASCII characters.*

Character set — A list of all characters that can be processed by a device. The system character set is a list of the characters that can be entered via the keyboard and displayed on the screen. Most systems can process 256 characters. Individual devices within the system—particularly printers—may not be able to process all the characters in the set. Therefore, the printer is said to have a smaller character set. See, also, *ASCII characters.*

Character-based printer — The character set of a mechanical typewriter consists of the characters on the keyboard and type bars and ordinarily does not change. The character set of a daisy-wheel typewriter consists of the characters on the daisy wheel itself, and can be changed by changing the daisy wheel. The same is true of daisy wheel computer printers, which usually have character sets consisting of capital and lowercase letters, numbers, punctuation marks, and a few common symbols—fewer than half of the complete ASCII set. Contrast with *graphics mode.*

Character-based screen — Contrast with *graphics screen.* See ¶ 5201.

Character-based word processor — See ¶ 5201.

Chip (microchip, silicon chip) — See ¶ 4004 and illustration 4106.1.

MORE

CONTINUED

Circuit board A flat plastic sheet on which circuits are located. Usually a circuit board contains microchips and other components. An **expansion circuit board** contains connections along one edge that allow it to be inserted into an expansion slot. See, also, *expansion slot* and ¶ 4107.

Client tracking See ¶ 4415.

Clip art Collections of illustrations stored on disk in graphic file formats that are compatible with word processing, desktop publishing, and presentation programs. In practice, the clip art file is first imported by the host program then integrated into the document being processed.

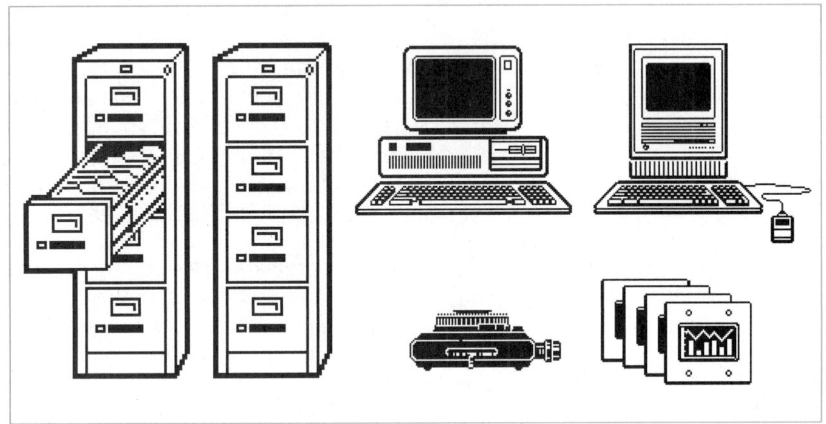

Illustration 4200.5 Clip Art

Coaxial cable See ¶ 4533.

Command An instruction that causes a computer system to perform a specific task. An instruction may be part of a batch file, may be keyed in, or may be selected from alternatives presented on the screen.

Communications program See ¶ 4418.

Compiler A program that translates programs written in a high-level language such as C into machine language. Once an application program has been written, debugged, and tested, a final compiled (machine language) version is sold. Although the programmer may make changes and recompile the program, the buyers or users of the application program normally purchase the machine-language version and have nothing to do with compiling the program. See, also, *interpreter* and ¶ 4300.

Compress The use of software to reduce the disk space required by files. See, also, *archive*.

Computer See ¶ 4101.

Computing speed Generally, programs written in **assembly language** run faster than compiled programs or interpreted programs because each machine operation in an assembly language program is spelled out as an instruction. **Compiled programs** are somewhat slower than assembly language programs because high-level programming language is less efficient than is a programmer at specifying machine instructions. **Interpreted programs** are somewhat slower than compiled programs because the interpreter must translate the high-level program to machine language each time the program is run.

Control code The first 32 ASCII characters, which are reserved for system hardware control. A program such as a word processing or desktop publishing program may send control codes to the printer to control the operation of the printer. See, also, *embedded control code*.

Control <Ctrl> key Provides an alternate use for each function key and for some other keys. See, also, *alternate key*.

Coprocessor An auxiliary processor chip that assists the microprocessor in specialized applications such as mathematics or graphics. Many computers are delivered with a built-in connector for a math coprocessor. The math coprocessor may be plugged in later if the user experiences a need for the extra mathematical computing power.

Copy See ¶ 5220.

CPU (**c**entral **p**rocessing **u**nit) See ¶ 4106 and 4306.

Crash A serious computer malfunction that makes it impossible to continue. A crash usually means loss of the data that has been processed since the last time the user saved to disk. A crash usually requires rebooting the system.

CRT (**c**athode-**r**ay **t**ube) The monitor's large vacuum tube in which a cathode (electron gun) repeatedly sweeps a phosphor screen with a beam of electrons to create images that allow the user to communicate with the system.

CTD (**c**umulative **t**rauma **d**isorder) See *RSI* (repetitive strain injury).

CTS (**c**arpal **t**unnel **s**yndrome) See *RSI* (repetitive strain injury).

Current The one now in use: the *current* directory; the *current* disk drive; the *current* program, and so on.

MORE

Cursor The indicator that moves around the screen under the control of the user. It indicates the point of current interest on the screen: where the last action took place, where the next character will be entered, and so on. Usually the cursor is shaped as a blinking underscore, but may be configured as a solid square or some other shape as dictated by the user or the program. The cursor is controlled by the cursor keys or a pointing device.

Cursor keys The cursor keys control the cursor (pointer on the screen). When **<Num Lock>** is off, the cursor keys are active. There are at least eight cursor keys: *<Up>, <Dn>, <Lt>,* and *<Rt>* are the arrow keys that move the cursor as the arrows indicate. The cursor moves one line at a time vertically and one character at a time horizontally. The arrow keys are repeat keys, so the cursor can be moved quite rapidly.

The *page up <PU>* and *page down <PD>* keys usually move the cursor up or down by about half a screen; the *<Home>* and *<End>* keys usually move the cursor to the top and bottom of the screen respectively.

Since the cursor keys are under program control, they behave differently under different programs: the *<Home>* and *<End>* keys, for example, may move the cursor to the beginning and end of the entire document. *<Scroll Lock>* may, under some programs, make the cursor keys behave differently. Holding down the *<Alt>* or *<Ctrl>* key while pressing the cursor keys will, under some programs, produce still different results. All of these combinations are programmed to make the cursor easy to move to various points on the screen as needed by the application program that controls them.

Illustration 4200.6 Cursor Keys

Cut-and-paste The on-screen deletion of a block of data in one location and insertion of the same block in another location. For example, a paragraph might be deleted from the screen image of page 12 of a document and inserted on page 7 of the same document—as though a physical cut-and-paste job had been done on a hard copy of the document.

Cut-and-paste is similar to moving a block of data—except that the block may be cut now and pasted later; whereas, a block move cuts and pastes simultaneously.

Many variations on these techniques are used in word processors, publishing programs, spreadsheets, macro programs, and elsewhere. See ¶ 5216-20.

Daisy-wheel printer An impact printer that employs a plastic or metal printing element consisting of spoke-like type bars, each with a type character at its outer end. To print, the wheel is rotated until the proper character is in the printing position. Then, the print hammer strikes the back of the type character, driving the face of the type into the ribbon creating the imprint of the character on the pape. Daisy-wheel printers operate in character mode only, having no graphics capabilities.

While the imprint of a daisy-wheel printer is of high quality, the device is slow and noisy. Improved quality of dot matrix printers and reduced prices of laser printers have all but driven daisy-wheel computer printers from the market. The daisy wheel is the printing device of choice, however, for typewriters.

Data See ¶ 4001.

Database See ¶ 4409-15.

Debug To identify and correct errors in a program.

Decompress See *archive* and *compress*.

Dedicated Reserved for a single use or purpose, as contrasted with general purpose or multipurpose. A *dedicated* file server in a network; a *dedicated* PC that is used only as a server for a fax library; a single purpose or *dedicated* word processor.

Default A specification made automatically by the program when the user elects not to choose a specification. For example, a word processor might choose the following default values if the user chooses not to override them:

- a generic printer table that works with most printers
- 10 character-per-inch (pica) type
- margins set at 1 and 80
- tab stops at 6 and 40
- 6 lines per inch
- 66 lines per page
- first line of text on line 6
- last line of text on line 60
- no automatic word division or hyphenation
- no justification
- no automatic reformatting

4

Desktop See ¶ 4329.

Desktop publishing See ¶ 5300.

Device Any hardware component of a computer system: disk drive, monitor, printer, modem, scanner, and so on.

Device driver See ¶ 4530.

Dictation See ¶ 5019-26.

Dictionary See ¶ 5234.

Digit An individual numeral; in the decimal system, the numerals 0-9. The digits in the number 143 are 1, 4, and 3. The high-order digit is 1; the low-order digit is 3.

Digital A type of measurement, description, or representation based on discrete (noncontinuous) signals—the signal on which a digital watch is based or the signals (impulses) that control the output of a remote-reading digital thermometer. The individual frames of a movie film are digital, but projecting the film produces in the viewer's mind a representation of the original movement that was filmed.

Most general-purpose computers are digital computers; i.e., they record data in digital form, usually by recording an *on* or *off* condition. See, also, *binary, bit,* and *byte.*

Digital computer See *binary, bit, byte, digit,* and *digital.*

Directory A category or name to which files can be assigned for organizing and indexing purposes. A directory does not contain data. See, also, *disk organization.*

Disk A round flat plate on which data is recorded. **Magnetic disk drives** record data as magnetic impulses. See, also, *fixed hard disk drive, floppy disk, hard disk drive,* and *removable hard disk.*

Optical disk drives employ a laser beam to burn very small holes in the surface of the disk. They are called optical disks because they are read by a laser beam that is sensitive to the small changes in reflectivity caused by the holes. See, also, *CD-ROM, floptical disk,* and *WORM.*

Disk drive The device that keeps the disk spinning. The circuitry that directly controls a disk drive is called a **disk controller.** A disk controller usually resides on a circuit board that is inserted in an expansion slot or otherwise connected to the bus and may control more than one drive. The most common arrangement is a single control board for a hard drive and two floppy disk drives.

A **disk drive bay** is a space set aside inside the system case for the installation of a disk drive. The use of **bays** for drives and **slots** for controllers makes it easy to replace or add a drive. The controller is plugged into a slot, the drive is installed in a bay, and the controller and drive are connected with a **ribbon cable**—a flat, flexible cable containing multiple conductors.

Disk organization

Each operating system provides a means of organizing disks. A large, unorganized hard disk containing thousands of files would be a nightmare for the user.

Computer disks are organized hierarchically; i.e., by rank. The highest rank is applied to the **root directory** of the disk on which the data is being stored. The disk drive and its root directory are identified by a letter of the alphabet, followed by a colon. A typical system configuration might look like this:

A: 5 ¼″ floppy disk drive

B: 3 ½″ floppy disk drive

C: Hard drive

D: Hard drive

A **directory** is a name or category to which files can be assigned for organizing and indexing purposes. A directory contains files, not data.

The highest-ranking directory is the **root directory.** If no other directories have been created, all the files on the disk will be in the root directory.

A **file** is a unit into which related data is organized. A software program may be divided into several, a few, or many files. Each file has a **filename** that, in DOS, consists of up to eight characters. The filename may have an **extension** consisting of a period and up to three characters. Files with the extension *.BAT, .EXE,* and *.COM* can be **executed:** when entered, they take over the system and implement a program.

Other files store data rather than program code: word processing and desktop publishing documents, for example.

If you are organizing a hard disk on which all of your programs are stored, *representative* files might look like the following tree chart. On a DOS system, this chart, for the disk on drive C, is displayed by entering TREE C:.

MORE

4

Tree Chart

Although there would actually be more directories and files, the illustration shows:

[1] 2 files and 2 directories in the root directory

[2] 3 files in the DOS directory

[3] 2 files and 2 subdirectories in the DTP directory

[4] 3 files in the DOCS subdirectory

[5] 3 files in the SHEETS.STY subdirectory

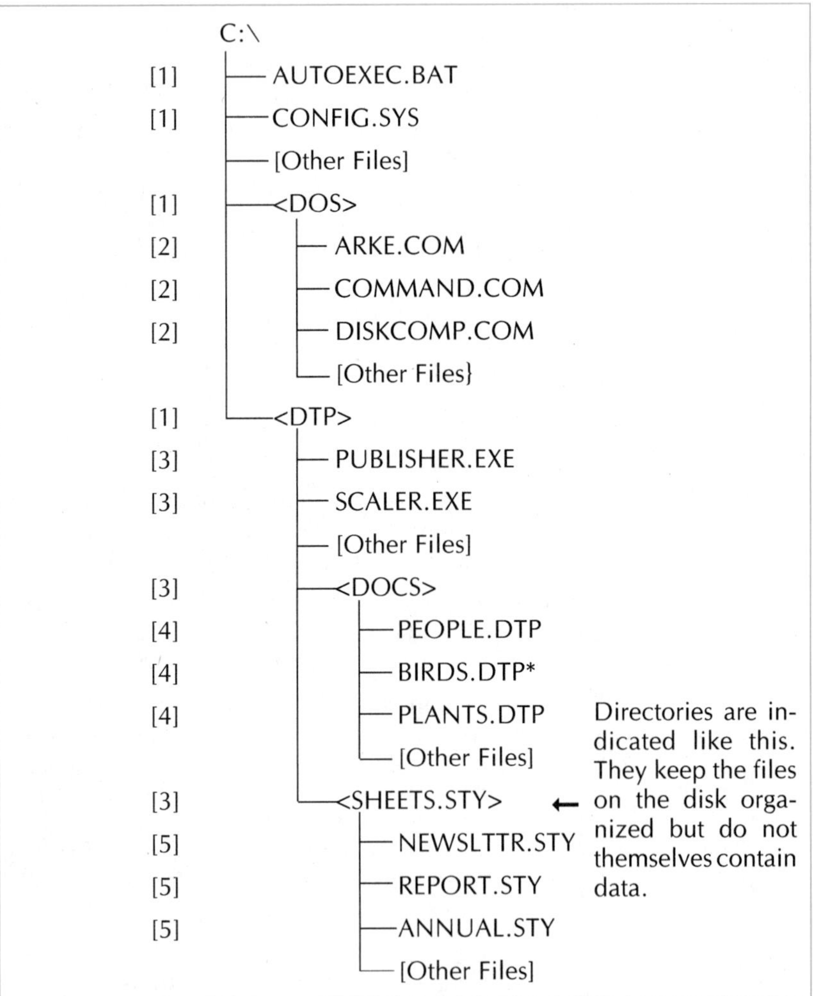

*BIRDS.DTP is the filename of a desktop publishing document entitled *Birds*. It is in the <DOCS> directory, which is in the <DTP> directory, which is in the root directory of drive C.

DOS locates a file by searching a **path** that identifies the disk drive, then the directory or directories in turn, and then the filename—using backslashes as separators. The path to the BIRDS.DTP file is C:\DTP\DOCS\BIRDS.DTP.

Diskette See *disk*.

Document A body of information—whether it is in memory, on disk, or on paper.

DOS (disk operating system) See ¶ 4315-25.

Dot matrix printer A printer that forms images on paper by selectively striking the pins of a print head, driving them against an inked ribbon. The print head of a dot matrix printer moves back and forth across a sheet of paper, printing one horizontal line with each pass. It can repeat the pass to darken the print or add characters such as underlining.

Most print heads contain either 9 or 24 wires or pins. For each pin, there is an electrical circuit. When the circuit is activated, an electromagnet repels or drives the pin forward. The pin strikes the ribbon, which prints a dot on the paper. The proper pins, fired in each print position, produce the characters that are printed. The dots produced by a 24-pin printer are smaller and closer together; the image is correspondingly smoother than that of a 9-pin printer.

Illustration 4200.7 Dot Matrix Print Head
(Photo courtesy of Dataproducts Corporation)

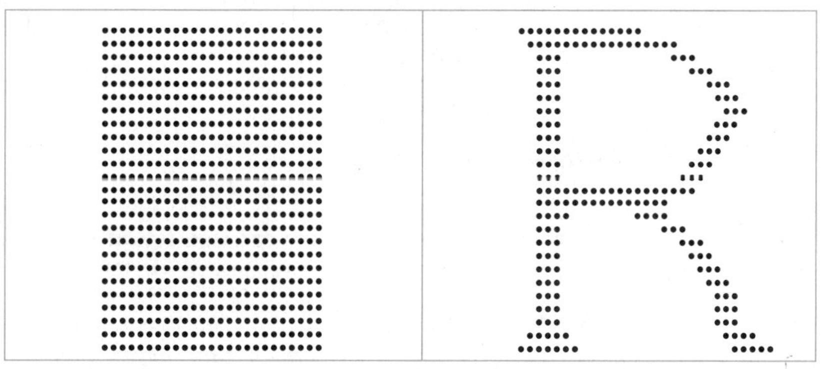

Illustration 4200.8 Dot Matrix Dot Matrix R

MORE

Download To copy a file or files from (1) disk to peripheral (e.g., from a hard drive to the memory in a laser printer), (2) network server to a computer in the network, or (3) an external source such as a bulletin board service. See, also, ¶ 4516 and 5681.

dpi (**d**ots **p**er **i**nch) A measure of resolution usually applied to printers. A basic laser printer may have a resolution of 300 dpi or 90,000 dots per square inch. See *pixel* for measuring the resolution of a display screen. See, also, *dot matrix printer*.

Drag-and-drop editing Moving a block of text by (1) highlighting it, (2) using a mouse to click-and-hold (drag) while moving the mouse pointer to the new location for the text, and (3) releasing the mouse button. The block of text disappears from the old location and appears in the new location.

Draw program See ¶ 5309.

Driver See ¶ 4530.

Drop-down menu See ¶ 4328, 5402, and 5417.

Editing Text, ¶ 5031-32.

Education application See ¶ 4421.

Electronic mail (E-mail) A communications service that (1) allows the subscriber to broadcast basis), (2) receives and stores messages for the subscriber, (3) alerts the subscriber when she or he signs on if there is a message waiting, and (4) allows the subscriber to download messages. See, also, ¶ 5682.

Elite type Fixed-pitch type with 12 characters per inch. See, also, *pica type*.

Embedded control code An ASCII character (usually one of the first 32) embedded (keyed and sent to the printer like any character that is to be printed) used to control a function of the printer. For example, ASCII 18 (↕), when embedded before and after a word (↕embedded↕) causes the characters between the two embedded commands to be printed in boldface (**embedded**).

Emphasizing type See ¶ 5213-15.

Enter <Ent> key Formerly called the **carriage return key** on typewriters, the **Enter** key is now marked **<Enter>** or **<Ent>.** As data is keyed, it appears on the screen in ASCII characters. The *<Ent>* key causes the data that has been keyed most recently (since the last time *<Ent>* was pressed) to be entered into RAM. In a word processor, the *<Ent>* is used to indicate the end of a paragraph or the hard return at the end of a line.

In word processors and many other programs, it is not necessary to press the <*Ent*> key at the end of each line. As the last word on the line is keyed, the word is wrapped around the end of the line. When the space following the last word is keyed, a program feature called **word wrap** pulls the last word back to the previous line if there is room for it or pushes the word forward to the current line if there is not. See, also, ¶ 5205-9.

EPS (Encapsulated PostScript) A graphics file format for PostScript printers and other high-resolution devices. EPS can include both a high-resolution image for printing and a low-resolution image for screen display.

Error message An on-screen message indicating that an error has occurred. The message may suggest remedial action or direct the user to a source of assistance such as an instruction manual.

Escape <Esc> key A key used by most application programs to abort the current operation or to return to the previous operation, program segment, or display.

Escape code A printer code prefaced by the ASCII 27 character (←). The characters that follow the escape character may be ordinary letters or numbers—but the presence of the escape code causes the printer to interpret them as instructions rather than printing them. See *ASCII characters*.

Execute To enter the filename of an executable program, causing it to take over the system and implement itself. The filenames of executable DOS programs include extensions of *.BAT, .EXE* or *.COM*. BASIC programs and individual BASIC commands can be executed under the control of a BASIC interpreter.

Expansion board See *circuit board*.

Expansion slot A slot-shaped receptacle designed for the insertion of a circuit board. The expansion slot connects the circuit board to the computer's bus. Full-sized desktop computers typically have eight expansion slots. Each can accept a circuit board that controls a component of the system. The purpose of adding a circuit board is to replace a component that has malfunctioned or to upgrade a component for better performance. See, also, *circuit board* and ¶ 4107.

Fax The shortened and altered form of *facsimile,* which means an exact copy. A fax is transmitted from a source fax machine to a destination fax machine via telephone connection. The destination fax machine reproduces the text and graphics of the original. See, also, ¶ 4517.

Fiber optics See ¶ 4009 and 4532.

MORE

Field

In database management, a subdivision of a *record,* which is a subdivision of a *file,* which is located in a *directory* that is located on a disk. Each field contains a specific kind of data (e.g., age, street address, city).

```
Disk drive          C:
   Directory           STUDENTS.CUR
      Filename            SENIORS
         Record              WANDER, WILLA
            Field               AGE
```

See, also, *disk organization, file,* and *record.*

The operating system and most application programs provide access to directories and files. Records and fields are established by and accessed through a database program. See, also, ¶ 4409.

File

A collection of data that has been stored under a filename. Program and system files are usually stored in binary format; text files are usually stored in ASCII format. See, also, *ASCII file, binary file,* and *disk organization.*

Filename

See ¶ 5229.

Fixed hard disk drive

Most disk drives are *internal* (mounted inside the system case); some are *external* (mounted in separate cases of their own). A full-sized system case contains as many as five disk-drive bays and eight expansion slots.

Hard disks are equipped with sealed covers that protect them from dust. Most hard disks are not removable and do not, therefore, require openings to the outside of the case. **Removable hard disks** do require openings on the outside of the case so that the removable part of the drive—the disk itself—can be removed and inserted.

A few hard disk drives are mounted on circuit boards; they are installed by simply inserting the circuit board in an expansion slot; no other connections are required.

Illustration 4200.9 Combination 5 1/4-inch and 3 1/2-inch Floppy Disk Drive

Illustration 4200.10 Hard Disk Drive Mounted on Circuit Board
Left: Cover removed from drive; Right: Cover in place.
(Photo courtesy of JVC Information Products Company of America)

Illustration 4200.11 Internal Hard Disk Drive (Cover Removed)
(Photo courtesy of Stephen McBrady/PhotoEdit)

Fixed-pitch font See ¶ 5320.

Flat-file database See ¶ 4411-12.

Floppy disk Flexible, removable magnetic disk. The familiar 5 ¼-inch floppy disk has been formatted for 180K, 320K, 360K, 720K, and 1.2MB as disk technology has improved. The flexible sleeve and open access hole make 5 ¼-inch floppy disks susceptible to damage, but their relative thinness makes them easy to carry and store.

The 3 ½-inch floppy is housed in a rigid plastic case with an automatic sliding door. It is much less susceptible to damage from dust or careless handling than is the older 5 ¼-inch disk. See, also, ¶ 4309-11.

MORE

Illustration 4200.12 3 ½-inch Floppy Disk

Floptical® disk Combines the precision of the laser and the recording ability of magnetic-media technology: a laser (optical) system guides a magnetic recording head, keeping it on track so precisely that the floptical drive can record at least 20 times as much data as can a floppy drive of similar size. A Floptical® drive can store 21MB of data on a 3 ½-inch cartridge-enclosed disk (similar in appearance to a 3 ½-inch floppy disk). Over 500MB can be stored on a special 5 ¼-inch disk. *Floptical®* or *magneto-optical* technology seems likely to emerge as a new industry standard for removable mass storage. See, also, ¶ 4010.

Font See ¶ 5316-24.

Foreground task See ¶ 4325.

Format See ¶ 5221-27.

Forth (**fourth**-generation programming language) A high-level programming language used for direct control of hardware devices such as robots, games, and computerized musical instruments.

FORTRAN (**for**mula **tran**slation) The oldest high-level programming language. Designed in 1956 for mathematical and scientific applications FORTRAN is still used for that purpose.

Freeware Copyrighted programs that the copyright owners have made available for unrestricted free use. Contrast with *public-domain software* and *shareware*. See, also, *BBS*.

Function keys A set of programmable keys used for different functions by different application programs. Most keyboards contain twelve function keys *<F1>* - *<F12>*. All function keys work as assigned by the program. In some programs, *<F1>* is the help key. Here are some of the other things function keys are assigned to do:

- Open a **window:** insert a rectangle in the screen image. The window might contain a **menu** or a **dialogue box.** A **menu** is a list of operations the system can be instructed to perform in the current segment of the program, usually a multiple choice question. A **dialogue box** is similar to a menu, except that the system asks for more than the answer to a single multiple choice question.
- Activate a spelling checker or thesaurus and look up the word on which the cursor rests. See ¶ 5232-33.
- Start or stop underlining, boldface, italics, and so on. The function key, alone or with *<Alt>* or *<Ctrl>,* inserts embedded control characters. See, also, *embedded control code.*
- Control any other system function assigned by the program.

G or **GB** (**gigabyte**) — Approximately one billion bytes of memory: one GB = 1,073,741,824 bytes.

Grammar checker — A TSR program that checks for certain errors, particularly for expressions that should be avoided. The grammar checker also checks for certain errors in spelling and punctuation.

Graphical interface — See ¶ 4328.

Graphical word processor — See ¶ 5202.

Graphics — Two-dimensional art consisting of pictures, symbols, and designs. A graphic is a single such representation (e.g., a picture, design, or similar representation).

Also, the field of representing objects or ideas on two-dimensional media such as paper or a computer screen. Representation may involve the creation or reproduction of drawings, paintings, photographs, engravings, and the like, or the use of computer programs that create similar screen and printed representations.

Graphics file format — See ¶ 5310.

Graphics mode — PC screen images occur while the PC system is in **graphics mode** or **character mode.** Early PCs were equipped for character mode only and could not display anything other than the ASCII character set.

Graphics mode is made possible by special circuitry called a **graphics adapter,** usually located on a **video adapter board.** See, also, *video adapter* and ¶ 4107.

MORE

In graphics mode, the system can reproduce virtually any graphic representation by illuminating selectively the pixels on the screen. Since each pixel, or dot, must be controlled separately, processing graphics requires much memory and is very slow compared to processing characters.

Any image displayed on the screen is also in memory. It can be stored on disk, where it will also be a pattern of dots. It can be printed on a graphics printer (any laser or ink-jet printer and some dot matrix printers). The printed image will be a pattern of dots.

Graphics program See ¶ 5307-09.

Graphics screen See ¶ 5202.

GUI (**g**raphical **u**ser **i**nterface) See ¶ 4328.

Halftone A graphic made up of dots that are dense in some areas and sparse in others. In black-and-white printing, darker shades of gray are created by dense dot structure; lighter shades by the sparse dispersal of dots. See, also, ¶ 5313.

Illustration 4200.13 Halftone

Handshake See ¶ 4532.

Hanging paragraph A paragraph that has a reverse indentation; i.e., the first line extends farther to the left than do the subsequent lines.

Hard copy A copy that is written, drawn, or printed on paper or similar material. *Hard copy* is usually used in reference to a printed copy of information stored electronically in a computer system.

Hard disk drive A mass storage device using rigid magnitic disks. A hard disk drive (hard drive) typically stores 40-1000MB (1GB) or more and operates much faster than do floppy disk drives. See, also, ¶ 4312.

Hard hyphen See ¶ 5209.

Help key The help key is not a specific key on the keyboard. It is *any* key designated by the program to display an appropriate message when the user calls for help by pressing the designated key. Some programs that provide a help key use *<F1>*.

Just what the help message contains depends on which part of the program is active when the help key is pressed. When the help key is pressed during file retrieval in a word processing program, the help message will pertain to file retrieval. If the same help key is pressed when a word is being looked up in the thesaurus, the help message will pertain to using the thesaurus.

Hierarchical Organized by rank and order—as a table of organization, outline, or subject filing system.

High-end The most elaborate, sophisticated, and expensive items in a category offered for sale. A *high-end* word processing program; a *high-end* printer. Contrast with *low-end*.

High-level programming language The abstract programming languages furthest removed from machine language and easiest for people to understand. High-level languages such as BASIC, C, and Pascal are more abstract than lower-level languages such as machine language (the lowest level) or assembly language.

Contrast with *low-level programming language*.

Highlight See ¶ 5216.

Hub See ¶ 4522.

Hyphenation zone See ¶ 5206.

Icon See ¶ 4328.

Imagesetter A specialized typesetting machine that produces high-resolution reproduction copy on photographic film or paper. An imagesetter is compatible with the PostScript printer language used in desktop publishing.

Impact printer Any printer that transfers images to paper by driving type against an ink or carbon ribbon. See, also, *daisywheel printer* and *dot matrix printer*.

Information See ¶ 4001.

Information Age See ¶ 4000.

Information processing See ¶ 4001.

MORE

4

Ink-jet printer A nonimpact printer that fires very small droplets of ink in precise patterns to form high-quality printed images. Like that of a dot matrix printer, the print head of an ink-jet printer moves back and forth across the paper, printing one horizontal line with each pass. Either can overprint; i.e., print the same line more than once.

The print head contains 50 ink jets, each of which is capable of ejecting a minute droplet of ink that forms a dot on the paper, achieving a resolution of about 300 dpi.

Like the dot matrix printer, the ink-jet printer forms each character by printing some dots in the matrix and not printing others. See *dot matrix printer*.

Input Data expressed in characters and entered into the computer.

Insert <Ins> key See ¶ 5210-12.

Interactive processing Processing in which the user can monitor the progress of operations on the screen, select programmed options, and correct errors—all while the program is being used. Contrast with *batch processing*.

Interpreter A program that (1) translates programs written in a high-level language such as BASIC into machine language and (2) executes such programs immediately. Unlike a compiler, an interpreter does not make a permanent machine-language translation.

Most microcomputers are equipped with a BASIC interpreter that enables the user to write and run BASIC programs. The interpreter is part of the operating system and must be present each time the BASIC program is run since this method requires the interpreter to reinterpret the program each time it is run.

ISBN (International Standard Book Number) See *bar code*.

Italics See ¶ 5214 and 5324.

Jaggies See *aliasing*.

Justification See ¶ 5322.

K or KB (kilobyte) Approximately one thousand bytes of memory: one KB = 1,024 bytes.

Kerning See ¶ 5323.

Keyboard See ¶ 4308 and 5203.

Keyboarding See ¶ 5203-12 and 5400.

LAN (**l**ocal **a**rea **n**etwork) See ¶ 4501 and 4524.

LAN adapter See ¶ 4532.

Laptop computer See *portable computer*.

Laser See ¶ 4006.

Laser printer Combines laser technology with that of the electrostatic (xerographic) copying machine to print high-resolution images under the control of a microcomputer.

Layout In word processor documents, see ¶ 5225. In desktop publishing, see ¶ 5311.

LCD (**l**iquid **c**rystal **d**isplay) A constantly operating display (as time in a digital watch) that consists of segments of a liquid crystal.

Line art See ¶ 5312.

Load See ¶ 4320.

Low-end The least elaborate, least sophisticated, least expensive items in a category offered for sale: a low-end word processing program; a low-end printer. Contrast with *high-end*.

Low-level programming language The least abstract programming languages: machine language and assembly language. Contrast with *high-level programming language*. See, also *assembly language* and *machine language*.

M or **MB** (**m**ega**b**yte) Approximately one million bytes of memory: one MB = 1,048,576 bytes.

Machine language Language recognized and used by the computer's CPU; it is binary code consisting of 1s and 0s.Contrast with *high-level language*. See, also, *assembly language, base, binary, bit, byte,* and *number systems*.

Macro A recorded series of keystrokes that are played back when the **macro command** is pressed. The *macro command* can be a keystroke or combination of keystrokes. The *playback* is the series of characters you want to appear on the screen without having to key them individually. See, also, ¶ 4612 and 5231.

Macros can be recorded and held available in memory by

- A TSR that is loaded before the word processor, spreadsheet, or other application program. A **TSR** (**t**erminate and **s**tay **r**esident) program, loaded into RAM when the system is booted, leaves a latent module in memory ready to perform when its **hot key** is pressed—even from within another program. Examples are Newkey and SuperKey which provide

MORE

macro capabilities within word processors, spreadsheets, and other application programs.

- Macro capability on the part of the operating system, shell, or GUI, such as DOS's Doskey.
- Macro capability built into an application program such as a word processor or spreadsheet program. For example, Microsoft Word, WordPerfect, and Lotus 1-2-3 are among the application programs that have macro capabilities.

Macros for boilerplate

Macros are used to insert **boilerplate**—standard sentences, paragraphs, or passages—in letters, memos, reports, and the like. Form letters, for example, can be customized by varying the paragraphs included or the order of the paragraphs.

To reproduce a paragraph on *cost control* whenever you need it, you could enter the *record* mode of your macro program, choose a command key or keys you will associate with the paragraph—perhaps *<c> <c> <Enter>*—and record the paragraph. Now, pressing *<c> <c> <Enter>* will cause the paragraph to play back whenever you need it.

Be careful to avoid accidental playback. Anyone following the example above and subsequently entering *<c> <c> <Enter>* by mistake would be surprised to see an unwanted paragraph appear, letter-by-letter, on the screen. See, also, *boilerplate* and *merge*.

Macros for short expressions

Key combinations that are not used for any other purpose can be used as macro command keys. For example, if the combination *<Alt> F* does not command anything on your system, you may wish to assign it to a long firm name (the firm for which you work, perhaps) that you enter repeatedly. Then you could enter *<Alt> F* and watch *Higginbotham, O'Shaughnessey, Stephanopoulis,* and *Weyerhauser, Limited* run quickly and automatically across your screen.

Magnetic media

See *disk, disk drive, disk organization,* and ¶ 4010.

Mainframe

See ¶ 4102 and 4337.

Margins

See ¶ 5207, 5222, 5503, and 5617.

Math coprocessor

Circuitry designed to increase the speed of processing calculations, as in a spreadsheet application. Math coprocessor circuitry increases the speed of calculation by as much as 100 times. Many motherboards include a math coprocessor socket. In illustration 4107.1 (page 233), the math coprocessor socket is visible at the bottom center of the picture. The socket and the math coprocessor are similar in appearance to the microprocessor and its socket.

Some manufacturers choose to include the math coprocessor in the computers they deliver. In other cases, a math coprocessor can be plugged in by the user.

Some of the newer microprocessors (the Intel 80486DX for example) include math coprocessor circuitry in the microprocessor itself.

Memory

Computer circuitry that receives, retains, and permits the retrieval of information. Memory is usually used to mean RAM, unless otherwise specified.

Volatile memory loses its contents when the electricity is turned off or fails. Main memory or RAM is volatile. **Stable memory** retains its contents even when the system is idle. Most ROM is stable; all storage media (disks, tapes, etc.) are stable.

RAM (**r**andom **a**ccess **m**emory) is the main memory of the system. It is volatile—active only when the system is on. Information in RAM is lost when the system is turned off.

Most new computers can use 16MB of RAM or more. However, many are equipped with only 1MB or 2MB when they are delivered. Adding memory is neither difficult nor expensive.

Most computers use **SIMMs** (**s**ingle **i**n-**l**ine **m**emory **m**odules). Since there are several types and more than one installation pattern, care should be exercised in purchasing and installing memory modules. See, also, illustration 4107.1.

ROM (**r**ead-**o**nly **m**emory) is memory in which the manufacturer has stored permanent data that is not altered by the user. Typical uses are data used to boot the system and resident fonts stored in a printer. See, also, *CD-ROM*.

Other types of read-only memory are not of general concern to users:

PROM (**p**rogrammable **r**ead-**o**nly **m**emory)

EPROM (**e**rasable **p**rogrammable **r**ead-**o**nly **m**emory)

EEPROM (**e**lectrically **e**rasable **p**rogrammable **r**ead-**o**nly **m**emory)

Memory, measuring

Memory is measured, or counted, in terms of the number of characters that can be stored: 1 position of memory can store 1 character and is called a **byte.** Bytes are counted in thousands (kilobytes), millions (megabytes), and billions (gigabytes).

Since computer arithmetic is base 2, one kilobyte is actually 2^{10} or 1024 bytes; one megabyte is 2^{20} or 1,048,576 bytes.

MORE

K = kilobyte = 1024 bytes
KB = kilobyte = 1024 bytes

M = megabyte = 1,048,576 bytes
MB = megabyte = 1,048,576 bytes

G = gigabyte = 1,073,741,824 bytes
GB = gigabyte = 1,073,741,824 bytes

Menu See ¶ 5221. Also, see *dropdown* and *pull-down menus*.

Merge See ¶ 5235.

MHz (Megahertz) A unit of frequency equal to one million cycles per second. MHz is widely used as a measure of the clock speed of computer systems and the operating speeds of other devices.

Microchip (silicon chip, chip) See ¶ 4004.

Microcomputer See ¶ 4104.

Microsoft Windows See ¶ 4326 and 4330.

Microwave See ¶ 4008.

Minicomputer See ¶ 4103 and 4336.

Modem See ¶ 4518 and 5681.

Monitor The display screen and circuitry housed with it. Most of the control circuitry for the monitor is located inside the system case. See, also, ¶ 4307.

Most sophisticated monitors are labeled *multisync* or *multiscan* to indicate that they conform automatically to several video standards. A video standard is achieved only when the software, adapter, and monitor all meet the standard. The screen image will reflect the *lowest* standard achieved by any one of the three. To get the best possible performance from an adapter-monitor combination, it is necessary to specify the video standard accurately when configuring software to the system. See, also, *CRT* and *video adapter*.

Motherboard (system board) See ¶ 4107.

Mouse A palm-sized input device that controls the cursor and enters simple yes-or-no commands. The name *mouse* was inspired by the resemblance of the instrument and its cable to a mouse and its tail.

A mouse rests on the tabletop—or on a special pad about the size of the screen—and can be moved in any direction on its horizontal plane via a rolling ball underneath it. Move the mouse, and the cursor follows. This is called an

analog function because any movement of the mouse produces a corresponding movement of the cursor—just as the hands of a clock are analogous to the passage of time and the needle of a speedometer is analogous to the speed of the vehicle.

Typically, the mouse is used with a GUI (**g**raphical **u**ser **i**nterface) that includes a number of buttons and control areas. Use the mouse to position the cursor over a button or control area, and the system will highlight the button or control area. **Click** the mouse (press its primary button) and the system will react accordingly (e.g., produce a drop-down menu, move a window to another position on the screen, etc.).

For example, moving the mouse to a button labeled *File* and clicking once may cause a corresponding menu to drop down. Use the mouse to move the cursor down through the menu to an action button labeled *Quit* or *Exit* and *Quit* or *Exit* will be highlighted. Click the mouse, and the program will terminate, returning the system to the control of the operating system.

Some buttons require a single click for one result and a **double click** (two clicks in quick succession) for another. A widely used double-click technique allows the expert user to move quickly through a program while protecting the novice or the careless user:

A double click on an action button causes the action to take place immediately; whereas, a single click produces a "last chance" question. For example, a double click on *Quit* terminates the program immediately. A single click on the Quit button produces a "last chance" question that asks **Are you sure? Yes No.** A single click on the Yes button then terminates the program.

Just as the ball makes the mouse an analog device, the buttons make it a **digital** device—one that employs distinct separate units to measure, control, or coordinate—because the clicks are digital impulses that control the computer system.

A mouse may have as many as three buttons, all under program control. The left button is usually the primary button used to click. The middle button may be programmed to equal a double click. The right button may be programmed to undo the last mouse command. Many programs employ the left button only, not assigning any function to the middle and right buttons.

A **trackball** is a specially designed mouse turned over to expose the controlling ball. Instead of moving the mouse, the user moves the ball with a thumb or finger. A trackball is built into some keyboards.

MORE

A **cordless mouse** is radio controlled; it does not have a cable connection to any other part of the system. See, also, ¶ 4313.

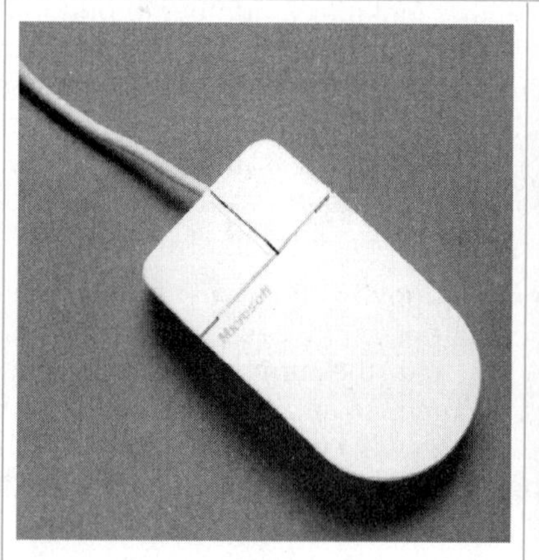

Illustration 4200.14a Mouse

Illustration 4200.14b Trackball (Photo courtesy of David Young-Wolff/PhotoEdit)

Move See ¶ 5218.

MS-DOS (DOS, PC-DOS) See ¶ 4315.

Multiloading Loading several programs with the ability to switch from program to program. Only one program is active at a time. See ¶ 4324 for single-tasking.

Multimedia program See ¶ 4417.

Multiprocessing See ¶ 4541.

Multi-programming A technique that permits two or more programs to reside in main memory together and, under control of the operating system, to be executed simultaneously.

Multitasking Executing more than one program at a time. Only one program is actively controlled by the keyboard. Another program can run in the background, but without direct keyboard control. Background execution is for operations that are time consuming, but require little of the CPU—primarily printing. See, also, ¶ 4325.

Network See ¶ 4500 and 5681.

Notebook computer See *portable computer.*

Number Systems

Decimal Base 10	Binary Base 2	Octal Base 8	Hexadecimal Base 16
0	0	0	0
1	1	1	1
2	10	2	2
3	11	3	3
4	100	4	4
5	101	5	5
6	110	6	6
7	111	7	7
8	1000	10	8
9	1001	11	9
10	1010	12	A
11	1011	13	B
12	1100	14	C
13	1101	15	D
14	1110	16	E
15	1111	17	F
16	10000	20	10

Numeric keypad

Located at the right side of the keyboard and arranged like the keyboard of a 10-key hand calculator. When the number lock *<Num Lock>* key is on, the number keys can be used.

When *<Num Lock>* is off, the number keys control the cursor (the indicator that moves around the screen under the control of the user). The cursor indicates the current point of interest on the screen: where the last action took place, or where the next action will take place.

<Num Lock> is a **toggle key:** it shifts back and forth between two conditions—numbers and cursor—as the shift lock on a typewriter shifts back and forth between uppercase and lowercase characters.

Object-oriented graphics (vector graphics)

Images stored as mathematical formulas for lines, shapes, and curves. Capable of perfectly smooth curves, limited only by the resolution of the printer. Can be enlarged or reduced without introducing distortions. Compare to *bitmapped images*. See, also, *vector graphics*.

OCR (**o**ptical **c**haracter **r**ecognition)

Use of a scanner to read and special software to recognize printed text. First, printed or typewritten text is read by a scanner and converted to digital data. Second, the digital data is translated by software to ASCII characters. In practical use, a third step is employed: editing by the user. Thus, a printed or typewritten page can be converted to an ASCII file that is available to a word processor—without rekeying it.

MORE

Off-line	Not connected to the system or switched to inactive status. An auxiliary copier not connected to the system is an *off-line* copier. A printer that is turned off or set to inactive (off-line) status is *off-line*. Contrast with *on-line*.
On-line	Connected to the system, switched to active status, or capable of interacting with other components of the system. Contrast with *off-line*.
On-line information service	See ¶ 4419.
Operating system	See ¶ 4300.
OS	See *operating system*.
OS/2 (Operating System/2)	See ¶ 4334.
Outlining	See ¶ 5007-14.
Output	Anything produced by the system, especially those things that are displayed, printed, or stored on disk. Output can also be stored in memory, or take the form of sound, light, electronic signals, and so on. Contrast with *input*.
Output device	Any peripheral device that produces output; e.g. monitor, printer, plotter, loudspeaker, or synthesizer.
Paint program	See ¶ 5308.
Parallel port	An external connection to the data bus on the motherboard; it is used primarily to connect a printer to the motherboard. A typical parallel connector has 36 pins, 8 of which are used for data and 9 for printer control signals. The 8 data channels permit simultaneous (**synchronous**) transmission of the 8 bits that represent a character. Contrast with *serial port*.
Parallel printer	A printer that is connected to the system case via a parallel port and receives synchronous data transmission. See, also, *parallel port*.
Pascal	A high-level programming language that requires highly structured programs. Useful in academic applications; less useful in business applications. Available for use with either an interpreter or a compiler. See, also, *compiler, high-level programming language,* and *interpreter*.
Path	See *disk organization*.
PC (**p**ersonal **c**omputer)	A desktop computer designed for a single user. Usually refers to DOS (IBM compatible) systems rather than Macintosh or other systems.
Peripheral device	A system device other than the CPU (e.g., disk drive, printer, keyboard, mouse, scanner, etc.).

Pica type Fixed-pitch type with 10 character per inch. See, also, *elite type*.

Pixel (picture element) The smallest unit in a screen display. Arranged in columns and lines, the pixels make up the screen. On a color monitor, each pixel consists of three dots (red, green, and blue). The system controls the pixels to produce the screen image. See, also, ¶ 4009.

Platform See ¶ 4305.

Pointing device An input device that controls the cursor, using it as a pointer. See, also, *mouse* and *trackball*.

Portable computer Small, light computer designed to operate from battery power as well as household current. Most of the general-purpose computers in each of the following size categories use the same CPUs as do their desktop counterparts or similar CPUs drawing less current. There are computers in most of these categories that use the most common operating systems and other software (e.g., DOS, Windows, Macintosh, Unix, etc.).

Sizes and weights are for typical general-purpose computers in each category.

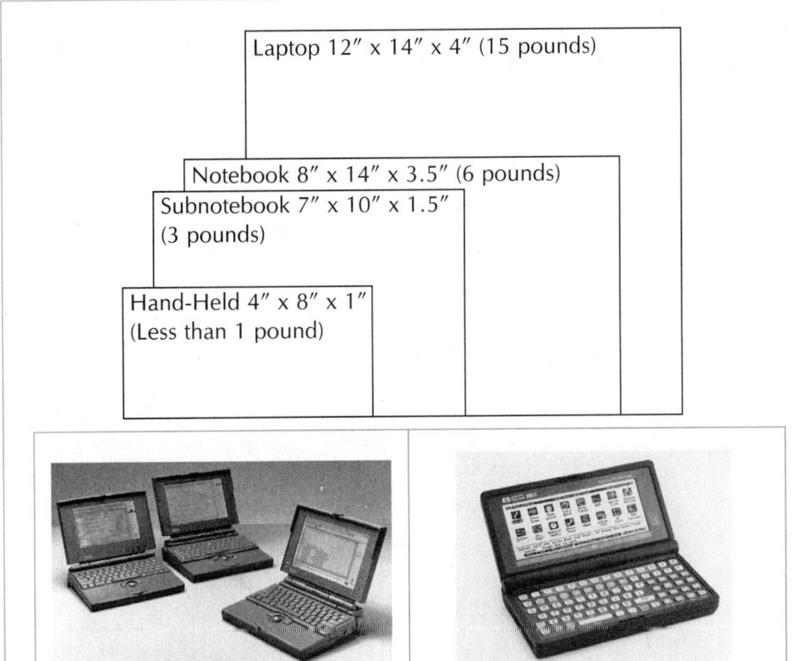

Illustration 4200.15a
Notebook Computer
(Courtesy of Apple Computer, Inc./ John Greenleigh, Photographer)

Illustration 4200.15b
Hand-held Computer
(Photo courtesy of Hewlett Packard Company)

MORE

4

4

Portals	See ¶ 4543.
PostScript	The dominant page description language not only in desktop publishing but in the printing industry as well. Controls laser printers and other high-resolution printing and typesetting devices (imagesetters, for example) to produce high-quality documents including text and graphics. See, also, *EPS*.
Presentation program	See ¶ 4416.
Print screen <Prt Sc> key	Causes the printer to reproduce, to the best of its ability, the image that is on the screen (in most cases, the screen can display some characters the printer cannot print). This is an easy way to "take notes." It may be necessary to hold down *<Alt>*, *<Shft>*, or *<Ctrl>* while pressing *<Prt Sc>*; see your operating system manual.
Processing	See ¶ 4001.
Program	A list of instructions written in a programming language. When loaded into the computer and executed, a program causes the system to operate in a predetermined manner.
Proofreading	See ¶ 5033-37.
Proportional spacing	See ¶ 5321.
Protocol	See ¶ 4519.
Public-domain software	Programs that are not copyrighted and may, therefore, be used freely by anyone. Contrast with *freeware* and *shareware*.
Pull-down menu	See ¶ 4328, 5402, and 5417. See, also, *drop-down menu*.
Queue	Pronounced as "cue." A waiting-line of tasks to be done by the system: typically a line or queue of printing jobs that the printer is doing one-at-a-time and in-turn while the rest of the system is put to another use, such as the composition of a document.
RAM (**r**andom **a**ccess **m**emory)	See *memory*.
Record	In database management, a subdivision of a file. A *file* of customers might contain a *record* for each customer. Each *record* might contain several *fields*, such as *address, telephone, sales,* and so on. See, also, *disk organization, field,* and *file*.
Recreation application	See ¶ 4422.
Redirector	See ¶ 4529.
Reformat	See ¶ 5226.

Relational database See ¶ 4410 and 4412.

Removable hard disk Hard disk drive in which the disk itself can be removed from the disk drive. Combines great speed and capacity with portability. The removable disk can be transported and stored almost as conveniently as can floppy disks. Although both the drive and the removable disks are more expensive than floppies, the greater speed of removable hard disks makes them an attractive alternative to floppies for truly voluminous applications—particularly among users who regularly work together and can, therefore, choose one type of removable disk. See, also, *Bernoulli box*.

Illustration 4200.16 Removable hard disk

Repeater See ¶ 4544.

Resolution The number of dots per inch that can be displayed or printed. The more dpi (**d**ots **p**er **i**nch), the higher the resolution and the sharper and clearer the image.

Ordinary newspaper halftones are printed at low resolution: 65-85 dpi (**d**ots **p**er **i**nch). With an ordinary magnifying glass, one can easily see each dot. Laser printers print at 300 dpi and more; professional imagewriting equipment operates routinely at high resolution: 1200 dpi and more.

Retrieve See ¶ 5230.

Ring configuration See ¶ 4523.

Router See ¶ 4546.

RSI (**r**epetitive **s**train **i**njury) Injury to the hands, wrists, arms, neck, and shoulders that results from the use of those body parts in repeated patterns. Those patterns are often associated with use of the computer.

Risk of injury is minimized when one uses ergonomic furniture and equipment, observes the rules for good posture, avoids rigid muscle set, and takes regular breaks.

MORE

Height and angle of the screen and keyboard and adjustment of the chair are particularly important.

Special keyboards, pointing devices, monitor mounts, and office furniture have been developed to help users avoid RSI.

RSI is also known as CTD (**c**umulative **t**rauma **d**isorder) and CTS (**c**arpel **t**unnel **s**yndrome).

Satellite See ¶ 4007.

Save See ¶ 5228.

Scalable font See ¶ 5319.

Scanner Converts the image of original copy or artwork to digital data that can be translated into any one of several standard file formats used for storing graphics. A scanner also converts the images of printed or typewritten characters to ASCII code that can be stored electronically.

A **flatbed scanner** scans an entire page in one pass; a **hand-held scanner** scans about half a page in one pass, depending upon software to stitch the halves of each page together if necessary. See, also, *Graphics* and *OCR*.

Illustration 4200.17a Flatbed Scanner

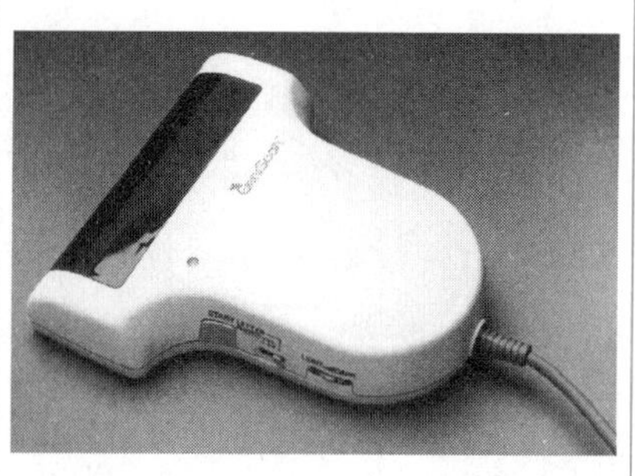

Illustration 4200.17b Hand-held Scanner (Photo courtesy of Stephen McBrady/ PhotoEdit)

Screen (monitor) See *monitor* and ¶ 5201-02.

Screen graphics See ¶ 5314.

Scroll bar See ¶ 4328.

Serial port A connector on the back of the system case through which **serial** or **asynchronous** (one-bit-at-a-time, in-line) data is transmitted and received. Serial-port connections are used for mdoems and for connecting computers and computer systems to one another. Contrast with *parallel port*.

Server See ¶ 4527-28.

Shareware Software distributed freely via BBSs, mail, shareware houses, and user-to-user. Unlike public domain software, shareware is copyrighted. The publisher (frequently a hobbyist or small entrepreneur) requests payment of a small fee from those who decide to use the software after they have tried it. Contrast with *freeware* and *public-domain software*. See, also, *BBS*.

Slot See *expansion slot, circuit board,* and ¶ 4107.

Soft font See ¶ 5317.

Soft hyphen See ¶ 5208.

Software Programs: system programs and application programs.

Spelling checker See ¶ 5232.

Spreadsheet See ¶ 4403-8.

Standards See ¶ 4519.

Star configuration See ¶ 4522.

Storage Mass read-write memory that retains the stored data after the system is turned off. See, also, *floppy disk, hard disk drive,* and *memory*.

Style sheet See ¶ 5225.

System A single computer installation—including its CPU and peripheral devices such as disk drives, keyboard, monitor, printer, mouse, and scanner.

System 7 The current version of the Macintosh operating system. See, also, ¶ 4332.

System case See ¶ 4105.

System software See ¶ 4300.

Tab stops See ¶ 5222.

Telecommunications See ¶ 4600.

Terminal See ¶ 4515.

Thesaurus See ¶ 5233.

Toggle, toggle key, toggle switch A switch or other control device that has two positions. For example, the *<Shift Lock (or Caps Lock)>* is a *toggle key* that allows the user to *toggle* between capitals and lowercase letters.

Token ring See ¶ 4523.

MORE

4

CONTINUED

Tower case Stands vertically next to the monitor rather than sitting horizontally beneath it. Tower cases usually have more room for expansion boards, disk drives, and other internal components.

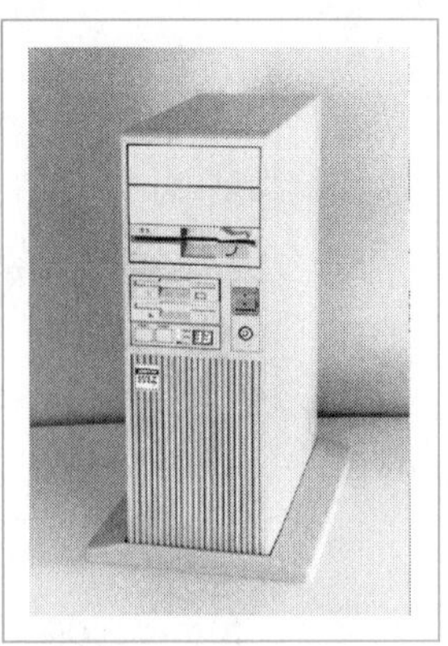

Illustration 4200.18 Tower Case (Photo courtesy of David Young-Wolff/PhotoEdit)

Trackball See *mouse*.

Transcription See ¶ 5021-22 and 5026-27.

Tree chart See *disk organization*.

TSR (terminate and stay resident) A program that (1) is loaded before an application program, (2) terminates, but leaves a latent module in memory ready to be called from within the application program, and (3) pops up within the application program when a specified key combination (hot key) is pressed. Among popular TSRs are spelling checkers, thesauri, and macro programs.

Twisted-pair wire See ¶ 4533.

Typeface See ¶ 5315.

Typewriter See ¶ 5101-03.

Typography See ¶ 5315-25 and references in ¶ 5400.

Underscore See¶ 5215, 5324.

UNIX See ¶ 4333.

UPC (Universal Price Code) *See bar code*.

Upload To send a file or files to another computer system via network or modem. See, also, *BBS* and ¶ 4516.

Utility program A program that supplements the operating system by performing housekeeping tasks related to the organization of the system or its work. Utility programs can help with disk organization, file management, and similar tasks. Recent versions of DOS incorporate several programs that were previously marketed as separate utility programs.

Vector graphics Also called **object oriented graphics** or **outline graphics,** images stored as mathematical formulas for lines, shapes, and curves. A **vector** is a quantity that has magnitude and direction; it is represented by a line. Vector graphics are capable of perfectly smooth curves; smoothness and accuracy are limited only by the resolution of the printer itself. Vector graphics can be enlarged or reduced without introducing distortions. See, also, *object-oriented graphics*.

Video adapter Circuitry that controls a monitor and transmits the signals necessary to produce the desired images on the screen. It is usually located on a circuit board that is plugged into an expansion slot, but may be located on the motherboard. See, also, *monitor* and illustration 4107.1.

Video display See, also, *monitor*.

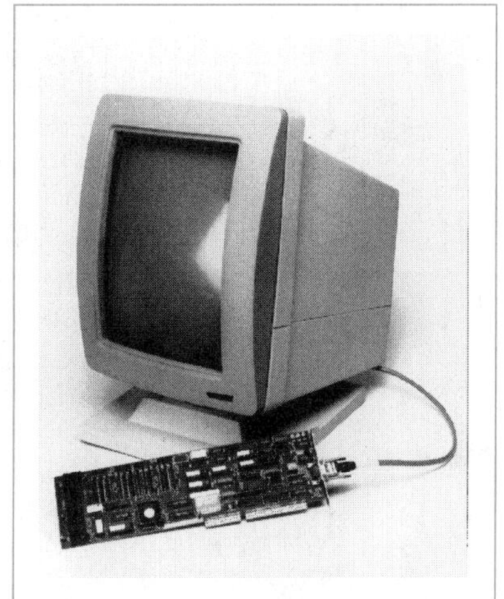

Illustration 4200.19 Multisync Monitor Connected to VGA Adapter (Photo courtesy of Stephen McBrady/ PhotoEdit)

Video standard A uniform method of producing images on the screen. Video standards range from the first, fuzzy one-color monitors of the first PCs to the sharp, clear, color monitors of today's high-end computer systems.

Each video standard has four components:

(1) Horizontal resolution: the number of dots or pixels across the entire screen.

(2) Vertical resolution: the number of dots or pixels on the screen vertically—or the number of lines of horizontal dots.

(3) Mode: text or graphics. Text mode supports the display of the 256 ASCII characters; graphics mode supports the display of an unlimited variety of shapes.

MORE

(4) Colors: the number of colors that can be displayed. In any video standard, additional colors require a sacrifice in resolution. Early PC monitors were **monochrome** monitors; although the word appears to mean "one color," it actually means two colors: one color for the background and one color for the foreground.

Like most other computer components, high-quality color monitors now cost much less than in the past. Most systems equipped for general office use, word processing, or desktop publishing have color monitors that meet or exceed VGA (**v**ideo **g**raphics **a**rray) standards. That means that they are capable of producing a sharp, clear image, displaying text or graphics in at least 16 colors.

Virus A program designed for use as a prank or for sabotage. The code attaches itself to other code in memory, causing the infected system to display or print predetermined messages or otherwise to behave erratically. A virus can cause errors and corrupt memory and disk storage. In extreme cases, a virus can destroy the contents of hard drives or corrupt all of the software in a system.

All viruses are designed by people. A virus may be embedded in input received by modem or disk. Programs are available for detecting and removing known viruses, but it is likely that new ones will emerge from time to time. See, also, ¶ 4535.

4

WAN (**w**ide **a**rea **n**etwork) See ¶ 4501 and 4542.

Windows See ¶ 4326-30.

Word processing See ¶ 5000.

Word processing program See ¶ 5200.

Word processor See ¶ 5103-05.

Word wrap See ¶ 5207.

WORM (**w**rite **o**nce **r**ead **m**any times) Optical disks that allow for one-time recording but can be read many times.

WYSIWYG (**W**hat **Y**ou **S**ee **I**s **W**hat **Y**ou **G**et) See ¶ 4331 and 5202.

Xerography See ¶ 4005.

4

SYSTEM SOFTWARE

Operating Systems

4301 **Definition.** The **operating system** consists of one or more programs that manage the operations of a computer. It acts as a bridge interface between the computer hardware, application software (See ¶ 4400), and the user. It provides the most basic instructions your computer needs to operate. It tells the computer how to interpret input from the keyboard and/or mouse; how to process data; how to produce output to the display screen, printer, or other devices; and how to store files. The operating system is the first program loaded when the computer is turned on.

4302 **Boot.** The process of loading an operating system into the main memory of the computer is called **booting** the system. This routine called **boot** (from the term *bootstrap,* pulling yourself up by yourself) has two functions: to complete the POST, and to load the operating system.

4303 **POST (power on self test).** The **POST** is the process the CPU uses to send signals over the *system bus*—the circuits that connect all system components with each other—to check all components of the system (hardware and software) for proper operation. It checks the display, the RAM (random access memory) chips, the keyboard, the disk drives, and searches for an operating system. When these functions are complete, the boot operation begins launching the operating system by reading the operating system files and copying them to the computer's RAM.

4304 **API (application program interface).** API is a language and message format used by a program to activate and interact with functions in software or hardware or with user interfaces (e.g., keyboard, mouse, menus).

4305 **Platform.** A **platform** is the system (hardware and software) necessary to run an application program. Platforms originally meant only the structure of a particular computer system. At that time the structures included platforms unique to particular computers such as IBM and IBM-compatibles, Macintosh, UNIX, minicomputers, and mainframes. Lately, because several operating systems are available to operate on the same machines (DOS, DOS with Windows, OS/2, NT), the term has been used to identify the operating system as well. In offering a new software package, a manufacturer now may claim it operates on the DOS, Windows, OS/2, NT, Macintosh, and UNIX *platforms*. All of these operating systems will be discussed in this chapter.

Computer Hardware

4306 **System unit.** The **system unit** holds all of the electronic components of your computer, also known as the central processing unit (CPU). The floppy and hard disk drives are *usually* mounted inside of the system case.

4307 **Monitor.** The **monitor** is the video display tube, CRT, or screen plus its case and associated circuitry. The monitor displays visually what is keyed on the keyboard and whatever the system provides as video output. This display *may* have an on/off switch.

4308 **Keyboard.** A **computer keyboard** is a board with keys that is similar to a typewriter keyboard. The keyboard is used to key entries and issue commands. The computer keyboard has alphabetic and numeric keys like the typewriter, but it also contains special keys to use with applications software. A variety of keyboards are available with different special keys.

4309 **Floppy disk drive.** The **floppy disk drive** is used to store information and to put information into the computer (applications programs or files from another computer, for example). From the floppy drive you can put information onto the hard drive or take information off the hard drive onto a floppy disk.

4310 **Sizes of floppy disk drives.** Floppy disk drives come in two *sizes*: 5 ¼-inch or 3 ½-inch relating to the size of the floppy disk they accept. Floppy disks differ in size and type (referring to the amount of information they can store). The disk drive you use must match the floppy disk you use in both size and type. The computer you use must be able to handle the type of disk (e.g., double sided, high density, both). For example, an IBM 386 will take high density, but not double density, disks.

4311 **Types of floppy disks.**

Size of Disk	Types of Disks: Capacity and Identifiers for IBM and IBM compatible machines		
5 ¼-inch disks	360 KB disks = 368,640 bytes double density (DD) double sided (DS)	1.2 MB disks = 1.2 million bytes double sided, high density (HD)	
3 ½-inch disks	720 KB disks = 737,280 bytes double density	1.44 MB disks = 1.44 million bytes	2.88 M disks = 2.88 million bytes

4312 **Hard disk drive (hard drive).** A **hard disk drive** is a mass storage device containing usually a rigid, nonremovable metal disk coated with a magnetic surface. The hard disk drive can be mounted internally inside the system unit box or be external and connected to one of the computer's ports via a cable. The hard drive contains several stiff metal disks called platters on which data is stored.

4313 **Mouse.** A **mouse** is a small input device used to control the movement of the cursor and to enable the user to select options displayed on the screen.

4314 **Printer.** A **printer** makes a paper copy (called **hard copy**) of documents created on the computer. The printer must be attached to the computer by a cable and *installed* (giving directions to the computer application software as to how to interface with the printer) to function.

Disk Operating System (DOS)

4315 **DOS, PC-DOS, and MS-DOS.** The **disk operating system** *(DOS)* created for the IBM personal computer (PC) is sometimes referred to as both *DOS* and *PC-DOS* to differentiate it from *MS-DOS*, the version created for *non*-IBM PCs. DOS and MS-DOS were developed by Microsoft and are almost identical. IBM has participated in the development of DOS in varying degrees.

4316 **DOS prompt.** The **DOS prompt** is the message DOS displays when it is ready to accept input. It identifies the current drive that the computer will read from or write to. The user keys a command at the DOS prompt and then presses the enter key to send the command to the operating system.

DOS Prompt Examples

A:>
C:>
D:>

4317 **DOS file.** A **DOS file** refers to any computer file created under DOS.

4318 **DR DOS (Digital Research DOS).** DR DOS is a DOS-compatible operating system from Novell noted for its many features.

4319 **AUTOEXEC.BAT (Automatic execute batch) file.** The **autoexec.bat** is a file of DOS commands that are automatically executed when the computer is turned on. This file can be easily modified by the user. For example, a user might want to modify this file to have a calendar program loaded and displayed when the computer is turned on.

4320 **Load.** To **load** is to copy a program or file into the computer's memory so that the computer can execute it. *Load* is also used to describe the process of filling up a disk with programs or data and the process of inserting a disk or tape into a drive.

4321 **.BAT (Batch) file.** **.BAT** files are files of DOS or OS/2 (see ¶ 4334) commands that are executed one after another from beginning to end. The .BAT is the file extension. It is preceded by a file name of not more than eight letters/numbers. A batch file allows processing of a group of commands at one time.

Operating Systems Development Beyond DOS

4

4322 **Installed base.** In moving beyond DOS (as well as within revisions of DOS) computer companies had to consider their installed base. The **installed base** for any computer company is the *existing customers* who have already purchased and are using a company's products. In developing new, advanced computer operating systems, companies need to make certain they have provided *backward compatibility* so that customers can continue to use all of their old programs with the new operating system.

4323 **DOS limitations.** Under DOS, one program is started at a time. Work cannot begin on a second task until the first task is complete. DOS is like a desktop with space for only one piece of paper. The user is never given the opportunity to spread out work on the desktop to work on many tasks at the same time.

4324 **Single-tasking, context switching, or task switching.** **Single-tasking, context switching,** or **task switching** are all terms describing the process that enables you to load multiple programs into a computer at the same time, but run only one program at a time.

4325 **Multitasking.** In **multitasking** a single system with a single CPU switches back and forth among programs so quickly that all of them appear to be running simultaneously. In multitasking, the program you are currently working with—the one that accepts keystrokes—is the *foreground task*. The programs that disappear into folders when minimized (see, also, ¶ 4328) are *background tasks*. While some operating systems (TopView, the original DOS 4.0, OS/2 1.x, etc.) were excellent efforts to create a powerful new platform for multitasking and running memory-intensive graphical programs, they failed with customers because they were unable to support existing applications (the installed base). IBM and Microsoft did not build anything to draw people away from DOS until Windows 3.0 (see ¶ 4330) was released by Microsoft.

Windows

4326 **Microsoft Windows definition.** Microsoft's Windows program is not an operating system, but rather a companion program to DOS. It must have DOS loaded to operate. It is a graphics-based operating environment that enables users to view applications in various "windows" on their screens.

4327 **DESQview.** DESQview from Quarterdeck Office Systems is another popular windows-environment program for DOS. It runs multiple DOS text and graphics programs in resizable windows.

4328 **Graphical user interface (GUI).** A graphics-based operating environment employs **graphical user interfaces** (GUIs), which are sometimes referred to as *WIMP interfaces*. WIMP is the abbreviation for the various parts of the GUI:

- **W = Windows**. The rectangles or squares on-screen known as **windows** that can be resized and rearranged by the user. If there are more options available through the window than can be viewed in the window size used, the window contains a *scroll bar* (which can be both horizontal and vertical) with arrows at each end. To view additional information, the user points to an arrow and scrolls through the window to view more options.
- **I = Icons**. **Icons** are small pictures that represent concepts or objects—such as programs, data, and peripherals (printers, CD Rom, etc.). An icon sometimes takes the place of the application or filename.
- **M = Mouse**. The **mouse** is the small input device used to control the movement of the cursor and to select an on-screen option.
- **P = Pull-down menus**. **Pull-down menus** are menus that pull or drop down, when a choice is selected, to reveal currently available options or unavailable options. Unavailable options are usually accessible once another step has been taken (such as highlighting text before choosing "cut") and when unavailable, are usually displayed in another color—such as light gray. (See ¶ 5417 for examples of pull-down [also known as drop-down] menus.)
- **Dialog boxes.** A GUI application also features dialog boxes that allow you to carry on a conversation with the computer by selecting various options or providing additional information:
- **Option buttons.** In a group of option buttons only one option can be selected. For example, in illustration 4328.1, "full document" is selected to print the entire file. Selecting "Current Page" would print the current page only.
- **Check boxes.** In a group of check boxes, you can select any or all of the options, as long as the choices are not contradictory. For example, in illustration 4328.2, you can choose to have your text printed with bold, underline, and italic in the options listed in the appearance and size boxes; however, you cannot select both underline and double underline—or large and extra large text size.

MORE

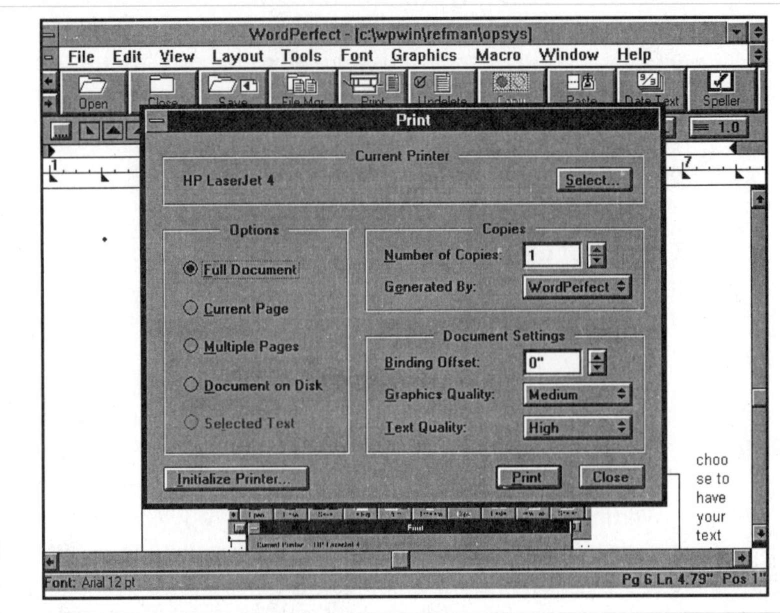

Illustration 4328.1 Option Buttons

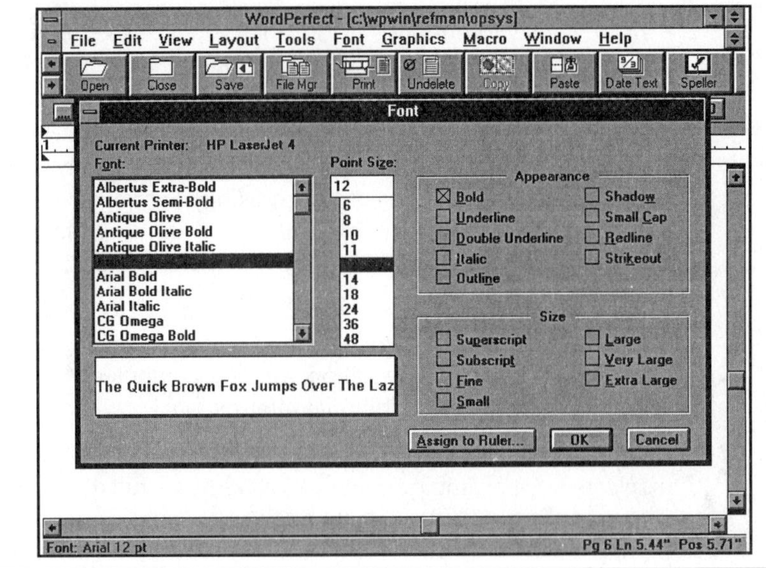

Illustration 4328.2 Check Boxes, Listed Boxes

- **Text boxes.** A text box allows text to be keyed, such as entering the name of a new file to be saved.
- **List box.** A list box contains a series of available choices. You can select an item from the list. For example, in illustration 4328.2, the Arial font is selected. In this case, selecting any other font would automatically deselect the Arial font. However, some list boxes allow you to select more than one item.

4329 **Desktop.** A **desktop** is an on-screen work area (so called because it resembles your desktop) in which each active application is displayed in a resizable, movable window, or in an icon.

4330 **Microsoft Windows 3.0.** Windows 3.0, released in 1990, did not include many more features than Windows versions 1.0 and 2.0. However, Windows 3.0 and later 3.x versions, were able to run not only existing DOS and Windows programs, but also provided the ability to load more than one existing program at the same time. Therefore, users could load and wait for the loading of each program only once each day and switch back and forth very quickly between programs already loaded. The immediate popularity of Windows 3.0 (it sold more copies in the first month, than OS/2 had sold in three years) reinforced developers' understanding of the consumer demand for backward compatibility and task switching in all new product development. Windows 3.0 does not provide true multitasking, rather it switches from one active program to another (preloaded) program giving the *appearance* that more than one program is active at a time.

Other Operating Systems

4331 **Macintosh computers.** Macintosh developed as a line of easy-to-use personal computers from Apple Computer. Macintosh computers first became popular because of

- **the graphic interface** based on the Xerox Star system.
- **WYSIWYG (What You See Is What You Get) graphics**; display on-screen image is exactly what you get when a document is printed.
- **ease of use**. All programs and files on a Macintosh are represented by on-screen, easy to identify pictures (icons).
- **program consistency**. All programs on the Macintosh have the same feel and look. Once you have learned one program on a Macintosh, learning other programs is easy.

4332 **Macintosh System 7.** Macintosh System 7 is a major upgrade of the Macintosh operating system (1991) and includes multitasking as well as virtual memory, increased memory addressing, TrueType fonts, and other advances.

4333 **UNIX.** UNIX is a multiuser, multitasking operating system from AT&T that runs on computers from micro to mainframe. While DOS and Windows are used primarily for single-user business applications that result in personal user productivity, UNIX is for multiuser applications—such as computer-assisted design/computer-assisted manufacturing (CAD/CAM), banking, and accounting. The result is increased group productivity. While powerful, UNIX has been slow in catching on with single users because of its high cost and difficulty of operation. UNIX is now owned by Novell, which is expected to position the UNIX operating system as a real competitor with OS/2 and NT.

4334 **IBM OS/2 (Operating System 2).** While DOS was designed as a single-user, single-tasking operating system, OS/2 is a single-user, multitasking operating system. It has a graphical interface (Presentation Manager) similar to Windows. Early versions were developed jointly by IBM and Microsoft. However, beginning with version 2.0, IBM began independent development. The 2.0 version has backward compatibility and runs OS/2, DOS, and Windows programs. One of IBM's missions in the development of OS/2 was to link the personal computer to the computer center.

4335 **Microsoft NT (New Technology).** Microsoft announced its version of OS/2, Microsoft NT in 1993. It is also a single-user, multitasking operating system.

4336 **Minicomputer.** A **minicomputer** is a medium-scale computer that can function as a single workstation or as a multiuser system with up to several hundred terminals. High-end microcomputers and low-end mainframes overlap minicomputer price and performance. Minicomputers have their own operating systems. (See ¶ 4515 for a comparison of personal computers, minicomputers, and mainframes.)

4337 **Mainframe computer.** A **mainframe** is the largest computer. It has hundreds of megabytes of memory and hundreds of gigabytes of storage. Mainframes are commonly used as the central computer in large corporations and universities and have their own operating systems. (See ¶ 4515 for a comparison of personal computers, minicomputers, and mainframes.)

4338 **Why switch?** For the majority of personal computer users on a network, upgrading to one of the newer, advanced operating systems may happen eventually because of the desire or need for true multitasking; the need to connect efficiently and exchange files easily between a PC, a minicomputer, a Macintosh, and a mainframe; and when software developers begin to place the most emphasis on cross platform connectivity and exchange of files between software programs.

4400 APPLICATION SOFTWARE

4401 **Application software described.** **Application software** enables computer users to perform specific tasks other than the operation and maintenance of the system itself: writing a report (word processor), preparing a budget (spreadsheet), or operating a client billing system (database). Contrast *application software* with *system software* (¶ 4300).

4402 **General application programs.** General application programs are those designed to serve a variety of users who have similar needs and to perform generic tasks that are common to most businesses, professions, and industries: word processing, spreadsheet, database, general accounting, and presentation programs, for example. Contrast these general applications with the specialized applications discussed in ¶ 4420-22.

Spreadsheet Programs

4403 **Spreadsheets and worksheets.** The multipurpose worksheet is the accountant's most useful form. Spreadsheets computerize the worksheet, making it easier to use because all the calculations are automatic and immediate.

4

4404 **The "what if?" feature.** A single change on a spreadsheet may cause a number of other changes. On a computerized spreadsheet, all changes are shown automatically as new information is entered. Therefore, it is possible to try many combinations of factors to get the desired results. In trying to balance a budget, for example, one can try every conceivable way to increase income or decrease expenses—without having to recalculate each time a change is made. The "what if?" feature can answer such questions as

- What if I get a 12 percent increase in salary?
- What if my income is decreased by 10 percent?
- What if I throw caution to the winds and take a Caribbean cruise this year?

4405 **Capacity of spreadsheets.** Huge quantities of numeric information can be entered and maintained on a single spreadsheet—and multiple sheets can be used to increase the capacity. Even modestly priced spreadsheet programs have 50 or more columns and 250 or more lines. The "sheet" is actually an imaginary sheet stored in computer memory. To understand how a computerized spreadsheet works, imagine a sheet of paper four feet wide and four feet high with 50 columns and 250 lines printed in regular pica type. Now imagine placing an empty eight-inch by ten-inch picture frame on the spreadsheet. The picture frame can be moved around to "see" every cell on the spreadsheet—but only a few cells can be seen at the same time. (A **cell** is the rectangular intersection of a column and a line. For example, the intersection of column d and line 12 is identified as cell d12).

4406 **Capacity of the screen.** Just as a picture frame can be moved around relative to a huge sheet of paper, the computer screen can be moved relative to the computerized spreadsheet. Typically, the screen can "see" at one time a section of the spreadsheet that contains about 8 columns and 23 lines—184 cells. The entire spreadsheet, 50 columns by 250 lines, contains 12,500 cells. Thus, the screen can "see" at one time 184 of the 12,500 cells, or less than 2 percent of the entire spreadsheet.

4407 **Spreadsheet example.** In the following example, a spreadsheet program has been used to design a simple budget report. We have used the spreadsheet program to retrieve a file named BUDGET from the disk on which it was stored in an earlier session. After retrieval, the spreadsheet in the BUDGET file is displayed on the screen.

Some of the cells are for input numbers, others are calculated according to formulas that are stored and retrieved as part of the spreadsheet. For example, a spreadsheet could have two input cells headed a and b and a third cell that displays at all times the current total of a + b (the formula).

Enter 5 in cell a and the Total cell automatically displays 5.

Cell a	Cell b	Formula Total a + b
5		5

Enter 19 in cell b and the Total cell automatically displays 24.

Cell a	Cell b	Formula Total a + b
5	19	24

Change the 5 in cell a to 14 and the Total cell automatically displays 33.

Cell a	Cell b	Formula Total a + b
14	19	33

The formulas are not shown in the spreadsheet itself but are shown one at a time at the bottom (or top) of the screen as the cursor is moved from cell to cell. If the cursor is in a cell that does not contain a formula, no formula is shown at the bottom (or top) of the screen.

When the cursor is in cell h2, a notation on the screen shows the formula: sum(b2...g2). The three dots mean "everything between." The formula says that cell h2 will contain the sum of everything between cell b2 and cell g2, or b2 + c2 + d2 + e2 + f2 + g2. A designated row of cells, horizontal or vertical, is called a **range.**

Spreadsheet Budget

a 1	b January	c February	d March	e April	f May	g June	h Total
2 INCOME							
3 ———							
4 Taxes							
5 Rent							
6 Food							
7 Misc Exp							
8 TOT EXP							
9 ———							
10 Savings							
11 Savings %							

Formula: sum(b2 . . . g2)

The formula for the current cell (h2) is shown at the lower left corner of the spreadsheet in the preceding illustration. As the cursor is moved from cell to cell, the formula for the current (highlighted) cell is shown—if the current cell has a formula.

In the following illustration, the formulas for *all cells that have formulas* are shown. The cells highlighted in color are those in which information must be entered if the budget is to be complete.

Spreadsheet Budget

a 1	b January	c February	d March	e April	f May	g June	h Total
2 INCOME		b2	b2	b2	b2	b2	sum (b2...g2)
3 ———							
4 Taxes	b2x.17	c2x.17	d2x.17	e2x.17	f2x.17	g2x.17	sum (b4...g4)

MORE

Spreadsheet Budget

a 1	b January	c February	d March	e April	f May	g June	h Total
5 Rent		b5	b5	b5	b5	b5	sum (b5...g5)
6 Food							sum (b6...g6)
7 Misc Exp							sum (b7...g7)
8 TOT EXP	sum (b4...b7)	sum (c4...c7)	sum (d4...d7)	sum (e4...e7)	sum (f4...f7)	sum (g4...g7)	sum (b8...g8)
9							
10 Savings	b2 - b8	c2 - c8	d2 - d8	e2 - e8	f2 - f8	g2 - g8	sum (b10...g10)
11 Savings %	b10/b2	c10/c2	d10/d2	e10/e2	f10/f2	g10/g2	h10/h2

To complete the example, we shall first enter 2000 for January income in cell b2. The calculated amounts in the 13 other cells shown will appear automatically.

Spreadsheet Budget

a 1	b January	c February	d March	e April	f May	g June	h Total
2 INCOME	2000	2000.00	2000.00	2000.00	2000.00	2000.00	12000.00
3							
4 Taxes	340.00	340.00	340.00	340.00	340.00	340.00	2040.00

Monthly income is $2000.00, total income for the 6-month period is $12,000. Taxes are calculated (by formula) at 17 percent of gross income.

Next we shall enter January rent, an expense of 520, in cell b5. The same amount ($520.00) will be recorded automatically for the five other months. Total rent will be calculated automatically; it will appear in cell h5.

5 Rent	520.00	520.00	520.00	520.00	520.00	520.00	3120.00

Food expenses vary from month to month; consequently, we shall use actual expenditures from last year. Therefore, there is no automatic calculation other than that for the total appearing in cell h6.

6 Food	321.52	267.57	346.10	283.52	275.26	315.04	1809.01

Miscellaneous expenses also vary from month to month; they are treated in the same manner.

7 Misc Exp	480.59	621.21	523.97	413.54	582.84	662.47	3284.62

The rest of the spreadsheet is calculated automatically.

Spreadsheet Budget

a	b	c	d	e	f	g	h
1	January	February	March	April	May	June	Total
2 INCOME	2000.00	2000.00	2000.00	2000.00	2000.00	2000.00	12000.00
3 ———							
4 Taxes	340.00	340.00	340.00	340.00	340.00	340.00	2040.00
5 Rent	520.00	520.00	520.00	520.00	520.00	520.00	3120.00
6 Food	321.52	267.57	346.10	283.52	275.26	315.04	1809.01
7 Misc Exp	480.59	621.21	523.97	413.54	582.84	662.47	3284.62
8 TOT EXP	1662.11	1748.78	1730.07	1557.06	1718.10	1837.51	10253.63
9 ———							
10 Savings	337.89	251.22	269.93	442.94	281.90	162.49	1746.37
11 Savings %	17	13	13	22	14	8	15

4408 **General spreadsheet applications.** Spreadsheets are used to computerize many traditional accounting reports including worksheets, statements of income and expense, and balance sheets. Spreadsheets may also be used as journals and ledgers by using only the traditional number of columns—typically debit, credit, and balance.

Spreadsheets are also used for **management information reports,** especially those that answer questions such as "What will happen to profits if we eliminate Product X?"

Database Programs

4409 **Database defined.** A **database** is a collection of data organized for efficient retrieval and processing. A computerized personnel file containing

MORE

individual personnel records is an example. The file is usually viewed in tabular form as shown in the following illustration. The entire table is the **file;** each line is a **record;** each column is a **field.**

Personnel File

Last Name	First	Middle	Street Address	City	ST	ZIP	Dept	Soc Security	Hired	Title
Angiolotti	Marvin	Albert	477 Oak Street	Cincinnati	OH	45222-2332	21	405-24-7093	11-19-83	Sales Manager
Berchentold	Rosalee	King	584 Maple Lane	Cincinnati	OH	45069-9435	24	402-22-2111	1-24-85	Personnel Manager
Contreras	Henry	W	5847 Elm Drive	Cincinnati	OH	45236-5227	21	261-61-6121	11-19-83	Salesperson

4410 **Relational database programs.** A **relational database program** can manage several databases, coordinating them through a common field or column. Compare this simplified view of the personnel file in ¶ 4409 with the payroll file used by the same firm. Without a database program, the files are maintained separately and the reports are prepared separately.

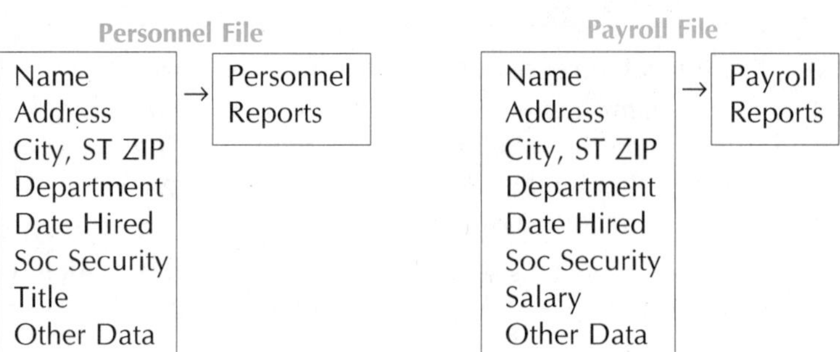

A relational database program can treat both of these files (and others) as a single database, using the social security column in each file to access, maintain, and coordinate the records in each file. The relational database program prepares all reports based on the expanded database, and performs other applications as well. (See, also, ¶ 4411.)

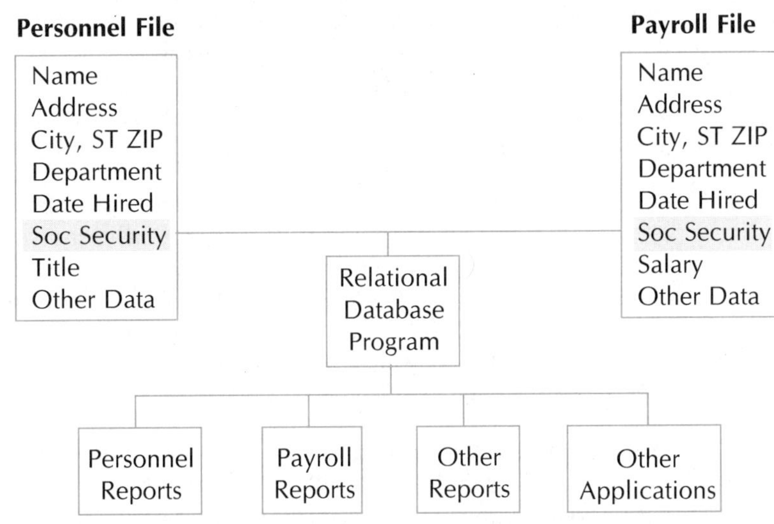

It is the common field, in this case the social security number, that allows the *relational* database program to retrieve all *related* records from all the files constituting the database. If your social security number is entered, the relational database program will scan all the records in all the files to find every record that pertains to you.

4411 **Flat-file database programs.** A **flat-file database program** works with one file at a time. To apply a flat-file (nonrelational) database program to the example used in ¶ 4409-10, the two files will be combined. The new database consists of a single file that contains the fields formerly residing in both the personnel file and the payroll file.

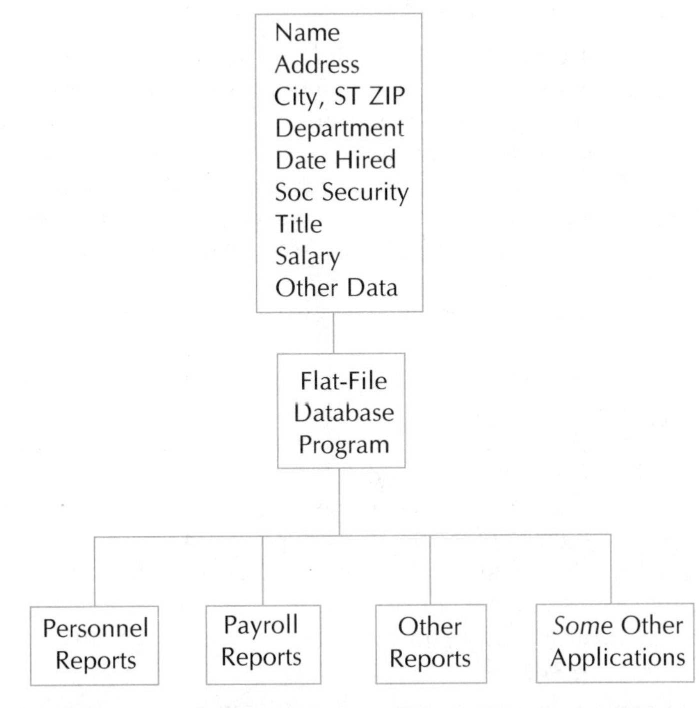

4412 **Relational and flat-file database programs compared.** Flat-file database programs are less expensive and easier to use. They do, however, lack some of the advanced features of relational programs—specifically, the ability to link several databases (see ¶ 4410) and perform advanced sorting, accounting, and printing tasks.

4413 **Confidentiality of records.** Access to some records should be confined to those with a specific need to know. Obviously, individual personnel records should be off-limits except to those in top management and personnel work who have a legitimate need for the information the records contain. Confidential files can be protected from unauthorized users by using access codes. **Access codes** are passwords that limit access to certain portions of the database.

4414 **Data integrity.** **Access codes** can also provide **limited access:** limited to certain records, certain fields, and/or limited to a read-only basis. This makes it possible for some users to read certain portions of the database, but not to revise the records. In larger database systems, responsibility for revising the data is usually centralized and restricted. Not only does centralization fix responsibility and minimize errors caused by carelessness or ineptitude, it also minimizes errors due to a lack of organization, coordination, or standardization. For example, if there are no controls, Amelia Bhern Cornwallis could be listed as Amelia Bhern Cornwallis, Amelia B. Cornwallis, Amelia Cornwallis, A. Bhern Cornwallis, Bhern Cornwallis, A.B. Cornwallis, A. Cornwallis, B. Cornwallis, or even as Amie Cornwallis (her nickname). If a cross-check is done on her address, she may be listed once at home, once at work, and once at her parents' address.

Obviously, some sort of standardization is necessary if duplication and other errors are to be avoided.

4415 **Client tracking.** One of the notable applications of database programs is **client tracking:** the maintenance of a record for each client in which the nature of each client contact is recorded. A contact may be a visit by the client to the office, a telephone call to or from the client, or some other business conducted on behalf of the client. A client tracking system may be the source for billing information. This system is used by attorneys, dentists, physicians, and others who need to keep track of their clients.

Presentation and Multimedia Programs

4416 **Presentation programs.** **Presentation programs** help the user prepare charts, graphs, illustrations, and other graphics on the computer. The computer image of each presentation graphic is stored in a file on a disk. That file can be displayed directly on the screen, imported into another program, inserted into a document, printed separately, made into an overhead projector foil, or sent via floppy disk to a service bureau for conversion to a slide, film, or any other compatible graphics medium. Although a presentation program can be used to prepare a single illustration for a printed report, it can also be used to prepare relatively sophisticated multimedia programs (see ¶ 4417).

4417 **Multimedia programs.** **Multimedia programs** integrate two or more media to present information in a manner calculated to capture and hold the attention of the audience. The information is usually presented as text, graphics, or sound, although exceptional applications have been designed to be felt or smelled. The media are usually computer screens, TV sets, slide projectors, overhead projectors, printed pages, or other compatible devices. Multimedia programs are usually controlled by general-purpose or specialized microcomputers.

Communications

4418 **Communications programs.** **Communications programs** are application programs that enable computers remote from one another to communicate, using telephone connections and modems. The simplest communications programs allow the user to select the settings for the modem, make the connection, send and receive files, and disconnect.

More-sophisticated communications programs employ elaborate user interfaces that are actually *simpler* for the user: macros that automate frequently used procedures, automatic connect and disconnect, and other user-friendly features.

4419 **On-line information services.** **On-line information services** use the communications capabilities of the microcomputer to provide on-line information via telephone connections and modems.

The subscriber to an on-line information service either pays a monthly fee or is charged by the minute (as in long-distance telephone billing) or both. On-line information services provide their subscribers with the necessary software as part of a one-time startup kit, usually made available to the new user for a modest fee.

Information varies by service; the following information and services are all available on one service or another:

Arts	Forums
Banking Service	Games
Bibliographic Database	Job Markets
Clubs	News
Computer Interest Groups	Shareware/Public Domain Software
Computerized Bill Paying	Shopping
Education	Special Interest Groups
Electronic Mail	Sports
Encyclopedia	Stock Market
Entertainment	Travel
Financial Service	Weather

Some of the outstanding on-line information services are CompuServe, Dow Jones News/Retrieval Service, GEnie, and Prodigy.

Specialized Application Programs

4420 **Business applications.** **Business applications** are those designed to serve the narrowly defined needs of users in a single business, profession, or industry. Contrast these with the general application programs discussed in ¶ 4401-19. Special-purpose application programs are available for the following fields and for others as well:

Architecture	Law office systems
Banking	Loan analysis for lending institutions
Bill collection	Maintenance scheduling
Church systems	Manufacturing inventory control
Condominium management	Medical office systems
Construction management	Opinion surveys
Dental office systems	Payroll management
Design	Ranching
Drafting	Shipbuilding
Engineering	Statistics
Estate planning	Structural engineering
Farming	Trucking
Fund accounting	Warehousing and inventory control
Land surveying	Will writing

4421 **Education applications.** Computers have a long-standing and continuing relationship with education. Apple and Macintosh, because of their easy-to-use graphical interface, have been particularly successful in the school environment. Education programs are helpful to those who want or need individual, self-directed study. Others are designed for group use in the classroom.

CD-ROM, with its ability to make available massive amounts of information and reproduce graphics and sound as well as text, now makes available entire books or sets of books, such as an encyclopedia—on disks that are indeed compact.

Education programs are available for most fields of study at most levels for most age groups. Since the list changes from month to month, the best sources are the listings in computer magazines, your favorite software stores, and the library of your choice.

4422 **Recreation applications.** **Recreation applications** range from educational programs that are so much fun that they hardly seem educational (*Flight Simulator, Where in the World is Carmen Sandiego*) to the utterly trivial that are unabashedly for-fun only. The for-fun-only market is the most volatile part of the software world. Here, the listings change from week to week.

4500 COMPUTER NETWORKS

4

COMPUTER NETWORKS

4501 **Computer network defined.** A **computer network** is a system in which two or more computers are linked, usually for the purposes of (1) exchanging information and (2) sharing common (network) resources such as files or expensive peripherals. A **local area network** (LAN) is a system in which two or more computers are connected in a single office or building. A **wide area network** (WAN) is a system in which two or more computers are connected over distances that may be as much as thousands of miles.

4502 **Communication via wire.** Although connecting computers via network cable is a relatively new science, the concepts used in building these networks date back to the nineteenth century. From the development of the *telegraph* and *Morse code* (by Samuel Morse) came the logic for ASCII, the modern-day computer alphabet and the concepts of sending data from one place to another using a series of electrical pulses. Alexander Graham Bell's telephone has burgeoned into a worldwide system that has improved rapidly over the years with fiber optics and microwaves replacing wire in many instances. The concepts of the **subscriber loop—**the analog audio line wire between your home and office—still provide the foundations for the telephone and computer network systems of today.

4503 **Printing telegraph.** The printing telegraph was the forerunner of the computer printer and computer terminal. Teletypewriters provided United Press International and Associated Press a wire service for fast-breaking news long before the computer networks they use today.

4504 **Telephone network.** The first network was actually that of Western Union, which was the first to span the North American continent following the westward growth of the railroads. As the demand for telephone service grew, Bell Telephone installed a complicated web of cables throughout the nation to provide the first telephone networks.

Telephones and Computers

4505 **Acoustic coupling.** The original use of telephone lines to transmit data involved workers in the field who used **acoustic coupling** to make and receive telephone calls via their company's existing two-way radio system. This first acoustical coupler was a device shaped like a foam bed that the telephone handset was put into. This made the telephone lines a highway for the radio communication. While the use of phone lines by third-party equipment was debated, the FCC ruled in favor of the use. This decision led to the FCC's 1975 publication of technical specifications—known as Rules and Regulations of the Federal Communications Commission, Part 68—and paved the way to ending AT&T's monopoly on telephones and telephone-related equipment.

4506 **Similarities between the telephone and the computer.** Although developed in different eras and with different technologies, the *telephone* and the *computer* seem to have been created for each other. The telephone network of today is supported by vast computer resources to aid in call processing, traffic routing, and call record keeping. Similarly, the existence of a worldwide telephone network provides the highway to allow computers to connect to one another for data transmission.

4507 **Differences between the telephone and the computer.** Even with these similarities, the telephone and the computer are still worlds apart. The world of the computer is digital; with all data passing through its central processing unit (CPU) in either a 1 or a 0 format. Telephones communicate by passing an analog audio signal over the line. Although much of the worldwide telephone network is now digital, the loop from the local telephone company office to the home is still the same two-wire circuit used by the Bell systems since the 1890s. It is these last few miles that the cable companies, telephone companies, television networks, and satellite providers are working so hard to standardize and modernize. The redesign of these final miles will greatly improve the video, audio, and computer services available in the home as well as access to worldwide services via the same system. For example, a video movie will be available 24 hours a day—beamed via satellite to a computer chip in a home cable box or television upon order and remaining there for instant, delayed, or partial viewing at the homeowner's convenience; as the movie is viewed, it will be erased from and clear the computer chip memory. Expanded shopping, library, foreign language, and other services will explode upon demand with the computer/telephone network connection.

4508 **Modem.** A **modem** *(modulator-demodulator)* converts the on-and-off digital pulses of computer data into on-and-off analog tones that can be transmitted over a normal telephone line. The first modems operated very slowly at a **baud** (signaling rate of a line) of 300 bits per second (bps) and made transmission of data a lengthy process. Recent improvements in modems allow speeds up to 57,600 bits per second. This development is important in providing the speed required for rapid transmission of data between the LAN (local area network within an office or building) and the WAN (wide area network providing connections fifty miles or thousands of miles away).

Communication between two individual computers:
computer↔modem↔telephone line↔modem↔computer

Communication between an individual computer and a network:
computer↔modem↔telephone line↔modem↔network↔computer

Communication between two computers on different networks:
computer↔[network]↔modem↔telephone line↔modem↔[network]↔computer

4509 **Modem communications interface.** Regardless of the communication speed, all modems share some common characteristics. Since they must connect to the telephone lines, they have a telephone-line interface (RJ-11) that looks like a regular telephone jack. For the connection to the computer, virtually all modems contain an RS-232C communications interface.

telephone line→RJ-11→modem→RS-232C→[network]-computer

4510 **Smart modems.** **Smart modems** were first introduced in 1981. The Hayes Company pioneered the use of microprocessor chips inside the modem itself. This technology provided automatic dialing and answering. The Hayes modem could virtually take the phone off the hook, wait for a dial tone, dial a number, wait for a connection, and implement the connection all by itself!

4511 **Mainframe computers.** The original **mainframe computers** were very large and very expensive. They required special air-conditioned and temperature-controlled facilities to function efficiently, as well as a dedicated staff of programmers and technicians to keep them running. Most of the early

MORE

systems were purchased by large businesses and universities; all data entry, access and retrieval was done in the computer center.

4512 **Video display terminal.** The modem and the **video display terminal** *(VDT)* provided a vehicle for terminals and computing to move out of the computer room and onto the desks of users throughout an organization. This distributed use of computers reduced costs per user significantly. Computer purchase and usage increased significantly as mainframe and minicomputers became affordable for many smaller companies and colleges.

4513 **Personal computer (PC).** Personal microcomputers first appeared in the late 1970s; the first IBM personal computer was introduced in late 1981 with a single-chip central processing unit (CPU). The personal computer gained immediate popularity with users who wanted to perform some mainframe-type data creation and manipulation without the difficulty, complexity, and limitations of the mainframe computer. Computer developers had learned many lessons from the mainframe; therefore, early personal microcomputers were easier to use, install, and upgrade without a staff of programmers and technicians. Still, they were a long way from the personal computers of today! These first personal computers were used primarily for stand-alone functions such as Lotus 1-2-3, VisiCalc, or WordPerfect. It was common to see both a personal computer and a mainframe terminal sitting on the same desk.

4514 **Microcomputers replace dumb terminals.** Soon it was discovered that the addition of a communications program to the personal computer would provide a connection to the company's mainframe or minicomputer. As mainframe "dumb" terminals wore out, they were replaced with personal computers.

4515 **Types of computers.** It is important to understand the differences between each type of computer from the smallest to the largest:

- **Dumb terminal.** A terminal that is connected to a powerful central computer. This "computer" cannot do anything if the central computer is shut down. It relies on the central computer for its processing power and storage.
- **Personal Microcomputer.** A computer that uses a single-chip microprocessor as its central processing unit. It is small enough to fit on a desk and powerful enough to carry out necessary operations on its own. Many of the current microcomputers are as powerful as some of the original mainframes!
- **Minicomputer.** A powerful computer often used as a central computer in a local area network. Minicomputers have a central processing unit comprised of more than one processing chip.
- **Mainframe.** The most powerful computer with hundreds of megabytes of memory and hundreds of gigabytes of storage. Commonly used as the central computer in large corporations and universities. The operating system of the mainframe is very complex and still requires a staff of programmers and technicians. The ease of use, graphic images, multiple

fonts, screen and menu design, and so forth, users are familiar with on a personal computer are unavailable with the mainframe operating system. Therefore, most of the recent developments in computer technology have been away from the mainframe and centered around the personal computer.

4516 **Upload/download.** The advantages of having all of the modern computer power is to connect electronically all components on a network and allow users to **upload** (send data to) and **download** (receive data from) each of the computers on the network—whether mainframe, mini, or personal computer.

4517 **Fax.** Ten years ago, the **facsimile machine** (better known as the *fax*) was almost unknown. Since that time, the fax has impacted every aspect of doing business from sending contracts between offices to sending in a business lunch reservation and order to a local restaurant. Unlike networked computers that transmit data in a computer alphabet (ASCII), the fax transmits images. A conventional fax is really two machines in one—a sender and a receiver. The sending machine incorporates an image scanner, a modem, and a microprocessor. The receiving machine reverses the process: the modem receives data from the phone and passes the data to the microprocessor; the microprocessor decompresses the data and sends it to the printer.

4518 **Fax modem.** The **fax modem** enables the computer to send and receive faxes. It is not necessary for a user to leave the desk and go to the fax machine. As a bonus, personal computer fax transmissions are clearer and sharper than regular fax transmissions, and they do not have any moving parts to cause paper jams. While working with any computer software program, a user will receive a message alert for an incoming fax. The fax can be read and discarded on the screen, or printed to the computer's local printer. In order for faxes to be received 24 hours a day, an individual computer and/or the network file server must be left on and the fax program left running (memory resident) at all times.

4519 **Communications protocols and standards.** Communications protocols are the hardware and software standards that govern transmission between two computer stations. As personal computer users increased in number, the demand for sharing of data on each hard drive grew. Networks were created for sharing files—word processing, database, and spreadsheet files, and devices (printers, fax modems, and electronic mail). Each sharing activity has its own rules; we call these rules standards and protocols. **Standards** describe how things should be; they set a minimum performance level. **Communications protocols** are sets of standards—rules and agreements describing how elements interact.

MORE

Conceptual example of a data transmission protocol:

Station one		Station two
I am here. Are you there?		**Yes I am.**
Are you ready to receive?		**Yes I am.**
Here comes part of the data	⟶	Xxxxxxxxxxxxxxxxxxxxx
Did you get it?		**Yes I did.**
Here comes the next part	⟶	Xxxxxxxxxxxxxxxxxxxxx
Did you get it?		**No I did not.**
Here it comes again	⟶	Xxxxxxxxxxxxxxxxxxxxx
Did you get it?		**Yes I did.**
That's all there is. Goodbye.		**Goodbye.**

To understand networking, you must understand the basic standards and protocols that make it possible for all network computers to be interoperable without losing or abusing the shared files and devices. Several large groups that influenced the development of standards and protocols are listed in ¶ 4520-4523.

4520 **Transmission Control Protocol/Internet Protocol (TCP/IP).** **The Department of Defense (DOD),** faced with an inventory of different computers that were not interoperable, pioneered the development of network protocols known as **Transmission Control Protocol/Internet Protocol (TCP/IP).** TCP/IP provides agreements for transmission across networks.

4521 **Ethernet.** **Xerox Corporation's Palo Alto Research Center (PARC)** developed protocols known as **Ethernet** to allow 1,024 nodes (network connection points—computers or terminals) to be connected and operate over local area networks (LANS). Ethernet has become a successful commercial product. Ethernet may use Standard Ethernet (10Base5); "ThinNet" or "CheaperNet" (10Base2); twisted pair, (10BaseT) using telephone wire; or Fiber Optic Ethernet. The latter two methods use a star pattern, considered easier for problem solving as networks expand.

4522 **ARCnet.** **Datapoint Corporation** developed a standard called **ARCnet** (**A**ttached **R**esources **C**omputer **Net**work), but kept it as a proprietary (unshared) set of specifications; therefore, it never enjoyed the success of Ethernet. ARCnet is known as a **star network** because it uses a cabling pattern in the shape of a star with active and passive hubs to extend cabling farther than Token-Ring or Etheret. A **hub** is a central switching device for communications lines; it is the center of the network. A file server often acts as the hub of a LAN. The hub may be passive (adding nothing to the transmission of the signal) or active (regenerating signals to boost strength as well as monitor activity.)

4523 **Token-Ring.** **IBM Corporation** developed the third major networking technology in use today, *Token-Ring*. The **Token-Ring** is one network with two physically separate wiring hubs. The hubs are connected by fiber optic cable and can be several thousand feet apart. The actual ring exists within the wiring hubs. This networking technology is called Token, or Token-Ring, because it uses a token passing access method to allow various components access to the network ring.

4524 **Work groups.** Work groups, people working together on common projects, need network applications to make sharing of their work easier. A work group may be located in the same office or building where computers are hard-wired in a LAN (see ¶ 4525) or located at a distance from one another in a WAN (see ¶ 4542). Networks are designed to serve work groups using common applications. These applications include sharing files, electronic mail (¶ 5682), group scheduling (meetings, rooms, and equipment), common database files (Rolodex, company directory, price listing,), bulletin boards (for exchange of information), sharing of files (regardless of software version or platform used), project management, on-line information services (e.g., Prodigy, CompuServe, and America Online), fax modem pool (¶ 4665), printer access, and forms processing.

For example, the latest in work flow and desktop software allows for *scheduling* a meeting for 25 individuals by setting the duration needed, time period, and subject of the meeting and *selecting* each participant's name in a company database. The software then conducts a search of all twenty-five calendars to determine the first available time when everyone can attend. The same software allows scheduling of the meeting room and any equipment needed within the same process! Imagine the time that is saved over the old system of trying to coordinate manually 25 calendars.

Other groupware features include automatic routing of forms to everyone who must authorize or receive copies. This process allows for a "hold" awaiting additional information, overriding to an administrator when special considerations dictate, and allowing everyone in the process to see where any item is at any given time.

4525 **Local area network (LAN).** A **local area network (LAN)** is a group of computers connected to a local network, often by no more than a thousand feet of cable. The growth of networks has inspired necessary developments in telephone technology, computer hardware design, software design, and even work group (two or more individuals who share files and databases) sociology. Because of the demand for flexibility, the original limited network specifications and protocols have been expanded to provide mix and match hardware, software, and operating systems (see ¶ 4300) to create a useful customized network.

Network Components

4526 **Network operating systems.** **Network operating systems** are programs that run in networked computers providing the ability to share files, printers, and other devices across the network. Computers that share their resources with others on the network are called **servers.** Servers can share hard disk drives, attached peripherals (such as printers and CD-ROM drives), and communications circuits. Servers check requests for proper authorization and for conflicts, then provide the requested service.

4527 **File servers.** **File servers** store files created by application programs. They provide simultaneous access to shared databases, such as a company phone directory.

4528 **Print servers.** **Print servers** accept print jobs sent by any network user. Since printers are slower than most application packages and network transmission, print jobs are spooled (stored in a disk file until the printer can accept them) in a print queue (a line of files waiting to be printed in the order in which they were received). The print server, however, can recognize a specific priority given to a particular job or user and move it up the queue for faster printing.

4529 **Client software.** **Client software** works with the operating system of the computer to route requests to file and print services. It is common to have client and server software running on the same computer. The **redirector** in the client software captures service requests it is programmed to recognize and routes them across the network for service.

4530 **Device driver.** The **driver** software works between the network interface card and the network communications software. This driver software tells the computer how to work with a device that is connected (internally or externally) to the computer. For example, a print driver tells the computer how to talk in a language that a particular printer understands.

4531 **Networked peripherals.** **Networked peripherals** include printers and modems with their own network connections. They do not have to be attached to the network via a computer.

4532 **Network interface card (LAN adapter).** The low-powered digital signals inside a computer are not powerful enough to travel long distances without help. The **network interface card** changes the signals inside the computer into more powerful signals for their trip across the network cable. This card also packages the data for transmission and acts as a gatekeeper to control access to the shared network cable. Inside the computer it moves data to and from the random access memory (RAM). Outside the computer it controls the data in and out of the network cable. When the digital signals establish a valid connection between two stations each can access the other if authorized. This connection is known as a **handshake.**

4533 **Network cabling.** The electrical signals from a computer can be sent over **network cables** of copper (unshielded twisted-pair, coaxial, or shielded twisted-pair), over fiber using light pulses, or through the air using radio or light waves. In fact, all of these techniques can be combined on any one network to take advantage of the features of each, while minimizing total costs. Illustration 4533.1 provides information on the speed, cost, cable size, and maximum relative cable length for each of the cable types.

Type of Cable	Speed	Cost	Cable Size	Maximum Cable Length
Unshielded twisted-pair	fast	least expensive	small	short
Coaxial cable	very fast	inexpensive	medium	medium
Shielded twisted-pair	very fast	expensive	large	short
Fiber optic	fastest possible	most expensive	very small	very long

Illustration 4533.1 Network Cable Comparison

4534 **Network management.** Network management software utilizes small management programs, known as **agents,** to monitor network activity. If data coming in from the agents exceeds certain criteria, the management software can detect and alert for viruses, monitor various software application activity by users (thus providing important information for licensing purchases), redirect traffic in case of unbalanced network utilization, and even dial a telephone number and summon human help via a pager. The network administrator monitors all of these activities to ensure that everything is working correctly on the network. Other important aspects of a network administrator's job include network security, virus control, file management, and network backup.

4535 **Network security.** Protection of data against unauthorized access is the purpose of network security. Programs and data are secured by issuing identification numbers and passwords (also known as **access codes**) to authorized users of a network computer. **Access privilege** involves various levels of security set up for programs and files including no access, read only, read and write. Users should be encouraged to protect their passwords and change them often; taught to log in each time they wish to use the network, and log off each time they leave their computer; and requested to alert the network administrator to any unauthorized use of a network workstation. Network administrators should routinely review network usage logs to pinpoint any obvious abuse of network privileges or any attempts to log in by unauthorized users.

4536 **Virus control.** A **computer virus** is software written and used to destroy data in a computer. After the virus code is written, it is often buried within an existing program. When that program is executed, or after a certain date, the virus is activated and attaches copies of itself to other programs in the system. Infected programs then copy the virus to other programs. Entire computer networks have had all data erased or corrupted because of a computer virus. When installed properly, network virus control programs automatically scan the hard drive and the file server for viruses. If a virus is detected, these programs take steps to eliminate and seal off the virus. Many network backup programs also have built-in virus detectors. However since every computer disk may potentially contain a threatening virus, network users should be trained to routinely scan any outside disk before use with networked computers.

4537 **File management.** With hundreds of users on an individual network, all wanting the latest in software programs to use and create new data files, the network file server manages thousands of files. File management software allows the network administrator to partition (reserve) part of the disk or memory for particular purposes. For example, software application programs may be kept in one section, user data files in another, utility programs in another, and so on. All of this is transparent to the network user, who simply accesses (starts up) programs, opens existing or creates new data files, and moves throughout the network "warehouse" of choices available to that user's password. Usually, networked data files are stored on the *<F:>* drive, and users are segmented. Thus, user Barb would find her files under the network directory *<F:\users\Barb\>*. (See ¶ 5635 for more information on user file management.)

4538 **Shared directory.** The network administrator may create an easy-to-use directory called **share** for users to easily copy files into and share with other users. All network users have acccess to this shared directory (e.g., *<F:\users\share\>*)

4539 **Maximizing network file server storage.** The network administrator may use some nightly batch programs to eliminate dated files in regular or shared directories, automatic back-up files (*.BAK), and corrupted files. Constant attention to network file management is necessary to avoid overloading the file servers.

4540 **Network backup.** **Network backup** is the process of creating duplicates of network files on different storage media for emergency purposes. The advantage of partitioning (see ¶ 4537) network files allows backup of selected portions of the network file server by partition and by date every night while the network is inactive. In the case of a hard disk failure, a network can be put back on-line (active) within a short period of time with all data (as of last night) intact. Because such backup does not include user hard disk files, users should be encouraged to store files on the network or complete their own backup.

4541 **Multiprocessing.** **Multiprocessing** provides simultaneous processing with two or more processors in one computer (also known as **mirror image**), or with two or more computers processing together. If one fails, the other takes over and no data or network time is lost.

4542 **Wide area networks (WANS).** A **wide area network (WAN)** is a communications network that covers wide geographic areas, such as states and countries. This network can be connected via telephone lines or via satellite. Because many organizations need to move data over distances greater than a few thousand feet, the capability for a wide area network to connect users over thousands of miles was developed. As copper cables stretch over great distances, they accumulate electrical noise from the environment and from each other. As pulses of light travel through fiber optic cables, they lose their sharpness and degrade in strength over long distances. Noise and signal degradation are the two most important limitations of LAN effectiveness over increased lengths. Increased distances for transmission require the use of Wide Area Networks , which use a combination of copper, fiber, and satellite transmission.

4543 **Portals and devices.** **Portals** are the places where the local (LAN) services and long distance (WAN) services meet. Portal devices (repeaters, bridges, and routers) extend and separate the network's high speed cable and assist in data handling.

4544 **Repeaters.** A **repeater** is a small box used to connect two segments of the network cable. The repeater retimes and regenerates the digital signal on the cable and sends it on its way. Repeaters are relatively inexpensive and easy to install, but are not capable of long distances.

4545 **Bridges.** **Bridges** read the station address of each data package being sent to determine the destination of the message and provide a bridge to that destination. They do not, however, delve into the data message itself.

4546 **Routers.** A **router** digs into the data message to find the destination, discards the outer package or frame provided by the LAN, and then repackages and retransmits the data in the fastest way possible. Routers are available to work between different types of LANs. The router can avoid transmission problems because it acts as a safety barrier between network segments. Data packages with errors do not make it through the router. While routers are the most expensive portal device, they make up for their cost in speed, quality, and problem elimination within complex networks.

4547 **Leased WAN lines.** The techniques chosen by an organization to link LANs will depend on network traffic, distances, speed required, network protocols in use, and corporate philosophy regarding owned versus leased facilities. Because everyone cannot afford to run copper wire or fiber optics all over the world, it becomes important to arrange for leased circuits for links between LANs. These leased circuits come in three varieties: circuit-switched, full-period, and packet-switched.

4548 **Circuit-switched services.** **Circuit-switched services** are those with a dial tone. The LAN equipment dials a connection, transfers data, and hangs up when transmission is complete. Charges include equipment and installation, a monthly service charge, and a per call, by the minute charge according to the distance. These systems are perfect for electronic mail, updating records, or other services that can be provided for only three to eight hours each day.

4549 **Full-period services.** **Full-period services,** such as leased telephone lines, provide a circuit dedicated to the lessee's use 24 hours a day. Charges are applicable at all times whether or not the lines are in use.

4550 **Packet-switched systems.** **Packet-switched systems**— such as CompuServe, SprintNet, and MCI Mail—allow LANs in many different locations to exchange data with one central location and with each other via that system. Charges are based on a monthly fee and an additional fee based on the amount of usage.

4600 TELECOMMUNICATONS

4

4601 **Telephones in the Information Age.** The number of channels available for telecommunications (voice, data, and video communications) has increased significantly with the development of microwaves, communication satellites, and fiber optics. Cheaper access to those telephone channels, computerized call-handling, and improved computer-telephone technology have increased the use of telephone facilities for the transmission of computerized information.

When practical and relatively inexpensive modems became available, many computer users envisioned a bright future for general-purpose computers in automating routine use of the telephone. Although people who use both telephones and microcomputers intensively may rely on their computers to maintain telephone lists, dial outgoing calls, and the like, smart telephones and answering devices have been the choice of most. Again, microchips have made these devices more compact, more sophisticated, and less costly. (See ¶ 4602.)

Features of Individual Telephones

4602 **Smart telephones.** The earliest commercial telephones consisted of a transmitter, a receiver, and a ringer. One lifted the receiver and cranked the ringer to establish contact with "central," the switchboard. The operator then used the switchboard to complete the connection manually.

The telephone dial made it possible for calls to be completed without the service of an operator—and was the first of the automatic and semiautomatic features now available on individual telephones. These features are discussed in ¶ 4602-14.

The telephone pictured in illustration 4602.1 has a traditional handset, and a built-in speaker as well. It stores, displays, and calls 100 numbers that are accessed alphabetically. It has the following additional features:

Automatic redial	Memory display
Call timer	Number-being-called display
Clock	Receiver volume control
Express dial buttons (3)	Ringer On-Off-Volume
Hold	Tone or pulse dialing
In-use light	Conference calling

MORE

Illustration 4602.1 Smart Telephone

A telephone with numerous automated features is sometimes called a **smart telephone.**

4603 **Amplifiers.** Some telephones have **amplifiers** and volume control built into the handset. Others have both features built into the base unit. Add-on amplifiers that plug in between the telephone base and the handset are also available. Amplified handsets can be substituted for standard handsets—but not all handsets are compatible with all bases. See, also, ¶ 4602 and ¶ 4668.

4604 **Automatic dialing.** Certain telephones can store frequently called numbers and dial them when the user enters an abbreviated code. Some store a few numbers; others store 100, 200, 500 or more numbers. Typically, a telephone that stores only a few numbers requires the user to maintain a written list of names and the corresponding codes. On such a telephone, if the third number stored is 555-1234, the user presses *<Memory><3>* to cause the telephone to dial 555-1234. (See ¶ 4668.)

Some telephones with larger storage capacity use alphabetic indexing. If the user wants to call *Jacobs,* the user presses *<J>* until the name *Jacobs* appears—scrolling past other names that begin with *J*. When *Jacobs* appears on the display, a touch of the *<Dial/Redial>* key displays the *Jacobs* number and dials it.

4605 **Clarifiers.** Certain special telephones contain clarifying circuitry for the benefit of those whose high-frequency hearing is impaired. Under the user's control, clarifiers selectively amplify high-frequency sound. Clarification helps many of those who are not helped sufficiently by amplification alone. (See, also, ¶ 4668.)

4606 **Cordless telephones.** A **cordless telephone** consists of two units: (1) a *base unit* connected to a conventional telephone line and (2) a *portable unit* "connected" to the base unit via a radio channel.

	Base Unit		Portable Unit
→ Incoming Telephone Transmission →	Converted to Radio Transmission	→ Via Radio Channel →	Earpiece
← Outgoing Telephone Transmission ←	Converted to Telephone Transmission	← Via Radio Channel ←	Mouthpiece

A cordless telephone may have access to 20 radio channels or more, and the ability to choose the best channel available when the call is placed. Transmission between base unit and portable unit may be scrambled to prevent eavesdropping.

Some portable units operate effectively up to half a mile from the base unit, depending upon weather conditions, interference from other transmissions, and physical obstacles.

The **base unit** may perform several other functions, such as

- charging the battery in the portable unit.
- serving as a second telephone complete with dial pad and speaker (but usually not a second handset).
- automatic dialing, express dialing, and last-number redial.

The **portable unit** may

- serve as an intercom unit with pager (between base and portable unit).
- provides additional features such as automatic dialing, express dialing, and automatic re-call.

Illustration 4606.1 Portable unit
(Photo courtesy of David Young-Wolff/PhotoEdit)

4607 **Emergency dialing.** See ¶ 4608

4608 **Express dialing.** Many telephones that require entering two or more numbers or letters for automatic dialing also provide two or three dedicated keys that serve no function other than to dial emergency or frequently used numbers as simply as possible. The selection of which numbers that are to have *express* status and the numbers that are actually stored and dialed are up to the user. Many users assign their express dialing capabilities to the numbers for police service, emergency medical service, and fire service. (See, also, ¶ 4668.)

4609 **Headsets.** A lightweight **headset** is not only a way to increase efficiency, but a means of avoiding painful and long-lasting injury to the head, neck, and shoulders.

Headsets are manufactured in a variety of designs. Most of them emphasize light weight and include amplifiers, volume controls, and mute controls (to turn the microphone on and off).

Cordless headsets are useful for those who need to move around the office while they are on the telephone. (See, also, ¶ 4668).

4610 **Large-number telephones.** Large-number telephones have oversized keys with large numbers for the benefit of persons with impaired vision. (See ¶ 4668.)

4611 **Last-number redial.** **Last-number redial** makes it possible to redial automatically the last number called when a designated key is pressed (usually the <#> key or a special dedicated key labeled *<Redial>*). Last-number redial is used primarily to re-call a number after getting a busy signal. (See, also, ¶ 4668.)

4612 **Macro dialing.** A **macro** is an expression that, when keyed, evokes a longer expression. On a telephone keypad, for example, the sequence *<Memory><1>* may cause the telephone to display a stored number of seven digits or more. Macro dialing is another name for advanced automatic or express dialing because it provides advanced features (such as pause) and a larger maximum storage of digits. These features are particularly helpful for business voice mail retrieval. (See, also, ¶ 4668.)

4613 **Noise suppression.** **Noise suppression** is circuitry that creates a small sound-sensitive area in front of the mouthpiece and filters out extraneous noise. The result is that the voice of the speaker is transmitted more clearly and with a minimum of interference and extraneous sound.

4614 **Speakerphones.** A **speakerphone** is a telephone with a speaker that can be used instead of the handset. The speaker works like the speaker in an intercom in the sense that it serves both as a transmitter and a receiver. A speakerphone allows the caller to hear and speak through the telephone from anywhere in the room. It can be used to bring a telephone call into a meeting or to free the hands of the user to take notes during a telephone conversation. (See, also, ¶ 4668.)

Private Telephone Systems

4615 **Automatic telephone systems.** **Automatic telephone devices** that increase the utility of telephones have had a profound effect on office work. Most of the caller assistance once provided by operators is now handled by electronic devices such as answering machines (¶ 4616), call processors (¶ 4619), and the like.

4616 **Answering machines.** An **answering machine** can perform most of the tasks performed by an *answering service:* answer the telephone (with a prerecorded outgoing message), record an incoming message, and repeat all recorded messages when the user calls in.

Some answering machines notify the user that a message has been recorded by calling the user at another number (paging). Alerted by pager, the user can call from any Touch-Tone® telephone and employ a private access code to listen to recorded messages, change the outgoing message, rewind the tape, and so on.

Most answering machines offer **call screening:** circuitry that allows a user to listen to the incoming calls being recorded and break in to answer a call at will. (See, also, ¶ 4658 on voice mail.)

4617 Decentralized systems. **Private decentralized systems** consist of telephones capable of functioning together as a system without the use of a central control unit. The necessary control circuitry is built into each telephone. Most decentralized systems function with one to three outside lines and two to eight telephones. In the telephone business, a 1 x 2 system has one outside line and two extensions; a 3 x 8 system has three outside lines and eight extensions, and so forth. The outside lines are often referred to as *DID* (direct inward dialing.)

The system automatically selects an unused outside line for outgoing calls. Although an operator is not required, those who use the system must switch incoming calls and take messages for one another. Answering machines can be used in conjunction with a decentralized system.

4618 Centralized systems. **Private centralized systems** range from simple packaged units designed to serve two outside lines and six extensions (a 2x 6 system) to full-scale, private custom-designed telephone systems. Most of the smaller systems use a call processor. Larger systems may employ an operator or use a call processor backed up by an operator. (See, also, ¶ 4619.)

Standard centralized systems for as many as eight outside lines and twenty-four extensions are available (an 8 x 24 system). Some of the features available are

- after-hours answering machine
- call processor
- call restriction
- conference calling
- credit card reader
- display (console telephones at all stations)
- hold
- intercom
- message waiting
- paging
- system speed dial

(Photo courtesy of David Young-Wolff/ PhotoEdit)

MORE

- transfer to fax
- transfer to modem
- volume control

Private centralized systems are known by several names: PBX (**P**rivate **B**ranch e**x**change), APBX (**A**utomatic **P**rivate **B**ranch e**x**change), PABX (**P**rivate **A**utomatic **B**ranch e**x**change), autoswitcher, call director, call processor and others.

4619 **Call processors.** A **call processor** plugs into an outside line or lines and provides ports for several devices—usually a fax machine, modem, and one or more extension telephones. The call processor answers the outside line or lines on the first ring and listens for a fax or modem signal. If it detects such a signal, the incoming call is routed to the proper device.

If no advance fax or modem signal is detected, the incoming call is routed to an extension telephone—or to an answering machine if one is on duty.

Some call processors permit the incoming caller to connect with a specific device or extension by dialing a Touch-Tone® number. The call processor might say, "Thank you for calling the OfficeInfo Company. To reach an extension number, enter the number now; to place an order, press 1; to leave a message, press 2; to send us a fax, press 3; to talk to customer service, press 4; for other assistance press 5."

4620 **Detail recorders.** A **detail recorder** collects and stores data on telephone use. Some units record comprehensive data on all outgoing calls: the number called, who made the call, duration of the call, and other pertinent information.

4621 **Dial restrictors.** A **dial restrictor** restricts the placement of long-distance calls. Long-distance calling can be blocked from a single telephone, a group of telephones, or the entire system. Dial restrictors can block out certain exchanges, certain area codes, or all long-distance calls. They can also restrict a particular extension in a public place to interoffice extensions only.

Local Telephone Service

4622 **Basic local service. Basic local service** consists of access to a local line. In most areas, the cost of basic service includes placement and receipt of local calls. In some areas, there is a charge for local calls—either a flat rate per call or a charge based on the duration, distance, and time of day.

4623 **Call forwarding. Call forwarding** service makes it possible for all incoming calls to be switched automatically to another telephone number. It can be the number of a conventional telephone or the number of an answering service that will take a message or reach the subscriber by pager. (See ¶ 4657.) The number to which the calls are switched can be changed remotely from any Touch-Tone® telephone.

4624 **Call forwarding, busy.** **Call forwarding, busy,** service will forward all incoming calls to another number when the subscriber's line is busy. The other number can be for an answering machine or answering service—or for a colleague.

4625 **Call forwarding, no answer.** **Call forwarding, no-answer,** service will forward all incoming calls to another number when the subscriber's telephone is not answered. The other number can be for an answering machine or answering service—or for a colleague.

4626 **Call waiting.** **Call waiting** service sounds a soft beep when there is an incoming call on a line that is in use. The beep tells the user that there is a call waiting and allows the user to switch to the second caller then switch back and forth between callers to complete both calls. The user cannot talk to both parties at once.

4627 **Caller ID.** **Caller ID** service displays on a special device or special telephone the number from which an incoming call is being made. The number is displayed between the first and second rings. This allows the user to know who is calling. It is a means of screening out unwanted calls and preparing for others by retrieving files or other information before answering. For those who keep a computer up and running, a client's file can be called to the screen as the telephone is answered.

4628 **Centrex service.** **Centrex service** is provided by the local telephone company with equipment housed in their facilities and offers many of the services provided by user-owned devices and systems (see ¶ 4601-60).

4629 **Direct inward dialing system.** A **direct inward dialing system** allows users within the system to be dialed directly from outside rather than receiving calls through a PBX or other private call-processing system. Outgoing calls are still routed through the user's PBX or other call routing system. (See, also, ¶ 4617-19.)

4630 **Directory assistance.** **Local directory assistance** is obtained by dialing a number listed in the front of the telephone book. The most widely employed system is for the user to dial **555-1212.** (See ¶ 4643 for information about long-distance directory assistance.)

4631 **Exchanges.** Each telephone is connected to the **exchange,** which is identified by the first three digits of the local telephone number. The exchange may be a separate switching facility or merely a physical or logical subdivision of a centralized automatic switching facility. Now that most connections are made by automatic switching systems, the location and separate identity of exchanges is not as important as it was when calls were processed manually.

4632 **Lifeline.** **Lifeline service** automatically dials a predetermined number when a physically challenged subscriber leaves the receiver off the hook for more than 15-20 seconds. This and similar services are designed to assist those most likely to need emergency medical service. (See, also, ¶ 4669.)

4633 **Message central.** Most local telephone companies offer services similar to those of private answering services. Typically, the physical arrangements are similar to those for a centrex system: all equipment is installed and maintained in telephone company facilities. **Message central** functions much as does a voice mail system (see ¶ 4658) and can be used to broadcast a single message to all of the telephones in the same message central system (usually a single firm or office) with one call.

4634 **Remote station answering.** **Remote station answering** service automatically switches incoming calls to a designated telephone. It is useful during times when a business is closed for switching all incoming calls to an alternative telephone—perhaps for a large business, that of the night watchman or guard, or in the case of a small business, the owner's home telephone.

4635 **Distinctive ring signal.** **Distinctive ring signal** service allows single-line users to have more than one number listed for the same line—usually as many as three numbers. Distinctive ring patterns (short, short-long, short-long-long) tell users which number is being called. This allows several people to use the same line, but answer only when *their* ring is heard.

4636 **Three-way calling.** **Three-way calling** service allows a telephone user to add a third party to an existing connection. In most areas, the existing call is placed on hold by pressing the receiver button for one second. Then, at the dial tone, the second number is dialed. When the third party answers, the receiver button is again briefly pressed thereby connecting all three parties into the three-way conference call.

4637 **Touch-Tone®.** **Touch-Tone®** service provides faster and more accurate dialing. It also allows the user to communicate easily with call processors that are used by many organizations that maintain their own private call-routing systems.

Long-Distance Telephone Service

4638 **Long-distance providers.** Long-distance service may be obtained through the local telephone company or by another telephone company that specializes in long-distance service.

4639 **Collect calls.** **Collect calls** require some operator assistance. In some areas, this process is automated through the use of a Touch-Tone® phone and computer-assisted directions. In many locations collect calls can be dialed as follows:

Operator	**0**
Area code	**617**
Exchange	**555**
Local number	**1234**

After the number has been dialed, the operator will assist the caller in completing the call. The operator will need to know the name of the caller and that the call is a collect call. When the telephone is answered, the operator will state that the call is collect and give the name of the caller. If the call is accepted, charges are billed to the receiving telephone number.

In other areas, collect calls are placed by dialing *00* for instructions from the operator. See the local telephone book.

4640 **Conference calls.** **Conference calls** connect more than two parties. They can be arranged from an individual telephone with three-way calling (see ¶ 4636), from an electronic smart telephone with a conference calling feature (in the same manner described in ¶ 4636, repeated for each new addition to the conference call up to the maximum available), or with assistance from the operator. (See, also, ¶ 4668.)

4641 **Credit card calls.** The caller places a **credit card call** by dialing zero, area code, and the local number being called. The call is routed to a computer where an electronic voice will request that the caller dial in the credit card number or the operator may obtain the information by asking the caller to read the necessary information from the credit card. In many new electronic smart pay phones, an opening is provided for the caller to slide the telephone calling card or credit card through the slot, thus allowing electronic reading of the credit card number. The call is then billed to the caller's credit card or telephone account, rather than to the telephone from which the call is made.

4642 **Control systems.** A **long-distance control system** can be installed as part of a private telephone system. It can place system-wide (but selective) restrictions on toll calls similar to those provided by dial restrictors (see ¶ 4621).

4

4643 **Directory assistance.** **Long-distance directory assistance** is obtained in most areas by calling 1 (Area Code) 555-1212. (see ¶ 4630 for local directory assistance.)

4644 **International calls.** Persons in the United States can call persons living in a border zone of Canada or Mexico by dialing a number in the regular long distance format (for example, **1-905-555-1234**). To reach other foreign nations, follow the instructions in your telephone book or those published by your long-distance carrier.

The usual procedure for dialing international calls requires three codes plus the local number. The following example is for the local number **123456** in Frankfurt, Germany:

International access code:	**011**
Country code (2-3 digits):	**49**
City code (1-4 digits):	**69**
Local number:	**123456**

If you are using a push-button telephone, depressing the pound symbol (#) after dialing will speed up the switching process and get your call through more quickly.

4645 **Mobile and marine calls.** **Mobile and marine calls** can be made to automobiles, trucks, boats, and ships that are equipped for mobile or marine service. Ask the operator for the *mobile operator* for land vehicles or the *marine operator* for vessels. Portable cellular telephones provide direct-dial access regardless of the location (see ¶ 4659).

4646 **Person-to-person calls.** **Person-to-person calls** require some operator assistance. In person-to-person calls, the initiating caller of a long-distance call wants to restrict the connection to a specific individual—and no one else. In some areas, a person-to-person call can be dialed as follows.

Operator	**0**
Area code	**617**
Exchange	**555**
Local number	**1234**

After the number has been dialed, the operator will need to know the name of both the caller and the person to whom the caller would like to talk. When the receiving telephone is answered, the operator states that the call is person-to-person and asks for the person being called. Charges begin when the person being called comes on the line. However, since the person-to-person rate is high, it may be cheaper to make several attempts to place a direct-dial call.

4647 **Rates.** Each long-distance carrier has its own rate schedule. One common element of the rate schedules, however, is the application of higher rates in peak calling hours and lower rates in off-hours.

The following chart is typical of long-distance rate schedules for the 48 contiguous states:

Time	Mon	Tue	Wed	Thu	Fri	Sat	Sun
8:00 a.m.-5:00 p.m.	WEEKDAY RATE						
5:00 p.m.-11:00 p.m.	DISCOUNTED RATE						DISCOUNTED RATE
11:00 p.m.-8:00 a.m.	LOWEST RATE						

4648 **Station-to-station calls.** The lowest long-distance rates apply to station-to-station calls dialed directly. Charges begin when the receiving telephone is answered.

To dial a long-distance call, first dial the long-distance prefix. The prefix depends upon the long-distance carrier you use; it may be as simple as dialing the digit **1**. Dialing the prefix connects you to your long-distance carrier, which will route your call. The following example is for local number **1234** in the **555** exchange of area code **813**:

Long-distance prefix:	**1**
Area code (three digits):	**813**
Local exchange (three digits)	**555**
Station number (four digits)	**1234**

4649 **Third-number calls.** To make a third-number call, the caller asks the operator to charge the call to a number other than the one from which the call is placed—usually the caller's home or business telephone number.

4650 **Time and charges.** To receive a report of the time and charges pertinent to a long-distance call, follow the instructions published by your long-distance carrier. If you do not have the instructions, call the long-distance carrier before placing the call.

4651 **WATS (Wide-Area Telecommunications Service).** **WATS** is provided via a special telephone line over which outgoing long-distance calls can be placed. Generally, frequent users of long-distance service will pay less using WATS than they would using regular long-distance service.

4652 **WATS extender.** A **WATS extender** can be incorporated into a PBX system. It enables any authorized user (usually employees of the subscribing firm) to call the PBX system from the outside and use the PBX's WATS lines.

4653 **800 numbers.** The subscriber who pays for *inward* WATS is assigned an 800 number. Those who call the 800 number do not pay a long-distance charge. This allows businesses to provide toll-free service to its customers, clients, and prospects.

4654 **900 numbers.** Calls to a number with a 900 prefix (instead of an area code) are charged to the caller; a per minute fee for the information provided is also charged to the caller. Most telephone companies allow business and residential customers to place restrictions on their lines to block anyone from making 900 calls.

On-the-Go Telephone Service

4655 **Basic answering services.** The basic service provided by all answering service companies is taking incoming calls on the client's telephone line (which may be shared with others) and taking messages. The client retrieves those messages by calling the answering service.

4656 **Expanded answering services.** Most answering service companies offer some of the following additional services: paging, voice mail, call forwarding, fax transmission and reception, PC file transfer, 800-number service, and order taking.

4657 **Pagers (beepers).** A **pager** is a pocket-sized, battery-operated device that alerts the user to a waiting message. Pagers are used by people whose work requires them to be on the move and those who are on emergency duty or standby status. The pager may simply alert the user to call in for a message, or it may display a number to be called. More sophisticated models display brief alphabetic and numeric messages or provide two way voice communication with the paging service company.

4658 **Voice mail service.** **Voice mail** service is similar to the service provided by an answering machine. Voice mail can, in addition, *broadcast* a message to a group of its subscribers (referred to as a *distribution list*). One person in an office can address a voice mail message to everyone in the same department, for example.

MORE

Voice mail service can maintain several private "mailboxes" for different people sharing the same outside line. Voice mail service is available through answering services, through the local telephone company, and by using answering machines. In addition, many large organizations have their own internal voice mail system, often referred to as *phone mail*. These systems have numerous advanced features such as different messages for internal and external incoming calls, extension identification of the individual called, personal and company distribution lists for broadcasting messages to many individuals at once, automatic access to a secretary should the caller not want to talk to a machine, automatic reply to or forwarding of messages received, and so on.

4659 **Cellular telephones.** **Cellular telephones** are mobile telephones that work as part of a nationwide network of transmitting towers that "hand off" the user who passes from one "cell" in the system to another. The cellular system has made mobile telephones both more reliable and less expensive than they were previously. Cellular telephones can be installed in a vehicle or handheld. They can be used on land, sea, or in the air (restrictions apply on commercial airlines.)

4660 **Mobile and marine service.** See ¶ 4645.

Fax

4661 **Fax defined.** Fax is the shortened and altered form of the word *facsimile,* which means an exact copy. A fax is transmitted from a source fax machine to a destination fax machine via telephone connection. The destination fax machine reproduces the form (image) of the original. Most faxed material consists of text or pictures.

Some fax machines use *thermal* paper, others use *plain* paper. The latter is superior in quality. It uses the same xerographic process that is employed in plain paper copiers and laser printers. On fax machines connected to a *network* of microcomputer users, faxes can be directed to print on a laser printer or directed to the electronic computer mailbox of the network user.

4662 **Fax detector.** A sending fax machine first transmits a signal that alerts the receiving station to an incoming fax. Some call processors receive and interpret this signal, automatically switching the line to a fax machine when it is detected. (See, also, ¶ 4619 and 4665-66.)

4663 **Fax library system.** Special fax equipment makes it possible for a fax user to maintain a library of printed material (sales material, for example) to be sent automatically to any other fax user who requests it. Some systems incorporate a dedicated PC; others are equipped with self-contained servers that eliminate the need for a separate PC. In either case, a fax user calls and requests by Touch-Tone® signal a copy of a document from the library. The document is then automatically faxed to the user who has requested it.

4664 **Fax for microcomputers.** A microcomputer can be used to send, receive, and store faxes. All that is required is a kit that includes the necessary expansion circuit board, and software. Faxes that are received on a computer can be stored as files, displayed on the screen, or printed.

4665 **Fax modem pool.** With a microcomputer network of many computer users, a **fax modem pool** is utilized to maximize the use of both modems and fax-dedicated lines. Each user desiring to send a fax forwards the fax to the modem pool over the network, much the same as a job would be sent to a particular printer. The software administering the modem pool then spools (collects) all of the fax documents to be sent and either forwards over the first available modem or holds for more inexpensive transmission in a less expensive long-distance time period. The same software advises the system administrator of the total utilization of the fax modem pool, allowing cost-effective decision-making as to when new modems and fax lines need to be added. Incoming faxes may also be routed to each network station via an extension number attached to the incoming fax.

4666 **Fax switch.** An automatic **fax switch** detects an incoming fax signal and automatically switches the call to a fax machine. A manual fax switch permits the user to switch manually from voice communication to fax communication and back.

4667 **International fax.** Since there is no extra charge for using a telephone channel to transmit fax data, an international telephone connection used for fax is probably the least expensive way to send hard copies of documents between nations and continents.

Equipment for Physically Challenged Individuals

4668 **Features useful to physically challenged individuals.**

Amplifier	¶ 4603	Express dialing	¶ 4608
Automatic dialing	4604	Headsets	4609
Clarifier	4605	Large-number telephones	4610
Conference calling	4640	Last-number redial	4611
Cordless telephone	4606	Macro dialing	4612
Emergency dialing	4607	Speakerphones	4614

4669 **Lifeline service.** In some areas, a physically challenged person can arrange to have an emergency telephone number dialed automatically when the receiver is left off the hook for longer than 15-20 seconds or when a special device is activated.

This service is designed for those most likely to need emergency assistance or medical service. In other areas, various kinds of lifeline service is available through hospitals, answering services, or volunteer groups. Some lifeline services request a client call in several times a day. If a call is missed, the service checks (usually with a volunteer neighbor) to see if the client needs special assistance. (See, also, ¶ 4632.)

Express dialing can be used for similar purposes. (See ¶ 4608.)

4670 **TDD (Telecommunications Device for the Deaf).** A **TDD** permits a deaf person (or a profoundly hard-of-hearing person who cannot use a voice telephone) to communicate with another TDD across town or across the continent by using an ordinary telephone connection. The TDD contains a keyboard and display screen that allows both caller and receiver to key and view their messages and replies.

CHAPTER

WORD PROCESSING

5001 **Word processing defined.** **Word processing** is the production of documents using electronic office equipment. It includes *planning, organizing, drafting, editing, proofreading, revising,* and *printing*. *Handling the mail* (¶ 5600) and *filing* (¶ 5700) are so closely associated with the production of documents that they are included in this chapter. Since word processing programs and desktop publishing programs grow more alike with each revision—and there is no clear line of demarcation between the fields—desktop publishing (¶ 5300) is included as well. Organizations large enough to centralize their production of documents often combine functions similarly.

5002 **The writer.** The author of a business document may be a professional writer, but is more likely to be a manager whose responsibilities are in sales, personnel, accounting—some field other than writing. Writing is a *necessary* skill in many management positions and a *highly desirable* skill in most others. It is difficult to imagine a management position in which writing is not at least a *useful asset*.

As word processing hardware and software are improved, more writers choose to key their ideas directly into word processors. They find the computer screen an ideal medium for the development of ideas and the organization of words. See ¶ 5019-30 for writing in other media.

5003 **Word processing specialists.** The writer may work alone at a word processor or may be assisted by others who perform the specialized tasks into which word processing can be organized. These specialists may take shorthand (manually or on machines), operate dictating and word processing equipment, or employ other skills such as proofreading, layout, and editing.

Planning a Document

5004 **Writing plan.** A good document starts with a good writing plan. A writing plan includes items such as the following:

- Precise identification of the audience
- A clear statement of the goals of the document
- Identification of the sources to be used
- Identification of those who will collaborate
- The approximate length of the document
- Production schedule or completion date
- Cost
- Distribution

5005 **Choosing a method.** There are several methods for developing ideas. *Methods* are also called *patterns, systems, styles,* and *models.*

Choose a method for developing the subject before you begin writing. Initially, the wrong method is better than no method. Change methods as frequently as you like, but never lose sight of what you are doing and where it is taking you. Some of the recommended methods are

- **Major to minor.** Working from the most important to the least important. Exemplified by **the newspaper method** in which the reporter is admonished to get the who, what, where, when, why, and how in the first few lines of the story and to write as though the story might be cut from bottom to top: no matter how many paragraphs are cut, it should still be a well-organized story.
- **Minor to major.** In this method one builds to a climax, as with an adventure story or mystery.
- **General to specific.** The **deductive** method starts with a generalization, supports it with specifics, and reaches a conclusion that supports the generalization.
- **Specific to general.** The **inductive** method starts with specifics that are used to discover the generalization.
- **Procedural.** This method illustrates steps in a process.
- **Chronological.** In this method, events are written in time sequence.
- **Learning.** Elementary-to-advanced progression is the standard method for teaching.
- **Alphabetical.** A-Z organization is the alphabetical approach.

5

5006 **Headings.** The **level** of each heading is determined by how it fits into the organization of the document. Typically, higher-level headings are more important or more general. They are more prominent on the page: centered, printed farther to the left, printed in larger type, boldfaced, italicized, highlighted, or otherwise delineated. (See ¶ 5004-05 on planning and ¶ 5007-14 on outlining.)

The **sequence** or order in which the topics appear depends on how the document is organized. A document entitled "My Vacation" may call for *chronological order*. A section of the same document that describes learning to bake homemade bread while visiting the farm might call for *procedural order:* explaining the steps in a process.

Outlining a Document

5007 **Listing topics.** Writing a first draft is much easier if you are following an outline. Begin writing an outline by listing the topics that occur to you. Keep them as brief as possible. Do not worry about order or organization in the

MORE

early stages. If you have difficulty, try a different medium: switch from computer to file cards to paper and back. Each medium gives your work a different look and may spark new ideas. (See ¶ 5011-14.)

The following topics are for a paper entitled "Pets in the Neighborhood." The first list identifies the pets. In the second list, the topics are edited for use as headings and listed on separate lines; duplication is eliminated.

Original List	Edited List
`Hobo, a beagle`	`Hobo`
`Dog`	`Beagles`
`Tom, a common cat`	`Dogs`
`Lassie, a collie`	`Tom`
`Feather, an Angora`	`Commons`
`Cats`	`Lassie`
`Snoopy, a beagle`	`Collies`
`Abbigail, a basset`	`Feather`
	`Angoras`
	`Cats`
	`Snoopy`
	`Abbigail`
	`Bassets`

5008 **Organizing major sections.** Organizing major sections requires three steps: (1) select major headings, (2) put the major headings in order, and (3) sort the remaining headings.

(1) Select Major Headings	(2) Put Major Headings in Order	(3) Sort Remaining Headings
Hobo	Cats	Cats
Beagles	Dogs	Tom
Dogs	Hobo	Commons
Tom	Beagles	Feather
Commons	Tom	Angoras
Lassie	Commons	Dogs
Collies	Lassie	Hobo
Feather	Collies	Beagles
Angoras	Feather	Lassie
Cats	Angoras	Collies
Snoopy	Snoopy	Snoopy
Abbigail	Abbigail	Abbigail
Bassets	Bassets	Bassets

5009 **Organizing second-level sections.** If there are second-level sections, these require the same three steps:

(1) Select Second-Level Headings	(2) Put Second-Level Headings in Order	(3) Sort Remaining Headings
Cats	Cats	Cats
Tom	Angoras	Angoras
Commons	Commons	Feather
Feather	Tom	Commons
Angoras	Feather	Tom
Dogs	Dogs	Dogs
Hobo	Bassets	Bassets
Beagles	Beagles	Abbigail
Lassie	Collies	Beagles
Collies	Hobo	Hobo
Snoopy	Lassie	Snoopy
Abbigail	Snoopy	Collies
Bassets	Abbigail	Lassie

5010 **Organizing other sections.** If there are other sections, these require repetition of the three steps used in ¶ 5008-09. If the outline is both long and complicated, there may be third-level and fourth-level headings. Outlines with more than four levels of organization are unusual.

The final step that completes the outline is to put the lowest-level headings in order within each section. In the foregoing example, that involves only *Hobo* and *Snoopy* under *beagles,* and they already happen to be in alphabetical order.

5011 **Outlining on paper.** Use a shorthand notebook or a similar format that provides a page with a vertical line down the middle. On the right side of that line, jot down the briefest possible description of paragraphs you intend to write. Write on every third or fourth line, leaving room for headings and additional paragraph topics.

Use the left side of the paper to compose headings. Follow the logic of ¶ 5007-10.

5012 **Outlining on cards.** Some writers prefer ordinary file cards for outlining. Print each topic on a card, then follow the logic of ¶ 5007-10.

5013 **Outlining on the computer.** It is possible to use any word processor for outlining. The procedure is much like that for outlining on cards or paper—except that the organizing process takes place on the screen, using the word processor's ability to move lines and blocks of text. Follow the logic of ¶ 5007-10.

Computer outlining programs are more sophisticated—and more helpful—writing tools. Some word processing programs include full outlining capabilities; others include partial support for outlining. Among the leading *separate* outlining programs are *MaxThink, Think Tank, Ready!,* and *FreeStyle.*

MORE

A key feature of outlining programs is their ability to **truncate** (make shorter) any section of the outline—then expand it to its full length again. This allows the writer to expand the current section and truncate the rest of the outline, keeping the current section in context and in perspective. Look at page 321, the first page of chapter 5, to see how this section on "Writing" is expanded to show the detail of the current section; notice that the other major topics of the chapter are truncated to provide merely a perspective and quick reference.

5014 **Hierarchical outlines.** **Hierarchical outlines,** so called because they are based on rank and order, are very useful. However, some of the restrictions attributed to them are, at times, of doubtful value:

- The rule is that every heading must be followed by text. It is better to use a heading **not** followed by text than to create trivia to fill the space.
- Another rule is that there must be at least two items in every division of an outline. The traditional practice of boosting single items one level works well in most cases. If it does not, the single item should simply be included as logic dictates—but the writer should be aware that this practice is not allowed in formal outlines (college and postgraduate papers and papers in any English class) and is not universally accepted.
- Despite the hierarchical regulation that items of equal *rank* are of equal worth, value, utility, and so on, the writer of a document on vehicles or transportation may wish to think twice before deciding to give jet aircraft and roller skates equal billing.
- The logic of a document may be more like a network than a hierarchy. The logic line does not necessarily connect boxes of equal size, shape, and level in perfect symmetry. If something else makes more sense than a hierarchy, use it.
- In all but formal papers, the art of organizing a document lies not in forcing the text into proper outline form, but in laying the track for a train of thought carefully designed to provide the reader with an interesting and informative trip.

5

The First Draft

5015 **How to get started.** Start with the outline. On a word processor, open a space below the first heading and start writing.

5016 **How to keep moving.** The purpose of the first draft is to capture all of your thinking on the topics in the outline. Start at the beginning and work topic-by-topic to the end. When you are at a loss for words, mark the spot so you can return to it. Strike **<Enter>** to create a line break and return to the left margin, then enter three asterisks, (***). Better still, insert a word or two that will remind you of the elusive thought. For example, if you cannot think of the breed of the dog you want to mention, just strike **<Enter>** to create a new line and key "***dog with long ears" or another short expression that will remind you of the thought. Later, the line will be easy to locate on a draft copy. If you are using a word processor, the **search** feature will find *** for you.

Picture yourself as talking the text through the keyboard into the computer, word processor, or typewriter. Do not bog down. Tell yourself to keep talking.

5017 **If you get stuck.** If you get stuck, move to a section of the outline that is easier for you and keep writing. The outline remains on the screen as you write and is eventually embedded in the finished document.

5018 **Fill in the blanks.** When you have done your best on the first draft, print a copy and look at it on paper. Look for gross errors only; this is not the time to start the final editing process. Just mark misplaced paragraphs, headings that do not work, and blank areas that indicate a need for further research—and do not forget the sections you marked with asterisks or asterisks and phrases. You may wish to use this draft for a trip to the library.

Choosing a Writing Medium

5019 **Writing equipment.** Personal computers are remarkably well-accepted by writers. The exceptional few persons who still write with pencil or pen and paper or with mechanical typewriters are generally viewed as eccentric. A small number of persons like to write by talking—dictating their work to recording machines or stenographers.

Dictation and Transcription

5020 **Dictation machines and word processors.** **Dictation machines** use magnetic tape in microcassettes that are less than half the size of standard audio tape cassettes. The smaller cassettes, and the smaller machines they make possible, are designed to be held in one hand. Some larger dictation machines use standard audio tape cassettes. Dictation machines and word processors are ideal companions. The right-off-the-tape first draft, keyed to the computer screen, is excellent input for a word processor.

5021 **Transcription machines.** **Transcription machines** play back recorded material so that it can be processed on a computer, word processor, or typewriter. The transcription machine uses microcassettes identical to those used in compatible dictating machines. Transcription machines are larger than dictating machines because they are designed for desktop use. Since the person who transcribes needs both hands for the keyboard and must be able to hear the recording clearly, transcribing machines are equipped with foot controls and headphones.

5022 **Dictation-transcription machines.** **Dictation-transcription machines** are similar in appearance to transcription machines, but are designed for both functions: dictation and transcription. They lack the portability of single-purpose dictation machines, but are suitable for those who prefer a desktop machine—writers who dictate their material and later transcribe it themselves, for example.

5023 **Indexing dictated material.** An electronic signal (beep) recorded by pressing a **<Cue>** button makes it possible for the person who is transcribing to locate the beginning and end of each document. Corrections, insertions, and other reference points can be cued as well. Some writers keep with each tape a brief list that identifies each cue.

5024 **Organizing for dictation.** Efficient dictation requires concentration. Try to set aside a time for dictation when you will not be interrupted. Organize your day to give yourself the time you need; organize your work to use that time efficiently.

1. Develop a system that brings the source documents you need for dictation to your desk when you are ready to dictate. One system, called a **tickler file,** requires 31 folders (numbered from 1 through 31) and 12 file dividers (one for each month). To use a tickler file

   a. Divide the numbered folders into two stacks: 1 through today's date and tomorrow's date through 31.

   b. Put the first stack (1 through today's date) behind *next* month's guide. They will not be brought up until next month.

   c. Put the second stack (tomorrow's number through 31) behind *this* month's guide. They will be brought up, one each day, for the rest of this month.

   From then on, put all documents that you want to bring up at a later date in the appropriate folder: source documents you will need for later dictation, reminder notes you write to yourself, and anything else you want to have available on a specific future date. Write yourself notes about future dictation, or collect documents for future reference. File them under the date on which you wish to bring each document back to your attention.

2. Before each document is filed, mark on it any notes that will be helpful at the time of dictation. Obtain any related documents ahead of time. Make sure that everything needed will be available when the document is brought up for dictation.

3. As you file documents in the tickler file, check the current folders to be sure you are not overloading some days. Make it a habit to check ahead periodically and move documents forward or backward to even out your work when necessary.

4. Each morning: open the folder of the day, remove its contents, and put the folder back in the file behind yesterday's folder. Tomorrow's folder will then be the next one up.

5. Check the organization of the day's dictation and do anything you can to minimize interruptions after you start dictating.

5025 **Dictating.** Dictating skills improve with practice. Use the following suggestions; do **not** give up and write your correspondence in longhand.

1. Think about the person or persons to whom your document is addressed. Tell your story as though they were present as you dictate. Not only will your writing sound natural and unstilted, you will avoid—almost without

having to think about it—the use of artificial phrases such as "will be forwarded under separate cover" (will be mailed) or "it is our sincere wish to thank you for . . . " (thank you for . . .).

2. Dictate freely. Do not attempt to make the first draft your best formal text. Dictate naturally and get a first draft on paper. Then edit your work to your own satisfaction. As your dictating skills improve, you will learn to edit mentally and less rewriting will be required. Remember, however, that good writing is mostly rewriting.
3. Dictate paragraph breaks and punctuation marks. When in doubt, create a paragraph break. Paragraphs that are a bit shorter than normal are more effective than paragraphs that are too long.
4. Use illustrations, tables, lists, and the like, freely. Give or send a copy to the person who will transcribe the dictation. Do **not** try to dictate tables, lists, and other technical information unless doing so is absolutely necessary.

5026 **Organizing for transcription.** Transcription is easier and more rewarding if you are properly organized. Several of the organizational techniques discussed under dictating in ¶ 5025 are equally applicable to transcribing.

1. Before you begin to transcribe, do anything you can to minimize later interruptions.
2. Check for and transcribe first any document the writer has identified as a priority document.
3. Review references, notations on enclosures, and so forth. Be sure you understand all special instructions. Locate any additional documents needed as enclosures or for reference; sort and correlate them to the materials to be transcribed.
4. If there is any doubt about an address, title, date, number, or other information, confirm the correctness of the information before transcribing the document.
5. Be sure you understand how each document is to be formatted.
6. Encourage each writer to use a separate tape cassette. Keep a separate folder or bin for each writer. You will soon get to know the individual characteristics of each person whose dictation you transcribe and how to deal with those characteristics: fast or slow pace, unusual pronunciation patterns, and so forth.
7. Before transcribing, decide whether to process a draft and then a finished copy or to try for a finished copy the first time. Whether or not you should process a draft depends on the difficulty of the material, the dictating skill of the writer, and your own transcribing skill. If you are in doubt, it is probably better to process a draft first, even if it is only for your own use. Some writers write best by editing a draft and will, therefore, require one or more drafts before the finished text is acceptable.
8. Once you are familiar with the style of each writer and with the characteristics of your equipment, you will be able to estimate the amount of work contained in each cassette by the amount of tape that has been used.

5027 **Transcribing.** When you are organized and ready to transcribe, try to concentrate and minimize interruptions.

1. If you are transcribing from shorthand notes, keep your eyes on your notes. If you are using a dictation machine, keep your eyes on the screen or the paper in front of you.
2. Listen or read ahead to identify trouble spots before you reach them. Develop a pace that allows you to work steadily and with a minimum of errors. A pace that is just a little beyond your ability to transcribe accurately can reduce your productivity greatly.
3. It is usually best for the writer to dictate punctuation marks and paragraph breaks. However, not all writers do so. It is a good idea for one who is transcribing to read ahead, remaining on the alert for punctuation that is needed but has not been dictated.
4. Unless you know that a writer does not encourage the use of tables, take every opportunity to tabulate. Tables are usually clearer and more effective than ordinary text. Text can be itemized using bullets (•), numbers, or letters. If your equipment does not reproduce bullets, make them by keying lowercase o's and then filling them in with a black pen.

• Bullets	1. Numbers	A. Capital Letters	a. Lowercase Letters
•	2.	B.	b.
•	3.	C.	c.

5. Keep a dictionary, reference manual, thesaurus, word division manual, and calculator within reach.
6. As each document is finished, recheck it for coherence and completeness. Be sure that all enclosures are in place and that copies have been prepared for those who are supposed to receive them.

5

Handwriting and Keyboarding

5028 **Handwriting.** Some authors prefer to write, draw, diagram, or outline their work directly on paper. In a few cases, the writer is so effective at mental organization that the first draft on paper is usable—or requires a minimum of editing before it becomes usable.

Most authors work more effectively when they get a rough first draft on paper as soon as possible. This is a step that is usually the first in a series of rewrites by which the writer gradually polishes the document until it is finished.

5029 **Typewriting.** The mechanical typewriter—with its abrasive eraser, sticky type bars, and carbon paper—has been replaced by electronic typewriters and low-end word processors. Even the least-expensive machines now have such advanced features as daisy-wheel printing mechanisms, automatic error correction, and spelling checkers. (See ¶ 5101-5.)

5030 **Using a word processor.** Electronic typewriters and low-end word processors are discussed in ¶ 5102-3. More advanced word processors and microcomputers used as word processors are discussed in ¶ 5104-5.

Editing

5031 **Editing described.** Editing goes beyond the correction of mechanical errors in spelling, punctuation, formatting, and the like, to the improvement of the text itself—refining it in order to achieve higher levels of accuracy, brevity, clarity, directness, effectiveness, and fluency. Most writers edit their own text as an integral part of the writing process.

A useful first draft can be quite rough as long as the important ideas are recorded. Careful and repeated editing through several additional drafts can shape a rough first draft into the polished text that careful writers require of themselves.

Good writers and editors are always in demand—not necessarily to write best-selling novels or Hollywood screen plays, but to write the countless documents that are vital to the success of business firms. Most people who do office work have a part in the paperwork that keeps the office going. One of the criteria by which they are evaluated, formally and informally, is the quality of their written work. In a very real sense, office workers who hold positions of responsibility must do some serious writing, and are, therefore, writers, editors, and proofreaders.

5032 **Editing the work of others.** If you edit the work of others, it is best to do so as diplomatically as possible. Offer suggestions, not sarcasm. Be sure of your facts. If you correct another person's writing and turn out to be wrong, you can expect resentment on that person's part and embarrassment on your own.

Use notes written in the margins to *explain* any unusual changes. Question, explain, and suggest; do not dictate. Unless you have the authority to make unilateral changes, make it apparent in your manner that you are *suggesting* changes to improve the text. This is particularly important if you are editing the work of your boss.

Finally, try to avoid editing the work of anyone who resists improvement. Given the best advice, some writers continue to disregard generally accepted methods and standards.

Proofreading

5033 **Proofreading defined.** **Proofreading** is the comparison of proof (printed material) to the copy from which it was printed—and the marking of any errors on the proof. Normally, the printer's rule is to follow the copy—and the proofreader is responsible only for noting inconsistencies between the proof and the copy. However, it is considered both prudent and helpful for proofreaders to call attention to anything in the copy that is questionable.

5034 **Everyone proofreads.** In most word processing, publishing, and printing operations, everyone who works on the material is expected to read it and call attention to any suspected errors.

5035 **Proofreading techniques.** The key to effective proofreading is working systematically. The following techniques will help you find errors.

1. Establish a routine for proofreading. Many persons who still use typewriters proofread each page before the sheet is removed from the typewriter. Word processor operators may proofread each screen before it is scrolled out of sight, but wait until a section or chapter is finished to run the text through a spelling checker. Some **real-time spelling checkers** check each word as it is keyed, beeping when the spelling checker does not recognize a word.
2. Check the proof against the copy. The **proof** is the page you have printed; the **copy** is the original that tells you exactly what should be printed.
   a. Lay the proof flat on the desk in front of you.
   b. Grasp the copy between the thumbs and fingers of both hands in normal reading position.
   c. Place the copy on top of the proof, rolling the bottom of the copy back and under your fingertips so that only the first line of writing is visible.
   d. Match this line with the first line of the proof, letter for letter.
   e. Roll the proof up each time you finish a line, matching proof to copy, until you reach the bottom of the page.
3. Read for content. After checking the proof against the copy, read the proof again (without referring to the copy) for coherence and completeness. Does it make sense? Is there anything missing? It is easy to check all the areas in which you expect to find errors (difficult or obscure words misspelled, errors in punctuation, and the like) only to find that you have overlooked more obvious errors: entire words omitted, words written twice, or simple words misspelled—in headings or other obvious places.
4. Some word processor operators, faced with large or complex proofreading tasks, prefer to read the original into a dictating machine and then compare the proof to the recording. Some prefer to work with another person: one reads from the copy while the other checks the proof for correctness.

5036 **Proofreader's marks.** **Proofreader's marks** are used not only by those who read proof for publishers and printers, but by almost everyone who needs to indicate corrections in text.

Proofreader's marks may be written at the location of the change:

Before Change	After Change
when i move	when I move
I when move	when I move

Alternatively, proofreader's marks may be written in the margins **and** supplemented by marks in the text that indicate the exact location of the change.

Change	Mark in Margin	Supplementary Mark in Text	After Change
Align	‖	words on a list	words on a list
Capitalize	cap	new york	New York
Close up space	⁀	win ter	winter
Delete	ℊ	leave out the	leave the
Delete and close up space	ℊ	peoople	people
Insert	out	leave the	leave out the
Insert apostrophe	'	Maries dress	Marie's dress
Insert asterisk	*	the end, but	the end,* but
Insert brackets	[/]	run fast now	run [fast] now
Insert colon	:	follow these steps	follow these steps:
Insert comma	,	ham, eggs and toast	hams, eggs, and toast
Insert diagonal	/	and or the former	and/or the former
Insert hyphen	-	do it yourself project	do-it-yourself project
Insert parenthesis	(/)	run fast now	run (fast) now
Insert period	⊙	the end	the end.
Insert quotation marks	"/"	the end.	the "end."
Insert semicolon	;	Row row row.	Row; row; row.
Insert space	#	thespace	the space
Let stand	Stet	best well-wisher	best well-wisher
Lowercase	lc	the Summer season	the summer season
Move down	⊔	n dow	down
Move left	[	move left	move left
Move right	]	move right	move right
Move up	⊓	u p	up
Spell out	sp	wouldn't run	would not run
Begin a paragraph	¶	The first line and the seond	The first line and the second
Straighten the line	=	the straighten line	straighten the line
Transpose	tr	first to strike	to strike first

5037 Typical errors found in proofreading.

1. Transposed letters.

`This is hte third time we`	`This is the third time we`

2. Transposed words.

`That is best the way to go`	`That is the best way to go`

3. Omitted letter.

l `When the wilow tree was the`	`When the willow tree was the`

4. Omitted word.

we `How were wearing our`	`How we were wearing our`

5. Repeated letter.

`There weere more than enough`	`There were more than enough`

6. Repeated word.

`When they they went to the`	`When they went to the`

7. Errors or inconsistencies in paragraphing or indentation.

¶ `This was the first time that` `the engine had failed to sta`	`     This was the first time` `the engine had failed to sta`

Revising

5038 **Rewriting.** The most significant difference between those who write well and those who do not may be the ability and willingness—sometimes compulsion—to rewrite. Contrary to folk stories, Abraham Lincoln did not write the "Gettysburg Address" on the back of an envelope on board the train to Gettysburg. He wrote at least five revisions, on ordinary paper, over a period of two weeks. Some professional writers agonize over unusually troublesome passages through forty or fifty revisions. Most people who write business documents find that they are reasonably well satisfied with their work by the time it has gone through six to ten revisions.

When there are several revisions, an operator who is processing copy written by someone else will be expected to follow the standards set by the writer at each stage of production. In the early stages, the writer may not require perfectly reproduced text—just a **working copy.** As the writer refines the document, however, the standards will be raised until the final copy represents the highest standards of which the writer and the operator are capable.

The paragraphs that follow (¶ 5039-44) suggest some categories into which needed improvements seem to fall: accuracy, brevity, clarity, directness, effectiveness, and fluency. Some writers and editors prefer to read through a document several times with a different category in mind each time. Remember, the "editor" may be a writer rewriting his or her own work; or the "writer" may be the sales manager.

5039 **Accuracy.** Question the accuracy of the text as you edit. Did the runner run the mile in 4.2 *seconds,* or should it be 4.2 *minutes?* How can net profit be greater than gross sales? Did the committee really *assume* their meeting after the recess, or should it be *resume?* Using the right word is very important. "No reading aloud" means that reading out loud is not permitted; "no reading allowed" means that reading, including reading to oneself, is prohibited.

The decedent who left her estate to be divided "equally between my niece and two nephews" intended that her estate be divided into three equal shares; however, the wording she used (*between* instead of *among*) dictates that the niece is to receive half the estate and the two nephews are to share the other half.

5040 **Brevity.** Among reasonably literate writers, wordiness is probably the most common fault. A very direct way to improve your work is to see how many words you can delete without changing meaning or weakening effect.

- **Ordinary redundancy.** Compare these sentences:

Wordy: A word processing computer software program used in conjunction with a general-purpose digital computer can make possible greatly facilitated and easier editing of text on the screen of the monitor of the computer.

Better: A general-purpose computer, programmed for word processing, makes the convenience of on-screen editing possible.

- **Redundancy of context.** Once you have established the context (framework) within which you are writing, do not restate it unnecessarily. Use *period* instead of *period of time* in a document on punctuality, scheduling, and the like, where a time period will not be confused with the punctuation mark. Use *tire* instead of *automobile tire* in a document on automobiles or automobile tires.

5041 **Clarity.** Text should be unambiguous.

Ambiguous: She slammed the book down on the table and struck it with her fist.

Clear: She slammed the book down on the table and struck the table with her fist.

Ambiguous: He removed the boat from the trailer and painted it.

Clear: Having removed the boat, he painted the trailer.

Ambiguous: Go to the second traffic light and turn left.

Clear: Go to the second traffic light (not counting the one overhead) and turn left.

5042 **Directness.** Text can be written in a brief and clear style but still be ineffective if it wanders indiscriminately toward its conclusions, distracting the reader with extraneous thoughts. Get directly to the point through the orderly development of ideas. To do this, you need a method (See ¶ 5005-06).

Decide where to begin (how much background is necessary) and where to end (how much elaboration, if any, is needed once you have reached your conclusions). Careful outlining is the best way to eliminate unnecessary detours on your way to a conclusion (See ¶ 5007-14.)

If you are writing a piece on cleaning up Jackson's Pond in Titusville, there is probably no need to begin with a history of the environmental movement and conclude with the importance of Titusville to the nation's economy.

In some cases, it is desirable to put the central portion of a document into historic or geographic perspective or to enrich the document by taking a few byways that add human interest or other elements. Digressions, however, should be purposeful and well planned. They should also be used with discretion.

A document may move logically from premise, through proof, to conclusion: "Proper Maintenance Reduces Costs." It may explain how a process, device, or principle works: "The Roundabout Process of Production." It may appeal first to the intellect and then to the emotions: "Why a Convertible Makes Sense to Me." It may be organized chronologically: "My Trip." It may proceed from front to back: "The Automobile." Or bottom to top: "Building a House."

The following passage on the building of a house proceeds chronologically **and** from bottom to top. It conveys the growing strength and solidity of the house as it is constructed.

The house gathered strength as it grew to fill the space between newly exposed rock and the future location of its ridgepole. One day, a 50-ton batch of concrete was poured into the footing forms, mating with the rough rock below and providing a level base for the foundation walls.

A few days later, another 200-ton batch of concrete was worked carefully into the foundation forms, filling them solidly to the level of the first floor.

Soon, wooden joists spanned the concrete walls of the foundation. Then, in rapid succession, came the subfloor, scantlings, rafters, and ridgepole. Each new member, carefully joined to its neighbors, added strength and solidity to the structure.

5043 **Effectiveness.** Writing, to be effective, must have a purpose. Typical purposes are to **inform, persuade, describe,** or **narrate.**

- **Exposition** explains or informs, helping the reader understand something about the subject. Although expository writing may persuade, tell or include a story (narrative), or rely partly on sensory perception (descriptive), its primary purpose is to explain: a process, a social problem, a political battle, and so on.
- **Argument** is written to persuade—to convince the reader. The appeal may be logical, using the informative techniques employed in exposition.

The appeal may also be emotional, based on psychological factors such as the desire for affection, status, comfort, or security. Patrick Henry used information, logic, and emotion to craft his now-famous argument.

- **Description** is the written sharing of the writer's sensory perceptions: a beautiful sunset, a feeling of power, an unpleasant experience.
- **Narration** portrays events, real or imaginary, within a framework of time—but not necessarily in chronological order.

Many documents have more than one purpose; many employ more than one writing style. While a novel may be primarily narrative, it is certain to include description—and likely to contain both exposition and argument.

An expository document on a machine or process may include discussion of the effect of the machine or process on the writer, its social or economic effect, and so forth.

It would be difficult to advance most arguments without explaining, describing, or using narrative examples.

5044 **Fluency.** **Fluency** is the ability to use language with ease and grace—to evoke explicit visual images and lucid abstractions that help the reader visualize what the writer has in mind.

- **Fluency and pretentious writing.** Fluency should not be confused with pretentious writing, the unnecessary use of elaborate language. Fluent writing has the grace, ease, and flowing quality that can be achieved through simplicity. Pretentious writing is ornate, but not necessarily graceful or useful.

Pretentious writing: `Contemplating, the youth reclined in a supine position and observed the visible nocturnal celestial bodies.`

Fluent writing: `Deep in thought, the boy lay on his back and watched the moon and stars.`

- **Fluent writing is evocative.** Fluent writing evokes *explicit, sequential, visual images,* as if the reader were leafing through a picture book or watching a slide show. The fluent writer uses words to make pictures in your mind.

Weak: `I was bitten on the leg by a large red dog.`

Visual images:

I was bitten	Difficult to visualize because the reader does not know where or by what (whom?) the writer was bitten. Avoid passive voice (was bitten); active voice is better.
on the leg	Now the reader can visualize a leg, but the image of the bite remains indistinct. If this is a piece on dogs, the reader may visualize a dog bite—only to find that the sentence reads *I was bitten on the leg by a flea.*
by a large red dog.	Finally the reader has the picture.

MORE

5

CONTINUED

Fluent: `A large red dog bit me on the leg.`

Visual images:

A large red dog	The reader visualizes a large red dog. (Notice the use of active voice.)
bit me	Now the dog opens its mouth, bares its teeth, and prepares to bite.
on the leg.	Now the reader visualizes the dog biting the writer's leg.

WORD PROCESSING HARDWARE

5101 **The choices.** There is an unbroken spectrum of choices in word processing equipment with a $100 electronic typewriter at the low end and a microcomputer system costing $5000 or more at the high end.

The categories in ¶ 5102-04 are representative of the abundant variety of typewriters and dedicated word processors available.

5

5102 **Electronic typewriters.** **Electronic typewriters** are the low-end word processing machines. Daisy wheel technology coupled with microchip circuitry give these $100-$150 machines their share of advanced features: automatic paper feed, boldface, 500-character correction memory, line-out correction, 10- and 12-character per inch pitch, 60,000-word spell checker, subscript, and superscript.

5103 **Low-end word processors.** **Low-end word processors** have features similar to those of electronic typewriters; plus editable memory of 5-7KB; LCD (**L**iquid **C**rystal **D**iode) screens that display 16-20 characters; and the ability to copy, move, and delete blocks of text.

5104 **High-end word processors.** **High-end word processors** increase editable memory to 64K; increase spelling words to 75,000; and add a 90-character by 15-line CRT (**C**athode **R**ay **T**ube) display, 3.5-inch disk drive, and a 50,000-word thesaurus. Some use file formats that are compatible with DOS and have spreadsheet capabilities.

High-end dedicated word processors employ daisy-wheel or inkjet printing mechanisms that produce quality work. The imprint of a good daisy wheel print mechanism through a one-time plastic ribbon produces an impression of high quality. An inkjet mechanism can approach the quality of a laser printer.

5105 **The computer as a word processor.** The microcomputer, loaded with a word processor program, is the most capable word processor in general use. See ¶ 5300 on professional typesetting and imagewriting equipment used by or for the desktop publishing industry.

The microcomputer has graphics capabilities, mass high-speed storage, the option of laser printing, compatibility with desktop publishing and professional typesetting and imagewriting equipment, and other advantages. The microcomputer—coupled with a laser printer—is the word processor of choice.

5200 WORD PROCESSING PROGRAMS

WORD PROCESSING PROGRAMS

5201 **Character-based word processor programs.** Early word processors, and many simple word processors still in use, are character based: under their control, the system can display 23 lines of 80 characters each, for a total

MORE

of 1840 characters. The **character set** consists of the 256 ASCII characters; no pictures, no additional fonts, no proportionally spaced typefaces, and so on.

Laser printers, and other graphics printers, can print large and small proportionally spaced fonts *whether or not they can be displayed on the screen*.

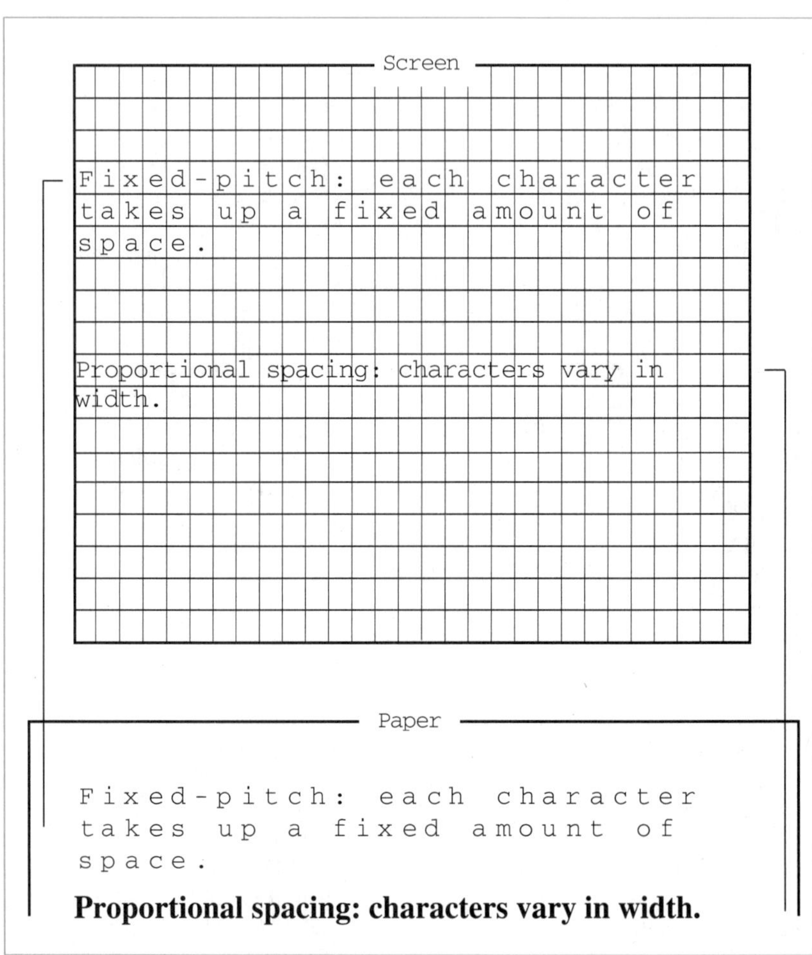

Illustration 5201.1 Character-Based Screen

In illustration 5201.1, the screen displays the only typeface it *can* display. The printer demonstrates that it can print the same typeface as the one on the screen (the first line on paper) *and* larger, proportionally spaced type as well (the second line on paper).

5202 **Graphical word processor programs.** A graphical word processor program, running on a system with a graphical display, displays realistically on the screen what the printer prints on paper: What You See Is What You Get (WYSIWYG—sometimes pronounced *wizz′-ēe-wig*). See illustration 5202.1.

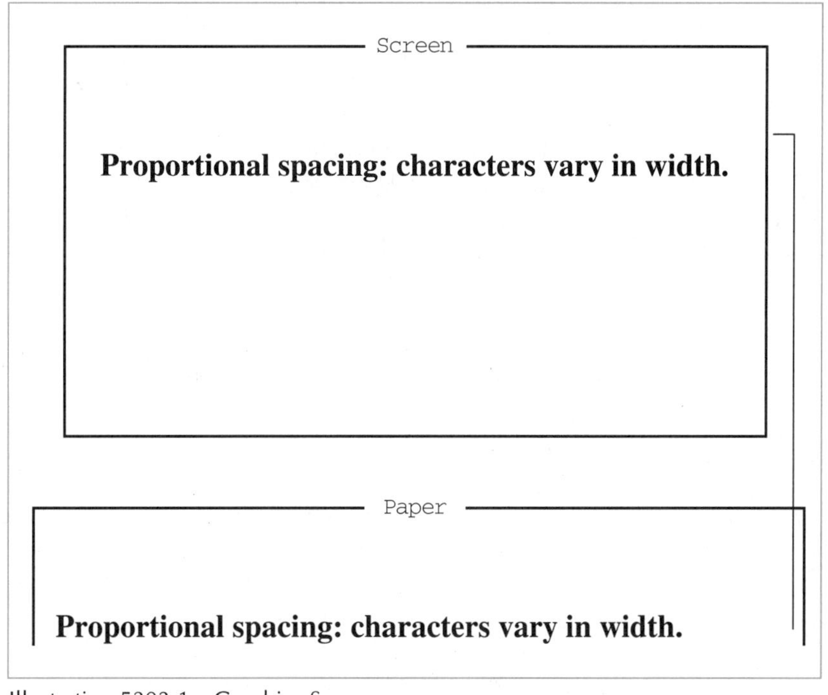

Illustration 5202.1 Graphics Screen

Keyboarding on a Word Processor

5203 **Writing at the keyboard.** Writing at the keyboard of a computer is much like typewriting. When a key is struck, however, the character the key controls appears on the screen rather than directly on the paper. Putting the character on paper comes later, when an entire page or an entire document is printed in a single operation.

5204 **Function keys.** Some computer keys are assigned to different functions by different programs; others retain the same functions under all programs. (See ¶ 4200: *function keys*).

5205 **Automatic line breaks.** The *<Enter>* key, located where typewriter keyboards have a carriage return key, is not normally used at the end of a line. Once the user has set the **hyphenation zone,** the return of the cursor to the left margin is automatic: the user continues keying and the end-of-the-line arrangements are managed by the word processor program.

5206 **Hyphenation zone.** The **hyphenation zone** at the end of the writing line determines which words will be considered for hyphenation. The hyphenation zone is set as part of the **writing line format** (See ¶ 5221).

```
Hyphenation zone of 3 characters:    ----------------|-/--
Hyphenation zone of 6 characters:    -------------|----/--
Hyphenation zone of 24 characters:
                                 ----|----------------------/--
```

MORE

Only words that begin before the beginning of the hyphenation zone (|) and extend beyond the right margin (/) will be hyphenated, and then only if they can be hyphenated in accordance with the hyphenation table of the word processor. A 3-character hyphenation zone will cause many words to be divided. A 6-character hyphenation zone will cause fewer words to be divided. A 24-character hyphenation zone will stop automatic hyphenation—no words will be divided automatically—unless words of more than 24 letters are used.

5207 **Word wrap.** Any word that crosses the right margin and is not hyphenated—either because it begins after the hyphenation zone (|) or because of the hyphenation table—is carried to the next line.

In the case of the 24-character hyphenation zone described in ¶ 5206, hyphenation is effectively precluded. Words that cannot be *completed* at or before the right margin (/) are carried to the next line. This feature is called **word wrap** because it appears to "wrap" the last word around the end of the current line, then pull it back to the current line if there is room for it or push it forward to the next line if there is not.

5208 **Soft hyphens.** **Soft hyphens** are those that are inserted when a word is hyphenated automatically at the end of the line. When the text is reformatted, any word containing a *soft* hyphen will be reunited, unless the word is automatically divided in the new format.

5209 **Hard hyphens.** **Hard hyphens** are those keyed by the user. They remain in place when the text is reformatted.

Correcting Individual Characters and Words

5210 **<Insert> key.** The **<Insert> key** is a toggle key (one that has two positions) that controls two keyboard modes: *replace* and *insert*. In *replace* mode, newly keyed characters replace old text that is in their way. In *insert* mode, newly keyed characters push forward (to the right) old text that is in their way.

5211 **Individual character.** An **individual character** can be corrected by simply keying another character over it. To replace a *z* with an *x*: first be sure the keyboard is in replace mode; then use the cursor keys to position the cursor under the *z;* then key an *x*.

If the keyboard is in insert mode, the same procedure will cause the *x* to push the *z* to the right, and the text will read *xz*.

5212 **Individual word.** An **individual word** or short expression can be corrected by putting the *<Insert>* key in replace mode and keying new characters to replace the old ones, by putting the *<Insert>* key in insert mode and pushing the old characters forward as new characters are keyed, or by replacing some characters and inserting others.

Emphasis: Boldface, Italics, and Underscore

5213 **Boldface.** **Boldfacing** is controlled by one of the function keys; which one depends upon which word processing program is in use. Usually, the same function key turns boldfacing on and turns it off. Press that key, and the characters keyed thereafter appear in boldface on the screen and in the printed document. Press the boldface key again, and the characters keyed thereafter will once again be entered normally—not boldfaced.

5214 **Italics.** **Italics** can be printed by some word processors on some printers. When an italic typeface is available, a designated function key turns italics on and off as described in ¶ 5213 for boldfacing.

5215 **Underscore.** **Underscoring** is turned on and off by a function key just as boldfacing and italics are. One function key causes *all* words, spaces, and punctuation to be underscored. Another function key causes just words, not spaces or punctuation, to be underscored.

Editing Blocks of Text

5216 **Highlighting.** **Highlighting** modifies a selected part of the text on the screen to make it stand out from the rest of the text on the screen. Highlighting is also called **selecting text.**

A **block** of text—word, line, sentence, column, paragraph or more—is usually highlighted to specify which part of the text is to be acted upon by the next command: moved, copied, or deleted.

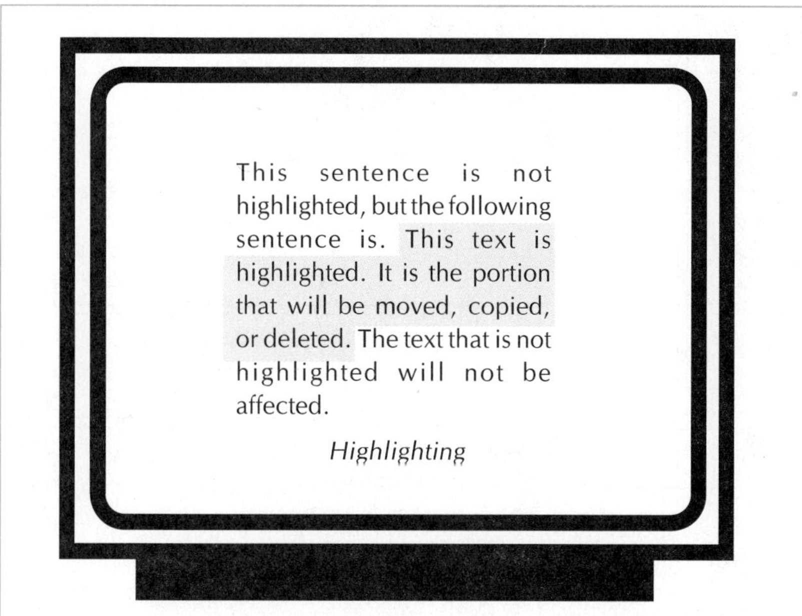

This sentence is not highlighted, but the following sentence is. This text is highlighted. It is the portion that will be moved, copied, or deleted. The text that is not highlighted will not be affected.
Highlighting

Illustration 5216.1 Highlighting

5217 **Deleting a block.** **Deleting a block** of text is a convenient way to clear a portion of the screen without disturbing the rest of it.

5218 **Moving a block.** **Moving a block** of text not only allows a few words, a line, a column, a paragraph, or more to be moved from place to place within the document, it allows the writer to restructure the document by moving badly located paragraphs to the end of the document temporarily, then reinserting them as they are needed. The *<End>* key moves the cursor quickly to the end of the document; the *search* function allows the user to return to the same spot in the text.

When a block of text is moved, it disappears from the old location and appears in the new location. (See ¶ 5219.)

5219 **Delete or blank?** When a block of text is deleted or moved, its former location may be left blank or closed up. In some cases, the user is given the option.

5220 **Copying a block.** **Copying a block** of text works just like moving a block of text, except that the block does not disappear from its original location; it is literally copied. (See ¶ 5218.)

Formatting

5221 **Formatting menu or window.** Special **menus** or **windows** allow a format to be specified for each document. The specified format is stored with the document. The format is automatically retrieved with the document whenever the document is retrieved. The formatting windows or menus can be brought to the screen (and the format revised) at any time during a writing or editing session.

```
HORIZONTAL                    PAGE CONTROL
Characters per Inch    12     Length of Paper       66     Reformat     Y
Proportional            N     Continuous Forms       N     Printer    199
Justification           N     Pagination             Y
                              First Page—Text starts on line        6
                              Other Pages—Text starts on line       6
VERTICAL                      All Pages——Text ends on line         60
Lines per Inch          6     Even Pages—Left border                1
Line Spacing            1     Odd Pages——Left border                1

                       MARGINS AND TAB STOPS
\----+-----+---------------------------|-/-----------------
```

Illustration 5221.1 Typical Formatting Window

The format shown in illustration 5221.1 specifies fixed-pitch type of 12 characters per inch (the same as elite type). Proportional spacing and justification (straight right margins) are turned off. Vertical spacing is 6 lines per inch with single spacing.

The paper is 66 lines long, not continuous (fanfold) but cut sheets. The computer will automatically reformat each paragraph (as it is entered) and divide the document into pages.

The number 199 identifies the make and model of the current printer allowing the word processing program to use the proper printer control table. Moving the cursor to highlight the current setting (199) and pressing *<Enter>* opens a window in which all widely used printers are listed. The user selects the proper brand and model, and the identification number of that printer becomes part of the format for the current document.

Text starts on line 6 and ends on line 60 on all pages. The left margin is set at 1 with tab stops at 6 and 12. The right margin is set at 70, with a 3-character hyphenation zone (see ¶ 5206).

With the left margin on the screen set at 1 and the left border in the format specifications set at 1, the printer will print as close to the left edge of the paper as possible—usually about 1/2-inch from the left edge.

The printed image can be moved to the right on the page by moving (increasing) the left border. This is called **paper offset** and should not be confused with moving the left margin on the screen. On some printers, paper offset can also be adjusted by moving the paper itself to the left or right.

5222 **Margins and tab stops.** **Margins and tab stops** are set as part of the format; the settings are stored with the document. In illustration 5221.1 (page 344), margins are set by \ and /; tab stops by + ; the hyphenation zone, three characters in this case, includes |-/ (see ¶ 5206).

5223 **Fixed format elements.** **Fixed format elements** remain unchanged throughout a document:

- Printer
- Type of paper (continuous form or cut sheets)
- Size of paper
- Pagination (yes or no)
- Margin specifications

The margins specified do not change the image on the screen. Rather, they adjust the entire printed image on the page, allowing the current document to be adjusted to the current printer.

5224 **Variable format elements.** **Variable format elements** can be changed from page to page within a document—or changed within a single page:

- Characters per inch
- Proportional-spaced or fixed-pitch font
- Justification (yes or no)
- Lines per inch
- Line spacing (single space, double space, triple space)
- Margins and tab stops

5225 **Layouts and style sheets.** A **layout** is a set of variable format elements that can be applied to a document or any part of a document. (See ¶ 5224.)

A **style sheet** is a set of layouts designed for a particular document or group of documents. Although the word processor program may furnish a default style sheet or several standard style sheets, most style sheets are created by the user and stored under individual filenames. Any style sheet can be called for by filename at any time during a word processing session.

In creating a new document, the user may either design a new style sheet or use one that has been stored previously. In either case, the style sheet can be modified as the document is created.

When the finished document is stored, the style sheet will be stored with it.

Some word processor programs permit the use of the filename extension to identify and call style sheets that are associated with groups of documents. For example, the extension *.LTR* might be used for a style sheet applicable to all letters, *.ENV* for a style sheet for all envelopes. See illustration 5225.1.

Layout 1	**Headline**
Layout 2	This is a layout for an overhanging paragraph. The left and right margins of the first line are equal. The left margin is indented on subsequent lines of the paragraph. The font is 10-character-per-inch Courier upright (fixed-pitch).
Layout 3	This layour specifies no paragraph indentation and printing in upright Courier medium at 15 characters per inch.
Layout 4	*This layout specifies normal paragraph indentation and printing in 12 point Times Roman italic medium—a proportionally spaced font.*

Illustration 5225.1 Style Sheet

5226 **Automatic reformatting.** When **reformat** is set to *Y* as it is in the example in illustration 5221.1 (page 344) each line is automatically formatted as the cursor returns to the left margin. The current paragraph is automatically reformatted when necessary. Entering an *N* in place of the *Y* turns automatic reformatting off.

5227 **Centering.** **Centering** is automatic. Just move the cursor to any position on the line to be centered and press the appropriate function key: which key depends upon which word processor program is in use.

Document Storage

5228 **Saving a document.** When a document is being keyed, it is a good idea to save it as each page is finished. Each time the document is saved (after the first time) the file on the disk is overwritten. Each word processor program has its own menu and key commands for saving on disk the work that has been entered into memory. The information in memory will be lost when the computer is turned off; the file on disk will not.

5229 **Filenames.** Each document is given a distinctive filename. Filenames conform to the format xxxxxxxx.xxx in which *x* stands for an alphabetic or numeric character. Your document about your vacation might be filed as *MYVACATN.DOC.*

5230 **Retrieving a document.** Menus or dialog boxes permit the user to **retrieve** from disk storage files that have been stored previously. Each document is called for by its filename.

Special Word Processor Features

5231 **Macro.** A **macro** is a recorded series of keystrokes available for playback when the macro command key is struck. The purpose of a macro is to avoid repetitive keying. High-end word processor programs have built-in macro functions. Those that do not can be provided with macro functions by a terminate and stay resident (TSR) macro program such as Newkey. (See ¶ 4200: *macro* and *TSR.*)

5232 **Spell checker.** A **spelling checker**, included in most word processor programs but also available as a separate TSR program, checks spelling sequentially, stops at any misspelled word, provides a list of correctly spelled words believed to contain the intended word, and replaces the misspelled word with the correctly spelled word when the user selects it. Spelling checkers contain as many as 150,000 words.

A **real-time spelling checker** checks each word as it is keyed and beeps when the spelling checker detects an error. On command, the real-time spelling checker assists in correcting the misspelled word just as the sequential spelling checker does.

The user can add words to the spelling list. This feature is particularly useful for often-used technical terms, names, and the like—words that are not on the spelling list, but are used frequently by the user of the word processor program.

5233 **Thesaurus.** A computer **thesaurus** provides a list of synonyms and near synonyms for use when the writer is unable to think of just the right word. To find a synonym, follow this procedure:

1. Key the best word you can think of for your purpose. Move the cursor to any letter in that word.
2. Press the function key designated for synonyms. The thesaurus will display a list of synonyms.
3. Select the best synonym for your purpose, and press the <*Enter*> key. The word you have chosen from the list of offered synonyms will replace the word with which you were not satisfied.

5234 **Dictionary.** A computer **dictionary** provides both definitions and synonyms. It may be part of the word processor program or a separate TSR program.

5235 **Merge.** A **merge** feature in a word processing program permits the automatic insertion of variable information (a different name and address for each copy of a letter, for example) into form letters or other **boilerplate** or **canned text.**

Literally, *boilerplate* means the semifinished metal sheets or plates from which boilers are made.

The term *boilerplate* probably originated in journalism, where *boilerplate* refers to newspaper mastheads, syndicated columns, and the like, that fill up space with no effort on the part of the newspaper staff.

Boilerplate is also attributed to the law profession, where "canned" paragraphs supply the routine parts of contracts, wills, and other documents. The attorney supplies the custom-written portion of the document that suits it to the particular circumstances.

5236 **GUIs and word processor programs.** The leading word processor programs use **Graphical User Interfaces** and permit control of some functions by **mouse.** (See ¶ 4328.)

5300 DESKTOP PUBLISHING

DESKTOP PUBLISHING

5301 **Definition.** **Desktop publishing** is the use of microcomputer hardware and software to design electronic page images that are (1) displayed on screen, (2) stored on disk, and (3) printed.

Generally, word processing programs are used for documents that traditionally have been produced on office machines: letters, memos, reports, and the like. Desktop publishing programs are used for documents that traditionally have been produced on printing equipment: newsletters, brochures, menus, and the like. (See ¶ 5001 and ¶ 5302.)

5302 **Description.** The desktop publishing process works as follows:

1. A word processing program is used to enter text and store it on disk.
2. Artwork is originated or modified using the paint or draw capabilities of a desktop publishing program and separate paint or draw programs. Artwork is also scanned or purchased as **clip art** (electronic images stored on disk for future use).
3. A desktop publishing program is used to produce a layout on the computer screen.
4. The artwork drawn or selected in step 2 is inserted electronically into the layout on the computer screen by the desktop publishing program. The desktop publishing program can revise, crop, and position the artwork after it is imported.
5. Text is imported into the layout and electronically "set" into the various typefaces prescribed in the layout for headlines, body type, captions, and so on. The desktop publishing program can make some revisions in the text, size it, flow it around illustrations, and so forth. The word processing program is used to make major revisions in the text itself.
6. Electronic images of the finished pages are stored on disk and used to produce output in one or more of the following forms:
   - A reproduction-quality master is printed by the computer printer. Duplicate copies of this master produced on a photocopy machine may suffice if a small number of copies are needed.
   - A reproduction-quality master is printed by the computer printer and used as camera-ready artwork for **photo-offset lithography**—the printing process used for most runs of more than a few copies. Although photocopying is less expensive for the first few copies, lithography is much less expensive once the set-up costs of lithography (camera work, platemaking, and press make-ready) have been absorbed.
   - Electronic page images are transmitted by fax. It is also possible to transfer those images and other files from one system to another—even if the systems use different operating systems—by using special disk drives, network software, or data transfer software. System-to-system transfers can also be effected by using modems and telecommunications software.
   - Electronic page images stored on disk or transmitted by modem are used by a production shop as input for an **imagesetter**—a typesetting

MORE

machine that produces high-resolution output on photographic film or paper. An imagesetter operates at resolutions of 1200 dpi (dots per inch) or higher. A typical laser printer operates at a resolution of 300 dpi.

Hardware

5303 **The computer.** Computers suitable for desktop publishing belong to three groups:

- Apple Macintosh computers
- IBM, PCs, PC clones, the PC compatibles
- Computers using the UNIX operating system.

5304 **Desktop publishing systems.** A typical desktop publishing system has a 386 or 486 CPU, 4MB or more of RAM, a 120MB-or-more hard drive, and operates at 20 MHz or faster. A laser printer is virtually standard equipment.

Software

5305 **Word processing programs.** A graphical word processing program, such as Ami Professional, Microsoft Word, or WordPerfect, used with hardware similar to that described in ¶ 5304, can print most routine business documents, adding embellishments—such as justified columns, headlines, simple graphics, and font management. For more complex documents, both a word processing program and a desktop publishing program (see ¶ 5306) may be required.

5306 **Desktop publishing programs.** If the full potential of the microcomputer is to be used for publishing long and complex documents, a desktop publishing (page-layout) program such as PageMaker or Ventura Publishing is needed. Even the low-end desktop publishing programs such as PFS: First Publisher and Publish It! have layout and page control features that go beyond the capabilities of word processing programs.

5307 **Graphics programs.** **Graphics programs** are used to create and modify artwork. The artwork may be created by "painting" or "drawing" on the screen—or by modifying the electronic images of existing photographs, drawings, paintings, or other artwork. (See ¶ 5308-09.)

5308 **Paint programs.** Programs that permit images to be "painted" on the screen and stored as electronic dots (bits) are called **paint programs.** The electronic images are called **bitmaps.**

The gaps between the dots that constitute bitmap images cause the ragged edges that characterize bitmap images. These "jaggies" are particularly noticeable in images reproduced at low resolution (72 dpi, for example), somewhat noticeable but not objectionable at the 300 dpi resolution typical of laser printers, and more difficult to detect at higher resolutions. (See ¶ 4200: *bitmapped images.*)

5309 **Draw programs.** **Draw programs** are object oriented: they use **vectors** (lines that have width and direction) and **shapes** (circles, ellipses, curves, etc.) instead of bitmaps to form electronic images.

Object-oriented graphics can be **scaled** (made larger or smaller) without distortion. Bitmapped images are distorted because the lines grow thicker and thinner as the image is enlarged and reduced. (See ¶ 4200: *object oriented graphics.*)

5310 **Graphics file formats.** There is no universal format for the storage of artwork. Different paint and draw programs are used for PCs and Macintoshes; different file formats are used for object-oriented and bitmap artwork; draw and paint programs have their own proprietary formats.

The **EPS** (Encapsulated PostScript) format is the nearest thing there is to an industry standard. An EPS file contains both a low-resolution bitmap image that is displayed on the screen and a high-resolution image that is sent to the printer. EPS files are compatible with most painting, drawing, and layout programs for both the PC and the Macintosh. They are also used with professional typesetting equipment (see ¶ 5302)

Artwork

5311 **Artwork and layouts.** The principles of design that have guided layout artists, illustrators, designers, and printers for centuries apply to desktop publishing. Even if your design work is limited to the occasional use of an illustration, time spent studying a few of the references on the subject is well invested. Stated briefly, some of the more useful principles are the following:

1. The **optical center** of the page is slightly above the geometric center. Therefore, a bottom margin that is slightly deeper than the top margin is more pleasing to the eye. Side margins are generally pleasing in proportion if they are the same width as the top margin is deep.
2. There are two ways a page or an illustration can be oriented:

Portrait Orientation
(Shorter Side Horizontal)

Landscape Orientation
(Longer Side Horizontal)

MORE

Use the orientation that better suits the artwork:

- a flag on its pole in portrait format.
- a long ship or airplane in landscape format.
- a head and shoulders portrait in portrait format.
- a class picture in landscape format.
- the Washington Monument in portrait format.
- the Golden Gate Bridge in landscape format.

3. Any illustration that *points* (a hand, arrow, horseback rider, etc.) should point to an area *on* the page, not *off* the page. Vehicles, people, and the like, traveling right to left seem more natural, possible because that is the way we picture the early westward migration in America. Generally, people should look *toward the center* of the page, not *off* the page. An illustration that points up directs the reader's attention backward or off the top of the page, whereas an illustration that points *down* directs the reader's attention to what you have to say next, or to the next page.

   An illustration that faces the wrong way can sometimes be *flopped* (reversed), but be careful not to reverse the text on signs, make right-handers into left-handers, and so forth.

4. Crop extraneous detail, but leave in anything that adds interest or focuses attention on the center of interest. An otherwise-extraneous person looking at, or pointing to, the center of interest can sometimes be a plus.

5. Watch the basic shapes. *Even* numbers of columns or other masses are generally more pleasing than *odd* numbers (count the number of columns, dormers, and the like on buildings that are generally admired). However, a balanced picture does not require regular or identical shapes; indeed, a balanced picture composed of a variety of shapes is usually more appealing than one composed of identical shapes.

6. Keep captions brief. Locate them as close to their illustrations as possible. Shape each to complement the shape of its illustration.

5312 **Line art.** **Line drawings** are made without any middle tones. Line art is usually printed black on white—without gray tones. High-key (high-contrast) photographs can similarly be produced without in-between tones. (See ¶ 4200: *halftone*.)

Line art, high-contrast photographs, and type images—having no gray tones—are printed as lines and shapes without the use of dots to produce in-between tones.

5313 **Photographs.** A properly processed color photograph can reproduce not only the primary colors, but hundreds of in-between shades as well. A high-quality reproduction lithographed on slick paper matches all these shades almost perfectly by using dots to mix the various colors printed on the page and to mix each ink with the white (or other color) of the paper.

In black-on-white printing, a photograph is reproduced by printing a screen of black dots that are dense in the black areas, sparse in the gray areas, and absent in the white areas. This dot image is called a **halftone.**

Similarly, dense dots printed in red ink can produce a brilliant red; fewer and fewer dots produce lighter and lighter shades of pink; absence of dots leaves the area white. Such a shading of tone in one color is called a **duotone.**

Halftones may also be used to print one color (usually black) reproductions of charcoal drawings, watercolors, airbrush work, and other non-photographic artwork containing in-between tones.

5314 **Screens and block graphics.** Screens were first used extensively to produce printed panels and borders by American printer Benjamin Day. The printing industry still refers to such screens as benday process. Benday background is specified as a percent of black. A 12-25 percent benday background is an effective way to highlight text.

The gray tones in black-and-white reproduction are made by mixing printed black dots with the white background. The denser the black dots (the screen), the darker the shade of gray.

If your system allows you to print ASCII characters 176, 177, 178, and 219, you may be able to keyboard and print screens like these:

12% 25% ░ 75% ▒ 100% █.

Other ASCII characters in the same range will produce single-line figures (┌ - ┘) and double-line figures (╔ = ╝), allowing you to enter and print figures such as these:

These are **block graphics,** so called because they are made up entirely of individual block characters. These are all included in the ASCII character set. (See ¶ 4200: *ASCII character set.*)

Use the macro capability of your word processor or a separate macro TSR, such as Newkey, to assign some of your unused keyboard combinations to ASCII block-graphics characters. The result can be a simple and useful character-based graphics system that works within your word processor. Block graphics are possible with most word processing programs.

More-advanced graphics require specialized software (a graphics, draw, or paint program) or a high-end word processing or desktop publishing program. See ¶ 5316 for the use of fonts to print block graphics on any system that can print fonts.

Typography

5315 **Typefaces.** A **typeface** is a collection of all the characters of a single type design. Because of the need for variations in size, posture, and weight, each typeface has several fonts. (See ¶ 5316.)

Most typefaces fall into one of the two major type families: **roman** (with serifs) and **gothic** (without serifs or **sans serif**). **Serifs** are the small embellishing strokes at the ends of the major strokes.

This is 14pt Times Roman Bold

This is 14pt Avant Garde Book

The height of type is measured in points (pt). There are 72 points to an inch.

5316 **Fonts.** A **font** is a complete set of characters of the same *size* (in points), *typeface* (Century, Helvetica, etc.), *posture* (upright or italic), and *weight* (light, medium, or bold). In the early days of the printing industry, the font of type the printer bought from the type foundry contained very few Zs, a few Ns, and several Es—an assortment that included a quantity of each character proportional to the frequency with which that character was used.

In desktop publishing, a font contains the *electronic image* of each character. That image is copied electronically as it is needed, much as a character on a typewriter is used over and over to produce image after image. Thus a font, as defined in desktop publishing, is *one* of each character in a given size, typeface, posture, and weight.

A font of 14pt Avant Garde Book:

! " # $ % & ' ( ) * + , / 0 1 2 3 4 5 6 7 8 9 : ; , = . ? @
A B C D E F G H I J K L M N O P Q R S T U V W X Y
Z ' (\ ) ^ a b c d e f g h i j k l m n o p q r s t u v w
x y z { | }

A font of 12pt Times Roman Italic Medium:

*! " # $ % & ' ( ) * + , / 0 1 2 3 4 5 6 7 8 9 : ; , = . ? @ A B C D*
E F G H I J K L M N O P Q R S T U V W X Y Z ' [\ ] ^ a b c d
e f g h i j k l m n o p q r s t u v w x y z { | }

5317 **Fonts on disk and in memory.** **Resident fonts** are stored in the printer's read only memory (ROM). **Cartridge fonts** are stored in hardware ROM cartridges. The fonts in a cartridge become available when the cartridge is inserted into a special slot in the printer. Soft fonts are stored on the computer's hard disk. They are **downloaded** (copied) to the printer's RAM, usually at the beginning of a printing session. (See ¶ 4200: *laser printer.*)

Special purpose fonts are used to print small block graphics, sometimes called **dingbats.** Unless special translation tables are prepared, the screen displays the alphabet,

A B C D E F G H I J K L

while the printer prints the corresponding graphics,

▶ ◀ • ↕ ♥ ♦ ♣ ♠ § ↑ ↓ ¶

Drawing fonts provide a system for drawing with block graphics similar to the one described in ¶ 5314.

```
A B C D E F G H I J K L
- | ┌ ┐ └ ┘ ═ ║ ╔ ╗ ╚ ╝
```

Like other special purpose fonts, block graphics fonts often display the letters of the alphabet and print the block graphics.

Displayed on Screen

```
CAAAAAAAAAD
B         B
B   IGJ   B
B   H H   B
B   KGL   B
B         B
EAAAAAAAAAF
```

Printed on Paper

5318 **Bitmapped fonts.** **Bitmapped fonts** can be purchased in hardware cartridges that plug into the printer or as soft fonts stored on disks. Bitmapped fonts are not scalable; i.e., creation and storage of a complete set of characters is required for each type size. Bitmapped fonts share the characteristics of other bitmapped images, lacking the resolution and smoothness of scalable fonts.

5319 **Scalable fonts.** **Scalable fonts** may be resident fonts, cartridge fonts, or soft fonts. In any case, the electronic images are stored as mathematical formulas specifying the shape of each character. When a certain size is specified (in points), special font-scaling software produces a font of that size. **Scaling** means making the type images larger or smaller.

5320 **Fixed-pitch fonts.** A font designed with a **fixed pitch** uses an area of the same size for printing each character. For example, all characters in a 12-pitch font are allowed 1/12-inch of space. Some characters will cover most of the standard area (M, W, etc.); others will leave more white space (i, l, etc.).

w	i	l	l		i	t	?

5321 **Proportional spacing.** The width of the printing area of each character in a proportionally spaced font is proportional to the width of the character itself. The printing area for a capital *W* is wider than that for a lowercase *i*; the printing area for a lowercase *m* is wider than that for a capital *I*. This equalizes the white space between characters, making the print more attractive and easier to read. It also increases the amount of text a given area of the page can hold.

W	i	l	l		i	t	?

5322 **Justification.** Full lines of text that are **justified** are flush with both the left and right margins. Partial lines that are justified are printed flush with the left margin. This paragraph is justified.

A **blurb** is a headline or brief quotation. Each line may be centered or all lines may be justified. A box may be used around the blurb to make it stand out.

This paragraph is **left justified:** all lines are flush at the left side of the column. This format is most often described as **ragged right,** since left justification alone leaves the right margin uneven. Left-justified (ragged right) text may be used to the right of an inset, illustration, or blurb box in a layout—thus resembling a banner flowing to the right.

This paragraph is **right justified:** all lines are flush at the right side of the column. Right justified type may be used to the left of an inset illustration or blurb box in a layout—thus resembling a banner flowing to the left.

When a blurb box appears at the right margin, the text in it may be set flush left (ragged right). Some studies have shown that ragged right is the easiest format to read.

5323 **Kerning.** It is impossible to design a typeface in which all the letters fit together perfectly. For example, the word *away*, printed in capital letters, may leave unwanted white space between the letters:

A W A Y

Kerning is adjustment of the space between characters to increase readability and improve appearance. Usually, adjacent letters are moved closer together to eliminate excessive white space:

AWAY

5324 **Emphasizing type.** Emphasis such as boldfacing and italicizing should be used systematically and with restraint.

boldface	*italics*	underlined
ALL CAPS	CAPS AND SMALL CAPS	

Boldface an individual word or expression to indicate that it is the subject of a definition or explanation, because it serves as a heading, and so on.

Italicize words that deserve unusual emphasis: those that should be accented if the sentence is read aloud. Also, italicize to indicate parallel structure in longer sentences.

First play the *three of spades;* then play the *two of diamonds* and the *four of clubs;* keep the *ace of hearts* in your hand.

Underscoring is used in informal publications and manuscripts to indicate words and expressions that are italicized in more formal publications.

5325 **Desktop publishing example.**

Desktop Publishing

Desktop publishing is a means of bringing the graphic arts to the office. The masthead or main heading above is printed as a *reverse*—white on black rather than the normal black on white. The capital *D* at the beginning of this paragraph is called a *dropped capital*.

The city scene at the right is an example of *clip art*. It is stored on a computer disk with other pieces of clip art in a directory referred to as a *library* of clip art. Clip art is called and inserted by a desktop publishing program much as any file is called from disk and used by other kinds of programs.

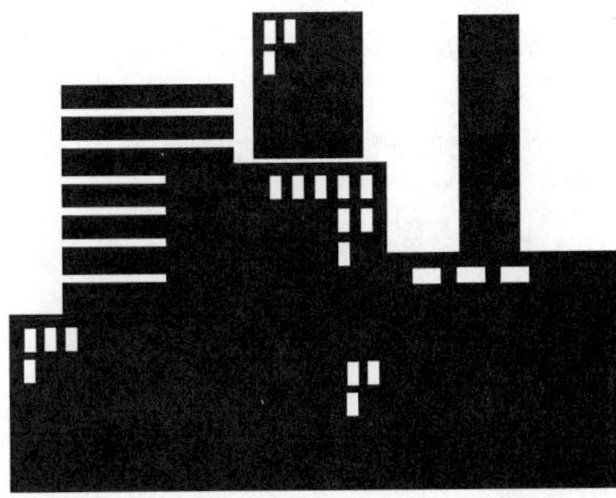

Clip Art: The City at Night

Desktop Computer: Monitor, System Case, & Keyboard

Reference Manual for the Office

FORMATTING

5401 **Keyboarding basics.** This chapter reviews some basic skills that you may recall from beginning keyboarding. An occasional refresher is a good idea when you have not used a particular skill for awhile. In addition, the latest word processing software simplifies many procedures. Steps reviewed here will cover the use of a computer in a nongraphics environment (G) (such as DOS) and in a graphics environment (G) (such as found using software on Apple/MacIntosh, Windows, OS/2, and NT platforms—see ¶ 4305 for additional information on computer platforms). However, automatic features vary so widely with hardware and software that hardware and software user's manuals are the only effective sources of information on automatic formatting. To review the steps required when using a typewriter, please refer to a basic typewriter text such as *Keyboarding/Formatting Style Manual* (stock #TA20EZM) or *Keyboarding Quick Reference Guide* (#TP01AA) available from South-Western Publishing Co.

5402 **Key definitions.** The following definitions will assist you in understanding the instructions to follow. (For more detailed explanations, refer also to ¶ 4200.)

Cursor—Indicator on the computer screen that shows the position where the next character will be entered, usually a blinking underscore or a solid square.

Drop-down menu—Listing of choices (usually at the top of the computer screen) that when selected expands to a larger menu "dropping down" on the computer screen to expand options for selection. Drop-down menus, which were once only available in graphics programs, are now also available in the more advanced nongraphics programs.

Function key <F>—One of the keys at the top or left side of the computer keyboard; these are labeled **F1 - F12**. (See also, ¶ 4200)

Icon button—A button square containing graphic pictures and/or text indicating a computer process that can be accessed by "clicking on" the icon button.

Click on—Process of placing the mouse indicator over an icon button or drop-down menu and depressing the left mouse button to select the process indicated. (See also, *mouse* in ¶ 4200.)

5403 **Horizontal centering.** **Horizontal centering** is the term used for centering a line in relation to the side edges of the paper. You probably use horizontal centering most often to center a line, such as a title.

Horizontal Centering

5404 **Steps for horizontal centering.**

- Key the word or phrase to be centered.
- Place the cursor anywhere on the word or phrase to be centered.
- (G) Depress the applicable function key for your software package (G) Click on the centering icon or select *center* from the appropriate drop-down menu.
- The word or phrase is centered within the previously set margins.

Note: For centering on odd-size paper and cards, reset the margins for the item to be printed and then follow the same steps.

5

5405 **Spread headings.** A spread heading looks like this:

A S P R E A D   H E A D I N G

To key a spread heading

- Key the heading, spacing once after each letter or character and three times between words.
- Center following the directions indicated for horizontal centering.

5406 **Vertical centering.** **Vertical centering**—also called top-to-bottom centering—is the term used for centering one or several lines in relation to the top and bottom edges of the paper. You probably use this skill most often in keying tabulated material.

5407 **Steps for vertical centering.** Vertical centering may be completed using one of three methods:

mathematical
backspace-from-center
automatic

5408 Mathematical method. (G) & (G)

- Count lines and blank line spaces needed to print information to be keyed.
- Subtract lines to be used from lines available (66 for a full sheet [11"] and 33 for half sheet [5.5"]). For odd-size paper, 1 inch = 6 vertical lines. When using word processing software, check the manual to determine the **vertical default**—the maximum number of vertical lines that will be printed on each paper sheet.
- Divide by 2 to get top and bottom margins. If a fraction results, disregard it.
- If an even number results, space down that number of times from the top of the computer page and begin keying the first line. If an odd number results, use the next lower number.
- Dropping fractions and using even numbers usually places copy a line or two above exact center—in what is often called **reading position.**

```
Formula for Vertical Mathematical Placement
lines available - lines used / 2 = top margin
```

- Begin to key material at vertical center.

5409 Backspace-from-center method. (G) & (G)

- Find total vertical lines available: full sheet, 11" x 6 lines per inch = 66 total lines available; half sheet, 5.5" x 6 lines to an inch = 33 total lines available. When using word processing software, check the manual to determine the *vertical default* (see ¶ 5408). Use this number to substitute for the *lines available* in the following formula; then proceed with other steps as described.
- Find vertical center of paper to be used.

```
total lines available/2 = vertical center
```

- Move the cursor down from the top edge of the page to vertical center.
- Use the **up arrow** to move back up the page once for every two keyed and/or blank lines.
- Begin to key material at vertical center.

5410 **Automatic Vertical Centering (G) & (G).** Many word processing programs allow you to vertically center automatically:

- Key in the material to be vertically centered.
- (G) Follow the instructions for vertical centering, usually a combination of a function key (e.g., **<F8>**) followed by other keys responding to computer prompts (answers to questions)—e.g., **2,1,Y**.
- (G) Place the cursor at the top of the page; choose appropriate drop-down menus for vertical centering for example, **Layout, Page, Center Page.**

5411 **Tabulation.** **Tabulation** is the term used to represent the keying of columns of information, often referred to as *tables*. Illustration 5411.1 shows a simple table with a main heading, secondary heading, and column headings. Illustration 5411.2 shows the same table using lines, shading (screens), a graphic, and different fonts available with word processing software to "dress up" the table. Tabulation is a way to present complex information in columns for easy reading and comparisons.

INFORMATION TECHNOLOGY DEPARTMENT
Outstanding Faculty
By Campus

Name	Campus	Employment Date
Lynn Forrester	Wolfson	September 15, 19—
Ida Gropper	Wolfson	April 20, 19—
Gloria Moutran	Wolfson	August 31, 19—
Georgie Willford	Wolfson	January 1, 19—
Pat Hodges	South	August 15, 19—
Billie Tomlin	South	January 3, 19—
Hazel Kates	South	January 2, 19—
Bob Ochs	South	August 15, 19—
Linda Hoffman	North	August 18, 19—
Martha Pinkston	North	August 21, 19—
Roz Reich	North	April 30, 19—
Shelia Long	North	August 29, 19—
Liz Forrester	North	January 3, 19—

Illustration 5411.1 Simple Tabulation

INFORMATION TECHNOLOGY DEPARTMENT
Outstanding Faculty
By Campus

Name	Campus	Employment Date
Lynn Forrester	Wolfson	September 15, 19—
Ida Gropper	Wolfson	April 20, 19—
Gloria Moutran	Wolfson	August 31, 19—
Georgie Willford	Wolfson	January 1, 19—
Pat Hodges	South	August 15, 19—
Billie Tomlin	South	January 3, 19—
Hazel Kates	South	January 2, 19—
Bob Ochs	South	August 15, 19—
Linda Hoffman	North	August 18, 19—
Martha Pinkston	North	August 21, 19—
Roz Reich	North	April 30, 19—
Shelia Long	North	August 29, 19—
Liz Forrester	North	January 3, 19—

Illustration 5411.2 Advanced Tabulation

5

5412 **Steps for tabulation.**

- Position the cursor where you want the table to begin.
- (G) & (G) Choose *Define Tables* from the drop-down menu or icon button.
- Choose *Create Table* (as opposed to *Edit Table,* which you use when you need to change an existing table.)
- Choose the number of columns you wish to use.
- Choose the number of rows you wish to use (remember to count column titles.)
- Create **Cells** (each individual area in a column where information can be entered).
- (G) To change the width of columns, choose *Edit* (often this is done by combining the **<Shift>, <Alt>, or <Ctrl>** key with one of the function **[<F>]** keys, highlighting the column, and using right **[→]** or left **[←]** arrow keys to widen columns.)
- (G) To change the width of columns, usually clicking on the tab arrows in the ruler bar and moving to the left or right will widen a column.
- (G) & (G) To change the vertical size of an individual cell in the column, simply press the enter key while in that cell.
- (G) & (G) To add or subtract columns and/or rows, choose *Table Edit* (instead of Create as in step 2).
- (G) & (G) To center column titles or the text in any cell of the table, highlight the text in that cell and follow the steps for horizontal centering (see ¶ 5404).
- Center the entire table vertically on the page by following the steps listed for vertical centering (see ¶ 5408-10).

5413 **Tabulation in business letters and manuscripts.** Detailed material in letters and reports may be easier to understand if it is tabulated. The tabulated material is keyed after double-spacing below the preceding paragraph. Double spacing is also used after the tabulated material, before continuing the remainder of the letter or manuscript. When you are ready to create a table within a letter or memorandum, move the cursor to where you want the table placed and follow the guidelines in ¶ 5412 for creating a table. See illustration 5413.1 for an example of a memo containing tabulated material.

Gonzalez & Company

TO: Dr. Horace Traylor, Employee Relations

FROM: Marie Hydress
Associate Vice President
Human Resources

DATE: July 3, 19–

SUBJECT: Ten-Year Pins

Thank you for offering to order the ten-year pins for employees celebrating their tenth anniversary with Gonzalez & Company. The same style pins as those used last year will be fine—with the exception of the change in color to blue, as we discussed.

Following is a listing of employees' names for the engraving on each pin:

Name	Date Employed	Department
Mary King	January 15, 19--	Human Resources
William A. Stokes	February 2, 19--	Purchasing
Bennie Moore	April 17, 19--	Customer Service
Gary Gosnell	July 21, 19--	Accounting
Arcie Ewell	October 18, 19--	Facilities Management

Please call me when the pins arrive, and I shall arrange to have them picked up and gift wrapped for each employee. Thanks again for your help.

Illustration 5413.1 Memo with Tabulated Information

5414 **Decimal tab.** Many advanced word processing software programs provide the ability to use a decimal tab. This tab stop aligns the decimals in columns of numbers as they are keyed. See the example in the second column.

Departments	Sales in Millions
Computer Games	845.5678
Comic Books	1.67
Dolls	1,348.801

5415 **Proofreading.** Finding errors is the first step to take *before* printing. See ¶ 5034-38.

5416 **Corrections.** Even the best keyboard operators make errors. Therefore, the operator, together with the employer, must decide the best type of correction techniques to be used. ¶ 5417 lists the important features of each correction technique.

5417 **Steps for corrections.** The fastest and most efficient method available for error correction is the use of word processing software. This software allows for rapid addition and deletion of letters, words, and paragraphs. Paper costs are definitely reduced when such corrections/revisions are made before a copy is printed. Through use of an *edit undo feature*, some software programs even allow you to change your mind and *recover* letters, words, or paragraphs that were just deleted.

1. **Use the spell/grammar check and thesaurus.** The latest software packages have spelling checkers that check all words keyed against 50,000-plus words in an electronic dictionary, and allow for the addition to the dictionary of common business terms (or names) specific to your organization. Once started, the electronic spelling checker stops at each word not recognized and provides suggested corrections. You may *<replace>*, *<skip once>*, or *<skip always>*. You may also *<add>* new words to the dictionary.

   Medical, legal, and financial dictionaries are also available. An electronic thesaurus with 200,000-plus synonyms provides assistance in enlarging your vocabulary while writing. Companion software programs that check written documents against simple grammatical rules are also available.

2. **Correcting individual letters or words.** An individual letter or word may be corrected in several ways:

   - (G) & (G) Check to see if *insert* is on or off. **Insert** is a toggle key (which means that if pressed once it is turned on and pressed again it is turned off). Different software programs have different initial (default) settings for whether the program starts with the insert off or on.

Original text:	`Now is time`
Add the word *the* (cursor position = ▒)	`Now is time`
Insert on:	`Now is` *`the`* `time`
Insert off:	`Now is` *`thee`*

   - (G) & (G) The delete key pressed once deletes the letter identified by the cursor:

Original text:	`Now is the time`
Cursor position = ▒ :	`Now is the time`
Press delete key:	`Now s the time`

   - (G) & (G) From the position of the cursor, the backspace key pressed once deletes the first letter to the left:

Original text:	`Now is the time`
Cursor position = ▒ :	`Now  is the time`
Press backspace key:	`No is the time`

3. **Moving/Deleting letters, words, sentences, or paragraphs.** Sometimes the fastest method of making corrections involves moving or deleting entire sentences or paragraphs. This is quickly accomplished using word processing software as follows: (See also, ¶ 5216-20.)

- (G) The first step is to mark the **block** (the words, sentences, or paragraphs to be moved). This is usually accomplished by moving the cursor to the beginning of the portion to be moved and marking *block beginning*; moving to the end of the block and marking *block ending*.
- (G) To delete, choose <*delete block*> once the entire text section is blocked.
- (G) To copy or move instead of delete, the cursor is moved (after blocking the text) to the point of insertion and the software is instructed to either <*copy*> or <*move*> block. If the words are *copied*, a copy appears at the position of the cursor and the original block is left untouched at the original location. If the words are *moved*, the copy appears at the position of the cursor and disappears from the original location.
- (G) The following steps (1-5) and accompanying screen examples indicate how to mark the block by highlighting the text:
- (G) To delete, simply press the <*delete*> key after the text is highlighted.
- (G) To move choose <*cut*> from the edit menu; move the cursor to the insertion position; and, choose <*paste*> from the edit menu.

Step 1. Highlight text

Place cursor at the beginning of word or phrase to be highlighted; hold down left mouse button and move to end of phrase to be highlighted. Release mouse button.

To delete text, press <*delete*> key now.

To move text, continue to step 2.

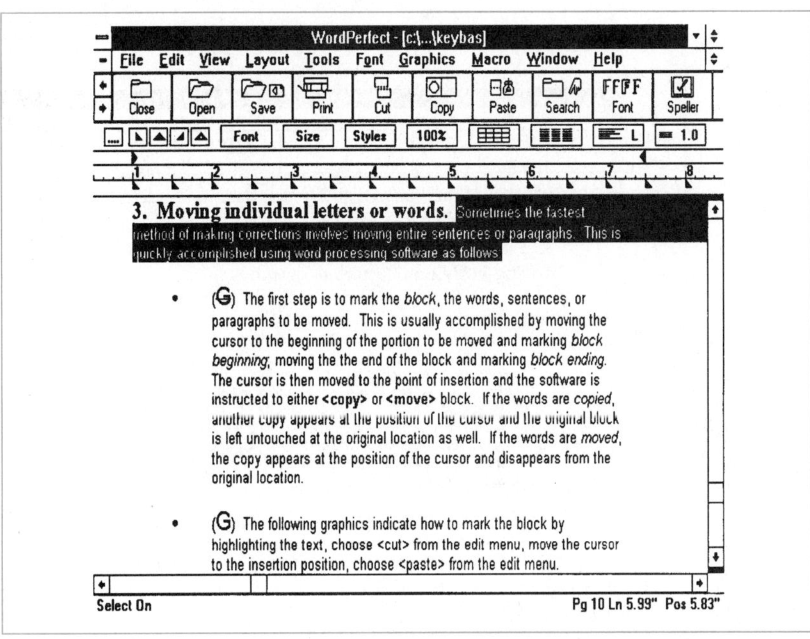

MORE

CONTINUED

5

Step 2. Edit menu: choose Cut

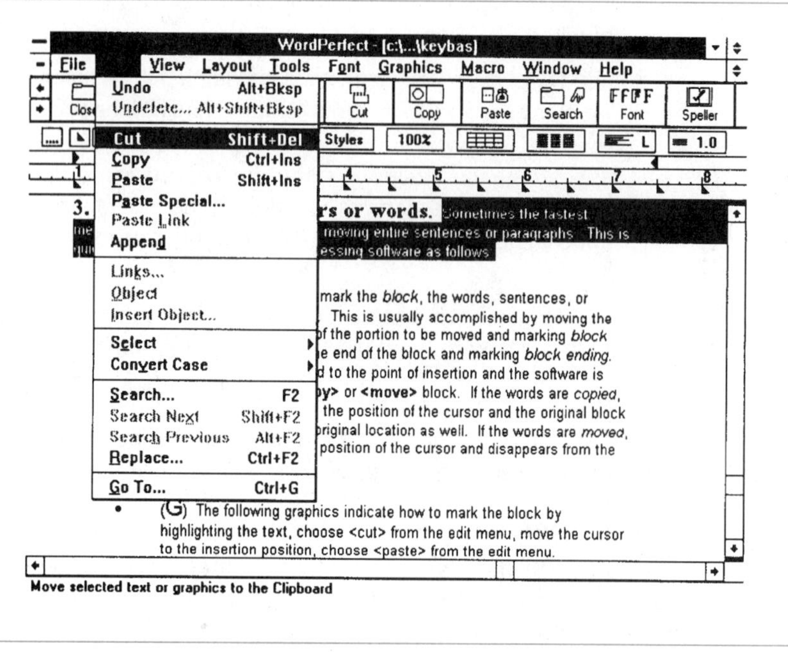

Step 3. Highlighted text disappears

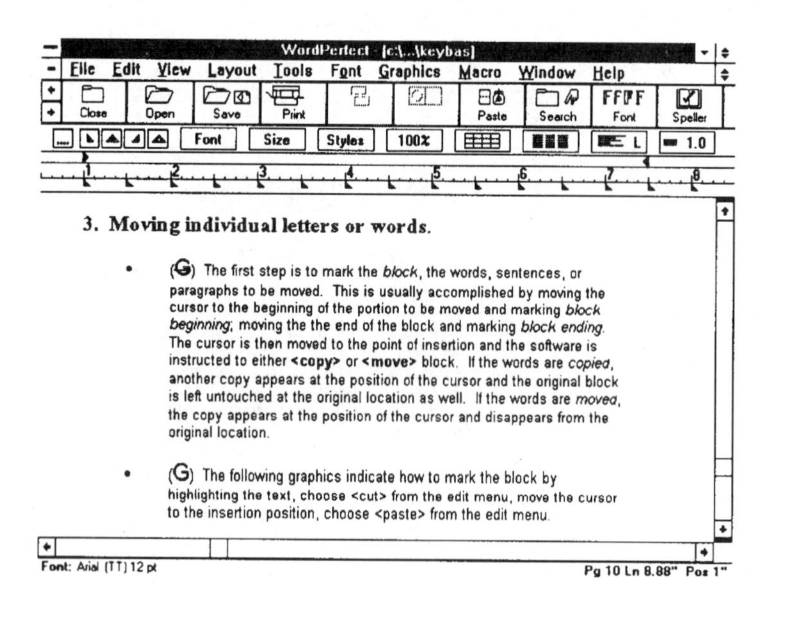

Step 4. Move cursor to insertion point; Edit menu: choose Paste

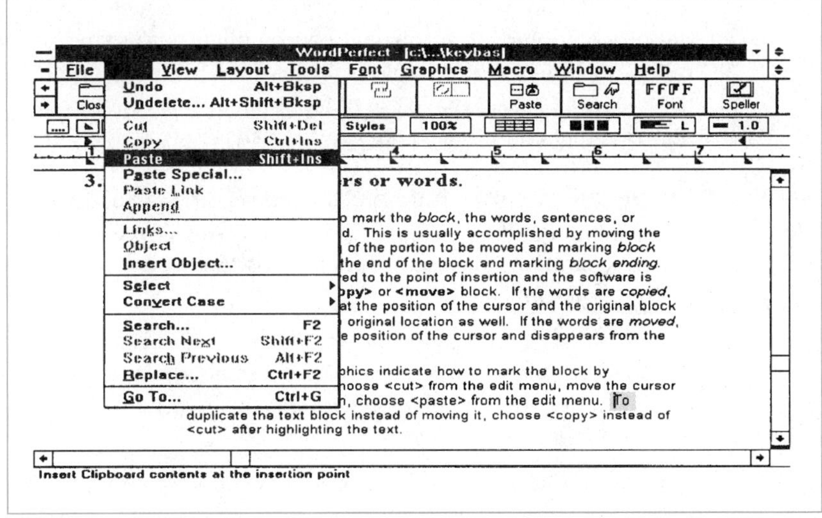

Step 5. Highlighted text in new position

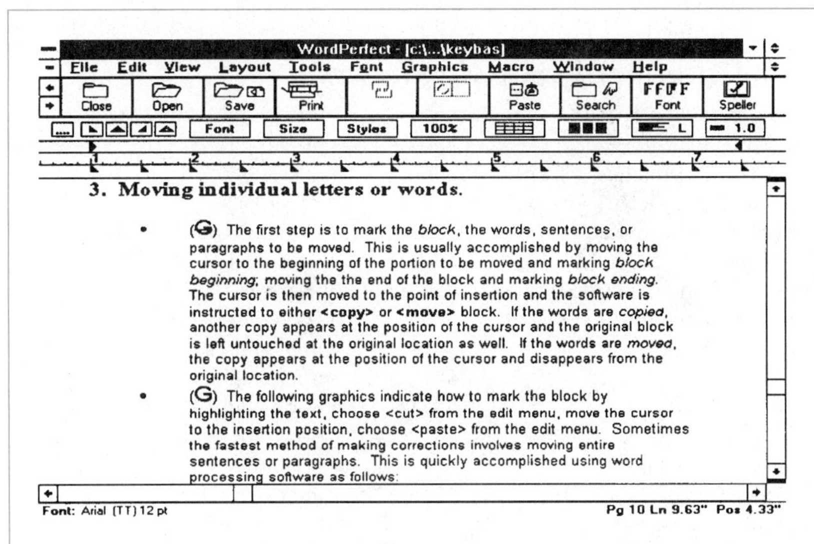

- (G) To duplicate the text block instead of moving it, choose *<copy>* instead of *<cut>* after highlighting the text.

5418 **Keying forms.** Information on forms—such as applications, invoices, bills of lading, and the like—should be keyed on the lines of the form so that only a slight space separates the letters from the underline (about the width of a hair). To give the forms you complete a professional look, align the beginnings of keyed lines where possible. Fill in all requested information, inserting *N/A* (not applicable) or a dash for lines that do not apply.

MORE

CONTINUED

Recent software releases of advanced forms packages provide the ability to design computerized forms that can be filled out on and printed from the microcomputer. Not only does this make it easier to complete forms, but these packages also make possible the recording of information entered in a format that can be used later in a database program.

5419 **Keying index cards and labels.** Index cards can usually be prepared on the computer and printed onto 8 1/2- by 11-inch sheets with perforations to allow separation and use as index cards. Such sheets are available in the local office supply store.

Similarly, labels are available in sheets of all sizes and all colors (even transparent). Most advanced word processing software programs provide an option under the layout menu to set up for printing labels and sending appropriate instructions to the printer.

However for a quick card or label, it is still very convenient to use a self-correcting or electronic typewriter. Since index cards and labels tend to slip as you key them, solve this problem by making a small pleat 1/4-inch wide in a full sheet of typing paper. Use cellophane tape to hold the ends of the pleat. Insert the index card or small label into the pleat and roll the sheet with the card or label in place into the typewriter. Slippage will be eliminated.

5500 REPORTS AND MANUSCRIPTS

REPORTS AND MANUSCRIPTS

5501 **Business reports.** **Business reports** are written to convey information in a clear, concise manner. They may be formal or informal—but should always retain their clarity and conciseness. You quite likely know something about writing reports because you probably have written reports or manuscripts or both as part of your job or as a class assignment.

5502 **Formal reports.** **Formal reports** may contain several parts. Some components are necessary; others are optional.

FORMAL BUSINESS REPORTS

Required Parts	Optional Parts
Title Page *or* Letter of Transmittal	*Both* the Title Page *and* Letter of Transmittal
Body of Report	Preface/Foreword
	Acknowledgments/Dedication
	Table of Contents
	Bibliography
	Appendix
	Footnotes

Each of the parts identified in the foregoing chart is discussed in detail in this section. Examples are provided for several parts.

5503 **Report and manuscript spacing.** Margins on reports are designed to allow for the binding that will hold the report together. Reports can be unbound, leftbound, or topbound.

- **Unbound**. When reports or manuscripts are short and informal, they are usually held together by a staple inserted in the top left corner; such reports are said to be **unbound.** Margins for unbound reports are indicated in illustration 5503.1.
- **Leftbound**. When reports are lengthy, they should be bound. When the report is bound (either with several staples, by spiral, by three-ring, by plastic cover, or other binding) at the left side, the report is **leftbound.** An extra half-inch of space is left in the margin at the left side. Margins for leftbound reports are indicated in illustration 5503.1.
- **Topbound**. If a similar binding is used at the top, it is a topbound report. An extra half-inch of space is left in the margin at the top. Margins for topbound reports are indicated in illustration 5503.1.

MORE

CONTINUED

Type of Page	Unbound					Leftbound					Topbound				
	Top	Btm.	Left	Right	Pg.no.	Top	Btm.	Left	Right	Pg.no.	Top	Btm.	Left	Right	Pg.no.
Title Page	N/A	N/A	N/A	N/A	none	N/A	N/A	N/A	N/A	none	N/A	N/A	N/A	N/A	none
Letter of Transmittal	N/A	N/A	N/A	N/A	btm.	N/A	N/A	N/A	N/A	btm.	N/A	N/A	N/A	N/A	btm.
Preface/Foreword	1.5	1	1	1	btm.	1.5	1	1.5	1	btm.	N/A	N/A	N/A	N/A	btm.
Acknowledgments/ Dedication	1.5	1	1	1	btm.	1.5	1	1.5	1	btm.	2	1	1	1	btm.
Table of Contents	1.5	1	1	1	btm.	1.5	1	1.5	1	btm.	2	1	1	1	btm.
List of Tables	1.5	1	1	1	btm.	1.5	1	1.5	1	btm.	2	1	1	1	btm.
Body of Report															
First Page; Major Page Subdivisions	1.5	1	1	1	none	1.5	1	1.5	1	none	2	1	1	1	none
All Other Pages	1	1	1	1	top	1	1	1.5	1	top.	1.5	1	1	1	btm.
Bibliography/Appendix															
First Page	1.5	1	1	1	none	1.5	1	1.5	1	none	2	1	1	1	none
All Other Pages	1	1	1	1	top	1	1	1.5	1	top	1.5	1	1	1	btm.

Note: All margins are given in inches.

Illustration 5503.1 Business Reports Margins

5504 **Title page.** The **title page** contains the report title, the writer's name (also title and department on a business report), and the date the report is submitted. Each item is centered horizontally; the title is keyed in capitals, with all capitals optional for the other lines. Vertical spacing is chosen for balance of the entire page. See illustration 5504.1.

However, if the title page is for a leftbound report, one-half inch should be added to the left margin before horizontally centering each line. With a topbound report, an extra half-inch of space should be left at the top of the title page.

TECHNOLOGY IN THE CLASSROOM

by

Jo Ann Falco, Professor
English Department

Bayside Community College
Central Campus

May 22, 19–

Illustration 5504.1 Sample Title Page

5505 **Letter of transmittal.** The **letter of transmittal** introduces the report to the intended reader. It can be used to summarize important information, point out certain comparisons, and so on. Preparation of the letter of transmittal follows the same guidelines as those for any business letter (see ¶ 5615-37). However if a letter of transmittal is to be part of a leftbound report, one-half inch should be added to the left margin of the letter; in a topbound report, one-half inch should be added to the top margin of the letter. See illustration 5505.1.

BAYSIDE
COMMUNITY COLLEGE
Central Campus
390 West Tenth Street
Oakland, CA 94320-3990

July 12, 19--

Mr. John Neely, Editor
EDUCATION TODAY
Central Publishing Company
1633 Western Avenue
Montrose, CA 92174-7293

Dear Mr. Neely:

Enclosed is an article entitled "Technology in the Classroom" for your consideration for possible publication in EDUCATION TODAY. This article is an examination of the improvements brought about by the use of technology in the business education classrooms of the high school, community college, and university.

The topic is timely for today's educators as they attempt to meet the needs of classrooms of students with varied abilities--all of whom have grown up with MTV. A variety of teaching tools for technology are discussed, with tips for the use of each.

Your publication committee's review of my article is most appreciated. I look forward to hearing from you.

Sincerely,

Jo Ann Falco

Jo Ann Falco, Ed.D.
Associate Dean

mos

Enclosure

Illustration 5505.1 Sample Letter of Transmittal

5506 **Preface/foreword.** The **preface** (*written by the author*) or **foreword** (*written by someone other than the author*) is a set of introductory remarks to the reader. It may provide special information on methods used in gathering information for the report, point out special parts of the report itself, or provide other information the author or reviewer of the report believes to be important and pertinent. See illustration 5506.1.

PREFACE

The information contained in this report was compiled from a survey of high schools, community colleges, and universities in the states of California, Michigan, Texas, Florida, and Wyoming. Seventy-eight percent of all public schools in these states returned the surveys.

Illustration 5506.1 Sample Preface

5507 **Acknowledgments/dedication.** The **acknowledgments** or **dedication** page is a personal message from the author to individuals who have provided special assistance or to whom the volume is dedicated, respectively. See illustration 5507.1.

DEDICATION

To students—those whom we have the privilege of teaching, from whom we learn much more than we teach, and with whom we keep searching.

Illustration 5507.1 Sample Dedication Page

As illustrations 5506.1 and 5507.1 indicate, the margins for both the preface/foreword and the acknowledgments/dedication pages are identical; they correspond to those used for the first page in the body of the report. A quadruple space follows the title; the remainder of the page is double-spaced with five-space paragraph indentions.

5508 **Table of contents.** A **table of contents** is a list of every major division in a report and the page number of the first page of each division. The table of contents is not required; when a report is lengthy, however, it serves to organize the information presented. The margins for the table of contents are indicated in illustration 5503.1. A double space follows the title and each major division, with single-spacing within subdivisions. See illustration 5508.1.

Illustration 5509.1
Sample List of Tables

LIST OF TABLES

Illustration 5508.1
Sample Table of Contents

TABLE OF CONTENTS

5509 **List of tables.** The **list of tables** is similar to the table of contents, except that it provides a listing of all tables contained within a report. Naturally, you would not have a list of tables unless there were *several tables* presented within the report. The spacing of the list of tables follows exactly that used for the table of contents. See illustration 5509.1.

5510 **Outline.** Just as the journey from one city to another is easier with a road map, the composition of a report is easier when you have an **outline** to guide you. Follow the suggestions in ¶ 5004 for planning a document to prepare an outline (see ¶ 5007-14) that will help you provide information on

- THE PROBLEM—Upon what is the report to focus? State the problem briefly.
- BACKGROUND—What situations have led to identification of this problem? Briefly, provide background information.
- PROCEDURES—What procedures were used to gather the information presented in this report? What people were involved in the preparation?
- RESULTS—What are the facts and figures of the situations analyzed? What have comparisons shown? What events have occurred?
- RECOMMENDATIONS—How can we use the results to make changes that will benefit the organization? What should we do differently with the knowledge we now have? What should we do in the same way?

If possible, share the outline with colleagues. Discuss ideas to expand on the original outline. Compare the outline to reports previously submitted in your organization.

With the outline before you, write the first draft of the report.

5

5511 **Body of report.** The **body of the report** is where the background facts, figures, findings, recommendations, and so forth, of the report are found. The *body of the report* is keyed in what is called **manuscript style** (double-spaced with five-space paragraph indentions) because it is easy to read. Margins for the first page and subsequent pages are indicated in illustration 5503.1. Illustration 5511.1 shows the first page of the body of a sample (unbound) report.

Double-space between the chapter reference and the title; a quadruple space is left between the report title and the first line of the body. First- and second-level subtitles are preceded and followed by a double space. Double-space the remainder of the body except for listed material and lengthy quoted material (see ¶ 5512-13).

Each paragraph need not have a separate subtitle. Subtitles are used to provide the reader with additional information or to provoke interest in and clarification of the subject matter to be discussed in subsequent paragraphs.

MORE

CONTINUED

CHAPTER I

CHAPTER TITLE

The main heading (usually a chapter or division heading) begins with a one-and-one-half-inch top margin (two inches for a topbound report) with "CHAPTER" and the number. A double space after this is the chapter title; both lines are centered and keyed in all capitals. The first paragraph begins with a quadruple space after the heading.

First-Level Subtitle

A first-level subtitle is placed a double space after the preceding paragraph and centered. Only the first letter of each important word is capitalized. The paragraph begins a double space after the subtitle.

Second-Level Subtitle

A second-level subtitle begins a double space after the preceding paragraph and is keyed at the left margin. Only the first letter of each important word is capitalized, but the entire subtitle is underlined. The paragraph begins a double space after the heading.

Third-level subtitle. A third-level subtitle begins a double space after the preceding paragraph. It appears in the position of a paragraph indention. The first letter is capitalized, and the entire subtitle is underlined. Begin the text on the same line.

Illustration 5511.1 First Page and Sample Headings, Unbound Report

5512 **Quoted material.** See illustration 5512.1 for **quoted material** within a report. When quoted material is more than two lines, it is indented five spaces from the left margin and single-spaced. A double space precedes and follows the quotation.

same time span will undoubtedly provide the greatest challenge to date with classrooms of students with the maximum diversity of skills and abilities.

Patricia Cross stresses the need for improvement in education:

> American higher education has worked hard for the past quarter of a century to achieve educational opportunity for all. It looks very much as though we shall spend the remaining 25 years of this century working to achieve education for each. The problems of attaining even minimal educational opportunities for everyone have been so consuming that we have not yet turned full attention to the greater challenge of designing educational experiences that will provide maximum learning for individuals. . . . We have not yet demonstrated that we can deliver an education that is attractive and useful to the majority of Americans.[6]

In his book Human Characteristics and School Learning, Benjamin Bloom discusses a theory of school learning that can account for most of the variation under a wide variety of conditions. Simply stated, this theory consists of the following:

1. Cognitive entry behaviors. The availability to the learner of requisite entry behavior determines the extent to which a specific task can be learned.

2. Affective entry characteristics. Affective entry characteristics determine the conditioning under which the learner will engage in a learning task.[7]

---

[6]K. Patricia Cross, "Accent on Learning: Beyond Education for All—Toward Education for Each" (Paper presented at the meeting of the Symposium on Individualized Instruction, Gainesville, April 8, 1976), pp. 21-23.

[7]Benjamin S. Bloom, Human Characteristics and School Learning (New York: McGraw-Hill Book Co., 1976), p. 108.

Illustration 5512.1 Sample Manuscript Page with Quoted and Listed Material, Topbound Report

5513 **Listed material.** An example of **listed material** within a report is shown in illustration 5512.1. Listed material is also indented five spaces from the left margin and single-spaced.

Refer to ¶ 5034-38 for additional information on polishing your final report through the use of proofreading.

Bibliography

5514 **Bibliography defined.** The **bibliography** identifies all sources used, quoted, or paraphrased within the report. Spacing for both the bibliography and appendix pages is identified in illustration 5503.1.

MORE

CONTINUED

A quadruple space follows the title, with single-spacing used within each bibliography item and double-spacing between items. The first line of each notation begins at the left margin; subsequent lines are indented five spaces.

Sometimes special forms are used when citing the name of the author or authors in bibliography entries. In footnotes when there are more than three authors of a single work, the name of the first author is given, followed by the phrase *et al (and others)*; in bibliographies it is preferable to list all names. When two or more works by the same author are listed, repetition of the author's name is unnecessary. Instead, a line five spaces long, followed by a period, is substituted. Examples of these and other bibliographical forms follow.

5515 **Book—one author.**

Grisham, John. *The Client*. New York: Doubleday, 1993.

5516 **Book—repeating author.**

_____. *The Firm*. New York: Doubleday, 1991.

5517 **Book—two authors.**

Stone, Bob, and Jenny Stone Humphries. *Where the Buffaloes Roam*. Georgia: Lapidum Press, 1993.

5518 **Book—more than three authors.**

Robinson, Jerry W., Jack P. Hoggatt, Jon A. Shank, Arnola C. Ownby, Lee R. Beaumont, T. James Crawford, and Lawrence W. Erickson. *Century 21: Keyboarding, Formatting, and Document Processing*. 5th ed. Cincinnati: South-Western Publishing Co., 1993.

5

5519 **Book—with editor.**

Segal, Rick (ed.). *Insider's Guide to Personal Computing and Networking*. Indiana: Sams Publishing, 1992.

5520 **Book—chapter reference.**

Watson, Danie. "Protecting Your Network from Virus Infection." *Insider's Guide to Personal Computing and Networking*. Indiana: Sams Publishing, 471-479.

5521 **Bulletins, pamphlets, or monographs.**

Gettings, Patrick W. *Methods of Teaching Computer Programming: A Research Analysis*. Monograph 134. Detroit: McNae Publishing Co., 1994.

5522 **Government publications.**

U.S. Superintendent of Documents, comp. *Checklist of United States Public Agencies*, Vol. I, 8th ed. Washington D.C.: U.S. Government Printing Office, 1994.

5523 **Journal/magazine article—with author.**

Anderson, Porter. "Fernando Bujones." *Profiles, The Magazine of Continental Airlines*, July, 1993, 38-42.

5524 **Journal/magazine article—no author.**

"Presentation Packages." *PC Marketing*, February, 1993, 74-75.

5525 **Newspaper.**

New York Times, 15 June 1994, p. 3a.

5526 **Paperback.**

Whitney, Phyllis A. *Woman Without A Past*. New York: Fawcett Crest, 1991.

5527 **Unpublished dissertation.**

Stringer, Pamela D. "An Experimental Study in the Use of Multimedia Education." Doctoral dissertation, Wayne State University, 1993.

5528 **Appendix.** The **appendix** is a consolidation of examples, charts, graphs, memorandums, and the like, to further support and illustrate the information provided and recommendations made in the report. Each appendix item may be different in format, depending upon the type of information included. As much as possible, however, format should follow that recommended for the bibliography.

Footnotes

5529 **Footnotes defined.** **Footnotes** are references used to cite for the reader the source of any quoted or paraphrased material. An example of traditional footnotes is included in illustration 5512.1 on page 377. Traditionally, footnotes are keyed a double space below a divider line after the last line of text on the page. The secret to keying footnotes is knowing how much space to leave so that the footnote(s) will appear between the manuscript material and the one-inch margin at the bottom of the page. At the left margin, an underline is keyed one-and-one-half inches long. A double space follows, and then the first footnote of the page is indented five spaces and typed single-spaced. Between two footnotes, there is a double space. Footnote numerical references are keyed as superscripts following the quoted material and in the reference at the bottom of the page. Most current word processing software packages assist in the keying of footnotes and superscript references. Consult the help menu with the software used.

5530 **Book—one author.**

[1]John Grisham, *The Client* (New York: Doubleday, 1993), pp. 107-112.

5531 **Book—repeating author.**

[2]John Grisham, *The Firm* (New York: Doubleday, 1991), p. 118.

5532 **Book—two authors.**

[3]Bob Stone and Jenny Stone Humphries, *Where the Buffaloes Roam* (Georgia: Lapidum Press, 1993), pp. 228-235.

5533 **Book—more than three authors.**

[4]Jerry Robinson et al., *Century 21: Keyboarding, Formatting, and Document Processing,* 5th ed. (Cincinnati: South-Western Publishing Co., 1993), p. 97.

5534 **Book—with editor.**

[5]Rick Segal, ed., *Insider's Guide to Personal Computing and Networking* (Indiana: Sams Publishing, 1992), p. 45.

5535 **Repeated footnote references.** When a footnote refers to *exactly* the same source as the previous footnote, the abbreviation *ibid.* (in the same place) can be used.

[6]Ibid.

When a footnote refers to a work by an author fully cited previously (*but not the one immediately preceding*), a shortened form for the footnote, including simply the author's surname and the reference page number, can be used.

[7]Douglas, p. 88.

At one time, scholarly references employed the abbreviations *loc. cit.* (in the place cited) and *op. cit.* (in the work cited) for subsequent references. However, this style is no longer recommended.

[8]Douglas, loc. cit.

(when reference is made to the same page in the work previously identified)

5

[9]Douglas, op. cit., p. 77.

(when reference is made to a different page in the work previously cited)

5536 **Internal citations.** A newer form of reference is called an **internal citation.** In the internal citation form of reference, the quoted material is cited within the report using just the author's surname and the year of publication.

Sample Internal Citation

. . . important when we deal with children." (Higgins, 1993)

The bibliography reference for the internal citation is similar to what it would be in the traditional bibliography, with the addition of the exact page number of the quoted material.

Bibliography Entry for Internal Citation

Higgins, Jack. *Thunder Point*. New York: G. P. Putnam's Sons, 1993, p. 5.

In the internal citation form, works by the same author are identified by the difference in the year of publication. Should quoted material include sources by the same author written within the same year, one reference would read "(Smith, 1994A)" and the second "(Smith, 1994B)."

5600 MAIL (Letters, Memos, and Envelopes)

(continued)

5

(continued)		WORD PROCESSING PROGRAMS	5200
• Mailgrams	5686	DESKTOP PUBLISHING	5300
• Overnight telegrams	5687	FORMATTING	5400
• Telex	5688	REPORTS AND MANUSCRIPTS	5500
• Teletex	5689	FILING	5700
WRITING	**5000**		
WORD PROCESSING HARDWARE	**5100**		

MAIL (Letters, Memos, and Envelopes)

5601 **Incoming mail.** The task of opening and preparing the daily mail is an important responsibility. In a small firm, the mail carrier may simply give incoming mail to a designated person who will sort and distribute it.

Larger firms, managing larger quantities of mail, usually have centralized departments and more formal procedures for processing the mail. Usually, the mail for the entire office is delivered to a designated location—the mail department if there is one. There, it is sorted for internal delivery to the addressees—specific persons, departments, or offices.

5

5602 **Mail not addressed specifically.** Some mail is addressed to the company or office rather than to a specific department or individual. In each office, someone (frequently a person in the mail department or the chief executive's office) opens and routes all mail that cannot be routed by the address on the envelope.

5603 **Opening the mail.** Some executives prefer to open their own mail; most have it opened by an assistant. Before you open the mail, first separate it into any obvious categories such as publications, business correspondence, and advertising.

Business correspondence—which includes letters, memos, and reports—should be opened first. Use a letter opener for ease, as well as to preserve the mailing envelope.

Confidential mail or any mail marked **personal** should be delivered unopened to the addressee.

5604 **Checking enclosures.** Many executives prefer to have their assistants quickly scan all letters to make sure that noted enclosures were actually sent. If enclosures are missing, attach a small note or make a pencil notation on the letter indicating the enclosure was missing. Then, call the sending office to make arrangements to have the enclosure sent as soon as possible—noting the date, the name of the person called, and the telephone number called with the original notation.

5605 **Saving the return address.** As mail and all enclosures are reviewed, look to see if the return address of the sender is included on the correspondence before discarding the envelope. If not, save the envelope to provide the return address for the file.

Discard envelopes, wrapping, and other waste, after being sure that they do not contain addresses or other information that may be needed later.

5606 **Date-stamping the mail.** Most offices will have a **date stamp** to use with the mail. The stamp may include office/department information and even the time. It is important to know when mail is received in order to monitor office efficiency, especially how quickly customer inquiries are answered. Date-stamp mail on the back or in a specific location on the front. Check with a supervisor to determine office preference. Never stamp the date over keyed information.

On pictures or glossy brochures where the date stamp may rub off, stamp a small piece of paper and attach that to the item. Check the employer's preference for dating reference materials, magazines, and advertisements.

5607 **Sorting the mail.** If the mail is sorted for many individuals or several departments, sort mail first by individual or department. Next, sort the opened mail according to the following categories:

Category I: Urgent or emergency mail

Category II: Unopened personal or confidential mail

Category III: Routine correspondence

Category IV: Bills or invoices

Category V: Magazines, journals, newspapers

Category VI: Advertisements

Familiarity with mail procedures will allow sorting when mail is being opened and dated.

5608 **Attaching related files.** Another useful mail-handling procedure is to retrieve related files and attach them to the mail. Quick reference can be made to the file and a rapid response prepared. Check with a supervisor for office preferences.

5609 **Directing/delivering the mail.** The mail should be opened, sorted, and delivered as soon as it is received. Always place opened mail in a folder to maintain confidentiality. If a large volume of mail is received, use separate folders for the various mail categories. Ask the employer where to place opened mail; the location suggested should be used consistently.

If the mail is to be placed in an employer's office, do not take it in while he or she is with a customer or on the telephone. Wait until the employer is free and then take in the mail.

Usually, bills and invoices may be directed to an office manager or bookkeeper, and general magazines may be placed in a reception area for visitors. When first opening the mail, find out how it should be directed in the office. Ask questions or consult the office procedures manual.

5610 **Recording incoming mail.** A **mail log** or **register** may be maintained for registered or certified mail, insured mail, special delivery mail, mail including payments, or legal correspondence. Depending on the regulations to be followed, an office may require that some mail be logged. (See illustration 5610.1.)

In	Out	Mo	Da	Yr	File Number	Document Name	Their Name	Our Person	Their Person	Response Mo/Da/Yr		
X		9	12	95	2345.67	Purchasing Report	Home Office	Calliero	D'Loto	9	16	95
	X	9	13	95	984.77	Sales Tax Information	State Revenue	Smithy	Bujones	9	16	95

Illustration 5610.1 Mail Register

5611 **Routing slips.** Any document that should be seen by several people can be controlled with a **routing slip,** which contains the names of those to whom the document is to be routed. The slip is simply attached to the document, which is then passed from person to person. A routing slip is used for documents that are neither urgent nor of critical importance. (See illustration 5611.1.)

Mary Calleiro Public Relations Department		
	Date:	
ROUTING SLIP		
Send to	Name	Date Forwarded
	Everyone	
	Bryant, Castell	
X	Guarch, Gerry	3/26
	Hydress, Marie	
X	Lipof, Irene	3/25
X	Mateo, Cristina	3/27
	Phillips, Roy	
X	Schlazer, Al	3/29
	Smith, Sis	
WILL YOU PLEASE:		
	Read and keep	
	Read and pass on	
	Read and return	
X	Read, pass on, and return	
	See me	

Illustration 5611.1 Routing Slip

5612 **High-priority correspondence.** One or a combination of the following methods may be used to fix the responsibility for answering high-priority correspondence and remind the person or persons responsible for meeting deadlines:

- Have a rubber stamp made to route and control high-priority documents. (See illustration 5612.1.)
- Circulate photocopies of the document (after it has been marked with the rubber stamp on which the blanks are filled in) to all who have an interest in or responsibility for response to the document.
- Register high-priority documents in a mail log. Include a check-off column to record in the log book the mailing of a response. Check the log book daily to be sure that deadlines are being met. Remind anyone who may be in danger of missing a deadline.
- Use a tickler file or computerized "to do" list to prompt yourself to remind others of deadlines for reports, renewals, and the like, before each deadline.

MORE

CONTINUED

URGENT Date received	File
Document	
From	
Routed to	
Response required by	
The person to whom this document is routed is responsible for the response as indicated.	
Comments _____ _____ _____ _____ _____ _____	

Illustration 5612.1 Rubber Stamp for Routine High-Priority Correspondence

5613 **File-coding incoming correspondence.** If a standard filing system is used throughout the office, department, or company, the logging procedure for incoming mail may include coding documents for filing purposes.

5614 **Mail expected under separate cover.** Whether or not other mail is logged, some firms keep a record of mail expected under separate cover. They do so to make sure that all the pieces of a mailing (letter and packages, several packages, and so forth) reach the addressee. This procedure should trigger a follow-up when an expected piece of mail does not arrive.

Preparing Business Correspondence

5615 **Appearance.** The appearance of the correspondence leaving your office is very important. How a letter looks to the recipient—the way it is centered on the page, the grammar and punctuation, and the skill with which the message is conveyed—will create an immediate mental impression of the office. From the initial preparation to the final review before mailing, your responsibility in preparing business correspondence is to make certain that you have created the best possible impression. Grammar and punctuation guidelines are discussed in other sections of this manual; this chapter will review the basic guidelines for keying business letters.

5616 **Office letterhead.** **Letterhead** is used for letters sent outside the organization. A letterhead is printed on good-quality bond paper. It contains essential information identifying the organization, its location, its telephone number(s) and key personnel. Since both the printing and the quality of paper make letterhead expensive, you should use it carefully.

Several different letterheads may be used within the same office. For example, in a small legal partnership each attorney may have an individual letterhead as well as the letterhead used by the entire firm. In a large organization, such as a manufacturing firm, the same basic letterhead may be used throughout the organization with a variety of listings added for specific departments or individuals. (See illustration 5616.1.)

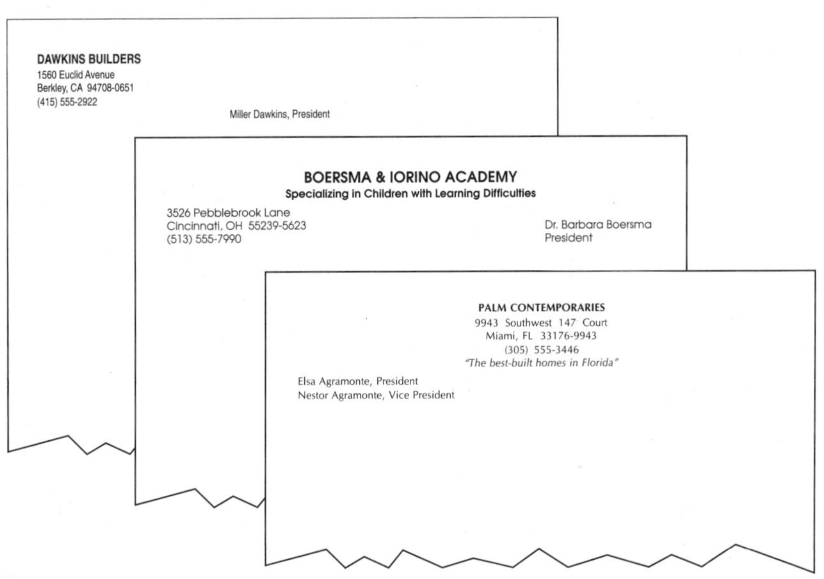
DAWKINS BUILDERS
1560 Euclid Avenue
Berkley, CA 94708-0651
(415) 555-2922
Miller Dawkins, President

BOERSMA & IORINO ACADEMY
Specializing in Children with Learning Difficulties
3526 Pebblebrook Lane
Cincinnati, OH 55239-5623
(513) 555-7990
Dr. Barbara Boersma
President

PALM CONTEMPORARIES
9943 Southwest 147 Court
Miami, FL 33176-9943
(305) 555-3446
"The best-built homes in Florida"
Elsa Agramonte, President
Nestor Agramonte, Vice President

Illustration 5616.1 Sample Office Letterhead

5617 **Letter margins.** Just as a picture is centered within a picture frame for attractive placement, you should center the text of each letter within the margins of the page. After you have practiced judging margins for a while, it is easier to visualize the placement of a letter. Until you have perfected this technique, however, a few guidelines will be helpful.

Typewriters traditionally used one of two sizes of type—pica or elite. Pica type is larger and fits ten letters into one horizontal inch. Elite type is smaller and fits twelve characters into each horizontal inch. Vertically, both styles print six lines to each inch. Word processing software has expanded the use of a variety of fonts in many different sizes by providing a basic selection of fonts and sizes with each software package.

MORE

In addition, most software facilitates the addition of other font packages as well. To accommodate this variety of fonts and sizes, a good selection for letter margins is one that balances all text on the page: one-inch top, bottom, left, and right. This is the default (start-up) margin setting for many of the top-selling software packages. For a longer letter, margins can be changed to one-half inch; for shorter letters, one and one-half inches on all sides. (See illustration 5617.1.)

Some letterheads take up more than one inch at the top of the page. In this case, remember to enlarge the top margin to accommodate the letterhead, while leaving the other margins at one inch.

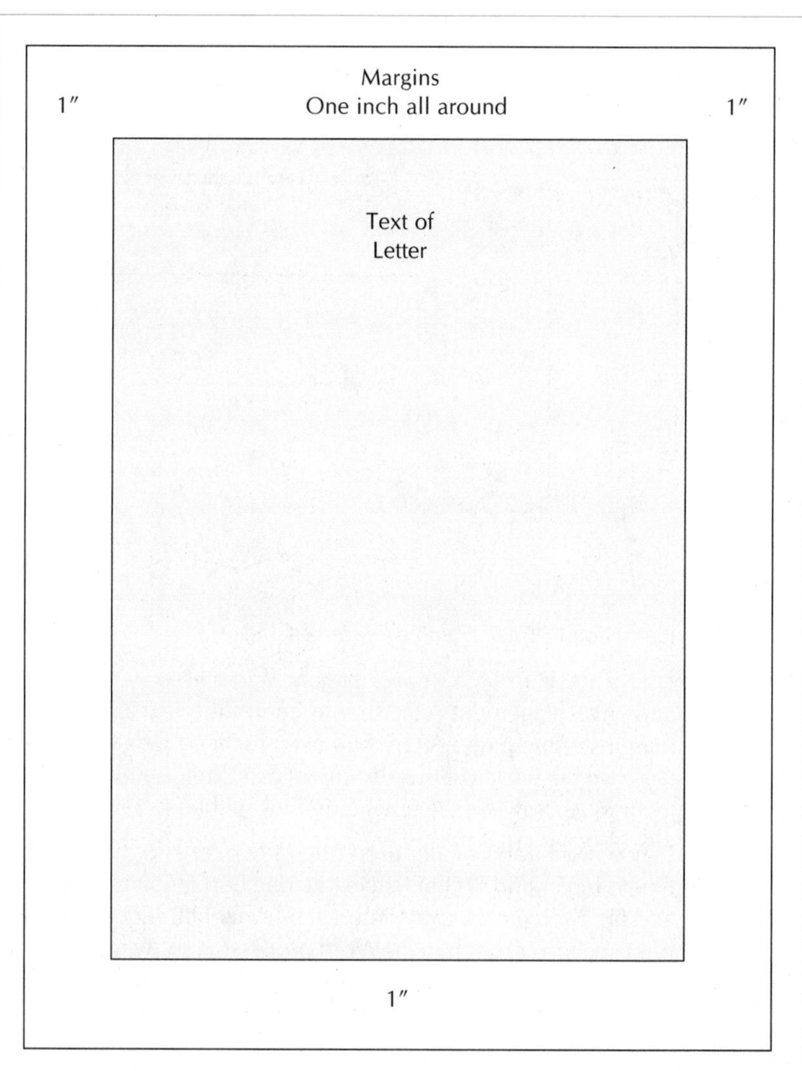

Illustration 5617.1 Letter Margins

5618 **Personal business letter.** If you are keying a **personal business letter,** use your home address in place of a letterhead. (See illustration 5618.1.) All other guidelines for business letter preparation apply.

```
4408 Glen Rose Street
Fairfax, VA  22032-8044
January 15, 19-


Academic Advisement Department
Santa Fe Community College
111 Southeast First Avenue
Gainesville, FL  33333-1110

Ladies and Gentlemen:

I am interested in enrolling in the legal assistant training program
offered at Santa Fe Community College.

I should appreciate receiving information regarding admission
requirements and financial assistance available at Santa Fe. Also,
please send me a copy of your college catalog containing information
on course requirements and course descriptions for the legal assistant
and executive secretary programs.

Do you have dormitories available on your campus? If not, are there
student apartments near the campus? Since I shall be coming from
Virginia to attend Santa Fe, I shall need some help in finding a place
to live.

Thank you for your assistance.

Sincerely,

Karen McMeekin

Karen McMeekin
```

Illustration 5618.1 Personal Business Letter

5619 **Business letter styles.** Most business letters are keyed in the **block, modified block,** or **simplified** style.

- **Block**: *All* lines begin at the left margin. (See illustration 5619.1.)
- **Modified block with block paragraphs**: All lines begin at the left margin except date, complimentary close, and signature lines—which begin at the center of the page. (See illustration 5619.2.)
- **Modified block with indented paragraphs**: Identical to the modified block, except that the first word of all paragraphs is indented five spaces. The subject line may be centered or indented five spaces (to match the paragraphs). (See illustration 5619.3.)
- **Simplified**: All lines begin at the left margin. To *simplify* the keying of this letter: the inside address is keyed all in caps, the salutation is omitted and replaced by a subject line keyed in all capital letters on one line, and open punctuation is always used. (See illustration 5619.4.)

5620 **Business letter punctuation styles.** Two punctuation styles are used in today's office correspondence.

MORE

CONTINUED

- **Mixed punctuation:** This is the most widely used punctuation style. It requires a colon after the salutation and a comma after the complimentary close. (See illustrations 5619.1 and 5619.2.)
- **Open punctuation**: No punctuation is used after the salutation or the complimentary close. (See illustration 5619.3.)

Illustration 5619.1
Block Letter Style with Mixed Punctuation

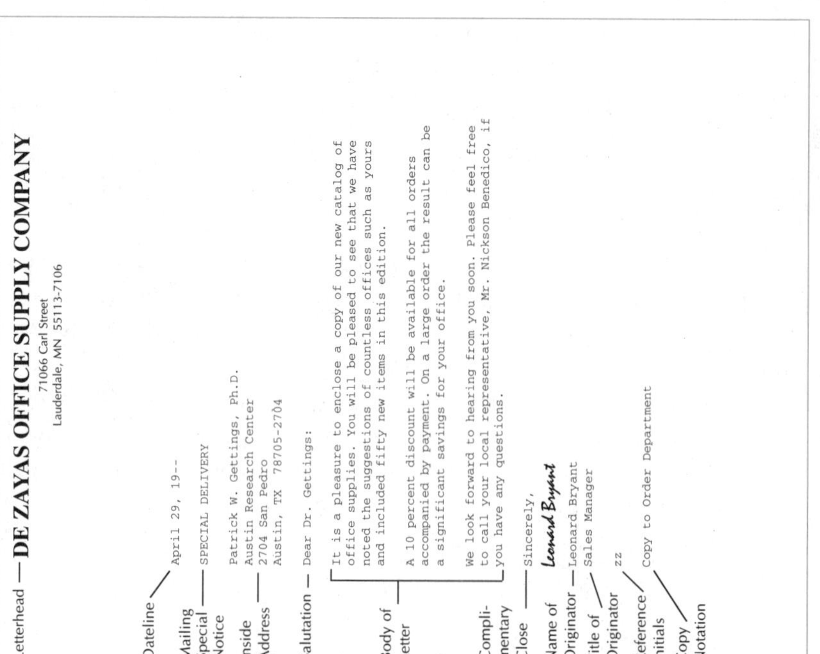

DE ZAYAS OFFICE SUPPLY COMPANY
71066 Carl Street
Lauderdale, MN 55113-7106

April 29, 19--

SPECIAL DELIVERY

Patrick W. Gettings, Ph.D.
Austin Research Center
2704 San Pedro
Austin, TX 78705-2704

Dear Dr. Gettings:

It is a pleasure to enclose a copy of our new catalog of office supplies. You will be pleased to see that we have noted the suggestions of countless offices such as yours and included fifty new items in this edition.

A 10 percent discount will be available for all orders accompanied by payment. On a large order the result can be a significant savings for your office.

We look forward to hearing from you soon. Please feel free to call your local representative, Mr. Nickson Benedico, if you have any questions.

Sincerely,

Leonard Bryant

Leonard Bryant
Sales Manager

zz

Copy to Order Department

Illustration 5619.2
Modified Block Letter Style with Block Paragraphs and Mixed Punctuation

Attention Line · Subject Line · Company Name · Enclosure Notation · Copy Notation · Postscript

THE BIOENGINEERING EXAMPLE COMPANY
990 Brade Road
Bartlett, TN 38154-0099

June 18, 19--

PERSONAL AND CONFIDENTIAL

Take Charge Restaurant Industries
Attention Mrs. Marta Quintana
255 Blue Hill Avenue
Boston, MA 02187-0255

Ladies and Gentlemen:

MODIFIED BLOCK LETTER STYLE

This letter is an example of the modified block letter style with block paragraphs. It is one of the most popular business letter styles in use today. You will note that the dateline and closing lines are indented and blocked at the center of the page. Mixed punctuation is frequently used with this letter style: a colon after the salutation and a comma after the complimentary close.

When the modified block letter style is used, the dateline, the complimentary close, the company name, and the keyboarded name and title of the originator are begun at the center of the page.

This letter is unusual in that it is loaded with special features. Normally, all of the elements shown here do not appear within one business letter. However, they are included to show you their proper sequence.

Sincerely,

THE BIOENGINEERING EXAMPLE COMPANY

William McNae

William McNae
Chief Executive Officer

mos

Enclosure

c Georgianna Stringer, CPA

Please request additional information on business letter stationery from our home office.

Illustration 5619.3
Modified Block Letter Style with Indented Paragraphs and Open Punctuation

Bay Area Marine Company
2232 Waterfront Drive
San Francisco, CA 31178-2322

April 10, 19--

REGISTERED MAIL

Nancy A. List, D.O.
1754 Maple Ridge Road
Bassett, MI 48840-4571

Dear Dr. List

It is a pleasure to confirm May 22, 19--, as the delivery date for your new 32-foot Starlight cruiser. The factory representatives assure me that the special options you ordered can be worked into the production schedule without any difficulty.

Our original quotation of $198,600 is now a firm price. It is payable at the time the title is transferred. Please let me know if you want any assistance with financing.

You have selected a fine boat! I hope you will spend many enjoyable hours aboard.

Very truly yours

Eugene McDonald

Eugene McDonald, President

sq

As you know, a member of our staff will be available to assist you on a shakedown cruise at your convenience any time within sixty days of delivery.

Illustration 5619.4
Simplified Letter Style

SEASIDE BUSINESS SCHOOL
100 Bay Boulevard
Miami, FL 33130-0101

February 1, 19--

ALMA GUERRA
CHANNEL 23-WLTV
2600 CORAL WAY
MIAMI, FL 33135-0260

SIMPLIFIED BLOCK LETTER FORMAT

This letter illustrates the features that distinguish the simplified block letter format from the standard block format.

1. The date is placed on line 12 so that the letter address will show though the window of a window envelope when used.

2. The letter address is keyed in the style recommended by the U.S. Postal Service for OCR processing: all-cap letters with no punctuation. Cap-and-lowercase letters with punctuation may be used if that is the format of addresses stored in an electronic address file. Personal titles may be omitted.

3. A subject line replaces the traditional salutation (which some people find objectionable). The subject line may be keyed in all-cap or cap-and-lowercase letters. A double space is left above and below it.

4. The complimentary close, which some people view as a needless appendage, is omitted.

5. The writer's name is placed on the fourth line space below the body of the letter. The writer's title or department name may appear on the line with the writer's name or on the next line below it. The signature block may be keyed in all-cap or cap-and-lowercase letters.

6. A standard-length line is used for all letters. A six-inch line is common length.

The features listed and illustrated here are designed to bring efficiency to the electronic processing of mail.

Kathie Sigler

KATHIE SIGLER, DEAN FOR ADMINISTRATION

mos

5

Parts of a Business Letter

All business letters have certain essential components. In addition, other components may or may not be included depending upon letter requirements.

5621 **Required business letter parts.**

- Letterhead or return address
- Date
- Inside address
- Salutation (**not** used in simplified style)
- Body
- Complimentary close (**not** used in simplified style)
- Originator's identification
- Reference initials

5622 **Optional business letter parts.**

- Mailing/Special notations
- Attention line
- Subject line
- Keyed company name
- Title of originator
- Enclosure notation
- Copy notation
- Postscript

5623 **Date.** The date is an important and required part of business correspondence. It indicates to the reader when the letter was written. As shown in illustrations 5619.1 - .4 (pages 390-391) placement of the date may change with different letter styles and different letter sizes.

Date placement. However, a good rule of thumb is to leave one and one-half inches blank at the top of a page before beginning the date (line 10). This usually allows adequate room for the letterhead. Remember, if your page already has been set for a one-inch top margin (six blank lines), you should leave only another one-half inch (three blank lines) and begin keying the date on line 4.

5624 **Mailing notations and other special notations.** Special mailing notations (AIRMAIL, REGISTERED, SPECIAL DELIVERY, CERTIFIED) and other special notations (PERSONAL, CONFIDENTIAL) are keyed all in capital letters at the left margin a double space below the dateline.

5625 **Inside address/salutation.** The inside address provides all the necessary information for delivery of the business letter: the addressee's name, title, company name, street number and name, city, two-letter state abbreviation, and zip code. For two-letter state abbreviations, see ¶ 3020. The inside address also provides the information needed to determine the correct salutation.

Following are several examples of inside addresses and appropriate salutations for each. Note that the city, state abbreviation, and zip code are keyed on one line. One or two spaces (but **no** comma) follow the state abbreviation before the zip code.

To an individual. (Colon after salutation indicates mixed punctuation)

Mr. Ted Livingston
Tulane University
31 McAlister Drive
New Orleans, LA 85555-3100

Dear Mr. Livingston:

Ms. Vicki Kissling
4 Linden Place
Cincinnati, OH 45227-2222

Dear Ms. Kissling:

To an individual at a business address. (Absence of punctuation after salutation indicates open punctuation)

Horace E. Traylor, Ed.D.
Instructional Resources
Los Angeles Pierce College
6201 Winnetka Avenue
Woodland, CA 91364-6200

Dear Dr. Traylor

Vice President
School of Architecture
University of Miami
1600 N.W. 10 Avenue
Miami, FL 33136-0006

Dear Sir or Madam

To a company/organization.

The Upjohn Company
Pharmaceutical Sales Office
1974 Lashly Court
Snellville, GA 30278-9741

Ladies and Gentlemen:

Two-line address.

Mrs. Leota Schramm
Rogers City, MI 49779-3370

Dear Aunt Leota

With apartment number.

Ms. Paula Epstein
7131 Wood Drive, Apt. 151
Austin, TX 78731

Dear Paula

Two people, different addresses.

Arthur Asher, M.D.
P.O. Box 2143
Riverview Road
Riverton, WY 82501-2143

and

Ileana Gonzalez, D.O.
4408 Glen Rose Street
Fairfax, VA 22032-8040

Dear Drs. Asher and Gonzalez:

Two people, same address.

- Eliminate official titles, unless they are short and can fit on the same line with the name.
- Put names in alphabetical order.

MORE

- Eliminate department, unless both are from the same department.
- On individual envelopes, key full addresses.

Mr. Tom Petersen
Ms. Pam Stringer
Legal Services Association
1150 North Franklin
Dearborn, MI 48128-1105

Dear Tom and Pam:

Titles.

- Change the position of titles to balance the inside address.

Dr. Pat Hodges, Director
Betancourt Health Center
15432 Kit Lane
Fort Worth, TX 75240-5324

Dr. Billie Marie Tomlin
Vice President
Betancourt Health Center
15432 Kit Lane
Fort Worth, TX 75240-5324

Roz Reich, M.D.
Vice President and General Manager
Betancourt Health Center
15432 Kit Lane
Fort Worth, TX 75240-5324

Note: Use figures for the numbers of houses or buildings—except for house or building number one, which is spelled out. (See ¶ 3318.)

One Woodward Avenue
134 Maple Lane

Room, suite, building in address.

Ms. Renee Betancourt
Attorney at Law
429 Broad Street, Suite 13
Richmond, VA 23219-4329

Dear Ms. Betancourt:

Columbus Employees Federal
Credit Union*
Penobscot Building, Room 118
1800 King Avenue
Columbus, OH 48216-0011

Ladies and Gentlemen:

*Long company names can be placed on two lines.

Husband and wife.

```
Dr. and Mrs. Doug Andrews
Plaza Center Building
2050 Massachusetts Avenue
Washington, D.C. 20503-0500

Dear Dr. and Mrs. Andrews:
```

Foreign country.

```
Mr. Ryan Stringer
Trapp Interiors, Ltd.
27 Monks Close
Leeds, York ALY-372
ENGLAND*

Dear Mr. Stringer:
```

*Key the name of a foreign country in all caps.

In care of.

```
Alberta Goodman, D.O.
In care of John Roueche, D.O.  or c/o John Roueche, D.O.
University of Texas at Austin
Austin, TX 78731-7001

Dear Dr. Goodman:
```

5626 **Attention line.** Usually, an **attention line** is used to route a letter to a particular person when the letter is addressed to an organization. The attention line indicates that the letter concerns company business and that the writer prefers that the letter be handled by the individual named in the attention line (or by another individual in a similar role if the individual named is no longer with the company.) The attention line is keyed as the second line in the inside address. Note that the salutation agrees with the inside address, **not** the attention line.

```
Carolina Construction
Attention Ms. Sally Buxton
1005 Ala Lililoi Street
Honolulu, HI 96818-5000

Ladies and Gentlemen:
```

```
Extra Super Food Centers
ATTENTION Mr. Dan Derrico
2525 W. Armitage Avenue
Melrose Park, IL 60164-2005

Ladies and Gentlemen:
```

5627 **Subject line.** When a **subject line** is included, it serves as a title to the body of the letter and should be keyed a double space below the salutation. The subject line may be keyed at the left margin. In a modified block letter, the subject line may be centered, begun at the left margin, or be indented five spaces (if the paragraphs are so indented). The word *SUBJECT* or *RE* is sometimes used with the subject line, but neither is required. The subject line can be keyed all in caps, in capitals and lowercase, or in capitals and lowercase underlined. A double space follows the subject line leaving one blank line between the subject and the body of the letter.

MORE

CONTINUED

```
Detroit, MI  48219-9106

Dear Mr. Gathercole:

ANNUAL DATAFLEX CONFERENCE
```

```
Detroit, MI  48219-9106

Dear Mr. Gathercole:

     SUBJECT: Annual Dataflex Conference
```

```
Detroit, MI  48219-9106

Dear Mr. Gathercole:

                RE: Annual Dataflex Conference
```

5628 **Body.** The message of the business letter is in the **body** of the letter. Each paragraph should be single-spaced with double-spacing between paragraphs. Paragraphs begin at the left margin (except with the modified block, indented paragraph style).

Efforts should be made to balance paragraph size, with at least two paragraphs in a letter. A very short letter (six lines or fewer) may be double-spaced or extra blank lines may be inserted between letter parts to achieve balance (or both may be done). See illustration 5628.1.

Quoted or tabulated material within a letter is set off by double-spacing (one blank line) before and after the quotation or table, and a five-space indention from each margin.

CARIBE MARKETPLACE

Loews Anatole Hotel
Dallas, TX 76135-1012

September 8, 19–

Ms. Rene McCullers
Post Community College
5301 Campus Drive
Ft. Worth, TX 76119-5030

Dear Rene:

Congratulations on your appointment as Vice President for Development of Post Community College. Please call on us if we can be of assistance in your new role.

Sincerely,

Janet Seitlin

Janet Seitlin
Conference Manager

mos

Illustration 5628.1 Very Short Letter Double-Spaced for Attractive Alignment and with Mixed Punctuation

5629 **Complimentary close, company name, and originator's identification.** A recent survey of businesses found that the majority use "Very truly yours" or "Sincerely." Two other popular **complimentary closes** were "Sincerely yours" and "Yours very truly."

- Key the complimentary close a double space below the body. In block style, begin the complimentary close at the left margin; in modified block style, begin the complimentary close at the center.
- Capitalize only the first letter of the first word of the complimentary close.
- In *mixed punctuation*, place a comma after the complimentary close. In *open punctuation*, no punctuation is used.

MORE

In some offices, the **company name** is keyed all in capital letters a double space after the complimentary close. The company name begins in the same place (left margin or center) as the complimentary close.

The **originator's identification lines** are those lines that identify the writer of the letter and often the writer's title or department or both. They follow the complimentary close (or company name, if one is used) by four line spaces. The signature line also begins in the same place (left margin or center) as the complimentary close.

```
Sincerely,

PERSUTTI ASSOCIATES

Delphine Persutti

Delphine Persutti
President
```

```
Very truly yours

PRIDE INTERNATIONAL

Robert Ochs

Robert Ochs, Ph.D.
Dean of Students
```

- Titles may be on the same line as the writer's name or on the following line.
- The titles *Miss, Ms.*, or *Mrs.* may be shown in the printed name. Parentheses are optional.

```
Sincerely yours,

Lina Cuan
(Ms.) Lina Cuan
Manager
```

```
Sincerely

Rene Garcia

Rene Garcia, Ph.D.
Vice President
```

5

5630 **Hyphenated last names.** Some hyphenated names are representative of other cultures. A hyphenated name such as Rivera-Wiggins is used by a male or female. The two names represent the father's and mother's side of the family. They are both used to indicate a pride in heritage. When a hyphenated name is used, the signature will always reflect the same hyphenation.

```
Sincerely yours,

Diana Rivera-Wiggins
Diana Rivera-Wiggins
Public Relations Director
```

Hyphenated last names are also a trend with many married people of all cultures who wish to use both the wife's family name and the husband's family name. Thus, Miss Bonnie Landsea who married Mr. Peter Diehl would become:

```
Bonnie Landsea-Diehl
Mrs. Bonnie Landsea-Diehl
Mrs. Peter Landsea-Diehl
```

And he would become:

```
Peter Landsea-Diehl
Mr. Peter Landsea-Diehl
```

Note: The wife's family name is first and the husband's second.

5631 **Reference initials.** **Reference initials** identify the person who keyed the correspondence. They are keyed a double space below the final originator's identification line at the left margin. Reference initials are keyed in a variety of ways:

- Indicating the keyboard operator:

```
kds                 zz                 map
```

- Indicating the writer* (first set of initials) and the keyboard operator:

```
ALR:kss             TRD/POE            SR:cm
```

*The writer's initials are included in this way only if the writer's name is not printed at the end of the letter.

- Sometimes the author of the letter (if different than the signer) is indicated in the reference initials:

```
CRWhite/pg          kss:pg
```

5632 **Enclosure notation.** When additional information is to be enclosed in the envelope with business correspondence, an **enclosure notation** should be used. This notation is placed at the left margin a double space below the reference initials. (See illustration 5632.1 and its enclosure, illustration 5631.2.) Enclosure notations are keyed in a variety of ways:

```
Enclosure        Enclosures (2)     Check Enclosed
Enc.             Enc. 2             Enclosures:  Invoice
                                                 Order Form
```

Illustration 5632.1
Letter of Application

NELSON A. BENEDICO
11621 Southwest 112th Street
Miami, Florida 33176-1621
(305) 555-4107

April 6, 19–

Mr. Hank Meyer
Hank Meyer & Associates
2990 Biscayne Boulevard
Miami, FL 33131-9900

Dear Mr. Meyer:

What do the words PUBLIC RELATIONS mean without being followed by the words HANK MEYER? Regardless of whether I am in class, at a PRSSA meeting, or at work, your name enters the conversation. In the face of such omnipresence, one might be too intimidated to write you. However, with the encouragement of Bill Stokes, I am taking that step. By way of my employment at Harrison Community College and through my mother, Zoila de Zayas, I have grown to know Dr. Stokes closely and value his opinion.

I am a student at the University of Miami and shall be graduated in approximately two months. I shall receive my bachelor of science in communications degree in public relations and English.

I am interested in an entry-level public relations position and should like the opportunity to discuss such a possibility with you. What makes me different? I love hard work. I love pressure. I love results.

I have completed internships with Beber Silverstein and Burson-Marsteller this semester and have grown accustomed to the environment that requires long hours and has unexpected problems, but offers the satisfaction of results. Some may call it an "ulcer factory." I call it thrilling.

I can offer you the experience I have acquired from my internships. In addition, I can offer my bilingual skills, writing abilities, and zealous energy.

I should appreciate the opportunity to speak with you concerning any suggestions you may have about the notorious job search. I am enclosing a copy of my résumé for your consideration and shall call you next week to schedule an appointment at your convenience.

In addition, Dr. Stokes asked me to offer him as a reference. He may be able to provide you with more information. I appreciate your taking the time to read my letter.

Sincerely,

Nelson A. Benedico

Nelson A. Benedico

Enclosure: Résumé

MORE

5

Illustration 5632.2
Sample Resume

NELSON A. BENEDICO
11621 Southwest 112th Street
Miami, FL 33176-1621
(305) 555-4107

EDUCATION

Bachelor of Science in Communication
University of Miami School of Communication
Coral Gables, Florida
May 1994

MAJORS: Public Relations/English

Tulane University
New Orleans, Louisiana
September 1990 - December 1991

INTERNSHIPS

Beber Silverstein & Partners
Public Relations Division
Miami, Florida
December 1993 - May 1994

Responsible for reviewing publications for client articles; maintaining clipping files; establishing a computer system for generating mass mailing labels; updating media contacts; producing a clipping file on Beber Silverstein; preparing paste-up of articles into camera-ready work for reproduction; assisting in the planning and execution of special events; assisting with technical aspects of presentations; writing, editing, and preparing releases, proposals, and correspondence for a variety of clients.

Burson-Marsteller
Chicago, Illinois
February 1992 - March 1993

One of six UM students to represent Burson-Marsteller in a local project for Procter & Gamble. Responsible for serving as Miami representative for Chicago-based Burson-Marsteller; serving as liaison between the company and local merchants, media, and public; executing events, including advance preparation, and follow-up of events at over 80 stores in three Florida counties; supervising work teams at each site; preparing paperwork, activity records, and logs of expenses.

WORK EXPERIENCE

Harrison Community College
Department of Public Affairs
St. Paul, Minnesota
1991-1992

Typesetter
Responsible for typesetting brochures, class bulletins, and flyers for campus activities; providing specifications on unlabeled work; maintaining traffic schedule to insure deadlines.

PERSONAL

Languages: Ability to read, write and speak Spanish fluently. Working knowledge of American sign language.

Office Skills: Keyboarding, word processing, computer operation.

AFFILIATIONS Public Relations Student Society of America

REFERENCES

Dr. Eduardo Padron
Campus President
Harrison Community College
(305) 555-3000

Dr. William M. Stokes
Campus President
Harrison Community College
(305) 555-2000

Note: Illustrations 5632.1 and 5632.2 show an actual letter and résumé sent by a student who did get an interview—and the job!

5633 **Copy notation.** When copies of a business letter are to be sent to individuals other than the addressee, a **copy notation** should be placed at the left margin, a double space below the enclosure notation or reference initials, whichever is last.

```
c  Dr. Hansen                pc  Research Department
   Dr. Kelly                     Personnel
```

Note: c=copy; pc=photocopy; cc=carbon copy

Also used:

```
Copy to:  Ms. Meg Laughlin          Copy to Purchasing
          Dr. Joan Schaeffer
```

It is helpful to indicate when enclosures are (or are not) sent to those copied:

```
pc (w/enclosures)  Dr. Harriet Spivak
                   Dr. Charlotte Gallogly

cc   Dr. Harriet Spivak (w/enclosures)
     Dr. Charlotte Gallogly (w/o enclosures)
```

Sometimes the letter writer wants to send a copy of a business letter to someone without the addressee's knowledge. In this case, a **blind copy** notation should be used on the file copy *only*.

```
bc:  Mr. Osvaldo Lopez     or     bpc:  Mr. Oswaldo Lopez
     Legal Department                   Legal Department
```

5634 **File copies.** Whether stored on paper, or electronically, copies of all business correspondence should be available in the office.

Paper file copies, still the most widely used storage medium, may be made by printing an extra copy on a laser or dot matrix printer or copying the printed original using a copy machine. On an impact dot matrix printer copies may be made with carbon paper or with NCR (no carbon required) paper. Some offices have special sheets with simplified letterheads for copies sent outside the office. Paper copies are filed in a convenient cabinet for quick retrieval.

Electronic file copies are made automatically when letters produced using word processing software are saved. While the original letter is printed (and copies to be sent to others are usually made on a photocopier), the office file copy should be electronically stored. This practice will save much office storage space and allow for future electronic transmission of the document to other offices.

You, of course, store paper file copies according to most accepted filing procedures (see ¶ 5700). However, thought should be given to the organization of electronic storage for easy retrieval.

5635 **Organizing electronic files.** On a hard drive on a personal computer, only one user is saving files. Generally, the hard drive is labeled **C:**

MORE

CONTINUED

On a network, many computer users are connected. The network file server distinguishes between the files of each user by setting up subdirectories of users and giving each user a unique name. In the example below, the <*f*> drive is used for the network, and the <*user*\\> is <*Barb*\\>. To avoid mixing up years of files (whether using her own hard drive or the network file server for storage), Barb needs to develop a plan for organization of word processing files. Most network administrators and most word processing software programs look in a certain directory for files to be retrieved. In the example following (using WordPerfect), files are stored under a directory named <*WPWIN*\\>.

Without doing anything else, a user of either of these computers would be set up, either automatically by the software or by the network administrator, to store files in this subdirectory. However, within a year or less, many computer users realize they have many, many documents (files) in their directories. It quickly becomes difficult to find files.

One method of organization is to set up sub-directories by *subject and year*. In the example that follows, the subject area for the word processing document is a memo regarding the dedication of a new building. Since Barb works with facilities a great deal, she has set up a subdirectory for <*facil*\\> (facilities) and extended the maximum eight digit name with _93 to indicate these will be facilities files for the year 1993. Finally, Barb has named the specific document being saved <*dedicate*>.

Many of the advanced word processing software packages have menu selections that assist you in making new directories or renaming old ones. You can also follow directory instructions in a DOS or Windows manual.

On a Hard Drive

```
C:\wpwin\
facil_93\
dedicate
```

On a Network

```
F:\users\barb\
wpwin\
facil_93\
dedicate
```

The complete name of Barb's file on the hard drive would be **c:\wpwin\facil_93\dedicate**.

The complete name of Barb's file on the network would be **f:\users\barb\wpwin\facil_93\dedicate**.

Note that directories are separated in the filename with a backslash (<\\>).

Since each filename can also have a three-character extension (e.g.,<.123>), many users name this extension as well. However, since many software packages automatically add this extension to a file to identify their program files (for example, <*dedicate.sam*> in AmiPro), using this extension is not recommended. Your organization can be different based on the files you store, and the subdirectories you most use. The key is to set up some organized way to store the files.

As your files grow and the need for unexpected subdirectories becomes apparent, use of a file manager program can aid you in easily moving files into new subdirectories and out of old ones.

5636 **Additional pages.** When a letter extends to a second page, a plain piece of bond paper of the same quality as the original letterhead should be used. Using the same side margins, the second page of a two-page letter should begin an inch from the top with a heading that identifies the addressee, the date, and the page of the letter. (See illustrations 5636.1 and 5636.2.)

```
Schaeffer Medical Research Group
Page 2
September 15, 19--

Now this letter will continue to completion. This format is only
one of those that can
```

Illustration 5636.1 Second Page Letter Heading

```
Mr. Hank Meyer                      2            April 6, 19--

     In addition, Dr. Stokes asked me to offer his name as a
reference. He may be able to provide you with more information. I
appreciate your taking time to read my letter.

                                    Sincerely,


                                    Nelson A. Benedico
```

Illustration 5636.2 Second Page Heading

Following the second-page heading, triple space and resume keying the body of the letter.

- Do not divide a paragraph between pages unless at least two lines remain on the first page and at least two lines of the paragraph are carried to the second page.
- Leave a margin of at least one inch at the bottom of all letter pages (except, perhaps, the last, which may be larger).
- Do not hyphenate the final word on a page.
- Do not use the second page to key only the complimentary close and following lines. At least two lines of the final paragraph should begin the second page.

To shorten a long letter that is not quite long enough to become two pages, some blank lines between the letterhead and date, between the date and inside address, or before the signature line may be eliminated. In addition, single-spacing may be used before reference initials, enclosure notations, and copy notations.

5

5637 **Postscripts.** A **postscript** is an additional word, line, or paragraph added after a letter has been completed. It is keyed as the *last* item in the letter—a double space below the reference initials, enclosure notation, or copy notation, whichever is last. The postscript should begin at the left margin, or be indented five spaces, depending upon the letter style chosen. (See ¶ 5619 and illustration 5619.2.)

Correspondence Within the Company

5638 **Keying an interoffice memorandum.** Letters sent to individuals within the same company or organization are often formatted as interoffice memoranda. This practice allows for the use of less expensive stationery, as well as identifies immediately that the correspondence is from within the organization.

Interoffice memoranda are printed on memorandum forms or on plain paper. The headings TO, FROM, DATE, and SUBJECT usually begin the memorandum. The subject line may or may not be capitalized. There are no complimentary close or signature lines in the interoffice memorandum. The writer signs (using name or initials) next to his or her name at the top. Reference initials, enclosure notations, and copy notations remain the same as in business letters. (See illustrations 5638.1 and 5619.2.)

Illustration 5638.1
Interoffice Memorandum

Gonzalez & Company

MEMORANDUM

TO: Jeff Brezner
Facilities Department

FROM: Bettie Thompson (BT)
Human Resources

DATE: April 10, 19--

SUBJECT: EMPLOYEE PICNIC

Thank you for agreeing to serve on our committee to organize the employee picnic next month. With the group of individuals who will be working on the arrangements, I am sure our picnic this year will be the best ever!

Enclosed with this letter are the following items from last year's efforts:

Planning Committee Report
Picnic Budget
Picnic Employee Flyer
Picnic Program
Picnic Evaluation

The first meeting of our planning committee will be in the executive dining room on Tuesday, July 17, 19--, at 2:00 o'clock. My secretary will be calling you to confirm your attendance at this meeting.

Bring all of your best ideas—let's make this picnic one that will be long remembered.

mos

Enclosures (5)

pc Dr. Maria Hernandez

5639 **Composing for the supervisor's signature.** The office worker should become familiar with typical answers to routine correspondence, whether by letter or memorandum. In the electronic office, canned paragraphs can be stored for later rearrangement and use in subsequent correspondence. It will be helpful to the supervisor if you can draft routine correspondence. The supervisor will then review, make any necessary corrections or revisions, and sign the final, revised document.

Outgoing Mail

5640 **Proofreading.** Regardless of the standards adopted by others, professional secretaries assume personal responsibility for the accuracy of their work. A final proofreading before each document is put into its envelope is the last opportunity to locate and correct errors. (See ¶ 5033-37 on Proofreading.)

5641 **Signature.** Develop a procedure for having the outgoing correspondence signed. Ideally, correspondence ready for signing should be taken in a batch to the executive. The secretary should stand by to answer questions and take last-minute instructions pertinent to the correspondence. A clipboard or folder may be used to organize the documents for signing. Stick-on notes may be used to indicate the proper location of signatures (particularly for complex documents) and to remind the executive of anything special about each document. If the secretary signs the executive's name to a document, the signature should be followed by the secretary's initials.

5642 **Enclosures.** Enclosure notations should indicate all the enclosures that will be included with a letter. If there is more than one enclosure, enclosures should be itemized in the notation. Double-check to be sure that enclosures are actually sent. The enclosure notation is placed flush with the left margin a double space below the reference initials or a double space below the signature block if reference initials are not used. (See ¶ 5632 for additional information on keying the enclosure notation.)

5643 **Courtesy copies.** Whether c (copy), cc (carbon copy), or pc (photocopy) is used, be sure that copies are made and sent to the proper persons when the original is sent out. Use a check mark on the file copy or some other notation to record systematically the fact that such copies have actually been sent. Even though there is no notation on the original that blind copies have been sent, there should be a notation on the file copy. The notation on the file or electronic copy is usually bc (blind copy), or bpc (blind photocopy). The copy notation should be placed a double space below the signature block, reference initials, or enclosure notation—whichever is last.

Be sure to save a file copy. When word processing software is used for letter preparation, a standard procedure should be adopted for saving hard copies or saving the text on the hard drive or network, or both. (See ¶ 5633 for more about copy notations, ¶ 5635 for information on electronic file organization, and ¶ 5700 for information on filing.)

5644 **Envelopes and mailers.** Stock a variety of envelopes—at least one of the large sizes and one of the small sizes. Mailers of several types are available; they are made with a variety of padding materials. If your firm does not have a department to prepare the outgoing mail, keep some brown wrapping paper and tape on hand to wrap packages that cannot be accommodated by standard mailers. It is important that mail be *machine readable* by the equipment used by the U.S. Postal Service.

5645 **Preparation of envelopes.** *Envelopes* should be prepared for outgoing letters before the letter is presented to the writer for signature. To speed mail delivery at the most economical rates, this section will emphasize the recommendations of the U.S. Postal Service for mail preparation.

5646 **Proper address formats.** The sequence of the address on any envelope or package should be:

- **Nonaddress data**
- **Name of recipient**
- **Information/attention**
- **Delivery address**
- **City, state, and zip + 4 code**

Nonaddress data. The nonaddress data is optional and, if used, should be on the first line of the address. It may contain advertising, account numbers, subscription or presort codes, small logos, and the like.

Name of recipient. The name of recipient line contains the name of an individual or company.

Information/Attention. The information or attention line is an optional line for additional address information. It may be used to direct mail to a specific person when the business name has been used and it *follows* the line containing the name of the business.

Delivery address. This line tells the postal service where to deliver the mail. It should always be immediately above the city, state, and zip + 4 code line. It should contain one of the following:

- street address
- post office box number
- rural route number and box number
- highway contract number and box number

For *multi-unit buildings,* one of the following should be placed immediately after the street address on the same line:

- apartment number
- suite number
- room number
- other unit designation

City, state, and zip + 4 code. The name of the city, two-letter state abbreviation, and zip + 4 code should be the bottom line of the address. (See ¶ 3020 for information on United States two-letter state abbreviations and Canadian province abbreviations.)

For maximum efficiency and lower cost in processing mail, use these standards when addressing envelopes:

- left margin should be uniform

- address should be printed parallel to the bottom of the envelope
- use only uppercase characters
- use no punctuation
- elements of the address should be placed in their correct positions.

5647 **Zip + 4 code.** The U.S. Postal Service has added four more digits to the standard five-digit zip code This expanded zip code provides faster processing and directing of all mail, which should also result in faster delivery. Speed is important in view of the larger volumes of mail processed each year by the postal service. Most offices know their expanded zip code. If you do not know your office's zip + 4 code, call or write your local postal center.

5648 **Optical character readers (OCR).** The postal service uses optical character readers to electronically scan the mail and direct it for rapid processing. These OCR machines can read over 36,000 pieces of mail an hour. For the OCR to work, it must be able to locate and read the delivery address. The eye of the OCR looks for the address within an imaginary rectangle on each piece of mail called the OCR read area. Nonaddress printing or marking should be kept above the delivery address line. The dimensions shown in illustration 5648.1 reflect optimum locations for reading the delivery address for a standard envelope.

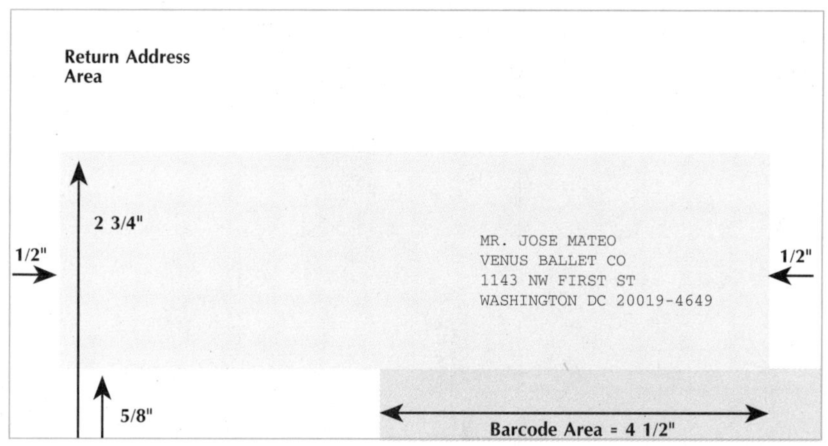

Illustration 5648.1 OCR Read Area

The large shaded area represents the rectangle of the OCR read area. To print within this area on a large envelope, begin the address four inches from the left edge of the envelope and on line fifteen from the top. On a small envelope, begin two and one-half inches from the left edge and on line twelve. Following these instructions will assure that the address will be in the OCR read area. Illustration 5648.2 shows the correct way to key both small and large business envelopes with a variety of mailing notations.

MORE

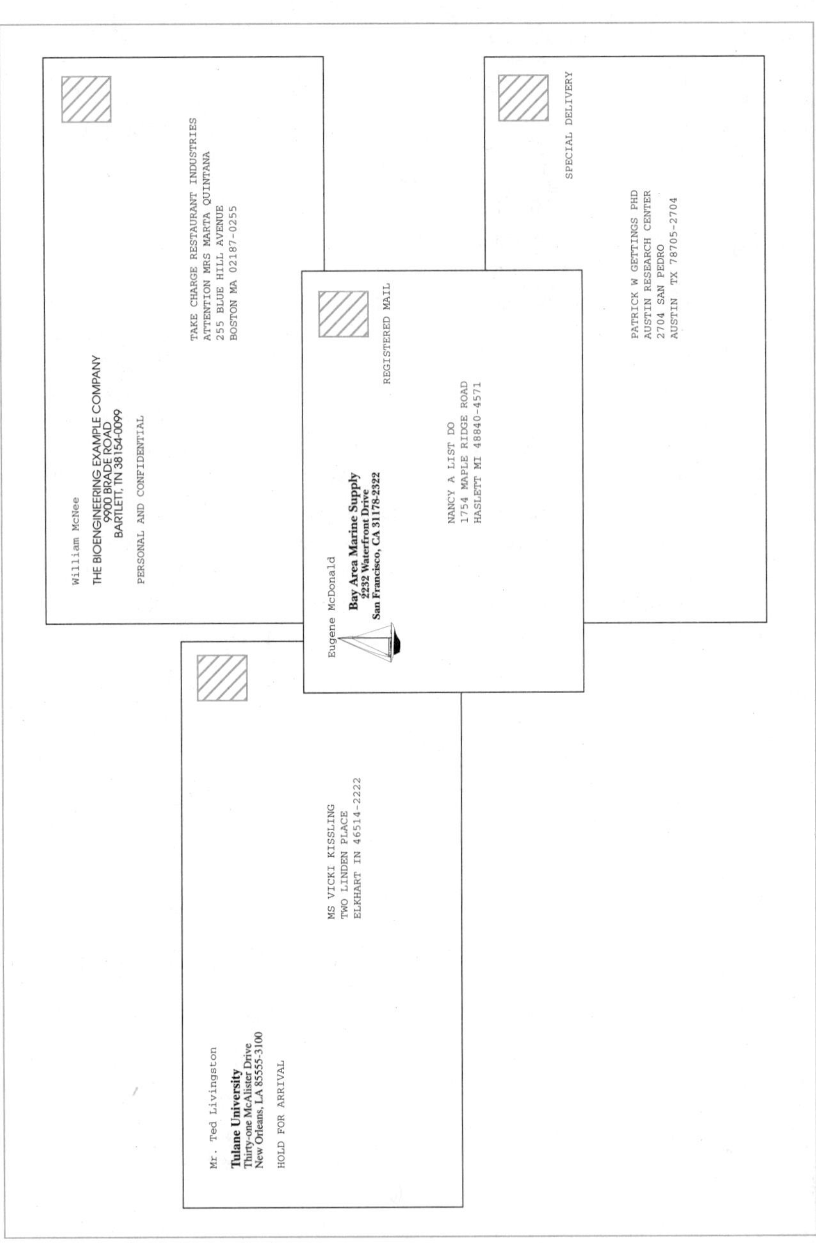

Illustration 5648.2 Envelopes with Notations

5649 **Electronic envelopes.** The most advanced word processing software packages provide automatic envelope preparation by merging the inside address on the letter with the envelope formatting. As is shown in illustration 5649.1, the envelope preparation screen pops up on top of the already-prepared business letter when the envelope macro is run. In this example from WordPerfect Corporation (illustration 5649.1), you have many envelope options—including the ability to add a barcode, add a return address, change envelope size, and so on.

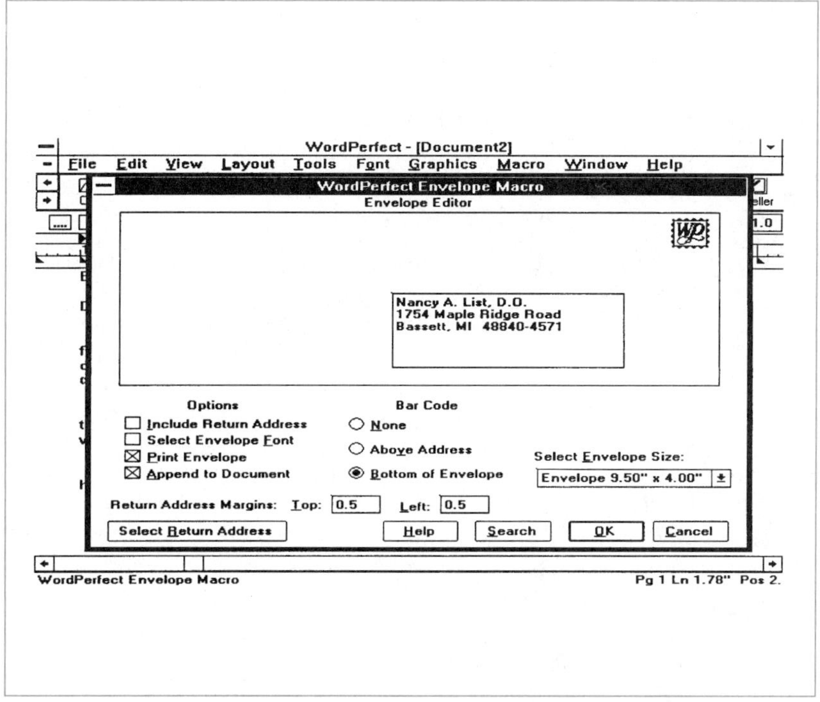

llustration 5649.1 Sample Electronic Envelope Screen, WordPerfect

The envelope is stored in the disk file with the letter. After the letter is printed, a message prompts the operator to insert an envelope.

5650 **Bar-coding envelopes.** After reading an address, the OCR will print the appropriate POSTNET bar-code (representing the zip code or zip + 4 code) in the lower right-hand corner of the envelope (see illustration 5648.1). This bar-code area must be kept free of any print. If the bar-code is preprinted on envelopes, one entire step at the post office can be avoided, thus speeding up mail delivery. Offices completing large mailings also qualify for lower rates by pre-bar-coding all mailing pieces. Word processing software that adds this bar code automatically will be much sought after. Once the bar code is on an envelope, that piece of mail can be read by less expensive, faster bar-code readers as it passes through additional sorting points on its way to its destination.

5

5651 **Return address.** Most offices use business envelopes with the name and address of the office printed in the upper left-hand corner of the envelope. It may, however, be necessary for you to key the name of the letter writer and/or department or account number (if you work for a large office). This information should be keyed above the printed return address (see illustration 5648.2).

For personal business correspondence, or if your office does not use preprinted envelopes, the return address should be keyed a double space from the top edge of the envelope and three spaces from the left edge.

5652 **Envelope notations.** Notations that are intended for the office receiving the mail are called **addressee notations.** These notations are to be used by the person(s) delivering mail *within* the office and include information such as PERSONAL, CONFIDENTIAL, HOLD FOR ARRIVAL, or PLEASE FORWARD. Such addressee notations should be keyed in all capital letters a triple space below the return address and three spaces from the left edge. (See illustration 5648.2 for examples of such notations printed on envelopes.)

5653 **Mailing notations.** Those mailing directions intended for the U.S. Postal Service—REGISTERED, RETURN RECEIPT REQUESTED, and SPECIAL DELIVERY, are **mailing notations.** Such notations identify special mailing requirements for postal personnel and should be keyed in all capital letters below the postage stamp (or postage meter mark) and at least three line spaces above the envelope address. (See illustration 5648.2)

5654 **Folding business letters.** The correct procedure for folding business letters for insertion into envelopes varies according to the size of the envelope you are using. Illustration 5654.1 shows how to fold a business letter for a large and small envelope. Also included are illustrations for folding business correspondence for use with a window envelope; make certain that the complete address shows clearly through the window of the envelope after insertion.

5655 **Metered mail.** In a large office, postage will probably be added to an envelope by a postage metering machine. This machine can add differing amounts of postage required depending upon the weight of the envelope or package being mailed. To facilitate rapid metering of such mail, envelopes should be left open (the meter machine automatically seals all envelopes) with all envelope flaps up and addresses facing the same way. CONFIDENTIAL mail can be sealed before sending to a mailroom, if desired. To avoid machine damage, letter envelopes containing bulky items, such as paper clips, should be sealed and marked "Hand Stamp" by the originating office.

5656 **Recording outgoing mail.** Some firms have all pages of each piece of outgoing mailing photocopied in order to have a complete record of everything sent. Others photocopy only the most representative pages of each mailing (the first and last pages of a multipage letter with enclosures, for example). Still other firms use a log or register to record outgoing documents. Any one of these methods provides a chronological record of the outgoing mail. (See illustration 5610.1 for an incoming/outgoing mail register.)

Classes of Mail

5657 **First-class mail.** **First-class mail** includes letters, bills, statements, invoices, checks, postal cards, business reply cards and envelopes, and greeting cards. First-class mail is delivered by the fastest transportation available. Normally such mail posted by 6:00 p.m. local time will be delivered to local addresses the following day, to destinations within 600 miles the second day, and to other destinations in the 48 contiguous states the third day. First-class mail cannot be opened for postal inspection. It is also the most expensive class of mail.

Stationery	Envelope	Fold	Window Envelope Fold
Standard (8 1/2″ x 11″)	No. 10 (9 1/2″ x 4 1/8″) No. 6 3/4 (6 1/2″ x 3 5/8″)	3 2-3	W3 —
Monarch (7 1/4″ x 10 1/2″)	No. 7 (7 1/2″ x 3 7/8″)	3	W3
Baronial (5 1/2″ x 8 1/2″)	No. 5 3/8 (5 15/16″ x 4 5/8″)	2	W2

Fold 2

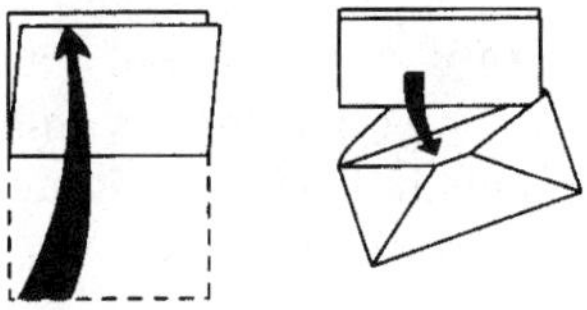

Fold into 2 parts.

Fold 2-3

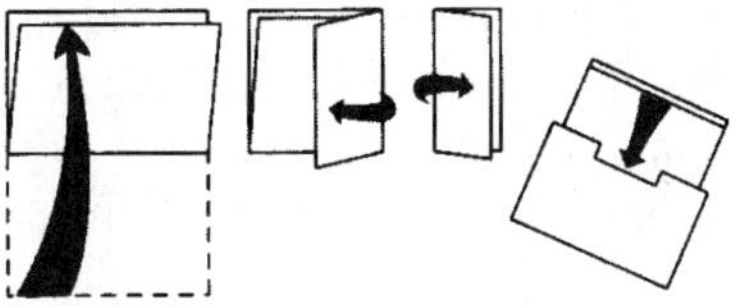

Fold into 2 parts, then fold into 3 parts.

Fold 3

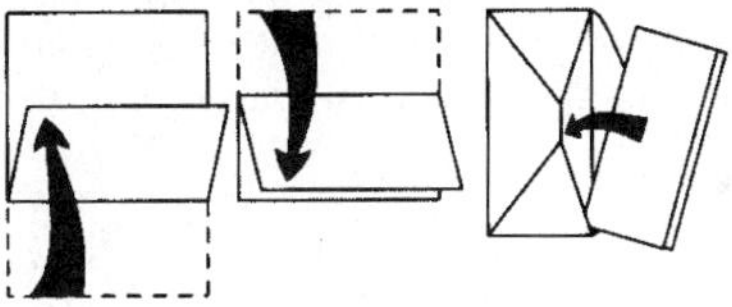

Fold W2 (Window Envelope)

Fold into 2 parts.

Fold W3 (Window Envelope)

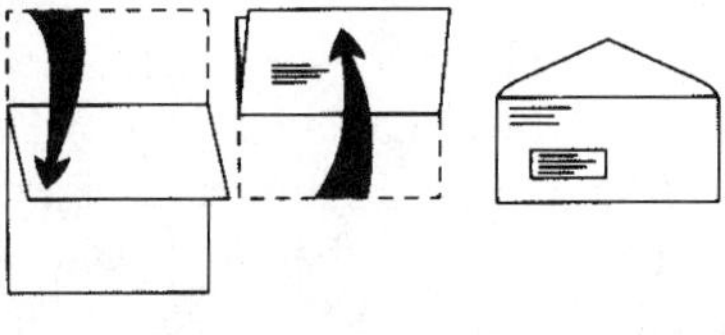

Fold into 3 parts.

Illustration 5654.1 Choosing Envelopes and Folding Letters

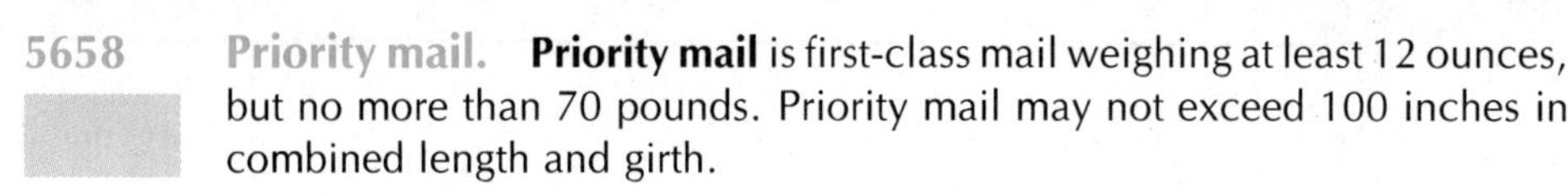

5658 **Priority mail.** **Priority mail** is first-class mail weighing at least 12 ounces, but no more than 70 pounds. Priority mail may not exceed 100 inches in combined length and girth.

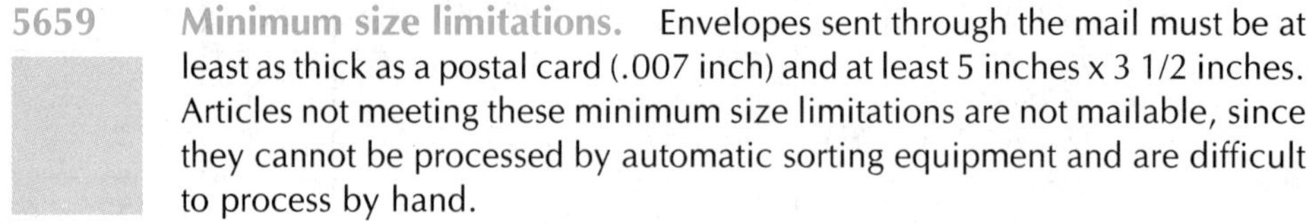

5659 **Minimum size limitations.** Envelopes sent through the mail must be at least as thick as a postal card (.007 inch) and at least 5 inches x 3 1/2 inches. Articles not meeting these minimum size limitations are not mailable, since they cannot be processed by automatic sorting equipment and are difficult to process by hand.

5660 **First-class minimum weight surcharges.** A **surcharge** is levied on any envelope that weighs one ounce or less *and* exceeds 6 1/8 inches in height or 11 1/2 inches in length or 1/4-inch in thickness.

5661 **Second-class mail.** **Second-class mail** is generally used for newspapers and magazines. It is a cheaper method of shipment. A special permit is required to send newspapers and magazines by second-class mail. Within the second-class category, there are separate classifications for single copies and bulk mailings (multiple copies of the same publication).

5662 **Second-class minimum weight surcharges.** A **surcharge** is levied on any article that weighs two ounces or less and exceeds 6 1/8 inches in height or 11 1/2 inches in length or 1/4-inch in thickness.

5663 **Third-class mail.** Although **third-class mail** may be used for any merchandise or printed material, it is used primarily for the mass mailing of advertising material. It employs two rate structures: one for one-of-a-kind, one-at-a-time mailings; another for batches of identical pieces. Sealed envelopes may be sent by third-class mail only if they are marked "Third-Class" on the address side. Third-class mail can be insured.

5664 **Fourth-class mail (parcel post).** **Fourth-class mail** accommodates parcels weighing one pound or more. There are maximums on size and weight. Charges are scheduled by weight and distance: higher rates for heavier parcels and more-distant zones. Parcels may be sealed or unsealed, but correspondence other than invoices or statements is prohibited. A common practice is to stamp or meter an envelope containing correspondence as though it were to be posted separately by first-class mail—then, fasten the envelope to the outside of the fourth-class package. First-class rates apply to the correspondence; fourth-class rates apply to the package itself.

5665 **Express mail.** **Express mail** is designed for rapid delivery. It is insured against loss at no extra charge. Several types of service are available:

	Picked up at Sender's Office	Mailed at Sender's Airport	Delivered to Addressee's Airport	Delivered to Addressee's Office
Same day airport service		X	X	
Airport to addressee service		X		X
Office to airport service	X		X	
Pick-up and delivery service	X			X

Next-day service. Post the letter or parcel (or have it picked up at your office) by 5:00 p.m.; it will be delivered no later than 3:00 p.m. the next business day.

International express mail. Three-day service to major cities in foreign nations is available.

5666 **Special delivery.** **Special delivery** service is available for first-, third-, and fourth-class mail. It provides delivery during regular business hours, during certain extended daily business hours, and during certain hours on Sundays and holidays.

Special delivery mail moves with the regular mail in its class until it reaches the post office in the destination city. Normally, it is delivered to the addressee the day it reaches the destination post office.

5667 **Certificate of mailing.** For a small fee, paid at the time an article is posted, the postal service will provide a *certificate* stating that the item was mailed. This certificate does not, however, insure the item against loss or damage.

5668 **Return receipt.** For a small fee, the postal service will provide a *receipt* signed by the addressee or the addressee's agent at the time of delivery. A return receipt may be obtained as proof of delivery for insured mail valued at more than fifteen dollars, certified mail, registered mail, and COD mail.

5669 **Insurance.** First-, third-, and fourth-class mail can be *insured* up to a value of $400. First-class mail includes priority mail (all first-class mail weighing at least 12 ounces); fourth-class mail is also called parcel post.

5670 **Registered mail.** Articles that cannot be replaced and those valued at more than $400 should be shipped by **registered mail.** Insurance of the actual value of the article up to $25,000 is included in the registration fee on all domestic deliveries (those inside the United States).

To ship an article by registered mail, the customer must declare the actual value of the article at the time it is posted. The article receives special care under controlled conditions all the time it is in the hands of the U.S. Postal Service (USPS). When the article is posted, the customer receives a receipt stating that it has been accepted for delivery by the USPS. For an extra fee, the USPS will provide a return receipt that indicates when, where, and to whom the article is delivered.

5671 **Postage meters.** **Postage meters** can be purchased or leased from private manufacturers or leased from the USPS. The machine is taken to the post office periodically by the customer, who pays to have the meter reset (i.e., have it indicate more postage). Each time the user applies postage to an envelope or to a label for a parcel, the amount of postage necessary is set by the user. That amount is printed on the envelope or label and deducted from the postage indicated by the meter. The meter indicates the postage used since the machine was reset and the postage remaining for use. Misprints can be taken to the post office to obtain a refund.

For volume mailers, there are several advantages to the use of a postage meter. It is faster than stamping. It provides improved security—postage is centralized; the imprint can be identified and traced. Cancellation is not required as it is in the case of stamps. Postage meters can include a promotional message in their imprint.

5

5672 **Postage permits.** Organizations can obtain a permit that allows the organization to have the postage printed on the envelope in the same impression used for printing the return address. One special kind of permit imprint is valid only for bulk mailing by the organization holding the permit; envelopes or other articles imprinted for bulk mailing cannot be mailed individually. Bulk mailing permits are available for first- through fourth- class mail. Postage permits make it unnecessary to affix stamps or run the pieces to be mailed through a postage meter.

5673 **Collect on delivery (COD) service.** The USPS will deliver an article to the addressee, collect at the time of delivery the amount specified by the sender (up to $300), and return the money to the sender. Charges may include all or part of the cost of the article, the postage, and the insurance. COD service is available for first-, third-, and fourth-class mail. COD service is also available from most of the private sector carriers that compete with the USPS.

5674 **Money orders.** Postal money orders for payment in the United States are available at any post office. Most large post offices can arrange for money orders payable in foreign nations. The limit on an individual money order is $400, but more than one money order can be purchased if larger amounts are to be sent. Lost or stolen money orders will be replaced by the USPS if the user can establish ownership of the money order. Copies of money orders can be obtained for two years after the date of the payment.

5675 **Forwarding mail.** Individuals or organizations changing addresses should use the change of address kits provided by the USPS. Each kit contains forms with which to notify the USPS and those with whom the individuals or organizations correspond of the new address. First-class mail received at the old address is forwarded without charge for a period of one year; other classes are forwarded postage-collect.

5676 **Business reply mail.** Individuals or organizations can obtain permits to distribute self-addressed envelopes imprinted to indicate that the permit holder will pay the postage for the returned envelope. This allows business firms to distribute business reply envelopes freely with their advertising matter, hoping that a postage-free response will help persuade the potential customer to respond. Postage is collected from the permit holder when the envelope is returned. The permit holder may establish an account through which postage for individual items is deducted from a deposit for advance payments, thus eliminating payment in cash at the time of delivery.

5677 **International mail.** Any post office will accept items for foreign delivery and answer individual questions about international mail. A USPS publication, *International Mail Manual,* is a helpful guide, as are the other USPS publications on the subject.

5678 ***Postal Service Manual.*** Postal laws, regulations, services, and rates change from time to time. It is a good idea to have a copy of the *Postal Service Manual* in the office or mailroom. It is available from or through your post office. *The Domestic Mail Manual (DMM)* is a computerized version that provides instant searches, easy reference, the latest in cost-cutting mail techniques, and continued updates of changing information.

5679 **Private carriers.** Courier services, parcel services, airlines, bus companies, and taxicab companies offer a variety of delivery services. The yellow pages of the telephone book contain information on the services available.

5

Electronic Mail and Wire Service

5680 **Cablegrams.** **Cablegrams** are international telegrams that may travel by cable—or by microwave (satellite or relay-tower), radio, and the like. Cablegram service is available from Western Union and several other companies.

5681 **Computer networks.** Almost any computer can be equipped inexpensively with a **modem** (modulator-demodulator) that permits the computer to send and receive data by regular telephone lines.

The computer user can "talk" to another user on the same network, check to see if there are any messages addressed to him or her, or "download" information. In **downloading,** the user simply copies over the telephone line data that is kept available in files maintained by the network. (See ¶ 4500 for more information on networks.)

If you have a computer equipped with a modem, you can reach anyone else equipped for telecommunication. If you know the person has a computer that is part of a network, you will go through that network unless that computer also has a separate telephone connection. (See ¶ 4500 and 4600 for more information on communicating between computers via networks.)

5682 **Electronic mail.** **Electronic mail** (E-mail) is offered both within a firm as well as nationwide. Within a firm, E-mail allows all network users to send messages, files, and graphics back and forth to each other. Users of many nationwide services also enjoy the same features, often communicating with colleagues, via bulletin boards, and even with complete strangers.

5683 **Facsimile devices.** A **facsimile transmission (fax) machine** is a scanning device that sends page-sized images by wire to similar machines throughout the world. Some operate over regular telephone lines; others are operated by various telephone companies and by Western Union. A fax machine operates like a photocopy machine that sends the image by wire. At the receiving end, a similar machine receives the electronic code for the image and translates it into the finished copy. The sending and receiving machines may be any distance apart so long as they are joined by a good connection. (See ¶ 4517-18 for more information on sending and receiving faxes over a network.

5684 **Full-rate telegrams.** A **telegram** is a message sent by telex (see ¶ 5688) to someone who does not have a telex machine. It is sent to a Western Union office near the addressee by telex, then telephoned to the addressee. Delivery of the hard copy produced by the receiving telex machine is available for an extra fee.

5685 **Inmarsat.** **Inmarsat** is the marine satellite system. It allows shore-to-ship, ship-to-shore, and ship-to-ship voice communication. Direct dialing is possible, using an area code for each ocean and a seven-digit number for each ship.

5686 **Mailgrams.** **Mailgrams** are made available through a cooperative effort of Western Union and the U.S. Postal Service. The sender sends a telex message (through the sender's own teletypewriter [or computer] or by calling Western Union) to the USPS telex installation nearest the recipient. At the receiving post office, the hard copy telex message is removed from the telex machine and delivered as mail. If the message is sent early in the day, it will be delivered the same day; if not, it will be delivered the following day.

5687 **Overnight telegrams.** An **overnight telegram** is a telegram sent after regular business hours to arrive at the opening of business the next day. Since the charge is considerably less than that for a full-rate telegram, overnight telegrams are frequently used for longer messages.

5688 **Telex.** The **telex system** is a network of teletypewriters and computers connected through automatic exchanges that make it possible for one user to communicate with another. Telex service is available in most of the major cities of the world. It is important to international trade because it helps overcome time and language differences and because it produces a hard-copy record. Western Union operates the largest telex network in the United States.

5689 **Teletex.** **Teletex** is an international system that permits properly programmed computers to serve as telex machines. It is operated by Western Union in the United States.

5700 FILING

5

FILING

Filing Systems

5701 **Filing defined.** **Filing** is the orderly arrangement of records for retention and retrieval. Records may be written, printed, copied, photographed, or recorded by another method. They may be on paper, film, disks, tape, or another medium.

5702 **Purposes of filing.** Records are maintained for two general purposes. First, for transactions purposes: conducting the day-to-day affairs of the organization. Typical documents containing data on transactions are cash register tapes, sales slips, purchase orders, time cards, payrolls, and routine letters regarding the day-to-day operation of the organization.

The second purpose of maintaining records is the compilation of management information. Management information—derived from transactions data and other sources—reflects past, present, and projected (future) sales, costs, profits, staffing, facilities, and the like; it provides a factual basis for management decisions.

5703 **Need for rules.** The orderly completion of transactions and effective use of management information are among the most important functions in any organization. In a small organization, they may be relatively simple; they can probably be undertaken informally with some degree of success. In larger organizations, they are not simple—and *must* be undertaken methodically.

5704 **Who makes the rules?** When only a few people use the files, and they can easily communicate with one another, some common practices usually develop. These practices may work reasonably well—so long as they are used by everyone who has access to the files.

If some of those who use the files insist that their individuality be reflected in their work, the system will not work effectively. Worse still, a haphazard filing system makes periodic record-by-record searches for lost documents inevitable.

The records of larger organizations demand a more sophisticated approach—both because the problems of filing are more complex and because the results of misfiling or failure to retrieve are more difficult and costly to fix. The planning, organization, operation, and control of more-sophisticated filing systems is called **records management.**

In a large organization, many people may have access to the files. They *must* use the same rules for filing. Those rules are usually recorded in a manual; they are taught to each new employee who is given access to the files.

On a larger scale, many of those who work in records management belong to ARMA (the Association of Records Managers and Administrators). From time to time, ARMA publishes rules for alphabetic filing, such as *Alphabetic Filing Rules* and *Filing Procedures Guidelines*.

5705 **Alphabetic-by-name systems.** Most organizations file alphabetically by the name of the person or organization the document concerns. A letter to or a letter from Suzanne Masters is filed in the *M* section under *Masters, Suzanne*. A bill from the Arvey Cable Company is filed in the *A* section under *Arvey Cable Company*.

5706 **Subject files.** The military services, some other government agencies, and nongovernment organizations with special needs file by subject. Their systems are divided first into broad categories such as *Planning, Training, Intelligence,* and *Supply*. As in an outline, the system is divided into narrower and narrower categories until there is a file category for the subject of every document. The procurement of flour might be filed under

```
Supply
        Procurement
              Food
                    Flour
```

5707 **Numeric Files.** Although subject files can be arranged alphabetically, the various subjects are usually numbered. A few systems employ numbers separated by hyphens (12-2-23) or alphanumeric coding (A-23-G). However, most numeric systems are decimal systems, similar to those used in libraries and in the military services.

When a subject filing system contains correspondence or other material pertaining to individuals or organizations, the filing order is *subject first,* then *alphabetically by name.* A typical decimal filing system is organized something like the following example:

```
100 Plans and Training

200 Personnel
    201    Applications
    201.1  Current Applications
              Franks, Lucille Irene
              Thompson, Sheila Ann
    201.2  Inactive Applications
```

Although those who work with files soon get to know the numbers they use most frequently, a separate alphabetic card file is maintained as a key to the number system. The alphabetic card file in a library is the key to the decimal subject system used for the books themselves.

In a typical computerized application, a single database system can be accessed in any way that makes sense to the user. The computer can search at electronic speeds for a single subject, name, volume, or the like. In large applications, the most efficient system is a numeric arrangement of the physical objects (usually documents or volumes) and a matching computerized database that permits manipulation of the database information for the convenience of users.

5708 **Subject sections in alphabetic files.** Organizations employing alphabetical-by-name systems frequently use a few subjects within the alphabetical system. Since the names of individual applicants are not long remembered, an *applications* section is frequently maintained. It is filed in alphabetic order under *applications*. Within the applications section, the names of applicants are filed alphabetically.

Similarly, a subject section within an alphabetic file may be set aside for sources of supply, a current construction project, a branch office, and so on.

5709 **Geographic files.** Some organizations prefer to file some records geographically. The home office of a decentralized organization may choose to maintain geographic files arranged alphabetically by state, then city, then personal or organizational name.

At first it might seem that such a system would operate very inefficiently when the home office receives a letter directly. In reality, a quick look at the address of the correspondent reveals the territory or branch office to which the letter should be assigned.

5710 **Filing Segments.** A **filing segment** is the complete name, subject, or number used to file a record.

Adeline R. Sweet (Personal name)

Webster Word Company (Organizational name)

Applications (Subject, filed alphabetically)

407.38 (Subject, filed by number)

Personal Names and Addresses

5711 **Indexing unit.** An **indexing unit** is a single character or group of characters (word, letter, number, or symbol) considered separately for filing purposes. The name *Connie B. Tien* has three indexing units: *Connie, B,* and *Tien*.

5712 **Alphabetizing records.** In alphabetizing records for the files, the key unit is considered first, then the second unit, then the third unit, and so on. Within each unit, the letters are considered from left to right.

Name	Key Unit	Unit 2	Unit 3
	123456789	123456789	123456789
Thaddeus R. Calvino	Calvino	Thaddeus	R
Alberta Y. Canelli	Canelli	Alberta	Y

Filing order is determined at the third letter by the *l* in *Calvino* and the *n* in *Canelli*.

5713 **Nothing before something.** When all letters in a unit are identical to the first letters in a longer unit, the shorter unit is filed first.

Name	Key Unit	Unit 2	Unit 3
	123456789	123456789	123456789
Henry John Judman	Judman	Henry	John
Henry Johnson Judman	Judman	Henry	Johnson

5714 **Alphabetizing generally.** In other applications of alphabetizing, the indexing unit system is not generally used. In the dictionary, for example, a compound word is treated as a single word (indexing unit) even if it actually consists of several words written open (with spaces between them). Thus *doubleheader* is listed before *double standard*. In filing practice, *doubleheader* is a single indexing unit; *double standard* is two indexing units. In filing practice, *double standard* is filed before *doubleheader* because the key indexing unit *double* comes before the key indexing unit *doubleheader*.

Word	Key Unit	Unit 2
	123456789	123456789
double standard	double	standard
doubleheader	doubleheader	

5715 **Key indexing units identical.** When key indexing units are identical, filing order is determined by the letters in the second units (presuming that they are not identical, also).

Name	Key Unit	Unit 2	Unit 3
	123456789	123456789	123456789
William P. Cuthbert	Cuthbert	William	P
Wilma R. Cuthbert	Cuthbert	Wilma	R

5716 **Second indexing units identical.** When first and second indexing units are identical, filing order is determined by comparing the letters of the third unit (presuming that they are not identical, also).

Name	Key Unit	Unit 2	Unit 3
	123456789	123456789	123456789
Dina Marie Ellis	Ellis	Dina	Marie
Dina Mary Ellis	Ellis	Dina	Mary

5717 **All indexing units identical.** When all indexing units are identical, the addresses determine the filing order. (See ¶ 5725-29 for identical personal names and ¶ 5744 for identical organizational names.)

5718 **Initials in personal names.** Each initial in a personal name is considered a separate indexing unit.

Name	Key Unit	Unit 2	Unit 3
	123456789	123456789	123456789
B. B. Biltmore	Biltmore	B	B
B. Bobbie Biltmore	Biltmore	B	Bobbie
Betty B. Biltmore	Biltmore	Betty	B

5719 **Surname prefixes.** A prefix (particle) is combined with the word that follows it to form a single indexing unit. If a space separates the particle and the following word, the space is ignored for indexing purposes. Some common particles are *a la, d', da, de, De, del, De la, della, Den, Des, di, Dos, du, El, Fitz, la, Les, Lo, Los, Mac, Mc, O', St., Ste., Saint, San, Santa, Santo, van, Van der, von,* and *Von der.*

Name	Key Unit	Unit 2
	123456789	123456789
Anthony DeSarro	DeSarro	Anthony
Carla Desarro	Desarro	Carla
Ilio De Sarro*	DeSarro	Ilio

* Names written with a space between the prefix and the base are indexed as one unit without a space.

5

5720 **Hyphenated surnames.** A hyphenated surname is considered a single indexing unit. (Compound surnames written open are indexed as separate units. See ¶ 5721.)

Name	Key Unit	Unit 2
	123456789	123456789
Hugh Smith-Ardmon	SmithArdmon	Hugh
Jilla Wynn-Hartke	WynnHartke	Jilla

5721 **Compound personal names written open.** Compound personal names written open are treated as separate indexing units. (A hyphenated surname is indexed as a single unit. See ¶ 5720.)

Name	Key Unit	Unit 2	Unit 3	Unit 4
	123456789	123456789	123456789	123456789
Jani Ann Dill-Maran	DillMaran	Jani	Ann	
Hugh John Armon Watts	Watts	Hugh	John	Armon

A compound name written open (Armon Watts) may be cross-referenced (under *Armon*).

A hyphenated surname (Dill-Maran) is treated as a single unit. If the second element (Maran) might be used to identify the person, the name should be cross-referenced under the second element.

If the first word in a compound surname is one of the standard surname prefixes (the *St.* in *St. John,* for example), the surname is indexed as a single unit. (See ¶ 5719.)

5722 **Names of married women.** The name of a married woman is indexed as she writes it. If more than one form of the name is known, it may be cross-referenced.

Name	Key Unit	Unit 2	Unit 3	Unit 4
	123456789	123456789	123456789	123456789
Miss Sheila R. Adler	Adler	Sheila	R	Miss
Ms. Sheila R. Adler	Adler	Sheila	R	Ms
Mrs. Arthur S. Wood	Wood	Arthur	S	Mrs
Mrs. Sheila Adler Wood	Wood	Sheila	Adler	Mrs
Mrs. Sheila R. Wood	Wood	Sheila	R	Mrs

5723 **Royal or religious title followed by single name.** A name consisting of a royal title (King, Princess, and the like) or a religious title (Sister, Brother, and the like) and a single name (given name or surname, but not both) is filed *as written* with the title as the first indexing unit and the name as the second.

Other titles applied to full names are treated normally. (See ¶ 5727, ¶ 5742.)

Name	Key Unit 123456789	Unit 2 123456789
Brother Edgar	Brother	Edgar
Father Vincent	Father	Vincent
Princess Grace	Princess	Grace
Sister Lorraine	Sister	Lorraine
Sister Mildred	Sister	Mildred

5724 **Unusual names.** If it is difficult to distinguish between the given name and the surname, consider the name written last as the surname. Cross-reference if doing so will be helpful.

Name	Key Unit 123456789	Unit 2 123456789	Unit 3 123456789
Min Lan Sing	Sing	Min	Lan
Hu Soong	Soong	Hu	
Yeh Zababa	Zababa	Yeh	

5725 **Seniority (Sr., Jr., III).** When names are identical, seniority designations (if any) are used to determine filing order.

Name	Key Unit 123456789	Unit 2 123456789	Unit 3 123456789	Unit 4 123456789
Spencer Demare III	Demare	Spencer	III	
Spencer Demare IV	Demare	Spencer	IV	
Edward Thompson, Jr.	Thompson	Edward	Jr	
Mrs. Edward Thompson, Sr.	Thompson	Edward	Sr	Mrs

Seniority designations are indexed in their abbreviated forms (Jr., Sr., and so forth). The order is as follows:

First:	Arabic numbers in numerical order (2d, 3d)	2 3
Second:	Roman numbers in numerical order	II III
Third:	Words in alphabetic order, abbreviated form	Jr. Sr.

See also, ¶ 5728.

5726 **Abbreviations (CPA, MBA).** When names are otherwise identical, academic degree or professional designations (if any) determine filing order. Abbreviations for academic degrees and professional designations are indexed alphabetically as written.

MORE

CONTINUED

Name	Key Unit	Unit 2	Unit 3	Unit 4
	123456789	123456789	123456789	123456789
Mavis B. Stewart, A. B.	Stewart	Mavis	B	AB
Mavis B. Stewart, C.P.A	Stewart	Mavis	B	CPA
Mavis B. Stewart, MBA	Stewart	Mavis	B	MBA
Mavis B. Stewart, M.D.	Stewart	Mavis	B	MD
Mavis B. Stewart, Ph.D.	Stewart	Mavis	B	PhD

See also, ¶ 5728.

5727 **Titles (Miss, Mr., Mrs., Ms., Dr.).** When names are otherwise identical, personal or professional titles (if any) determine filing order. Abbreviations of personal and professional titles are indexed alphabetically as written.

Name	Key Unit	Unit 2	Unit 3	Unit 4
	123456789	123456789	123456789	123456789
Dr. Jean Parker Smith	Smith	Jean	Parker	Dr
Miss Jean Parker Smith	Smith	Jean	Parker	Miss
Mr. Jean Parker Smith	Smith	Jean	Parker	Mr
Mrs. Jean Parker Smith	Smith	Jean	Parker	Mrs
Ms. Jean Parker Smith	Smith	Jean	Parker	Ms

In a rare case, one might find names that are identical including seniority designations, abbreviations, and personal titles. Consider the units in this order:

Name	Key Unit	Unit 2	Unit 3	Unit 4	Unit 5	Unit 6
(Dr.) Avil R. Band III, P.A.	Band	Avil	R	III	PA	Dr
(Mr.) Avil R. Band III, P.A.	Band	Avil	R	III	PA	Mr

See also, ¶ 5728.

5728 **Identical names with identical titles, degrees, etc.** When names are identical and titles, degrees, seniority designations, and the like, are also identical, filing order is determined by the address.

Identical Units	City	State or Province	Street	House or Building Number
(Dr) R G Tate CPA	Atlanta	Georgia	Southern Avenue	122
(Dr) R G Tate CPA	Columbus	Georgia	Fifth Avenue South	531
(Dr) R G Tate CPA	Columbus	Ohio	State Street	1022
(Dr) R G Tate CPA	Columbus	Ohio	Tucker Avenue	22
(Dr) R G Tate CPA	Columbus	Ohio	Tucker Avenue	237

5729 **Identical names without differentiation.** When names are identical and there are no distinguishing titles, degrees, or other such units, filing order is determined by the address.

Identical Units	City	State or Province	Street	House or Building Number
W T Black	Dallas	Texas	Longhorn Road	222
W T Black	Kansas City	Kansas	Walnut Avenue	313
W T Black	Kansas City	Missouri	Ellington Avenue	4309
W T Black	Kansas City	Missouri	Walnut Avenue	439
W T Black	Kansas City	Missouri	Walnut Avenue	4309

See also, ¶ 5728.

5730 **Names of numbered streets.** The names of numbered streets are filed in ascending numerical order before street names expressed in words. Ordinal endings (*st, d,* or *th*) are disregarded. (See ¶ 5731 for examples.) Remember that street numbers of ten and less are spelled out in ordinary text.

5731 **Compass directions in street names.** A compass direction in a street name is indexed as it is written.

Name	First Unit In Street Name	Second Unit In Street Name	Third Unit In Street Name	Fourth Unit In Street Name
3d Street	3	Street		
7th Street	7	Street		
7th Street SE	7	Street	SE	
7th Street Southeast	7	Street	Southeast	
South East 7th Street	South	East	7	Street
Southeast 7th Street	Southeast	7	Street	
Southeast Seventh Street	Southeast	Seventh	Street	

5732 **House and building numbers.** House and building numbers written in figures are filed in ascending order. If an address contains both a street address and a building name, the building name is disregarded.

Building Designation	First Unit in Building Designation	Second Unit in Building Designation
Allison Arms	Allison	Arms
Building 1	Building	1
Building 2	Building	2
Building C	Building	C
Cheltenham Club	Cheltenhan	Club

Organizational Names

5733 **Order of indexing units in organizational names.** The words in the name of an organization are indexed in the order in which they are written. There is, however, one exception: When the word *The* appears as the first word of a business name, it is considered the last indexing unit. The same rules apply to business firms, financial institutions, religious institutions, clubs, associations, and the like. The organizational name is filed as it appears in the letterhead, trademark, or the closing lines of letters.

Name	Key Unit 123456789	Unit 2 123456789	Unit 3 123456789
American Historical Association	American	Historical	Association
Collier County Bank	Collier	County	Bank
Community General Hospital	Community	General	Hospital
East Seattle Nursery	East	Seattle	Nursery
East Side Carpet Company	East	Side	Carpet
First Methodist Church	First	Methodist	Church
First National Bank	First	National	Bank
Long Island Lumber	Long	Island	Lumber
The Ritz-Carlton Hotel	RitzCarlton	Hotel	The
Truxton Department Store	Truxton	Department	Store
University of Florida	University	of	Florida

5734 **Personal name within an organizational name.** Organizational names containing personal names are indexed as written; personal names are not transposed. (See, also, ¶ 5749.)

Name	Key Unit 123456789	Unit 2 123456789	Unit 3 123456789	Unit 4 123456789
Juan Estero Insurance Agency	Juan	Estero	Insurance	Agency
Mario Deconda Pizza Parlor	Mario	Deconda	Pizza	Parlor

5735 **Compound words in organizational names.** Compound words in organizational names are indexed as written. Hyphenated words are treated as though written solid.

Name	Key Unit 123456789	Unit 2 123456789	Unit 3 123456789	Unit 4 123456789
New York Deli	New	York	Deli	
Pan American Travel Company	Pan	American	Travel	Company
South West Properties	South	West	Properties	
Southwest Property Management	Southwest	Property	Management	
South-West Property Management Co.	SouthWest	Property	Management	Co

5736 **Married woman's name within an organizational name.** A married woman's name in an organizational name is filed as it is written.

Name	Key Unit 123456789	Unit 2 123456789	Unit 3 123456789	Unit 4 123456789
Mrs. Abbie Dabney's Place	Mrs	Abbie	Dabneys	Place
Mrs. Henderson's Candies	Mrs	Hendersons	Candies	

5737 **Minor words in organizational names.** All words in an organizational name—including minor words such as articles, conjunctions, and prepositions—are indexed in the order in which the organizational name is normally written, except for an initial *the*, which is considered as the last indexing unit. Each word—including minor words—is indexed as a separate unit.

Name	Key Unit 123456789	Unit 2 123456789	Unit 3 123456789	Unit 4 123456789
At the Village Green	At	The	Village	Green
The Green Banana	Green	Banana	The	

5

5738 **Numbers in organizational names.** Numbers written in figures are filed before numbers written in words. Arabic numerals are filed before roman numerals. Numbers written in figures with ordinal endings (1st, 2d, and so on) are indexed without the endings (1, 2, and so on). Inclusive numbers (24-47) are indexed by the lower number only (24).

Numbers spelled out in organizational names are indexed as written and filed alphabetically—after numbers that are written in figures.

Name	Key Unit	Unit 2	Unit 3
	123456789	123456789	123456789
1st Texas Grill	1	Texas	Grill
6-9 Shop	6	Shop	
Chapter 13	Chapter	13	
Chapter XIII	Chapter	XIII	
Fifty-Four Forty Club	FiftyFour	Forty	Club
First Texas Grill	First	Texas	Grill
One Twenty-Three Restaurant	One	TwentyThree	Restaurant
Shipmates' Marker 8	Shipmates	Marker	8
Shipmates' Marker 28	Shipmates	Marker	28
Shipmates' Marker South	Shipmates	Marker	South
Size 6-9 Shop	Size	6	Shop

5739 **Symbols in organizational names.** Each symbol in an organizational name is indexed as a unit and treated as though it were spelled out (¢ = cents, + = plus, and so forth).

Name	Key Unit	Unit 2	Unit 3	Unit 4
	123456789	123456789	123456789	123456789
2 @ 1 Price	2	at	1	Price
The $ Wise Shop	Dollar	Wise	Shop	The
#1 Shop	Number 1	Shop		
Take #s Off	Take	Pounds	Off	

5740 **Hyphenated and coined organizational names.** Each hyphenated or coined word in an organizational name is treated as a single indexing unit.

Name	Key Unit	Unit 2	Unit 3	Unit 4
	123456789	123456789	123456789	123456789
E Z Way Stores	E	Z	Way	Stores
E-Z On Brace Co.	EZ	On	Brace	Co
EZ Ride Cab Co.	EZ	Ride	Cab	Co
Ezzard Charles Gym	Ezzard	Charles	Gym	
Southwestern Properties	Southwestern	Properties		

Name	Key Unit 123456789	Unit 2 123456789	Unit 3 123456789
South-Western Publishing Co	SouthWestern	Publishing	Co
Two-For-The-Show Theater	TwoForTheShow	Theater	

5741 **Punctuation in organizational names.** All punctuation is disregarded when indexing organizational names.

Name	Key Unit 123456789	Unit 2 123456789	Unit 3 123456789	Unit 4 123456789
H. W. Baker Co.	H	W	Baker	Co
Hart, Wynn, and Baker	Hart	Wynn	and	Baker
Hart-Wynn Co.	HartWynn	Co		
Hart-Wynn, Inc.	HartWynn	Inc		

5742 **Titles in organizational names (Miss, Mr., Mrs., Ms., Dr.).** Titles in organizational names are indexed as written.

Name	Key Unit 123456789	Unit 2 123456789	Unit 3 123456789
Doctors' Hospital	Doctors	Hospital	
Dr. Well	Dr	Well	
Miss Bangles Fashions	Miss	Bangles	Fashions
Mr. Bob	Mr	Bob	

5743 **Abbreviations and single letters in organizational names.** Abbreviations and single letters in organizational names are indexed as written. Each is indexed as a separate unit.

Single letters separated by spaces are indexed as separate units. An **acronym,** a pronounceable word formed from the first letters or first few letters of several words (radar, BASIC, laser) is indexed as a single unit regardless of how it is written: closed, with spaces, with or without periods. The call letters of a radio station or television station are indexed as a single unit.

Cross-reference the spelled-out form of the abbreviated form if that will be helpful (*Alcoholics Anonymous* to *AA*; *American Automobile Association* to *AAA*, and so on).

MORE

CONTINUED

Name	Key Unit 123456789	Unit 2 123456789	Unit 3 123456789	Unit 4 123456789
A. A. Able TV	A	A	Able	TV
A Able Inc.	A	Able	Inc	
A. Able Incorporated	A	Able	Incorporated	
Mad Harry's Used Cars	Mad	Harrys	Used	Cars
MADD	MADD			
Madison Ave Theater	Madison	Ave	Theater	
Madison Avenue Bowling	Madison	Avenue	Bowling	
WBBH	WBBH			
WBBH-TV	WBBHTV			
WIXI	WIXI			

5744 **Identical organizational names.** Identical organizational names are indexed by address. The elements of the address are indexed as follows:

Identical Units	City	State or Province	Street	Building Number
Hamburger Hideaway	Covington	Georgia	Hamilton Ave	8436
Hamburger Hideaway	Covington	Kentucky	Garrard St	343
Hamburger Hideaway	Covington	Kentucky	Greenup St	822
Hamburger Hideaway	Covington	Kentucky	Greenup St	1833
Hamburger Hideaway	Denver	Colorado	Walton Ave	245

Governmental Names

5745 **Federal government.** All federal government agencies are indexed under *United States Government.* Each agency is then indexed under the most distinctive word at each governmental level listed in the agency's name, starting with the level (subdivision) of highest rank and working down to the name of the agency itself. If the words *Department of, Bureau of,* and so on, appear at any level, they are indexed as separate units if they are needed.

Written As	Indexed As
Bureau of the Census Department of Commerce	United States Government Commerce Department of Census Bureau of the
Federal Aviation Administration Department of Transportation	United States Government Transportation Department of Aviation Federal Administration

5746 **State and local governments.** The name of the state, province, county, parish, city, town, township, or village is indexed first. If words such as *State of, County of, City of, Department of,* or *Bureau of* are included in the official name of the political entity or agency, and those words are needed for filing purposes, they are considered as separate indexing units.

Written As	Indexed As
Bureau of Plant Inspection Division of Plant Industry Agriculture & Consumer Services Department State of Florida Tallahassee, Florida	Florida State of Agriculture and Consumer Services Department Plant Industry Division of Plant Inspection Bureau of Tallahassee Florida
Division of Meat Inspection Department of Agriculture State of Ohio Cincinnati, Ohio	Ohio State of Agriculture Department of Meat Inspection Division of Cincinnati Ohio
Division of Meat Inspection Department of Agriculture State of Ohio Columbus, Ohio	Ohio State of Agriculture Department of Meat Inspection Division of Columbus Ohio
Detective Division Police Department City of Rochester Rochester, Minnesota	Rochester City of Police Department Detective Division Rochester Minnesota

5747 **Foreign governments.** The first indexing unit of the name of a foreign government entity or agency is the English name of the nation itself (Canada, Mexico, and so forth). If the official name of the nation includes words such as *Republic of* or *Dominion of,* each of these words is included as an indexing unit if needed. Political entities and agencies of foreign governments are indexed in descending hierarchical (rank) order.

At each level, use the most important word as the first indexing unit; other words at that level are used if necessary. The city in which an agency is located (if needed for filing purposes) is the last element to be indexed. However, if all other elements are identical and the same agency has more than one location in the same city, the street address is indexed also.

Written As	Indexed As
Department of Transportation Dominion of Canada	Canada Dominion of Transportation Department of

Cross-Referencing

5748 **The need for cross-referencing.** No set of rules for filing could possibly designate a single category for filing every name and subject so clearly that

MORE

5

everyone would understand and agree upon it. Not every document is confined to a single subject or even to a single name.

Suppose you are neatly set up to file customer names and job applicants by subject; however, a customer writes to place an order *and* apply for a job. Or suppose that you work for a theatrical agency and Thelma Bledsoe writes to say that from now on her professional name will be Rita LaTour. Each of these documents requires cross-referencing.

5749 **Organizational name including personal name.** There are circumstances under which personal names included in organizational names should be cross-referenced. If your firm employs as an attorney the Zwick of the firm Alton, Zwick, and Milton, the correspondence should be filed under *Alton* and cross-referenced under *Zwick*.

The firm of A. B. Kensington, Inc., usually called "Kensington's," should be filed under *A* and cross-referenced under *Kensington* or *Kensington's* or both. (See ¶ 5734.)

5750 **Compound names.** A hyphenated compound name is indexed as a single unit. Each element of a compound name written open is treated as a separate indexing unit. In either case, if there is a possibility that the person or organization may also be known by part of the compound name, the name should be cross-indexed accordingly. For example, the name *Sandi Frazer-Hilton* would be filed under *FrazerHilton* and cross-indexed under *Hilton*. (See ¶ 5720-21 and ¶ 5740.)

Computer Filing Systems

5751 **Computer filing systems.** **Computer filing systems** are used for many large applications. (See the following topics in ¶ 4200: *directory, field, file, filename, path.*)

CHAPTER

INTERNATIONAL BUSINESS AND TRAVEL

INTERNATIONAL BUSINESS AND TRAVEL

International Business Relationships

6001 **International business.** **International business** is no longer characterized as buying foreign goods (importing) and selling domestic goods abroad (exporting); it is an integrated activity in which trading partnerships, joint ventures, mergers, and acquisitions bring people who are initially foreign to each other into close and continuing business relationships.

6002 **Learning about other nations.** Success in any business endeavor requires an understanding of the people with whom one works. It is difficult enough to understand the people we know best; understanding people about whom we know very little is even more difficult. Knowledge about those with whom one is or is to be associated should be the first order of international business.

6003 **Business customs.** Each nation has its customary ways of doing business. Whether you are a host or visitor, misunderstanding can be minimized by the timely discussion of How is it done in your country, How is it done in my country, and How are *we* going to do it?

6004 **Social customs.** Every nation has its own social customs. The best way to cope with them is the timely discussion of What is expected of me in this situation?

6005 **Language.** Only those who have experienced it know the profound feeling of isolation that goes with being the only person in a group who does not know the language being spoken. Take every opportunity to improve your knowledge of languages. Start with a phrase book or electronic interpreter if necessary. Do not be afraid to gesture (being aware that the gesture may *not* be universal), act out, use sign language, ask for help.

If you know the language and others do not, be the one to help them understand. If you are responsible for arrangements, provide an interpreter when one is needed.

International Travel Documents

6006 **Passport.** A **passport** is a document issued by a country's government to its nationals to identify them and certify that they may legally travel to other nations. U.S. nationals are those who owe their allegiance to the U.S. and depend upon it for protection—usually U.S. citizens. U.S. passports are issued by the Department of State. The initial contact in obtaining a passport is as simple as looking for the *Department of State* under *U.S. Government* in the telephone book of a major city or going to the main post office in a city. A travel agent can also provide assistance.

Physically, a passport is a small booklet similar in appearance to the passbooks issued by banks for savings accounts. (See also, ¶ 6007 on visas.)

6007 **Visa.** A **visa** is the permission of a host nation for a visitor to enter for a specific purpose and to remain for a specific period.

Physically, a visa is most usually a rubber-stamped image applied to a page in a passport. It may, however, be a signed, official document.

A U.S. citizen traveling in Europe may need a U.S. passport containing visas provided by Germany, France, and Spain. See ¶ 6006 on passports.

6008 **Tourist card.** **Tourist cards** are issued rather informally at international borders, by airlines, and at the consulates of nations that require them. Currently, Mexico and several South American nations require them. Regulations change from time to time, so it is a good idea to check with the embassy or a consulate of the host nation or with a travel agent or airline representative. Normally, tourist cards are issued where they are needed, with little or no delay, and without the need for a passport. One or two documents that prove citizenship or residence may be required: a birth certificate, voter registration, or driver's license.

6009 **Letter of authorization.** A **letter of authorization** is required by some nations when a child accompanies an adult across an international boundary. Information on letters of authorization is available from the embassy or a consulate of the host nation.

6010 **Money management.** Major credit cards are useful in international travel. Airlines, car companies, and many hotels and restaurants accept them. Check current charges and your credit limit before you leave to be sure you have sufficient credit available for the trip.

Traveler's checks are a safe and widely accepted means of payment when cash or its equivalent is required. Buy them at a U.S. bank before you depart. Expect to pay about 1 percent of the face value as a service charge, unless your bank offers them free as a promotional service. Think carefully about the denominations you buy. Many inexperienced travelers buy too many small-denomination checks.

6011 **Sources of foreign currency.** Foreign currency can be obtained in exchange for U.S. dollars in several places:

- a U.S. bank before departure (although you may have to go to a special department of the main headquarters of the bank).
- a U.S. international airport upon departure or before.
- a **gateway** airport: the international airport through which one enters the host nation.
- a hotel at your destination.
- a bank at your destination.
- money exchange specialists catering to visitors at your destination or in a large metropolitan U.S. city.

Since significant differences in exchange rates among these sources are normal, your travel agent, another travel planner, other travelers familiar with the destination nation, or a current guidebook can be useful in deciding which source to use.

6012 **Foreign exchange rates.** Exchange rates change, not just daily but from hour to hour. Despite their constant fluctuation, changes that are significant to the traveler who is concerned only with personal expenditures usually take place rather slowly. The following table illustrates average exchange rates for the period 1970-1990.

The amount of each foreign currency that could be bought with one U.S. dollar:

		1970	1980	1990
Australia	dollar	1.1136	1.1140	.7813
Canada	dollar	1.0103	1.1693	1.1668
France	franc	5.5200	4.2250	5.4453
Germany	deutsche mark	3.6480	1.8175	1.6157
Italy	lira	623.	856.	1198.
Japan	yen	357.60	226.63	144.79
United Kingdom	pound	.4174	.4302	.5603

MORE

CONTINUED

The cost of one unit of each foreign currency stated in U.S. dollars:

		1970	1980	1990
Australia	dollar	.8980	.8977	1.2799
Canada	dollar	.9893	.8552	.8570
France	franc	.1811	.2367	.1836
Germany	deutsche mark	.2741	.5502	.6189
Italy	lira	.0016	.0012	.0008
Japan	yen	.0028	.0044	.0069
United Kingdom	pound	2.3958	2.3245	1.7847

6013 **Insurance.** A review of your insurance coverage should be part of planning any trip abroad. The place to start is with your personal insurance agent. Additional coverage may be available through your travel agent. First be sure that your normal, personal coverage is adequate and *will be effective while you travel abroad.* Check these categories:

a. regular personal insurance coverage that remains in effect when you travel abroad, offering some (but not all) of the coverage in items c through h following.

b. short-term travel policies that offer some (but rarely all) of the coverage in items c through h following.

c. personal accident and illness.

d. baggage and personal effects.

e. trip cancellation and interruption.

f. default and bankruptcy of travel providers.

g. flight insurance.

h. automobile insurance.

Dates

6014 **Writing dates.** Care should be exercised in writing and interpreting dates, since the most common method of abbreviating dates in the U.S. is not used in other parts of the world. Americans are accustomed to writing *month/day/year*. In most other nations, the custom is to write *day/month/year*. In the first case (U.S.), 9/12/26 means September 12, 1926. In the second case (U.K.), 9/12/26 means 9 December 1926. In the military and abroad, the *day/month/year* format is also used when the month is spelled out: 9 September 1926 or 9 September 26.

6015 **International date line.** The **prime meridian** runs north and south through Greenwich, England. It is the starting point for the worldwide system of time zones. That system consists of 24 zones, each 15 degrees of longitude wide. Halfway around the world, at the center of the +/-12 time zone, is the **international date line:** the 180th meridian. The date changes when one crosses the international date line: add a day going west; subtract a day going east.

Time

6016 **Time zones.** Illustration 6016.1 on page 438 shows differences in times (and dates) that are useful in air travel. There are no columns for sparsely populated time zones in which there are no international airports: +4, +5, +6, +11, -1, -2, -4. Time zones are identified by their major international airports. These airports are listed in ¶ 6021.

The chart can be used to determine corresponding local times and dates. For example, when it is noon in Chicago (ORD), it is 6:00 p.m. in London (LHR) and 3:00 a.m. tomorrow in Tokyo (NRT).

A section of the chart in illustration 6016.1 can be highlighted to show all the times pertinent to an airline flight. The following example charts a 5:20 a.m. flight from LHR that arrives at JFK at 7:32 a.m. and connects with an 8:40 a.m. flight from JFK to SFO. The latter flight arrives at SFO at 9:52 a.m. When the 5:20 a.m. flight leaves LHR, it is 9:20 p.m. *the previous day* at SFO.

-11	-10 HNL	-9 JNU OME	-8 LAX SFO SEA	-7 DEN PHX YYC	-6 ORD DFW MEX	-5 JFK ATL MIA	-3 RIO SAO AEP	0 LHR LGW CAS	+1 ORY FRA OSL	+2 ATH TLV CAI	+3 SVO LED RUH
5p-	6p-	7p-	8p-	9p-	10p-	11p-	1a	4a	5a	6a	7a
6p-	7p-	8p-	9p-	10p-	11p-	Mdnt	2a	5a	6a	7a	8a
7p-	8p-	9p-	10p-	11p-	Mdnt	1a	3a	6a	7a	8a	9a
8p-	9p-	10p-	11p-	Mdnt	1a	2a	4a	7a	8a	9a	10a
9p-	10p-	11p-	Mdnt	1a	2a	3a	5a	8a	9a	10a	11a
10p-	11p-	Mdnt	1a	2a	3a	4a	6a	9a	10a	11a	Noon
11p-	Mdnt	1a	2a	3a	4a	5a	7a	10a	11a	Noon	1p
Mdnt	1a	2a	3a	4a	5a	6a	8a	11a	Noon	1p	2p
1a	2a	3a	4a	5a	6a	7a	9a	Noon	1p	2p	3p
2a	3a	4a	5a	6a	7a	8a	10a	1p	2p	3p	4p
3a	4a	5a	6a	7a	8a	9a	11a	2p	3p	4p	5p
4a	5a	6a	7a	8a	9a	10a	Noon	3p	4p	5p	6p
5a	6a	7a	8a	9a	10a	11a	1p	4p	5p	6p	7p
6a	7a	8a	9a	10a	11a	Noon	2p	5p	6p	7p	8p
7a	8a	9a	10a	11a	Noon	1p	3p	6p	7p	8p	9p
8a	9a	10a	11a	Noon	1p	2p	4p	7p	8p	9p	10p

←[+] [-]→

+7 BKK JKT	+8 HKG SIN TPE	+9 NRT HND OSA	+10 SYD MEL VVO	+/-12 AUK WLZ	DATE	-11	-10 HNL	-9 JNU OME	-8 LAX SFO SEA	-7 DEN PHX YYC	-6 ORD DFW MEX	-5 JFK ATL MIA	-3 RIO SAO AEP	0 LHR LGW CAS	+1 ORY FRA OSL	+2 ATH TLV CAI	+3 SVO LED RUH	
7p-	8p-	9p-	10p-	Mdnt		1a-	2a-	3a-	4a-	5a-	6a-	7a-	9a-	Noon-	1p-	2p-	3p-	Y
8p-	9p-	10p-	11p-	1a		2a-	3a-	4a-	5a-	6a-	7a-	8a-	10a-	1p-	2p-	3p-	4p-	E
9p-	10p-	11p-	Mdnt	2a		3a-	4a-	5a-	6a-	7a-	8a-	9a-	11a-	2p-	3p-	4p-	5p-	S
10p-	11p-	Mdnt	1a	3a		4a-	5a-	6a-	7a-	8a-	9a-	10a-	Noon-	3p-	4p-	5p-	6p-	T
11p-	Mdnt	1a	2a	4a		5a-	6a-	7a-	8a-	9a-	10a-	11a-	1p-	4p-	5p-	6p-	7p-	E
Mdnt	1a	2a	3a	5a		6a-	7a-	8a-	9a-	10a-	11a-	Noon-	2p-	5p-	6p-	7p-	8p-	R
1a	2a	3a	4a	6a		7a-	8a-	9a-	10a-	11a-	Noon-	1p-	3p-	6p-	7p-	8p-	9p-	D
2a	3a	4a	5a	7p		8a-	9a-	10a-	11a-	Noon-	1p-	2p-	4p-	7p-	8p-	9p-	10p-	A
3a	4a	5a	6a	8a		9a-	10a-	11a-	Noon-	1p-	2p-	3p-	5p-	8p-	9p-	10p-	11p-	Y
4a	5a	6a	7a	9a		10a-	11a-	Noon-	1p-	2p-	3p-	4p-	6p-	9p-	10p-	11p-	Mdnt	
5a	6a	7a	8a	10a		11a-	Noon-	1p-	2p-	3p-	4p-	5p-	7p-	10p-	11p-	Mdnt	1a	
6a	7a	8a	9a	11a		Noon-	1p-	2p-	3p-	4p-	5p-	6p-	8p-	11p-	Mdnt	1a	2a	
7a	8a	9a	10a	Noon		1p-	2p-	3p-	4p-	5p-	6p-	7p-	9p-	Mdnt	1a	2a	3a	
8a	9a	10a	11a	1p		2p-	3p-	4p-	5p-	6p-	7p-	8p-	10p-	1a	2a	3a	4a	
9a	10a	11a	Noon	2p		3p-	4p-	5p-	6p-	7p-	8p-	9p-	11p-	2a	3a	4a	5a	
10a	11a	Noon	1p	3p		4p-	5p-	6p-	7p-	8p-	9p-	10p-	Mdnt	3a	4a	5a	6a	
11a	Noon	1p	2p	4p		5p-	6p-	7p-	8p-	9p-	10p-	11p-	1a	4a	5a	6a	7a	
Noon	1p	2p	3p	5p		6p-	7p-	8p-	9p-	10p-	11p-	Mdnt	2a	5a	6a	7a	8a	
1p	2p	3p	4p	6p		7p-	8p-	9p-	10p-	11p-	Mdnt	1a	3a	6a	7a	8a	9a	
2p	3p	4p	5p	7p		8p-	9p-	10p-	11p-	Mdnt	1a	2a	4a	7a	8a	9a	10a	T
3p	4p	5p	6p	8p		9p-	10p-	11p-	Mdnt	1a	2a	3a	5a	8a	9a	10a	11a	O
4p	5p	6p	7p	9p		10p-	11p-	Mdnt	1a	2a	3a	4a	6a	9a	10a	11a	Noon	D
5p	6p	7p	8p	10p		11p-	Mdnt	1a	2a	3a	4a	5a	7a	10a	11a	Noon	1p	A
6p	7p	8p	9p	11p		Mdnt	1a	2a	3a	4a	5a	6a	8a	11a	Noon	1p	2p	Y
7p	8p	9p	10p	Mdnt+		1a	2a	3a	4a	5a	6a	7a	9a	Noon	1p	2p	3p	
8p	9p	10p	11p	1a+		2a	3a	4a	5a	6a	7a	8a	10a	1p	2p	3p	4p	
9p	10p	11p	Mdnt+	2a+		3a	4a	5a	6a	7a	8a	9a	11a	2p	3p	4p	5p	
10p	11p	Mdnt+	1a+	3a+		4a	5a	6a	7a	8a	9a	10a	Noon	3p	4p	5p	6p	
11p	Mdnt+	1a+	2a+	4a+		5a	6a	7a	8a	9a	10a	11a	1p	4p	5p	6p	7p	
Mdnt+	1a+	2a+	3a+	5a+		6a	7a	8a	9a	10a	11a	Noon	2p	5p	6p	7p	8p	
1a+	2a+	3a+	4a+	6a+		7a	8a	9a	10a	11a	Noon	1p	3p	6p	7p	8p	9p	
2a+	3a+	4a+	5a+	7a+		8a	9a	10a	11a	Noon	1p	2p	4p	7p	8p	9p	10p	
3a+	4a+	5a+	6a+	8a+		9a	10a	11a	Noon	1p	2p	3p	5p	8p	9p	10p	11p	
4a+	5a+	6a+	7a+	9a+		10a	11a	Noon	1p	2p	3p	4p	6p	9p	10p	11p	Mdnt+	
5a+	6a+	7a+	8a+	10a+		11a	Noon	1p	2p	3p	4p	5p	7p	10p	11p	Mdnt+	1a+	
6a+	7a+	8a+	9a+	11a+		Noon	1p	2p	3p	4p	5p	6p	8p	11p	Mdnt+	1a+	2a+	
7a+	8a+	9a+	10a+	Noon+		1p	2p	3p	4p	5p	6p	7p	9p	Mdnt+	1a+	2a+	3a+	
8a+	9a+	10a+	11a+	1p+		2p	3p	4p	5p	6p	7p	8p	10p	1a+	2a+	3a+	4a+	
9a+	10a+	11a+	Noon+	2p+		3p	4p	5p	6p	7p	8p	9p	11p	2a+	3a+	4a+	5a+	
10a+	11a+	Noon+	1p+	3p+		4p	5p	6p	7p	8p	9p	10p	Mdnt+	3a+	4a+	5a+	6a+	T
11a+	Noon+	1p+	2p+	4p+		5p	6p	7p	8p	9p	10p	11p	1a+	4a+	5a+	6a+	7p+	O
Noon+	1p+	2p+	3p+	5p+		6p	7p	8p	9p	10p	11p	Mdnt+	2a+	5a+	6a+	7p+	8a+	M
1p+	2p+	3p+	4p+	6p+		7p	8p	9p	10p	11p	Mdnt+	1a+	3a+	6a+	7p+	8a+	9a+	O
2p+	3p+	4p+	5p+	7p+		8p	9p	10p	11p	Mdnt+	1a+	2a+	4a+	7p+	8a+	9a+	10a+	R
3p+	4p+	5p+	6p+	8p+		9p	10p	11p	Mdnt+	1a+	2a+	3a+	5a+	8a+	9a+	10a+	11a+	R
4p+	5p+	6p+	7p+	9p+		10p	11p	Mdnt+	1a+	2a+	3a+	4a+	6a+	9a+	10a+	11a+	Noon+	O
5p+	6p+	7p+	8p+	10p+		11p	Mdnt+	1a+	2a+	3a+	4a+	5a+	7p+	10a+	11a+	Noon+	1p+	W
6p+	7p+	8p+	9p+	11p+		Mdnt+	1a+	2a+	3a+	4a+	5a+	6a+	8a+	11a+	Noon+	1p+	2p+	
7p+	8p+	9p+	10p+	MDNT		1a+	2a+	3a+	4a+	5a+	6a+	7a+	9a+	Noon+	1p+	2p+	3p+	
8p+	9p+	10p+	11p+	1A		2a+	3a+	4a+	5a+	6a+	7a+	8a+	10a+	1p+	2p+	3p+	4p+	
9p+	10p+	11p+	MDNT	2A		3a+	4a+	5a+	6a+	7a+	8a+	9a+	11a+	2p+	3p+	4p+	5p+	
10p+	11p+	MDNT	1A	3A		4a+	5a+	6a+	7a+	8a+	9a+	10a+	Noon+	3p+	4p+	5p+	6p+	
11p+	MDNT	1A	2A	4A		5a+	6a+	7a+	8a+	9a+	10a+	11a+	1p+	4p+	5p+	6p+	7p+	
MDNT	1A	2A	3A	5A		6a+	7a+	8a+	9a+	10a+	11a+	Noon+	2p+	5p+	6p+	7p+	8p+	
1A	2A	3A	4A	6A		7a+	8a+	9a+	10a+	11a+	Noon+	1p+	3p+	6p+	7p+	8p+	9p+	
2A	3A	4A	5A	7A		8a+	9a+	10a+	11a+	Noon+	1p+	2p+	4p+	7p+	8p+	9p+	10p+	
3A	4A	5A	6A	8A		9a+	10a+	11a+	Noon+	1p+	2p+	3p+	5p+	8p+	9p+	10p+	11p+	
4A	5A	6A	7A	9A		10a+	11a+	Noon+	1p+	2p+	3p+	4p+	6p+	9p+	10p+	11p+	MDNT	
5A	6A	7A	8A	10A		11a+	Noon+	1p+	2p+	3p+	4p+	5p+	7p+	10p+	11p+	MDNT	1A	
6A	7A	8A	9A	11A		Noon+	1p+	2p+	3p+	4p+	5p+	6p+	8p+	11p+	MDNT	1A	2A	D
7A	8A	9A	10A	NOON		1p+	2p+	3p+	4p+	5p+	6p+	7p+	9p+	MDNT	1A	2A	3A	A
8A	9A	10A	11A	1P		2p+	3p+	4p+	5p+	6p+	7p+	8p+	10p+	1A	2A	3A	4A	Y
9A	10A	11A	NOON	2P		3p+	4p+	5p+	6p+	7p+	8p+	9p+	11p+	2A	3A	4A	5A	
10A	11A	NOON	1P	3P		4p+	5p+	6p+	7p+	8p+	9p+	10p+	MDNT	3A	4A	5A	6A	A
11A	NOON	1P	2P	4P		5p+	6p+	7p+	8p+	9p+	10p+	11p+	1A	4A	5A	6A	7A	F
NOON	1P	2P	3P	5P		6p+	7p+	8p+	9p+	10p+	11p+	MDNT	2A	5A	6A	7A	8A	T
1P	2P	3P	4P	6P		7p+	8p+	9p+	10p+	11p+	MDNT	1A	3A	6A	7A	8A	9A	E
2P	3P	4P	5P	7P		8p+	9p+	10p+	11p+	MDNT	1A	2A	4A	7A	8A	9A	10A	R
3P	4P	5P	6P	8P		9p+	10p+	11p+	MDNT	1A	2A	3A	5A	8A	9A	10A	11A	
4P	5P	6P	7P	9P		10p+	11p+	MDNT	1A	2A	3A	4A	6A	9A	10A	11A	NOON	

Illustration 6016.1 Time and Date Chart

6017 **Military time.** The 24-hour clock is used by the U.S. military, by several other nations (as the official system), and by the U.S. travel industry.

Civilian Time	Military Time	Civilian Time	Military Time
1a	0100 (oh-one-hundred)	1p	1300 (thirteen-hundred)
2a	0200 (oh-two-hundred)	2p	1400 (fourteen-hundred)
3a	0300	3:15p	1515 (fifteen-fifteen)
4a	0400	4p	1600
5a	0500	5p	1700
6a	0600	6p	1800
7a	0700	7p	1900
8a	0800	8p	2000 (twenty-hundred)
9a	0900	9p	2100
10a	1000	10p	2200
11a	1100	11p	2300
12 Noon	1200	12:00 Midnight	2400
		12:01a	0001 (triple-oh-one)
		12:20a	0020 (double-oh-twenty)

Air Travel

6018 **Airline tickets.** **Airline tickets** are written by employees of each individual airline and by some 37,000 agents, mostly travel agencies. The agents are authorized by and write tickets through Airlines Reporting Corporation, a consortium of participating airlines.

Several ticket forms are used by the airlines and supplied to authorized agents by ARC, but all are similar in format. Each ticket is actually a booklet consisting of

- **Front Cover** — The ticket is not valid unless the front cover is affixed.
- **Notice Page** — Sets forth the terms of the agreement binding the carrier and the passenger and applicable laws, rules, and regulations.
- **Auditor's Coupon** — Contains the information necessary for financial settlement.
- **Agent's Coupon** — Retained by the agent who writes the ticket.

MORE

ENDORSEMENTS/RESTRICTIONS (CARBON) | ORIGIN/DESTINATION | BOOKING REFERENCE | FROM/ TO
CONJUNCTION TICKET(S) | AUDITOR'S COUPON | CARRIER | FARE CALCULATION
NAME OF PASSENGER NOT TRANSFERRABLE | ISSUED IN EXCHANGE FOR | DATE OF ISSUE | PLACE OF ISSUE - AGENCY
COUPONS NOT VALID BEFORE 1 | 2 | CARRIER FORM & SERIAL NO. PLACE DATE AGENTS CODE
COUPONS NOT VALID AFTER 1 | 2 | TICKET DESIGNATOR | TOUR CODE
X/O | NOT GOOD FOR PASSAGE | CARRIER | FLT/CLASS | DATE | TIME | STATUS | FARE BASIS | ALLOW
FROM
TO
TO | COMMISSION | TAX
PRESS FIRMLY—PRINT CLEARLY
COMM. RATE | FARE
FORM OF PAYMENT
IT IS UNLAWFUL TO PURCHASE OR RESELL THIS TICKET FROM/TO ANY ENTITY OTHER THAN THE ISSUING CARRIER OR ITS AUTHORIZED AGENTS
PASSENGER TICKET & BAGGAGE CHECK - ISSUED BY
SUBJECT TO CONDITIONS OF CONTRACT ON PASSENGER COUPON
FARE | TAX | TAX | ENCODE
EQUIV. FARE PD. | TAX | TOTAL
TAX

Illustration 6018.1 Form for Auditor's Coupon: Two-Flight Ticket

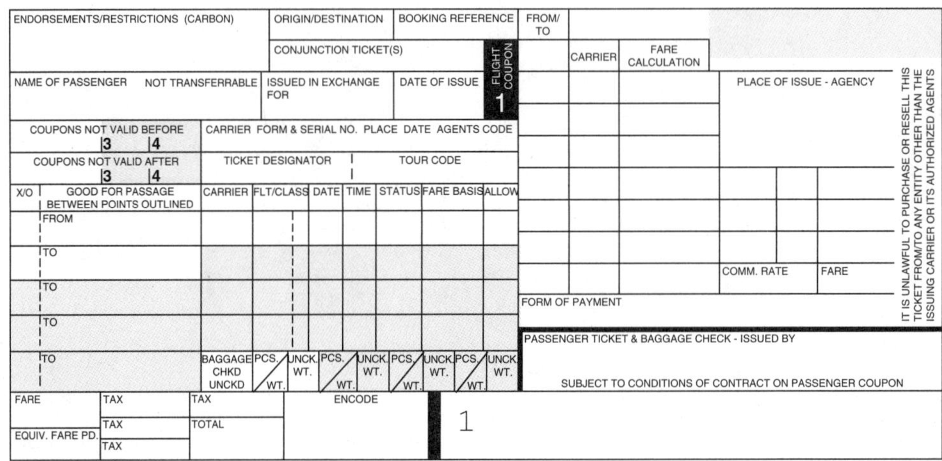

ENDORSEMENTS/RESTRICTIONS (CARBON) | ORIGIN/DESTINATION | BOOKING REFERENCE | FROM/ TO
CONJUNCTION TICKET(S) | FLIGHT COUPON 1 | CARRIER | FARE CALCULATION
NAME OF PASSENGER NOT TRANSFERRABLE | ISSUED IN EXCHANGE FOR | DATE OF ISSUE | PLACE OF ISSUE - AGENCY
COUPONS NOT VALID BEFORE 3 | 4 | CARRIER FORM & SERIAL NO. PLACE DATE AGENTS CODE
COUPONS NOT VALID AFTER 3 | 4 | TICKET DESIGNATOR | TOUR CODE
X/O | GOOD FOR PASSAGE BETWEEN POINTS OUTLINED | CARRIER | FLT/CLASS | DATE | TIME | STATUS | FARE BASIS | ALLOW
FROM
TO
TO
TO
TO | BAGGAGE CHKD UNCKD | PCS. WT. | UNCK. WT. | PCS. WT. | UNCK. WT. | PCS. WT. | UNCK. WT. | PCS. WT. | UNCK. WT.
COMM. RATE | FARE
FORM OF PAYMENT
IT IS UNLAWFUL TO PURCHASE OR RESELL THIS TICKET FROM/TO ANY ENTITY OTHER THAN THE ISSUING CARRIER OR ITS AUTHORIZED AGENTS
PASSENGER TICKET & BAGGAGE CHECK - ISSUED BY
SUBJECT TO CONDITIONS OF CONTRACT ON PASSENGER COUPON
FARE | TAX | TAX | ENCODE | 1
EQUIV. FARE PD. | TAX | TOTAL
TAX

Illustration 6018.2 Form for Flight Coupon 1: Four-Flight Ticket

6

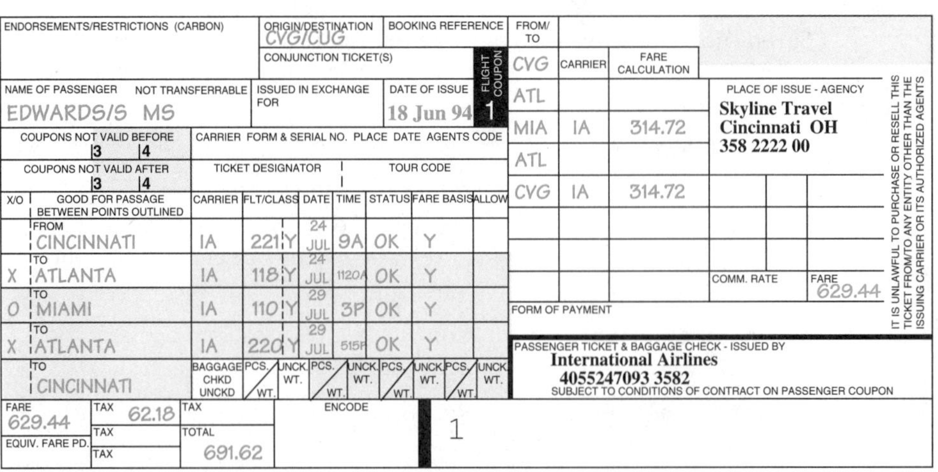

ENDORSEMENTS/RESTRICTIONS (CARBON) | ORIGIN/DESTINATION CVG/CVG | BOOKING REFERENCE | FROM/ TO
CONJUNCTION TICKET(S) | FLIGHT COUPON 1

FROM/TO	CARRIER	FARE CALCULATION
CVG		
ATL		
MIA	IA	314.72
ATL		
CVG	IA	314.72

NAME OF PASSENGER NOT TRANSFERRABLE: EDWARDS/S MS | ISSUED IN EXCHANGE FOR | DATE OF ISSUE: 18 Jun 94

PLACE OF ISSUE - AGENCY: **Skyline Travel Cincinnati OH 358 2222 00**

COUPONS NOT VALID BEFORE 3 | 4 | CARRIER FORM & SERIAL NO. PLACE DATE AGENTS CODE
COUPONS NOT VALID AFTER 3 | 4 | TICKET DESIGNATOR | TOUR CODE

X/O	GOOD FOR PASSAGE BETWEEN POINTS OUTLINED	CARRIER	FLT/CLASS	DATE	TIME	STATUS	FARE BASIS	ALLOW
	FROM CINCINNATI	IA	221 Y	24 JUL	9A	OK	Y	
X	TO ATLANTA	IA	118 Y	24 JUL	1120A	OK	Y	
O	TO MIAMI	IA	110 Y	29 JUL	3P	OK	Y	
X	TO ATLANTA	IA	220 Y	29 JUL	515P	OK	Y	
	TO CINCINNATI	BAGGAGE CHKD UNCKD	PCS. WT.	UNCK. WT.	PCS. WT.	UNCK. WT.	PCS. WT. UNCK. WT.	PCS. WT. UNCK. WT.

COMM. RATE | FARE 629.44
FORM OF PAYMENT
IT IS UNLAWFUL TO PURCHASE OR RESELL THIS TICKET FROM/TO ANY ENTITY OTHER THAN THE ISSUING CARRIER OR ITS AUTHORIZED AGENTS
PASSENGER TICKET & BAGGAGE CHECK - ISSUED BY **International Airlines 4055247093 3582**
SUBJECT TO CONDITIONS OF CONTRACT ON PASSENGER COUPON
FARE 629.44 | TAX 62.18 | TAX | ENCODE | 1
EQUIV. FARE PD. | TAX | TOTAL 691.62
TAX

Illustration 6018.3 Flight Coupon 1: Completed Four-Flight Ticket

- **Flight Coupons** — One coupon for each flight (leg/segment) of the trip covered by the ticket. One flight coupon is surrendered by the passenger each time he or she boards a flight.
- **Passenger's Coupon** — Retained by the passenger as a complete record of the transaction and the trip.

Illustration 6018.3 shows Flight Coupon 1 (Cincinnati → Atlanta) from a round-trip ticket from Cincinnati to Miami. The complete trip consists of four flights:

- Cincinnati (CVG) → Atlanta (ATL)
- Atlanta → Miami (MIA)
- Miami → Atlanta
- Atlanta → Cincinnati

6019 **Conjunction tickets.** Sequentially numbered *but otherwise identical* ticket forms may be combined. Such combinations are called *conjunction tickets*.

Highlighted areas indicate preferred combinations. Numbers in brackets indicate unused (voided) flight coupons.

Number of Flights	Number of Ticket Forms in Conjunction Ticket	
	Two-Flight Forms	Four-Flight Forms
1	1 [1]	1 [3]
2	1	1 [2]
3	2 [1]	1 [1]
4	2	1
5	3 [1]	2 [3]
6	3	2 [2]
7	4 [1]	2 [1]
8	4	2
9	5 [1]	3 [3]

Illustration 6019.1 Conjunction Tickets

Although **computer-generated tickets** are similar in size and format to manually-prepared tickets, the forms are not identical—nor are they interchangeable. Some computer systems use special four-flight forms, automatically voiding unused flight coupons. Other computer systems print flight coupons individually, producing only those that are needed.

6020 **Air travel itinerary.** An **itinerary** is an outline of a trip. It may include only the information on air travel or may be expanded to include information on lodging, cars, meals, meetings, and the like. It may be prepared by a travel agency, the traveler, or someone who assists the traveler (usually an administrative assistant).

Skyline
Travel
Agency

555 Oakley Square
Cincinnati, OH 45227
513-555-5511

June 18, 1994

Itinerary

Ms. Sheila Edwards

July 24 travel:	Leave Cincinnati 9:00 a.m.	International Flight 221 Boeing 737—Seat 15C Snack Arrive Atlanta 10:04 a.m.
	Leave Atlanta 11:20 a.m.	International Flight 118 Boeing 727—Seat 22D Lunch Arrive Miami 12:30 p.m.

July 24-28 lodging: Attaway Arms Motel Miami.

July 24-29 car: Avis economy, unlimited free mileage, confirmation number 907734526.

July 29 travel:	Leave Miami 3:00 p.m.	International Flight 110 Boeing 727—Seat 18B Snack Arrive Atlanta 4:12 p.m.
	Leave Atlanta 5:15 p.m.	International Flight 220 Boeing 737—Seat 16A Dinner Arrive Cincinnati 6:22 p.m.

6021 **International airports (selected).** Numbers in parentheses rank the world's busiest airports by number of passengers. Others are selected because of their strategic locations.

City	Location	Code	Airport
Amsterdam	Netherlands	AMS	Schipohl (16)
Athens	Greece	ATH	
Atlanta (8)	GA, USA	ATL	
Auckland	New Zealand	AKL	
Bangkok (19)	Thailand	BKK	
Buenos Aires	Argentina	AEP	
Cairo	Egypt	CAI	
Calgary	Alberta, Canada	YYC	
Casablanca	Morocco	CAS	
Chicago	IL, USA	ORD	O'Hare International (4)
Copenhagen (23)	Denmark	CPH	
Dallas/Ft. Worth (7)	TX, USA	DFW	
Denver (25)	CO, USA	DEN	
Frankfurt (3)	Germany	FRA	
Fukuoka (21)	Japan	FUK	
Hong Kong (13)	Hong Kong	HKG	
Honolulu	HI,USA	HNL	
Jakarta	Indonesia	JKT	
Juneau	AK, USA	JNU	
London	United Kingdom	LGW	Gatwick (10)
		LHR	Heathrow (1)
Los Angeles (14)	CA, USA	LAX	
Madrid	Spain	MAD	
Melbourne	Australia	MEL	
Mexico City	Mexico	MEX	
Miami	FL, USA	MIA	
Moscow	Russia	SVO	
Munich-Riem (26)	Germany	MUC	
New York	NY, USA	LGA	La Guardia
		JFK	John F. Kennedy
Nome	AL, USA	OME	
Osaka (6)	Japan	OSA	
Oslo	Norway	OSL	
Paris	France	CDG	Charles DeGaulle (9)
		ORY	Orly (5)
Phoenix	AZ, USA	PHX	
Rio de Janeiro	Brazil	RIO	
Riyadh	Saudi Arabia	RUH	
Rome	Italy	FCO	Flumicino (15)
St. Petersburg	Russia	LED	
San Francisco (20)	CA, USA	SFO	
São Paulo	Brazil	SAO	
Seattle	WA, USA	SEA	
Shanghai	China	SHA	

MORE

CONTINUED

City	Location	Code	Airport
Singapore (18)	Singapore	SIN	
Stockholm	Sweden	ARN	Arlanda (17)
Sydney (24)	Australia	SYD	
Taipei	Taiwan	TPE	
Tel Aviv	Israel	TLV	
Tokyo	Japan	HND	Haneda (2)
		NRT	Narita (12)
Toronto (11)	Ontario, Canada	YTO	
Vladivostok	Russia	VVO	
Wellington	New Zealand	WLG	
Zurich (22)	Switzerland	ZRH	

CHAPTER 7

GETTING THE JOB—GETTING AHEAD

GETTING THE JOB

Finding an Opening

7001 **Large office or small?** The modern office may vary in size and specialty; however, the kind of office work will be similar in each. Office workers may handle many and various duties including appointment scheduling, routine correspondence, general accounting, telephone, and reception.

Employment opportunities exist in many situations that require various abilities.

- **Traditional small offices.** Single doctor, lawyer, and CPA practices are still numerous today. Such small offices may have one to three individuals practicing the same, or different, specialties. Employees may handle a variety of duties each day.
- **Medium-sized offices where many employers work together.** These offices employ more workers who may share responsibilities, or specific tasks may be assigned to each office worker.
- **Large corporate offices.** In such office settings, office workers are generally assigned to specific departments or divisions with very specialized tasks. One employee might assist with the complex duty of organizing the delivery schedule, while another might work solely in the accounting department.

7002 **Personal interests.** The choice of fields in which to work is vast. Careful thought should be given to areas of enjoyment, knowledge, and interest. For example, enjoyment in working with people and an interest in sales may lead to job satisfaction by working in an automobile dealership, employment office, art gallery, or retail shopping mall.

7003 **Personal abilities.** To be successful in finding employment as an office worker, one of the first things to know is what employers are looking for. The following skills are the ones most requested by employers today:

- **Basic academic skills.** These are the ability to read, write, compute, and reason. Today, the lack of these skills is a problem for many office workers. Correct grammar usage and spelling are a must for the production of excellent office correspondence.
- **Secretarial skills.** These are the ability to keyboard quickly and precisely, to transcribe accurately from machine dictation, to arrange material attractively on a keyed page, to edit quickly and reformat previously entered text, to file and retrieve materials, and to use professional telephone techniques.
- **Human relations.** These skills involve the ability to deal with people (whether a supervisor, fellow worker, or customer) in a pleasant, friendly manner. It is important that all interactions be smooth and agreeable. Employers are looking for office workers who keep a positive and cheerful attitude, even in times of stress.
- **Specific job knowledge and experience.** It is a surprise to many to find that specific abilities, while desirable, are ranked as the least important for today's office employee to possess. It is not that such skills are unimportant. Rather, basic academic skills, secretarial skills, and human relations skills are a priority. If an employee has these basic skills, most employers are willing to train that employee for more specific skills related to each job. The employee is considered a good investment. Nevertheless, additional business skills (knowledge of business terminology and actual work experience in the specific field) will make any applicant the strongest possible candidate for a job opening.

7004 **Advertised openings.** During the job search, remember that job opportunities should be open to all persons—regardless of sex, race, ethnic heritage, religion, creed, age, physical disability, or other minority status.

Many job openings are advertised or posted. Such notices of office positions are found in many places.

- The classified section of a newspaper.
- Public or private employment agencies. (WARNING: When using an employment agency, know who pays the agency fee, if there is one. Many times the employer pays the agency to locate qualified individuals. It is not necessary for an individual to pay such fees.)
- School bulletin boards or placement offices.
- Magazines, professional journals, and periodicals.
- Bulletin boards in personnel offices.

7005 **Unadvertised openings.** There are several ways to find unadvertised openings.

- **Talk with family or friends.** They may know of employment opportunities in a particular field.
- **Visit personnel offices of employers.** Since personnel offices are responsible for posting and advertising all employment openings, a visit will often provide valuable advance information on upcoming openings.
- **Look for new or expanding office facilities.** The local newspaper often contains information regarding the opening of new offices, businesses, or departments within a university. The opening or expansion of any of these would require additional personnel. Once you know of such possibilities, a visit or job inquiry/application letter is the next step (see illustrations 7008.1 and 7008.2 on pages 450-451). The application letter may be printed on cream-colored, gray, or beige paper. Using such colored paper for the inquiry/application letter, envelope, and resume can make your application stand out from the rest; however, keep the overall look professional, not garish. The final package sent to the employer should contain no errors.
- **Review the yellow pages of the telephone directory to find potential employers.** Once a list of possibilities has been compiled, send a job inquiry/application letter along with a resume to each company on the list. (See illustrations 7007.1 [page 449] and 7008.1-08.2 [pages 450 and 451].)

Applying for the Job

7006 **Application steps.** There are several steps to be taken as part of the application process for any job. All steps will not be required by each employer. However, all steps will be required by some employers; therefore, it will help to be knowledgeable of each possible step.

7007 **Résumé.** The **résumé** should always be neatly keyed and printed. It provides a written picture of experience, skills, and abilities (see illustrations 7007.1 and 5632.2). The résumé is sometimes referred to as a personal data sheet. The résumé is usually sent with a job application letter (to apply for a specific position) or a job inquiry/application letter (to inquire as to possible openings).

If the job application letter is printed on light-colored stationery, the résumé should be printed on the same color and kind of paper. Putting the job application letter and résumé on colored paper can make your application stand out from the rest. In addition, the careful, tasteful, and creative use of a variety of fonts within the résumé will also add to the attention it may receive. (See illustrations 7007.1 and 5632.2.)

The résumé will consist of the following general sections:

MORE

CONTINUED

- **Personal information.** Include name, address, and telephone number. Review this information for accuracy. Once, information such as height, weight, marital status, number of children, birth date, health, and birthplace were included in the résumé. However, recent laws preventing discrimination in hiring have made these items optional.
- **Education.** Include the degrees earned (most recent first), dates of school attendance, institution (high school, college, or university name) where degree was awarded, location of school (city and state), educational major (minor optional), and month/year degree was awarded.
- **Work experience.** Include the dates of employment (most recent first), position title, company name, and location (city and state). Optional items in this category include name and title of your direct supervisor, job duties and responsibilities. When you do not have much paid work experience, list volunteer work in this category, clearly indicating that the work was *as a volunteer*.
- **Special skills.** Information in this category includes specific courses taken or skills mastered that are relevant to the job.
- **Other categories.** While education, work experience, and skills are always included on a résumé, the following categories are optional; choose among them to present the "written picture" in the best light possible.
  - High school or college activities. List membership in any organizations or clubs; indicate offices held, years of membership, special activities organized, and so forth.
  - Special honors or awards. List any special honors or awards received. This category helps your résumé stand out from the rest.
  - Service to the community. Include any community activities, professional memberships, and the like.
  - Military service. Include the branch of service, rank, muster dates, military occupation or specialty, and any awards or honors.
  - Hobbies or special interests.
- **References.** Obtain permission from all individuals before you use their names as references. You should feel certain that each one will know how to stress your particular skills. Indicate name, position, place of employment, business address, and telephone number for each reference.

Although each résumé contains similar categories, contents of the résumé may vary depending upon the available position. For example, a position in an accounting office would call for math, bookkeeping, and electronic spreadsheet skills. A position at the reception desk would call for human relations skills and good telephone techniques. Consider the employer reading the résumé; make certain that all questions are answered. As work experience and activities continue over the years, the résumé will grow. However, remember to maintain a brief and concise format.

Illustration 7007.1
Sample Résumé

SCOTT McMEEKIN
9090 Southwest 85th Avenue
Miami, FL 33156-1900
(305) 555-0511

Education

September, 19— to June, 19—	**Associate of Science,** Wolfson Campus, Miami-Dade Community College, Miami, FL Institute for Office Professionals Graduated June, 19—.
September, 19— to June, 19—	**Diploma,** Coral Gables High School, Coral Gables, FL, Business Education Major Graduated June, 19—.

Work Experience

August, 19— to Present	**Cook, CHICKEN SHACK,** Miami, FL Mr. Louis Monzon, Manager. This position has helped me pay for my college education.
April, 19— to Present	**Volunteer, BAPTIST HOSPITAL,** Miami, FL Dr. Castell Bryant, Volunteer Coordinator Duties: Data entry on the IBM personal computer, using WordPerfect, Lotus 1-2-3, and Pagemaker in a Windows environment; filing; telephone answering; deliveries; handling candy and magazine cart.

Special Skills

Keyboarding (60 wpm)
Windows experience on microcomputer.
Software used includes word processing (WordPerfect), spreadsheet (Lotus 1-2-3), and desktop publishing (Pagemaker).

SCOTT McMEEKIN
Page 2

College Activities

Fall, 19—	**Assistant Editor** **METROPOLIS** (school newspaper)
Fall, 19— to Summer, 19—	**Pi Theta Kappa Honorary Society** President (19—)

Special Awards

19—	**Silver Knight Winner, Business** THE MIAMI HERALD

References

Castell Bryant, M.D.
Volunteer Coordinator
Baptist Hospital
8900 Floral Avenue
Miami, FL 33156-8900
(305) 555-8076

Mr. Louis Monzon
Manager
Chicken Shack
11905 Magnolia Drive
Miami, FL 33176-1109
(305) 555-1191

Ms. Georgie Willford
Department Chair
Institute for Office Professionals
Wolfson Campus, Miami-Dade Community College
300 Northeast Second Avenue
Miami, FL 33132-3300
(305) 555-5800

7008 **Application letter.** The application letter introduces the résumé to the prospective employer. It points out special skills and abilities and requests an interview. There are two types of application letters. The first is a job

MORE

inquiry/application letter; this type of letter is written to determine if there are any employment openings that will fit your skills. (See illustration 7008.1.)

The second type is an application letter to a prospective employer written for a specific position that is vacant. The application letter in illustration 7008.2 is written in answer to the newspaper advertisement shown below. The application letter must get the reader's attention.

Look at the first paragraph in illustrations 7008.1 and 7008.2 for attention-getting ideas. Let creativity flow in attracting attention to YOU. Also, note in illustration 7008.2 the applicant, Scott McMeekin, took the time to call the number on the ad not only to get the address, but also to ask what kind of business it was so that he could emphasize the appropriate skills and training in his application letter.

EXECUTIVE SECRETARY
LET'S BUILD A FUTURE TOGETHER!

Good human relations skills,
Microcomputer skills
WordPerfect software
Top pay

ZCM PRODUCTIONS
Call 555-2789

Highlight special qualifications and special skills, education, or experience that make you the best candidate for the position. Elaborate on specific items in your résumé. Ask for immediate action in the final paragraph of the application letter. The request should be appropriate to the position. Such suggestions as "You may reach me during. . ." or "I can come for an interview on Friday" are good action phrases.

7

Illustration 7008.1
Job Inquiry/Application Letter

9090 Southwest 85th Avenue
Miami, FL 33156-1900
June 1, 19–

Ms. Annie Betancourt
Director of Human Resources
Jackson Memorial Hospital
1611 Jefferson Street
Miami, FL 33136-1106

Dear Ms. Betancourt:

The May 20, 19–, issue of The Miami Herald contained an article of interest to me about the upcoming expansion of the Pediatric Care Unit at Jackson Memorial Hospital. I am happy to hear of this expansion, as it will provide an opportunity to extend the excellent treatment now available to our ill and injured children.

Since such growth will require additional personnel, could the Pediatric Care Unit use a secretary who

... can work with little supervision, taking initiative in completing complex tasks?
... will be dependable in attendance and be punctual?
... can deal with the public in a positive manner?

If so, I am the medical secretary for you!

The Pediatric Care Unit needs reliable medical secretaries who recognize the importance of accurate records and who are concerned with the treatment of patients. These areas were stressed in my medical transcription training at Miami-Dade Community College. Jackson Memorial Hospital would be assured of a dedicated medical transcriptionist who sincerely cares for children, if you should decide to add me to your medical team.

In your hiring for the expanded Pediatric Care Unit, please give serious consideration to the enclosed résumé. An immediate interview can be arranged by calling 555-0511. I look forward to hearing from you soon.

Sincerely,

Scott McMeekin

Enclosure

Illustration 7008.2
Job Application Letter

9090 Southwest 85th Avenue
Miami, FL 33156-1900
June 1, 19–

ZCM Productions
10300 High Street
Miami, FL 33176-1030

Ladies and Gentlemen:

The future looks bright since your classified ad for an executive secretary appeared in the May 27 issue of THE MIAMI HERALD. You suggest "Let's Build a Future Together." As a bright, new, executive secretary, I should be happy to be a part of your television production agency.

As you will note from my enclosed résumé, THE MIAMI HERALD selected me as a candidate for future success by bestowing upon me the coveted Silver Knight award in business during my senior year in high school. While attending college, I have worked for several years as a volunteer at Baptist Hospital in south Dade County. Some of this work consisted of working in the public relations office on the computer using WordPerfect. In addition, my classes at Miami-Dade Community College provided me with daily practice in all aspects of microcomputer use. I have recently been working with desktop publishing in the layout and design of my college student newspaper.

The future success of ZCM Productions depends upon dedicated, competent assistance. You can count on me. Please call me at 555-0511 to set up an interview at your earliest convenience.

Sincerely,

Scott McMeekin

Enclosure

7009 **Application form.** Following a letter, call, or visit to an employer, the job applicant will usually be asked to fill out an **application form.** The form is usually printed by the employer and requests similar information to that given in the résumé. Have your résumé available when completing the application form so that all dates and other information are accurate. While much of the information requested in the form will duplicate information in the résumé, inquiry/application letter, and so on, many employers have a legal requirement for the job applicant to fill out *and sign* the application form, to certify the information provided is accurate.

Since the résumé, application letter, and application form will be the three written items considered before an interview is granted, it is important that all three represent the applicant well. If possible, ask to complete an application form at home, and then key the information requested. See illustration 7009.1 on page 453. If the application form must be completed in the employer's office, do so neatly and in ink. See illustration 7009.2 on page 454. Many employers now have computerized application forms that can be filled out on a computer in the personnel office.

Important points to remember when completing the application form are as follows:

- **Read through the entire form.** Before beginning to write, read through the entire form and note all of the questions asked. Review the form first to avoid putting answers in the wrong blanks. Follow directions carefully. Watch for special instructions, such as last name first.

MORE

- **Fill out the form completely.** Answer all questions fully and accurately. Complete all lines. If any questions cannot be answered (for example, information requested on military service if you have no military experience), put *N/A* on the blank line to show the question was not missed. All information provided on the application form and résumé should agree exactly.
- **Provide a salary range.** If a salary is requested on the application form, provide a salary *range* rather than a specific amount. Doing so will leave this subject open for later discussion during the interview. If you are unsure what the proper salary should be, talk to friends with similar jobs, school advisors, and so on.
- **Review the form carefully.** When the application form is complete, review it carefully to make certain that each line is completely filled out with the information requested.
- **Attach a copy of your résumé.** Finally, attach a copy of your résumé to the completed application form before submitting both to the employer.

7010 **Employment tests.** **Employment tests** may include one or several tests given to obtain additional information regarding each applicant. Scores from these tests are considered in selection of employees. Most often there is only one opportunity to be tested; however, sometimes the exam can be repeated to improve performance.

Employment tests may cover keyboarding, transcription, business terminology, general intelligence, personality, math, or specific business skills (such as use of a specific word processing or spreadsheet software.) Applicants attaining certificates of proficiency in any of these areas should take the certificates to the employment or testing office. A number of offices will accept such credentials and eliminate the test covering similar skills. Things to remember if asked to take an employment test:

- **Relax as much as possible.**
- **Read all instructions carefully.** When given a timed test, request a moment to read instructions before the clock is started. Ask questions to clarify any directions.
- **Use time wisely.** Divide allotted time for each section of the test. Do not waste time on one particular question. Skip the troublesome questions and come back to them later, *if* there is an opportunity.
- **Look for answers.** Answers to harder questions may be found in other parts of the test. It is sometimes surprising how many hints there are in other sections.
- **Write clearly and neatly.** Clear, neat writing assures that answers can be read.

Illustration 7009.1
Application Form—Typed

Jackson Memorial Hospital
the health team that cares.
Application for Employment

INSTRUCTIONS: This application must be filled out personally. Use black or blue ink. False or misleading statements are cause for rejection. All statements are subject to investigation. Answer all questions accurately and completely. PLEASE PRINT CLEARLY.

Position applied for:	Medical Secretary	Medical Transcriber

LAST NAME (Print in full)	First Name	Middle/Maiden Name	Social Security Number
McMeekin	Scott	N/A	263-74-3859

Present Address Street	Residence Telephone
9090 Southwest 85th Street	(305) 555-0511

City	State	Zip Code	Other phone numbers where you can be contacted
Miami	Florida	33156-1900	Mother 555-5122

Are you a citizen of the U.S.? Yes ☒ No ☐ If no, do you have a legal right to remain and work in the United States? Yes ☐ No ☐

EDUCATION - TRAINING
Place "X" in column indicating highest grade completed

5	6	7	8	9	10	11	12	GED	College
									A.S. X

Foreign Language Proficiency - Print the word "Good", Fair", or "Poor" in the boxes titled Read, Write, Speak which best describes your ability to use this language.

Language	Read	Write	Speak
Spanish	Good	Good	Good

	Name and Location	Dates From	Dates To	Graduated?	Major & Minor Subjects	Degree	Activities or Honors
High School	Coral Gables High School Coral Gables, Florida	19--	19--	yes	Business Education	diploma	National Honor Society; Student Council Vice President
College	Wolfson Campus, Miami-Dade Community College, Miami, FL 33132-3300	19--	19--	yes	Medical Transcription Major	A.S.	Asst. Editor, METROPOLIS; President, Pi Theta Kappa
College	N/A						
Other	N/A						

Occupational or professional license(s)
If you have one: Type Certified from MDCC Number none
Date obtained March, 19-- Renewal Date N/A
If one is pending: Type N/A Date to be received N/A

OTHER SKILLS: Typing 60 wpm Shorthand/Speedwriting 100 wpm
Other: Word Processing Equipment, Knowledge of Medical Terminology, Medical Transcription

Have you ever been a member of the Armed Services? ☐ Yes ☒ No
Dates: From N/A To
Type of Discharge ☐ Honorable ☐ Other (Explain) N/A

Date of Discharge Month	Day	Year
N/A		

V. Health Record
Do you have any reason that precludes you from performing any part of the job for which you are being considered?
None, excellent health

Since your 16th birthday, have you ever been convicted of a felonious offense? ☐ Yes ☒ No
If "Yes", state the court, nature of offence, disposition of case and date. N/A

Prior to employment, your fingerprints will be taken for routine check by the F.B.I. and other agencies.

Employment Record

Have you been previously employed by Jackson Memorial Hospital? Yes ☐ No ☒
If "Yes", state department and dates N/A

List in order, starting with present or last employer.

Dates (Month, Year)	
From: April 19-- To: Present	Company: BAPTIST HOSPITAL; Telephone: 555-8076 Street: 8900 Floral Avenue; City: Miami; State: FL; Zip: 33156-8900 Job Title: Volunteer; Department: Volunteer Services; Supervisor: Dr. Castell Bryant Major Duties: Data entry on IBM PC using WordPerfect, Lotus 1-2-3, and Pagemaker; telephone; deliveries Starting Salary $ N/A Per; Final Salary $ N/A Per; Reason for leaving: Still a volunteer
From: April 19-- To: Present	Company: CHICKEN SHACK; Telephone: 555-1191 Street: 11905 Magnolia Drive; City: Miami; State: FL; Zip: 33176-1109 Job Title: Cook; Department: Kitchen; Supervisor: Mr. Louis Monzon Major Duties: Food preparation Starting Salary $4.25 Per Hour; Final Salary $5.75 Per Hour; Reason for leaving: Still working
From: To:	Company; Telephone Street; City; State; Zip Job Title; Department; Supervisor Major Duties Starting Salary $ Per; Final Salary $ Per; Reason for leaving
From: To:	Company; Telephone Street; City; State; Zip Job Title; Department; Supervisor Major Duties Starting Salary $ Per; Final Salary $ Per; Reason for leaving
From: To:	Company; Telephone Street; City; State; Zip Job Title; Department; Supervisor Major Duties Starting Salary $ Per; Final Salary $ Per; Reason for leaving

CERTIFICATION: I hereby certify that all statements made on this form are true to the best of my knowledge. I fully realize that should an investigation disclose any misrepresentation, I will be subject to immediate dismissal.

Date: 6/29/-- Signature: Scott McMeekin

We are an Equal Opportunity Employer and participate in Affirmative Action Programs. Out application forms are designed to obtain an applicant's skills, knowledge and abilities based on specific job requirements. Questions are designed to elicit enough data for us to determine an applicant's abilities to successfully perform the job for which she/he is applying.

7

7

Illustration 7009.2
Application Form—Handwritten

Jackson Memorial Hospital
the health team that cares.
Application for Employment

INSTRUCTIONS: This application must be filled out personally. Use black or blue ink. False or misleading statements are cause for rejection. All statements are subject to investigation. Answer all questions accurately and completely. PLEASE PRINT CLEARLY.

Position applied for:	Medical Secretary	Medical Transcriber

LAST NAME (Print in full)	First Name	Middle/Maiden Name	Social Security Number
McMeekin	Scott	N/A	263-74-3859

Present Address Street	Residence Telephone
9090 Southwest 85th Street	(305) 555-0511

City	State	Zip Code	Other phone numbers where you can be contacted
Miami	Florida	33156-1900	Mother 555-5122

Are you a citizen of the U.S.? Yes [X] No [ ] If no, do you have a legal right to remain and work in the United States? Yes [ ] No [ ]

EDUCATION - TRAINING
Place "X" in column indicating highest grade completed

5	6	7	8	9	10	11	12	GED	College
									A.S. X

Foreign Language Proficiency - Print the word "Good", Fair", or "Poor" in the boxes titled Read, Write, Speak which best describes your ability to use this language.

Language	Read	Write	Speak
Spanish	Good	Good	Good

	Name and Location	Dates From	Dates To	Graduated?	Major & Minor Subjects	Degree	Activities or Honors
High School	Coral Gables High School Coral Gables, Florida	19--	19--	yes	Business Education	diploma	National Honor Society; Student Council Vice President
College	Wolfson Campus, Miami-Dade Community College, Miami, FL 33132-3300	19--	19--	yes	Medical Transcription Major	A.S.	Asst. Editor, METROPOLIS; President, PI Theta Kappa
College	N/A						
Other	N/A						

Occupational or professional license(s)
If you have one: Type Certified from MDCC Number none
Date obtained March, 19-- Renewal Date N/A
If one is pending: Type N/A Date to be received N/A

OTHER SKILLS: Typing 60 wpm Shorthand/Speedwriting 100 wpm
Other: Word Processing Equipment, Knowledge of Medical Terminology, Medical Transcription

Have you ever been a member of the Armed Services? [ ] Yes [X] No
Dates: From N/A To
Type of Discharge [ ] Honorable [ ] Other (Explain) N/A

Date of Discharge Month	Day	Year
N/A		

V. Health Record
Do you have any reason that precludes you from performing any part of the job for which you are being considered?
None, excellent health

Since your 16th birthday, have you ever been convicted of a felonious offense? [ ] Yes [X] No
If "Yes", state the court, nature of offence, disposition of case and date. N/A

Prior to employment, your fingerprints will be taken for routine check by the F.B.I. and other agencies.

Employment Record
Have you been previously employed by Jackson Memorial Hospital? Yes [ ] No [X]
If "Yes", state department and dates N/A
List in order, starting with present or last employer.

Dates (Month Year)			
From: April 19-- To: Present	Company: BAPTIST HOSPITAL		Telephone: 555-8076
	Street: 8900 Floral Avenue	City: Miami	State: FL Zip: 33156-8900
	Job Title: Volunteer	Department: Volunteer Services	Supervisor: Dr. Castell Bryant
	Major Duties: Data entry on IBM PC using WordPerfect, Lotus 1-2-3, and Pagemaker; telephone; deliveries		
	Starting Salary $ N/A Per	Final Salary $ N/A Per	Reason for leaving: Still a volunteer
From: April 19-- To: Present	Company: CHICKEN SHACK		Telephone: 555-1191
	Street: 11905 Magnolia Drive	City: Miami	State: FL Zip: 33176-1109
	Job Title: Cook	Department: Kitchen	Supervisor: Mr. Louis Monzon
	Major Duties: Food preparation		
	Starting Salary $4.25 Per Hour	Final Salary $5.75 Per Hour	Reason for leaving: Still working
From: To:	Company		Telephone
	Street	City	State Zip
	Job Title	Department	Supervisor
	Major Duties		
	Starting Salary $ Per	Final Salary $ Per	Reason for leaving
From: To:	Company		Telephone
	Street	City	State Zip
	Job Title	Department	Supervisor
	Major Duties		
	Starting Salary $ Per	Final Salary $ Per	Reason for leaving
From: To:	Company		Telephone
	Street	City	State Zip
	Job Title	Department	Supervisor
	Major Duties		
	Starting Salary $ Per	Final Salary $ Per	Reason for leaving

CERTIFICATION: I hereby certify that all statements made on this form are true to the best of my knowledge. I fully realize that should an investigation disclose any misrepresentation, I will be subject to immediate dismissal.

Date: 6/29/-- Signature: Scott McMeekin

We are an Equal Opportunity Employer and participate in Affirmative Action Programs. Out application forms are designed to obtain an applicant's skills, knowledge and abilities based on specific job requirements. Questions are designed to elicit enough data for us to determine an applicant's abilities to successfully perform the job for which she/he is applying.

7011 **The interview.** The best chance to convince a potential employer to hire you is during the interview. This is the opportunity to sit down and describe in detail how your knowledge, skills, and experience can benefit the employer. Also, the employer has a chance to evaluate your personality, attitudes, personal appearance, enthusiasm, and ability to communicate.

Furthermore, recognize that the interview provides an opportunity to evaluate the open position. Make certain that this office is one in which you would be happy.

- **Prepare first.** Before going to the interview, learn about the employer. Ask questions of teachers and friends about the normal skill requirements for such jobs, and make sure your qualifications match the requirements. Inquire about current salaries of similar positions within the same area to know what to expect or what to answer if asked. Be aware of fringe benefits provided by similar employers and rank their importance. Fringe benefits may include health insurance, dental insurance, life insurance, disability insurance, tuition reimbursement, vacation days, sick leave, maternity leave, and so on.

  Ask family and friends for possible interview questions and begin to practice good answers. Think about and write down questions to ask the interviewer about the position; arrange these questions in order of priority in case there is not time to ask them all.

- **Look your best.** Since this is the first opportunity the employer will have to judge your appearance, make sure you look your best. Decide in advance what to wear. Dress in your best business attire. Make certain your clothes are clean and wrinkle-free. Most importantly—remember to wear a smile!

- **Going to the interview.** Allow yourself plenty of time to dress and get to the interview. Call to find out exact directions before leaving home. If the route is very complicated, a test drive to determine time needed may be appropriate.

- **During the interview.** Try to appear relaxed. Although everyone is somewhat nervous during an interview, try not to show anxiety by moving often in your chair. Usually, an interview lasts approximately half an hour.

- **Focus on the interviewer.** He or she will take charge with the first question. Listen to all questions carefully and ask for clarification if you are confused. Reply honestly and briefly, but provide more than "yes" or "no" answers. Look the interviewer in the eye while speaking and smile often.

- **Remember to sell yourself.** Think about all of your skills and interests; discuss them in relation to the job requirements. Save questions about the

MORE

position and the employer until the end of the interview. Although pay and benefits are important concerns, do not focus all of your questions on salary, vacations, and bonuses.

- **Avoid any criticism about past work experience, teachers, or family members.** Keep the situation positive and expectant. Watch for indications that the interview is nearing an end. If you are interested in working for this company, close the interview by letting the employer know:

  "Ms. Stringer, you've been very kind to take time from your busy schedule to talk with me. The information provided about the position has been helpful. You can count on my dedication if I have an opportunity to work with you."

- **Check back.** Write a brief thank-you letter to the interviewer within a few days. Doing so will bring you and your qualifications once again to the interviewer's attention. Thank the interviewer for the time and courtesy extended. If there is anything you forgot to mention in the interview, include that fact briefly. Repeat interest in the position. See illustration 7011.1.

Illustration 7011.1
Thank-you Letter

9090 Southwest 85th Avenue
Miami, FL 33156-1900
June 5, 19—

Ms. Marcia Stringer, President
ZCM Productions
10300 High Street
Miami, FL 33176-1030

Dear Ms. Stringer:

Thank you very much for taking time from your busy schedule to meet with me last Wednesday. Your description of the job was quite comprehensive and very informative.

I am most interested in working in an office such as you described. If you decide to give me the opportunity, I shall strive to be always accurate and dependable.

Sincerely,

Scott McMeekin

GETTING AHEAD

Working Together—Fitting In

7101 **Attitudes and work habits.** When beginning a new job, you will find many things you do not know or understood. Take the time to be very observant, ask questions, and check carefully regarding instructions for new tasks. Remember advancement cannot be considered until there is mastery of the basic skills all employers expect. These include punctuality, good attendance, confidentiality, dependability, a good attitude, and a problem-solving approach to the business of the company.

7102 **Admit mistakes readily.** Approach the employer with a discovered error and discuss frankly how to solve the problem. Also, assure the employer the error will be avoided in the future.

7103 **Teamwork.** Complete all tasks by the deadlines assigned, even if it means working later than usual. Be positive and cheerful in dealings with other office workers. Volunteer to assist co-workers on high-priority projects. In times of stress, remain courteous. If there is a concern with a particular co-worker, discuss that concern directly with the co-worker *before* discussion with a supervisor.

7104 **Working independently.** Look for ways to prevent problems in advance; take the initiative to follow each task through to completion; and organize work in a way to allow speedy completion. When there is an unexpected roadblock to completing a task, try to find and implement a solution independently that will allow progress to task completion without returning to the supervisor; however, do not exceed your level of authority.

7105 **Move ahead with the organization.** As the organization grows, it will usually become more professional, more up-to-date, and more polished. It is important to grow with the company. Sometimes this requires considering new ideas or new possibilities. Try to look at the job with a fresh view—as a new employee would. In this way, different solutions will be found for complicated tasks.

7106 **Continuing education.** To advance within a profession, you must continue to improve and expand job knowledge. Because of their own dedication to the pursuit of knowledge in the field, most employers believe firmly in continuing education. The modern office worker should show a willingness to learn, even on weekends and "off" time. For instance, read as much as possible about recent trends and developments in your field.

Bring any notices of pertinent seminars offered to the attention of your supervisor. Continued interest in learning meaningful, job-related new techniques highlights you as a possible candidate for a higher level of responsibility. Frequently, employers will offer to pay tuition costs for seminars or classes. Local adult basic-education programs, community colleges, universities, and professional organizations offer continuing education programs.

7107 **The electronic office.** Be aware that office technology is changing so rapidly that everyone must work hard to stay abreast of the latest developments. Microcomputers networked to file servers, minicomputers, and mainframes can make the modern office environment more efficient, thus allowing more time for working with customers and staff.

Remain aware that everyone is learning about the impact of technology on every aspect of business. Do not be embarrassed to ask questions or take classes on the latest features of each new release of a software package commonly used in the office.

While new technology saves much time, provides information never before available, and customizes the processing of much routine paperwork, the software that runs it is complex and requires adequate training. To advance on the job: determine what training opportunities are available and take advantage of them; determine which individuals in the office are more knowledgeable about a particular software and ask them questions when you need help (when help is not critical to the moment, it is generally a good idea to write down several questions and wait to ask them at a nonpeak time); spend time checking out the help menu of the software for answers as well as unknown features; visit the local bookstore to find easy reference books to assist in understanding; and, take courses at the local community college.

Individual Initiative

7108 **How to advance.** Although your first years on the job will be for learning and perfecting job performance, begin to consider future goals. Sometimes it helps to think of more advanced positions for promotion within the same organization. Other times, upward movement requires changing employers. It is important to keep constantly in mind your goals for the future.

Good advice for those who wish to advance is to dress, act, and acquire skills for a position they aspire to, rather than for the position they have now.

7109 **Charting the future.** Remember to model the actions, behavior, work, job knowledge, and dress of those currently holding a position for advancement. Be realistic. Realize that on the average the first chance for promotion on a job is after a three-year period in the present position. Do not expect too much too soon.

7110 **Professional organizations.** Join the professional organizations most related to your new position. Many such organizations publish a periodical magazine with interesting articles on recent developments. Professional organizations also hold regular local, regional, and national meetings with expert speakers on particular topics. At these meetings, network with others and share experiences.

Follow these suggestions and advance up the career ladder. Always do the best you can on each task, and your efforts *will* be recognized. Best of luck!

CHAPTER 8

REFERENCES

REFERENCES

8001 **References in general.** Neither this book nor any other single source can possibly answer all the questions that arise in the typical office. However, the references that follow will enable you to identify and locate a wealth of additional information. Many of these publications (and others equally as useful) will be found in your school or community library.

Mergers and acquisitions in the publishing industry have resulted in moves and name changes for some publishing companies recently. Publishers and cities of publication are listed here as they are shown in the publications. If you have trouble in identifying or locating a publisher, go to your library and look up the title in *Books in Print,* R. R. Bowker Company. This listing will lead you to an 800-number (also in *Books in Print*) for the publisher.

8002 **Almanacs.** **Almanacs** are usually published on an annual basis. They contain a variety of general information. The emphasis is on statistical information for the previous year: athletic events and records, the names of government officials, memorable dates and holidays, events of historical significance, and the like.

Information Please Almanac. Boston: Houghton-Mifflin Company.

The World Almanac and Book of Facts. New York: Scripps Howard.

8003 **Biography.** The following publications contain brief biographical notes on prominent persons. More detailed biographical information, when available, is obtained by looking up the person's name in the card file or electronic file of the library.

Current Biography Yearbook. New York: The H. W. Wilson Company.

Dictionary of American Biography. New York: Macmillan, Inc.

International Who's Who. London: Europa Publications.

Official Congressional Directory. Washington, DC: United States Government Printing Office.

Webster's American Biographies. Edited by Charles Van Doren. Springfield, MA: Merriam-Webster, Inc.

Who Was Who. New York. St. Martin's Press, Inc.

Who Was Who in America. Chicago: Marquis Who's Who, Inc.

Who's Who. New York: St. Martin's Press, Inc.

Who's Who in America. Chicago: Marquis Who's Who, Inc.

8004 **Dictionaries, spellers, thesauri, and word division manuals.** **Unabridged dictionaries** (the largest ones, usually found in schools and libraries) contain most of the words in the language. **Abridged dictionaries** (shortened versions, about the size of a typical textbook) contain most of the *common* words in the language.

Spellers contain lists of words spelled correctly—and sometimes divided into syllables.

Thesauri (the plural of *thesaurus*) are books containing lists of synonyms and near synonyms arranged by subject. This arrangement allows the thesaurus user to select the best word for the intended purpose.

Word division manuals list words correctly spelled and provide indications of the points at which each word may properly be divided.

The American Heritage Dictionary of the English Language. Boston: Houghton-Mifflin Company.

Brown, Alvin R. *Spelling: A Mnemonics Approach*. Cincinnati: South-Western Publishing Co.

Byers, Edward E. *10,000 Medical Words*. New York: Gregg Division/McGraw-Hill Book Company.

Funk & Wagnalls' Standard Dictionary. New York: HarperCollins Publishers.

Kurtz, Margaret A. *10,000 Legal Words*. New York: Gregg Division/ McGraw-Hill Book Company.

Market House Books Staff. *The Oxford House Dictionary of Abbreviations*. New York: Oxford University Press.

Merriam-Webster's Collegiate Dictionary 10th ed. Springfield, MA: Merriam-Webster, Inc.

The Original Roget's Thesaurus of English Words and Phrases. New York: St. Martin's Press, Inc.

Perry, Devern J. *Word Studies*. Cincinnati: South-Western Publishing Co.

Perry, Devern J. *Word Division and Spelling Manual*. Cincinnati: South-Western Publishing Co.

The Random House Dictionary of the English Language. New York: Random House, Inc.

Roget's International Thesaurus. New York: HarperCollins Publishers.

Sisson, A. F. *Sisson's Synonyms: An Unabridged Synonym and Related-Term Locator*. West Nyack, NY: Parker Publishing Company.

Webster's Collegiate Thesaurus. Springfield, MA: Merriam-Webster, Inc.

Webster's Instant Word Guide. Springfield, MA: Merriam-Webster, Inc.

Webster's New Dictionary of Synonyms. Springfield, MA: Merriam-Webster, Inc.

Webster's Third New International Dictionary, Unabridged: The Great Library of the English Language. Springfield, MA: Merriam-Webster, Inc.

Zoubek, Charles E., and G. A. Condon. *20,000+ Words*. New York: McGraw-Hill Book Company.

8005 **Directories.** Just as the telephone directory for each community lists local businesses, other **directories** list people and organizations in specific categories (attorneys, banks, manufacturers, physicians, and the like) on a national basis. Each directory confines its listings to specific kinds of information: credit ratings, practitioners in a specific field, suppliers of specific products, and so forth.

American Medical Directory. Chicago: American Medical Association.

The Bank Quarterly. Austin, TX: Sheshunoff Information Services, Inc.

Directories in Print. Detroit: Gale Research Co.

The Martindale-Hubbell Law Directory. Summit, NJ: Martindale-Hubbell, Inc.

Reference Book of American Business. New York: Dun & Bradstreet, Inc.

MORE

The S & L Quarterly. Austin, TX: Sheshunoff Information Services, Inc.

Standard Corporation Records. New York: Standard & Poor's Corp.

Thomas Register of American Manufacturers. New York: Thomas Publishing Company.

8006 **Encyclopedias.** An **encyclopedia** is usually an entire set of books (typically about two dozen) explaining (usually in an introductory, general manner) virtually all branches of knowledge. Specialized encyclopedias treat a single branch of knowledge in greater depth. Encyclopedias are arranged alphabetically by subject.

The following encyclopedias are general references that treat virtually all branches of knowledge.

Academic American Encyclopedia. Danbury, CT: Grolier, Inc.

Collier's Encyclopedia. New York: Macmillan, Inc.

Encyclopedia Americana. New York: Grolier, Inc.

New Book of Knowledge. Danbury, CT: Grolier, Inc.

The New Columbia Encyclopedia. New York: Columbia University Press.

The New Encyclopaedia Britannica. Chicago: Encyclopaedia Britannica, Inc.

World Book Encyclopedia. Chicago: World Book.

8007 **Finding a job.** A search for a new job can be conducted more effectively if it is well planned. Information from the following sources can be helpful in planning.

Dictionary of Occupational Titles. Washington, DC: U. S. Government Printing Office.

Goble, Dorothy Y. *How to Get a Job and Keep It.* Austin, TX: Raintree Steck-Vaughn Company.

Molloy, John T. *Dress for Success.* New York: Warner Books, Inc.

Molloy, John T. *The Woman's Dress for Success Book.* New York: Warner Books, Inc.

Reed, Jean. *Resumes That Get Jobs.* New York: Arco Publishing Co., Inc.

8008 **Information processing, including word processing and desktop publishing.** The following sources provide a wealth of material on information processing, word processing, and other aspects of the computer world.

Albrecht, Bob. *Simply PCs.* Berkeley, CA: Osborne/McGraw-Hill.

Allen, Warren W., and Dale H. Klooster. *Automated Accounting for the Microcomputer.* Cincinnati: South-Western Publishing Co.

Clark, James F., Warren W. Allen, and Dale W. Klooster. *Computers and Information Processing: Concepts and Applications.* Cincinnati: South-Western Publishing Co.

Clark, James F., and Kathy H. White. *Computer Confidence—A Challenge for Today*. Cincinnati: South-Western Publishing Co.

Custer, Helen. *Inside Windows NT*. Redmond, WA: Microsoft Press.

Database Concepts. Edited by Hardgrave, et al. Cincinnati: South-Western Publishing Co.

Duncan, Charles, et al. *College Keyboarding*. Cincinnati: South-Western Publishing Co.

Easy Reference Guides (series). Cincinnati: South-Western Publishing Co.

Fosegan, Joseph S. and Mary Lea Ginn. *Business Records Control*. Cincinnati: South-Western Publishing Co.

Fuori, William M., and Lawrence J. Aufiero. *Computers and Information Processing*. Englewood Cliffs, NJ: Prentice-Hall.

Harris, Robert W. *DOS, WordPerfect & Lotus Office Companion*. Chapel Hill, NC: Ventana Press, Inc.

Harrison, William L. *Computers and Information Processing: An Introduction*. St. Paul, MN: West Publishing Company.

Inside Windows. Carmel, IN: New Riders Publishing.

Insider's Guide to Personal Computing and Networking. Edited by Rick Segal. Carmel, IN: Sams Publishing.

Kallus, Norman F., and Mina M. Johnson. *Records Management*. Cincinnati: South-Western Publishing Co.

Kraynak, Joe. *Plain English Computer Dictionary*. Carmel, IN: Alpha Books.

Long, Harry. *Introduction to Computers and Information Processing*. Englewood Cliffs, NJ: Prentice-Hall.

Margolis, Philip E. *Personal Computer Dictionary*. New York: Random House, Inc.

Mason, Jennie. *Introduction to Word Processing*. New York: Macmillan, Inc.

Minasi, Mark, et al. *Inside OS/2 2, Special Edition*. Carmel, IN: New Riders Publishing.

Morgenstern, Steve. *No-Sweat Desktop Publishing*. New York: American Management Association.

Murray, Katherine, and Rose Ewing. *Introduction to Personal Computers*. Carmel, IN: Que Corporation.

Nance, Barry. *Introduction to Networking*. Carmel, IN: Que Corporation.

O'Hara, Shelley. *Easy DOS*. Carmel, IN: Que Corporation.

O'Hara, Shelley. *Easy PCs*. Carmel, IN: Que Corporation.

MORE

Pfaffenberger, Barry. *Que's Computer User's Dictionary*. Carmel, IN: Que Corporation.

Robinson, Jerry, et al. *Century 21 Keyboarding, Formatting, and Document Processing*. Cincinnati: South-Western Publishing Co.

Robinson, Jerry, et al. *Keyboarding and Computer Applications*. Cincinnati: South-Western Publishing Co.

Rules for Alphabetical Filing. Chicago: Association of Records Managers and Administrators.

Schatt, Stan. *Understanding Local Area Networks*. Carmel, IN: Sams Publishing.

Stern, Robert A., and Nancy Stern. *Introduction to Computers and Information Processing*. New York: Wiley.

Stewart, Jeffrey R., Jr., et al. *Records and Database Management*. New York: McGraw-Hill Book Company.

White, Ron. *How Computers Work*. Emeryville, CA: Ziff-Davis Press.

8009 **Mail service and shipping; geography and travel.** The following references provide information on the movement of documents, goods, and people that is necessary to the transaction of business.

Address Abbreviations. Washington, DC: U.S. Government Printing Office.

Bullinger's Postal and Shippers Guide for the United States and Canada. Westwood, NJ: Bullinger's Guides, Inc.

Customs Regulations of the United States. Washington, DC: U. S. Government Printing Office.

Hammond Atlas of the World. Maplewood, NJ: Hammond, Inc.

Hotel and Motel Red Book. New York: American Hotel and Motel Association.

National Geographic Atlas of the World. Washington, DC: National Geographic Society.

National ZIP Code Directory. Washington, DC: U. S. Government Printing Office.

Official Airline Guide. Sausalito, CA: Official Airline Guide.

The Postal Manual. Washington, DC: U. S. Government Printing Office.

Rand McNally Contemporary World Atlas. Chicago: Rand McNally & Company.

Rand McNally New International Atlas. Chicago: Rand McNally & Company.

Rand McNally Zip Code Finder. Chicago: Rand McNally & Company.

Terpstra, Vern, and Kenneth David. *The Cultural Environment of International Business*. Cincinnati: South-Western Publishing Co.

Webster's New Geographical Dictionary. Springfield, MA: Merriam-Webster, Inc.

8010 **Personal and social development.** Appropriate personal manners and appearance can help you succeed in your present job—or help you get a new one.

Baldridge, Letitia. *The Amy Vanderbilt Complete Book of Etiquette*. Garden City, NY: Doubleday and Co., Inc.

Baldridge, Letitia. *Letitia Baldridge's Complete Guide to The New Manners of the 90s*. Garden City, NY: Doubleday and Co., Inc.

Eggland, Steven A., and John W. Williams. *Human Relations at Work*. Cincinnati: South-Western Publishing Co.

Post, Elizabeth L. *Emily Post's Etiquette*. New York: HarperCollins Publishers.

Reynolds, Caroline. *Dimensions in Professional Development*. Cincinnati: South-Western Publishing Co.

8011 **Publications in print.** Virtually all books and periodicals in print can be found in one or more of the following sources.

Books in Print. New York: R. R. Bowker Company.

Business Periodicals Index. New York: The H. W. Wilson Company.

Cumulative Book Index. New York: The H. W. Wilson Company.

Education Index. New York: The H. W. Wilson Company.

Gates, Jean Key. *Guide to the Use of Libraries and Information Sources*. New York: McGraw-Hill Book Company.

General Reference Books for Adults. Edited by Marion Sader. New York: R. R. Bowker.

The New York Times Index. New York: The New York Times.

The Publishers' Trade List Annual. New York: R. R. Bowker Company.

Reader's Guide to Periodical Literature. New York: The H. W. Wilson Company.

Sheehy, Eugene P. *Guide to Reference Books*. Chicago: American Library Association.

Ulrich's International Periodicals Directory: A Clasified Guide to Current Periodicals, Foreign and Domestic. New York: R. R. Bowker Company.

8012 **Quotations.** A good quotation is seldom out of place. It can be used to strengthen an argument, provide a change of pace, or improve text simply because someone has expressed an idea so well that no better way to express it has been found.

MORE

The Harper Book of Quotations. Edited by Robert Fitzhenry. New York: HarperCollins Publishers.

Magill's Quotations in Context. Edited by Frank N. Magill. New York: HarperCollins Publishers.

The Oxford Dictionary of Modern Quotations. Edited by A. J. Augarde. New York: Oxford University Press.

The Oxford Dictionary of Quotations. New York: Oxford University Press.

8013 **Secretarial handbooks.** For comprehensive, but sometimes brief, coverage of topics useful in the office, consult a secretarial handbook.

Anderson, Ruth I., et al. *The Administrative Secretary: Resource*. New York: Gregg Division/McGraw-Hill Book Company.

Clark, James L., and Lyn R. Clark. *How 6: A Handbook for Office Workers*. Boston: PWS-KENT Publishing Company.

Doris, Lillian, and Besse May Miller. *Complete Secretary's Handbook*. Englewood Cliffs, NJ: Prentice-Hall.

Holmes, Ralph M. *The Reference Guide: A Handbook for Office Personnel*. Boston: Houghton Mifflin Company.

Housel, Debra. *Keyboarding Quick Reference Guide*. Cincinnati: South-Western Publishing Co.

Humphrey, Doris, and Kathie Sigler. *The Modern Medical Office: A Reference Manual*. Cincinnati: South-Western Publishing Co.

Janis, J. Harold, and Margaret H. Thompson. *New Standard Reference for Secretaries and Administrative Assistants*. New York: Macmillan, Inc.

Miller, Besse May. *Legal Secretary's Complete Handbook*. Englewood Cliffs, NJ: Prentice-Hall.

Parker Publishing Company Editorial Staff. *Secretary's Desktop Library*. West Nyack, NY: Parker Publishing Company.

Sabin, William A. *The Gregg Reference Manual*. New York: Gregg Division/McGraw-Hill Book Company.

Taintor, Sarah, and Kate M. Monroe. *Secretary's Handbook*. New York: Macmillan, Inc.

Tilton, Rita S., J. Howard Jackson, and Sue C. Rigby. *The Electronic Office: Procedures and Administration*. Cincinnati: South-Western Publishing Co.

Whalen, Doris H. *The HBJ Office Handbook*. New York: Harcourt Brace Jovanovich, Publishers.

8014 **Writing.** Questions of grammar, style, punctuation, capitalization, abbreviation, and the like, arise from time to time in every office. The following sources contain the answers to many of these questions.

Brown, Leland. *Effective Business Report Writing*. Englewood Cliffs, NJ: Prentice-Hall.

Brusaw, Charles T., et al. *Handbook of Technical Writing*. New York: St. Martin's Press.

Campbell, William Giles. *Form and Style: Theses, Reports, Term Papers*. Boston: Houghton-Mifflin Company.

The Chicago Manual of Style. Chicago: The University of Chicago Press.

Cook, Claire Kehrwald. *Line by Line: How to Improve Your Own Writing*. Boston: Houghton-Mifflin Company.

Frailey, L. E. *Handbook of Business Letters*. Englewood Cliffs, NJ: Prentice-Hall.

Hodges, John C., et al. *Harbrace College Handbook*. New York: Harcourt Brace Jovanovich, Publishers.

Hulbert, Jack E. *Effective Communication For Today*. Cincinnati: South-Western Publishing Co.

Hulbert, Jack E. *English Skill Builder Reference Manual*. Cincinnati: South-Western Publishing Co.

Keithly, Erwin M., and Margaret H. Thompson. *English for Modern Business*. Homewood, IL: Richard D. Irwin, Inc.

Keyboarding/Formatting Style Manual. Compiled by Clifford R. House and Samuel Skurow. Cincinnati: South-Western Publishing Co.

Osborn, Patricia. *How Grammar Works: A Self-Teaching Guide*. New York: John Wiley & Sons, Inc.

Perkins, W. E. *Punctuation: A Simplified Approach*. Cincinnati: South-Western Publishing Co.

Perrin, Porter G. *Writer's Guide and Index to English*. Chicago: Scott, Foresman & Company.

Schachter, Norman, and Alfred T. Clark, Jr. *Basic English Review*. Cincinnati: South-Western Publishing Co.

Sigband, Norman B., and Arthur H. Bell. *Communication for Management and Business*. Chicago: Scott, Foresman & Company.

Strunk, William, Jr., and E.B. White. *The Elements of Style*. New York: Macmillan, Inc.

Style Manual. Washington, DC: U. S. Government Printing Office.

Turabian, Kate L. *A Manual for Writers of Term Papers, Theses, and Dissertations*. Chicago: The University of Chicago Press.

Wolf, Morris P., and Shirley Kuiper. *Effective Communication in Business*. Cincinnati: South-Western Publishing Co.

Writer's Resource Guide. Cincinnati: Writer's Digest Books.

PAGE INDEX

Numbers refer to page numbers

A

B

C

D

N

O

P

Q

T

U

V

CONTENTS